Quantitative Research for the Behavioral Sciences

Quantitative Research for the Behavioral Sciences

Celia C. Reaves
Monroe Community College

John Wiley & Sons, Inc.
New York • Chichester • Brisbane • Toronto • Singapore

Acquisitions Editor	Karen Dubno
Production Manager	Katy Rubin
Designer	Pete Noa
Cover Design	A Good Thing, Inc.
Production Supervisor	Sandra Russell
Manufacturing Manager	Lorraine Fumoso
Copy Editor	Elizabeth Swain
Illustration	Ishaya Monokoff

Cartoon on page 290 is from BLOOM COUNTY BABYLON:Five Years of Basic Naughtiness, by Berke Breathed. Copyright ©1986, by the Washington Post Co.

Library of Congress Cataloging in Publication Data:

Reaves, Celia C.
Quantitative Research for the Behavioral Sciences

Printed in Singapore

10 9 8 7 6 5 4 3 2 1

To my husband
with thanks and love
(not necessarily in that order)

Preface

Quantitative Research for the Behavioral Sciences introduces students to a broad range of research methods used by behavioral scientists. It attempts to provide an understanding of how quantitative research is conducted, analyzed, and used in such a way that it will remain with students until they themselves have to deal with the realities of research.

Although the text is suitable for all introductory level research methods courses and for graduate students who want a refresher, one of my goals in writing *Quantitative Research for the Behavioral Sciences* was to show students who plan to work daily to serve other people in some way the practical importance of research and to preach a little about how research ought to be done and evaluated. For this reason, of the more than 150 references cited, 75 percent are reports of actual research projects designed to address interesting questions of the sort that behavioral scientists may find themselves asking; and 30 percent of these research reports were written in the last five years. In this way, I hope to motivate students to see the research methods course as something more than an obstacle in their path. Instead, I want them to see it as a stepping-stone they will need to reach their goals. This attitude will make it more likely that the things they learn will stay with them beyond the final exam.

An important feature of *Quantitative Research for the Behavioral Sciences* is that it avoids a cookbook approach and instead gives the student the necessary theory that makes the practical aspects of research methodology comprehensible. For instance, chapters on the philosophy of science and on measurement theory give the foundation for understanding why control is necessary in experimentation, which in turn underlies the importance of random assignment. With enough theory to show the reasons behind the rules, students can fit the rules into logical, understandable structures, related to each other in meaningful ways.

Another significant feature of the text is how it covers the research report. Many students react to the notion of writing a report as they would to the notion of conducting their own appendectomy without anaesthesia. Students who have taken several English courses are less afraid of the idea, but they approach the scientific paper as they would a persuasive essay or a piece of creative writing. To counter these reactions, *Quantitative Research for the Behavioral Sciences* devotes an entire chapter to explaining the type of writing style needed in a research report, and how to write it, in a way that will enable most students to achieve creditable reports on the first try and to improve consistently thereafter.

Emphasis on writing the research report is one aspect of a commitment to good, clear writing in all aspects of science that is reflected throughout book itself. Numerous examples from real-life experiences and actual research create interest. It is important that students comprehend not only what they read, but why it was written, and why anyone should bother to read it.

Several features make Quantitative Research for the Social Sciences easy to use. Each chapter opens with a list of questions for the student to keep in mind while reading. Within each chapter, key terms are given in boldface. The arrangement of the text has been guided by the kind of organization that seems to work best for students in the classroom. However, each section is independent, and mention of material covered earlier or later is cross-referenced by chapter so instructors who prefer a different organizational structure can rearrange the material with relatively little difficulty.

Part 1, Fundamentals, offers an overview of general topics that underlie the rest of the book. These include chapters on the nature of research and the scope of the book, the philosophy of science, and research ethics. Part 2, Making and Using Measurements, covers topics that relate to the measurement process. Included in this section are chapters on measurement theory, measurement issues including sampling and specific techniques, and how correlations between variables are measured and used. Part 3, Experimental Methods, discusses this specific research technique. It includes an introductory chapter on basic experimental terms and ideas, and detailed chapters on experimental control and quasi-experimental research. Finally, Part 4, Dealing with Results, explores the links between the actual research and the rest of the world. Chapters in this section discuss statistical analysis, writing a research report, and the interactions between science, scientists, and society.

Each chapter closes with a detailed summary in outline form; a CheckPoint, that is, a list of questions the student should be able to answer after reading; and exercises that will require a little more creative, in-depth thinking. Appendices give information on computers in research, how to use charts and graphs, and statistical tests. The book closes with an extensive reference list, a glossary of terms, and a detailed index.

An Instructor's Resource Guide accompanies the text. It includes teaching tips, chapter outlines, lecture demonstration topics, examples of current research, exercises/homework problems, multiple-choice, true–false, matching, and essay questions, and transparency masters.

Acknowledgments

Among those who helped this book come into existence I must first thank the Social Sciences Division of Monroe Community College, which granted me a one-semester leave to begin its development. In particular, Charles Clark of the Psychology Department helped me design the course from which this book grew, and discussed it with me many times. I must also thank the editors at Wiley, whose patience should be legendary. Numerous reviewers provided thoughtful, detailed, invaluable advice, including B. A. Albiniak, *University of South Carolina, Coastal*; Cameron Camp III, *University of New Orleans, Lakefront*; Walter F. Carroll, *Bridgewater State College*; Janis W. Driscoll, *University of Colorado*; Susan E. Dutch, *Westfield State College*; Francis W. Flynn, *University of Wyoming*; Paula Ann Goolkasian, *University of North Carolina, Charlotte*; G. William Hill IV, *Kennesaw State College*; Erika Hoff-Ginsberg, *University of Wisconsin*; Paul C. Koch, *St. Ambrose University*; Kenneth O. McGraw, *University of Mississippi*; W. Trammell Neill, *Adelphi University*; Bradley C. Olson, *Northern Michigan University*; Michael J. Reich, *University of Wisconsin*; George S. Rotter, *Montclair State College*; Richard L. Rogers, *Georgia Southern University*; Robert J. Schneider, *Metroplitan State College*; Theodore C. Wagenaar, *Miami University*; Fred W. Whitford, *Montana State University*; Douglas C. Wiseman, *Plymouth State College*; and Klaus Witz, *University of Illinois*.

Finally, my husband Don provided more than technical, financial, and emotional support; he even listened when I discussed how the book was going.

Contents

Introduction: Why Study Research Methods? 1
   Evaluating the Research of Others 2
   Conducting Research of Your Own 3
CheckPoint 4
Exercises 4

Part 1: Fundamentals 5

Chapter 1. The Nature and Kinds of Research 7
   What Is Research? 8
   Different Research for Different Purposes 8
      Descriptive Research 8
      Exploratory Research 9
      Theoretical Research 10
      Applied (Evaluation) Research 11
         Types of Evaluation Research 12
         Special Difficulties of Applied Research 14
   Quantitative versus Qualitative Research 16
Summary 16
CheckPoint 17
Exercises 18

Chapter 2. The Nature of Science 19
   Goals of Science 20
      Description 20
      Prediction 21

Explanation 22
Control 23
Ways of Knowing 24
Traditionalism or Authority 24
Rationalism 25
Empiricism 27
Unscientific Empiricism 29
Falsificationism 29
How Falsificationism Works 31
Falsifiable Statements 31
Falsification and Confirmation 34
Summary 35
CheckPoint 36
Exercises 37

Chapter 3. The Ethics of Research 39
Ethically Questionable Activities 40
Physical and Mental Harm 41
Observing Hidden Behaviors 44
Invasion of Privacy 45
Loss of Anonymity and Confidentiality 47
Deception 49
Coercion 52
Plagiarism 54
Fabricating Data 55
The Ethics of Animal Research 56
Evaluating Ethical Issues 58
Cost–Benefit Analysis 58
Ethics Oversight Committees 59
Responding to Unethical Research 60
A Reminder to Students 61
Summary 62
CheckPoint 63
Exercises 64

Part 2: Making and Using Measurements 65

Chapter 4. The Theory of Measurement 67
What Is a Measurement? 68
Constructs and Observations 70
Variables and Variability 71
Operational Definitions 73
Levels of Measurement 75
Nominal Measurements 75
Ordinal Measurements 76

Equal Interval Measurements 77
Ratio Measurements 78
How Good Is The Measurement? 79
Reliability 79
Validity 80
Face Validity 81
Criterion Validity 81
Content Validity 82
Construct Validity 81
Describing Measurements 83
Describing Frequencies 83
Describing Central Tendency 84
Describing Variability 85
Summary 89
CheckPoint 90
Exercises 91

Chapter 5. Issues in Measurement 93
What to Measure 94
Sampling and Generalizability 94
Types of Samples 95
Nonprobability Sampling 96
Probability Sampling 97
Sample Size 99
Cross-Sectional versus Longitudinal Techniques 101
Types of Measures 103
Behavioral Measures 104
Surveys 104
Questionnaire Design 105
Survey Administration 107
Interviews 108
Types of Interview 108
Interview Techniques 109
Unobtrusive Research 110
Archival Research 110
Content Analysis 112
Trace Measures 113
Hidden Observations 113
Systematic Observations 114
Summary 116
CheckPoint 118
Exercises 118

Chapter 6. Measuring and Using Correlations 121
What Is Correlational Research? 122

Finding Relationships 122
Making Predictions 124
What Correlation Is Not 129
Expressing Correlations 132
Correlation Coefficients 132
Scatterplots 134
Summary 140
CheckPoint 140
Exercises 140

Part 3: Experimental Methods 143

Chapter 7. Fundamental Ideas in Experimental Methods 145
Goals of Experimental Research 146
Causation 147
Experimental Overview 148
Types of Variables 149
Independent Variables 150
Dependent Variables 152
Extraneous Variables 153
Subject Variables 154
Experimenter Variables 154
Situational Variables 155
Confounding Variables 155
More Complex Designs 158
Dealing with Three or More Groups 158
Factorial Designs 159
Multivariate Designs 163
Summary 165
CheckPoint 166
Exercises 167

Chapter 8. The Control of Extraneous Variables 169
The Nature of Equivalence 170
Simple Subject Variables 171
Random Assignment172
Related Versus Independent Groups 173
Types of Related Groups 174
Reduction of Variability 175
Reactivity Effects 176
Placebo Effects 176
Control Group Effects 178
Response Style Effects 180
Experimenter Variables 181
Simple Experimenter Variables 182

Experimenter Expectations 183
Summary 185
CheckPoint 187
Exercises 187

Chapter 9. Quasi-Experimental Research 189
Partial Control of Extraneous Variables 190
The Basic Before–After Design 192
  The Basic Design 193
  The Basic Problems 193
    History Effects 194
    Maturation Effects 194
    Testing Effects 194
    Instrumentation Effects 195
    Mortality Effects 195
    Regression Toward the Mean 196
  Variations on the Theme 197
Simple Variations on the Before–After Design 198
  Static Group Comparisons 198
  Before–After Nonequivalent Groups Designs 199
  Simulated Before-After Designs 201
Expanded Variations on the Before–After Design 203
  Interrupted Time-Series Designs 203
  Multiple Time-Series Designs 204
  Regression-Discontinuity Designs 205
Single-Subject Designs 208
  Reversal Designs 208
    The Importance of Reversal 210
    Reversal with Multiple Variables 211
  Multiple-Baseline Designs 213
Summary 216
CheckPoint 218
Exercises 218

Part 4: Dealing with Results 221

Chapter 10. Statistical Decisions 223
Inferential Statistics 225
  Statistical Reliability 227
  Understanding Errors 229
  Steps in Statistical Inference 231
Kinds of Statistical Test 233
  Levels of Measurement 233
  Research Design 235
  Parametric versus Nonparametric Statistics 236

Test Selection Summary Chart 238
Reporting Results of Statistical Tests 239
Summary 241
CheckPoint 242
Exercises 243

Chapter 11. The Research Report 245
Structure 246
Opening Material 247
Title Page 247
Abstract 247
What You Did, and Why 247
Introduction 247
Method 249
What You Found and What It Means 0
Results 251
Discussion 251
Closing Material 251
References 252
Appendices 252
Writing Techniques 253
Style 253
Sentence Construction 253
Terminology 255
Judging Your Writing 257
The Writing Process 259
Notes 259
Organization 261
Draft 263
Rewrite 270
Summary 272
CheckPoint 273
Exercises 274

Chapter 12. Science as a Human Activity 275
The Social Effects of Research 276
Effects on Participants 277
Effects on the Public 278
Effects on Policy Makers 280
Education 281
The Criminal Justice System 282
The Military 284
Private Industry 284
The Behavioral Science of Science 285
The Power of Patterns 285

Patterns as Positive Factors 287
Patterns as Negative Factors 289
When Theories Collide 291
Summary 295
CheckPoint 296
Exercises 297

Part 5: Appendices 299

Appendix A: Computers in Research 301
A Look at Computers 301
Uses of Computers in Research 303
Consulting the Literature 303
Conducting the Research 304
Analyzing the Data 305
Reporting the Results 307
Conclusions 308

Appendix B: Displaying Data 309
Frequency Data 309
Multivariate Data 312

Appendix C: Statistical Computations 315
A Note on Computations 315
Correlation Coefficients 316
Product–Moment Correlation (Pearson *r*) 316
Spearman Rank–Order Correlation (rho) 318
Four Common Statistical Tests 321
Testing a Frequency (Binomial Test) 321
Testing a Frequency Distribution (Chi-Square) 323
Testing a Difference in Means (*t*-Test) 327
Testing a Correlation (*t*-Test) 330

Appendix D: Statistical Tables 333
Random Numbers 333
Values of Chi-Square 335
Values of Student's *t* 336
Values of the Binomial Distribution 337
Values of the Standard Normal Distribution 338
Determining Needed Sample Size 338

References 341

Glossary 347

Index 363

Quantitative Research for the Behavioral Sciences

Introduction

Why Study Research Methods?

Questions to Consider as You Read

- Why is it important that I learn about research methods?
- Why might I be interested in research that has been done by other people?
- Why might I do research myself some day?

Some of you reading this book are already planning or conducting some sort of research project and want some help with how to go about it. A few of you may just be generally interested in understanding research and how it ought to be done. The rest of you, however, may be approaching this topic with, shall we say, a certain reluctance. In fact, students have been known to protest vehemently that they do not want to know about research methods, do not need to know about them, and furthermore never will need to know about them. Such people are, of course, entitled to hold that opinion if they choose. However, if they are planning further education or a career in the behavioral sciences, that opinion is probably wrong.

Behavioral scientists are interested in behavior, primarily the behavior of people. There are many different sorts of behavioral scientists, interested in the things people do, why they do them, and what we can learn by studying people and animals in many different situations, but they all are curious about the nature of behavior.

Perhaps you are planning to be a speical education teacher, or a parole officer working with juvenile offenders, or an advertising executive designing marketing strategies, or a social worker investigating accusations of child abuse for the family court system, or a campaign manager for a political candidate. Will you still need to know something about research methods? The answer is a definite yes, for two very important reasons. In the first place, you will probably need to evaluate research done by others at some point. In the second place, no matter what your work, you really are likely to do research yourself someday.

Evaluating the Research of Others

Suppose you are working at your career in the behavioral sciences, and performing research is the furthest thing from your mind right now. You are too busy setting up a suicide hotline or working with hyperactive children or planning the lobbying efforts of your political action committee. Then one day a colleague comes up to you and says, "I think we ought to change our program. We should incorporate some new features, so we can reach more people more effectively." What is the basis for thinking that a new program will be better than what you are doing now? Probably, research someone else has done. Your colleague may have read an article or heard a report about the new techniques. You must look at the report yourself to decide whether to follow the suggestions. If you do not know anything about research methods, you will have nothing but your own personal opinions about whether the research was done well enough to warrant the change, or whether it applies in your situation.

Or to take another example, when you are setting up your program you will have to make many decisions. How will you make them? You can go on gut instinct, or you can rely on research others have done about what works and what does not. But again, how will you decide which research to follow? Only an understanding of research methods will allow you to evaluate the research you use.

Even if you do not set out to address a particular question whose answer you must have to do your work, any practitioner in any profession has an obligation (and sometimes a requirement) to keep up with the newest work and ideas in the field. Teachers should keep up to date on methods of teaching and learning, social workers on the treatment and prevention of child abuse, police officers on the dynamics of inner-city youth gangs. This means reading about the latest research. Without some idea of how research is conducted and what it can tell us, reading all this research will be less than useful.

The point is, no matter what area of behavioral science you practice, you will probably have to be a consumer of research. Research performed by others will affect your work, directly and indirectly. Unfortunately, not all research that is done, and published, is done well. Furthermore, even the best research may not exactly fit your circumstances. You can protect yourself only by knowing enough to recognize bad research when you see it and to know when it is inappropriate to generalize from a given piece of research to your own conditions. That is one reason for the importance of studying research methods.

Conducting Research of Your Own

The other reason for studying research methods is to prepare to do research yourself. Most people, when they think of research, think of scientists in white lab coats pouring things from test tubes into beakers, peering into electron microscopes, or jotting obscure notations into big ledgers. Some research is like this, of course, particularly in physical sciences such as chemistry and physics. But in the behavioral sciences, most research is not like this. As a behavioral scientist, you will probably be involved in research of a very different type.

Research simply means answering questions. There are many different ways to answer interesting questions, and not all of them are considered to be scientific research. However, research is one important tool for answering questions. People who work in the behavioral sciences typically use research to find the answers to questions that affect themselves and the people they help. Perhaps you need to decide what sort of remedial program works best with disadvantaged children. Perhaps you are interested in why it is so difficult for battered wives to leave their abusive husbands. Perhaps you want to find out what the life of a homeless street person is really like. Perhaps you suspect that the shooting of Stonewall Jackson by his own men during the Civil War was not an accident. Perhaps you believe that there is a relationship between the number of uniformed police officers on the streets and the crime rate. Any time you begin thinking, "Gee, I wonder if—," you might find yourself doing some sort of research to find an answer.

That is what this book is about: showing you how to use research, your own or other people's, to answer your questions about human beings. We will explore what scientific thinking is and how it applies to social questions. We will consider the different types of research that exist and the kinds of questions each one is best at answering. We will cover some of the specific techniques that researchers use, such as random sampling and statistical analysis. Then, when you find yourself asking questions about people, you will be ready to start finding the answers.

CHECKPOINT

Check your understanding of the material in this introduction:

- What are the two major reasons for learning about research methods in the behavioral sciences?

- Why is it important to understand the research process before using the results of others' research?

EXERCISES

I-1 In your future education or career in the social sciences, what things do you think you will want to find out about people? List at least three different questions you might want to ask.

I-2 Do you think these are things other researchers have already studied? How might you find out?

I-3 Think of the one question you believe you are most likely to have to do research on yourself someday, as you work in the social sciences.

I-4 Write down a brief description of how you would do research on the question you just thought of, if you had to proceed based only on your current understanding of research. What problems do you think you might encounter? How would you solve them? Keep this description around to look at as you go through the course, so you can see how your ideas on research have changed.

Part 1

Fundamentals

Before studying research techniques and methodology, it is important to develop a general understanding of the scientific endeavor. Without such an understanding, you would be like an art student learning the chemistry of pigments and solvents without ever seeing a painting. You have to know what the techniques and methods are for—why they will be used—before they will make any sense.

This first section discusses some of the fundamental ideas that are important for any researcher in any field of science. Chapter 1, a brief overview of the what research is and why people do it, describes the sorts of research covered in this book. Chapter 2 discusses the nature of science, what makes scientific reasoning different from other types of reasoning, and what science can and cannot do for us. Chapter 3 presents some of the ethical issues that researchers, particularly in the behavioral sciences, have to keep in mind.

Once the foundation has been laid, we will be able to consider some more specific issues in research methodology.

Chapter 1

The Nature and Kinds of Research

Questions to Consider as You Read

- What is research?

- What do we mean when we say that research is scientific?

- What are some of the different types of research? What different purposes do they serve?

- What are some of the different ways in which a program could be evaluated?

- What are some of the special difficulties involved in certain types of research?

- What is quantitative research in particular? Why does this book focus on quantitative research?

Any textbook should begin by describing its subject matter. This book is about quantitative research, so quite logically it should begin by describing what quantitative research is and the different types of quantitative research that are used for different purposes. But in another sense, the entire book serves as a definition of research. The term "research" covers so much ground, and activities of so many different kinds, that it is not possible to come up with one simple definition that includes it all. Only by studying all the different types of research discussed in this book can you develop a real sense of what quantitative research is, why people do it, and how it should be done.

What Is Research?

Even though I cannot provide you with a good definition of quantitative research short of this entire book, I can still give you a sketchy idea, one that will serve as a starting point. It is useful to begin by understanding what research is in general and then look at quantitative research in particular. Research is one way of answering questions about the world. Not all questions that we might ask can be answered by research, and not all ways of answering questions are examples of research. What makes something research?

The most important way in which research is different from other ways of answering questions is that it is systematic. That is, you set out to answer your question with a plan in mind, deliberately collecting information you expect to lead you to an answer and arranging this information in a logical, sensible way. This gives us our preliminary definition: **research** is a systematic way of answering questions about the world.

If this definition leaves you feeling unsatisfied, do not despair. As you read and learn, you will build on this definition yourself, until you have a good idea of what research is and is not. You might not be able to put this idea into a few words or sentences, but that is all right. I cannot do it either.

Different Research for Different Purposes

Defining research as a systematic way of answering questions leads to even more questions. What sorts of questions does research address? What sorts of answers can research supply?

There is not one simple answer to what research does, because there are many different types of research that can be used for different purposes. In general, research can be divided into four broad categories according to the purpose for which it is conducted. These broad categories are descriptive, exploratory, theoretical, and applied research.

Descriptive Research

Descriptive research is research that has no purpose other than to describe a particular situation or event. Purely descriptive research does not involve any attempt to understand or explain the situation or to predict what it might be in the future or how it might be changed. For example, the U.S. Census is purely descriptive research, because its only purpose is to take a "snapshot" of the population of the country at a certain time. Another example of descriptive research is a study by Sommer, Estabrook, and Horobin (1988) on instructors' awareness of the cost of the textbooks they chose for their courses. This study showed a strong tendency for instructors to underestimate these costs.

Purely descriptive research is relatively rare, because researchers can seldom avoid the urge to draw some conclusions or make some recommendations on the basis of their observations. Even the study cited above (Sommer, Estabrook, & Horobin, 1988) ended with a section on suggestions for reducing textbook costs to the students. However, descriptive research is useful both for the picture it gives us of how the world is now, and for the insights it can offer into what it might be and how to accomplish this change.

Exploratory Research

The word "exploratory" makes you think of adventurers wending their way across new and unfamiliar territory to find out what it is like. This is an appropriate image for understanding this type of research. The purpose of **exploratory research** is to investigate phenomena or situations that are not familiar. When scientists are just beginning to examine a question, and there is not much information to give an idea of what sorts of answers might be found, they may do exploratory research. Exploratory research tends to be primarily descriptive: that is, directed more toward simply describing what happens in certain situations and less toward explaining why it happens or testing theories about it. Still, it differs from purely descriptive research by virtue of its interest in going beyond simple description to understanding or explaining the situation.

As the population of this country ages, producing a larger percentage of elderly people each year, researchers are becoming interested in the experiences of those who care for an elderly friend or relative. Simon (1988) discusses several exploratory studies of why certain people become caregivers rather than placing elderly relatives with other relatives or in an institution, and their reactions to their experiences as caregivers. The investigators discovered that many people do these things because there is no choice, since there are no other relatives and the caregiver cannot afford a nursing home. Many others, perhaps the majority, care for their spouses or parents because they feel it is right and find it very rewarding. The positive effects of caring for ill, frail, and often totally helpless relatives was something the researchers had not expected to find. This research is exploratory because it was begun not to prove or disprove early ideas, but to find out what the experience of caregivers is like. The researchers were exploring new territory, mapping it out for future research.

Another example of exploratory research involves computer-mediated communication. Kiesler, Siegel, and McGuire (1984) set up several groups to come up with group decisions in specific problem situations, either face to face or through a computer link-up, and found that there were differences in how efficiently the groups worked and how the members of the groups interacted with one another. When using a computer, the group members participated more equally in the group decision and were less inhibited, but they were less efficient in reaching a consensus. The researchers were not trying to test specific theories of communication in these studies. Instead, they were exploring a new area of research, one that may affect many of us in the near future.

When conducting exploratory research, the information one is after is rich and complex, not specific or predictable. This means that it is important to approach exploratory research with as open a mind as possible, free of too many preconceived ideas or expectations about what there is to be found. Exploratory research, when well done, will produce surprises, insights, and many more questions than answers. Few scientists will be satisfied to finish a project with exploratory research. They want to go on to answer some of the new questions, test some of the new insights, and explore yet more territory. Exploratory research is a beginning, the opening of a new frontier for researchers.

The difficulty in exploratory research is that the researchers frequently have little control over their subject matter. They often observe things as they are in their natural state, because to deliberately manipulate the situation might be to cut off some promising line of inquiry that no one has yet recognized. But this means that some of their observations may prove to be misleading or simply statistical flukes when examined more closely by more structured research. Exploratory research is not very useful if what you are looking for is dependable answers. But if you want interesting questions, exploratory research is a good way to begin. So it seems that already we must expand on our preliminary definition of research and say that it is a systematic way of generating and answering questions about the world.

Theoretical Research

One of the purposes of exploratory research is to generate theories about some new field of interest. **Theoretical** (or **basic**) **research**, on the other hand, is research whose main purpose is to test and evaluate theories by finding causal relationships among variables. Specifically, theoretical research is about the causes of things. Why do some people care for their elderly relatives themselves? Why do some impoverished people become criminals? Why do some people faced with traumatic events become stronger, while others retreat into some form of madness? All these questions might be addressed by theoretical research.

Cox, Paulus, and McCain (1984) report a number of studies demonstrating the effects of crowding on inmates in prisons and jails. One of their purposes was to evaluate separately what they called social density (the number of people in a specific space) and spatial density (the amount of space available for a single person). Increasing social density reduces the amount of privacy a prisoner has and increases the chances of harassment or interference from others. Increasing spatial density reduces the amount of private space a person has, but it is still private space. These researchers conclude that social density has much more serious effects on the inmates than spatial density. That is, putting more people into one cell is worse than reducing the size of a single cell. Their studies bear out this conclusion. This is theoretical research, because it is designed to evaluate a theory of prison crowding. (Of course, it is also applied research, because it addresses an issue of current social concern. Categories of research are seldom exclusive, and individual studies often fit into more than one category.)

It is likely that when most research scientists think of research, it is theoretical research that comes to mind. Discovering causes is one of the main things scientists do, and theoretical research is primarily for just that. In fact, the term "pure research" is sometimes used to refer to theoretical research, as though exploratory and applied research were somehow contaminated. But questions about causes are not the only questions that research can answer. Other types of research can be just as important and just as scientific as theoretical research, as long as they are well done.

Applied (Evaluation) Research

Descriptive, exploratory, and theoretical research are ideally suited for satisfying simple scientific curiosity. They can be, and most often are, used to help us understand what something is like—why and how it happens—without necessarily suggesting anything that we should or should not do with that knowledge. Applied research, on the other hand, is typically done for the sole purpose of telling us what to do next. **Applied research** is any research aimed at solving real-world problems or making practical decisions about actions in actual situations. **Evaluation research** focuses on the effectiveness of some program or treatment, for the purpose of determining how the program is working or how it can be improved. The distinction between these two terms sometimes gets fuzzy. In theory, "applied research" is more general, and "evaluation research" denotes one particular type of applied research. However, in practice, just about any research aimed at solving a real problem will probably also be about evaluating some actual or potential solutions to the problem, and so it will also be evaluation research. Scientists use these terms more to reflect the emphasis or the intent of the research than to indicate major structural differences.

Applied research is a very important part of the behavioral sciences, because it affects real people in their real lives. It is also a very important topic for students of research methods, because it is the type of research you are most likely to have to conduct even if you have no research training at all. If you look back at the introduction and reread the examples of research behavioral scientists might be expected to perform, you will notice that they are all applied research (in fact, they are all evaluation research). When you must choose which of two programs to implement, decide where to cut back to save funds, or look for places to improve services, evaluation research can help you make your decisions.

Types of Evaluation Research

Evaluation research is divided up in different ways, depending on the major goals the research is designed to address. The lines between the different categories of evaluation research are somewhat blurry, and a specific example of research may not fall neatly to one side or the other of a division. Nevertheless, thinking of these different types of research can be useful, because it can help you become clearer about just what it is the research is supposed to accomplish.

One way of categorizing evaluation research is to distinguish between summative and formative research. **Summative evaluation research** focuses on the current effectiveness of a program. That is, it emphasizes the sum, the total, the bottom line. How many suicides has the hotline actually prevented? Is the college professor ever available to the students outside of class? What is the profitability of a division of the company? How many people actually watched the new television commercial, and how many of them could remember it five minutes later? Summative evaluations may help people make decisions about whether to continue a program or to terminate it, or whether to look more closely at a program that needs improvement. **Formative evaluation research**, on the other hand, focuses on diagnosing areas of the program that are weak and making recommendations for improvement. The question of formative research is not whether the program should be canceled or kept, but what should be done differently. Formative evaluation is especially important when what is being evaluated is not a program, but a person. Employees are much more likely to accept an evaluation whose purpose is to help them improve their performance than an evaluation whose purpose is to determine whether they keep their jobs. It makes sense for the employer, too, because it is cheaper and more productive to improve an existing worker than to fire that one and hire a new one. Formative and summative evaluation are truly independent in that you can have either one without the other, or both together. It is not necessary to compute how the hotline functions with those who call before figuring out the number of potential suicides who dial the hotline number, or vice versa. Nevertheless, a summative evaluation is frequently another part of the formative evaluation process.

Another way of categorizing evaluation research is to distinguish between impact and process evaluation. (These are two different classification systems that can be applied to the same piece of research. Thus a study may be, for example, both summative and impact.) One way of looking at this distinction is that impact evaluation tells us *whether* something works, while process evaluation tells us *how* it works. **Impact evaluation research** uses primarily information about the actual effect, or impact, that a program has had. An impact evaluation of a program to give sterile needles to drug addicts to slow the spread of AIDS would focus on whether the program had any measurable effect on the number of new AIDS cases among drug addicts. **Process evaluation research**, however, focuses on the details of how the program functions in an attempt to determine what parts of it are successful and what parts of it are not. Suppose an impact evaluation showed that the sterile needle program has no effect at all on the spread of AIDS among drug addicts. Process evaluation might help us determine why not. Perhaps the drug addicts will not come in for the needles, because they are afraid of being arrested. Perhaps they share the new needles and get infected anyway. Perhaps drug addicts pick up AIDS in other ways, such as sexual contact, at such a rate that the sterile needles make no difference. Perhaps the company that packages the needles was not careful enough and the needles were not sterile in the first place.

Finally, there is an aspect of evaluation research called cost-benefit analysis. **Cost–benefit analysis** compares the total effect of the program in terms of what good it has done (the benefits) and the expenses and any harm it has done (the costs), to determine whether the benefits are large enough to outweigh the costs. This is similar to summative evaluation in that it looks mostly at what the program is actually accomplishing, not at how it could be improved, and it is similar to process evaluation in that it examines all the details of how the program functions, but it is not the same thing as either one.

Cost–benefit analysis is difficult to do well for two main reasons. First, *all* costs and *all* benefits must be evaluated: direct and indirect, deliberate and accidental, expected and unexpected. In the sterile needle program, costs would include not only the price of the needles and the staff to distribute them, but the amount spent on the education campaign to make the addicts aware of the program, the potential for increasing the public's fear of AIDS, and even the cost of the evaluation program itself. The benefits would include not only reduced human suffering and medical costs, but also the increased contact between drug addicts and "straight" society, which might improve the staff's awareness of the addicts as human beings and might get some of the latter in for treatment.

It is difficult in any analysis to be sure that every important cost and benefit has been included. But even if they are all included, another problem still exists in that costs and benefits are often difficult to measure. Comparing the price of the needles and the payroll of the staff on the one hand with the estimated hospital costs of AIDS victims on the other is fairly straightforward. But how do you fit the other variables into the equation? How many dollars is improved contact with addicts worth? What will you pay to avoid increasing the public fear of AIDS? Perhaps increasing public fear of AIDS is not a cost at all, but a benefit; fear can be a rational response to a fatal epidemic. These sorts of questions have no easy answer and they make cost–benefit analysis difficult to do.

Special Difficulties of Applied Research

There are other factors that can make any applied research more difficult to carry out than other forms of research. They stem from the fact that applied research deals with real-world problems, and the real world is seldom as neat and orderly as the research laboratory. The problems fall generally into three categories: those dealing with lack of control over the situation, those dealing with the reactions of the people involved, and those dealing with measurement and interpretation. While all these problems can apply to any type of research, they are more often important in applied research.

Lack of control means that the researcher may not be able to make decisions about how a program is to be implemented or how people will be chosen to become involved in the program, and without such control the results of the research will generally not be completely definitive. This is especially likely to happen when a program is implemented without thought to how its effectiveness will be evaluated, so that research to determine how well the program works must be designed after the program is in place. Suppose you want to know whether a certain program makes a difference. Compared to what? Compared to the situation before the program began? But perhaps other factors that have changed could account for the difference, not the program itself. Compared to other groups (cities, countries, schools, whatever) that do not have the program? But perhaps they are different in other ways and cannot really be compared to your situation. The problem of control is a critical one in any research that attempts to discover *why* something happened. This point is discussed in much more detail in Chapters 7–9, but for now just remember this: if you want to be sure that a specific change is due to the program itself and not to an extraneous factor, you will need a great deal of control over the situation, control that may be impossible in your research.

Whatever the results of an applied research study, it will usually affect someone in some way. This means that the people involved in the research program will often have a definite preference for how the research comes out and may attempt to bias the results. The *reactions of the people involved* may range from making suggestions about what sorts of things your research could consider, through reporting only the information that fits their biases, to actively distorting records and reports. It is important to be alert for this problem when conducting applied research. It is even more important to be sensitive to the feelings of the people who are involved in your research. Remember that they might be affected in important ways by your report. If you were to conclude that the sterile needle program was not effective and should be discontinued, the addicts would be denied services, people who have supported the program would be contradicted, and employees might lose their jobs. If such an outcome is a possibility, be sure to approach the situation with tact and consideration.

The final problem is actually true of any sort of research, but it is exaggerated in applied research because more people have a stake in what the research means. *Measurement problems* deal with applying numbers to situations that are very complex, such as the public fear of AIDS; *interpretation problems* deal with deciding what a particular measurement is saying to us, such as whether greater public fear of AIDS is a good thing or a bad thing. Almost no matter how you conduct your research, some people are likely to say that you did not measure the important factors at all or that your measurements are faulty or that you misinterpreted your results. This also happens with exploratory and theoretical research, but it is much more widespread with applied research, because applied research is more likely to be reported publicly and to trigger a strong reaction in more people. A newspaper headline is more likely to say "Scientists Conclude AIDS Prevention Program Ineffective" than "Scientists Falsify Interference Theory of Memory."

As an example of applied, evaluation research, consider a study done by the Massachusetts Department of Public Welfare to evaluate the mental health services provided to the poor under Medicaid (Davenport & Nutall, 1979). They compared the services supplied to Medicaid participants in a number of different mental health facilities with the services supplied to non-Medicaid participants in the same facilities. This very large and complex study involved aspects of most of the different types of research discussed above. Although the study evaluated the services currently provided to Medicaid recipients, it was more formative than summative research in that it was aimed at making recommendations for future improvement, not at determining whether to shut the whole program down. It contained aspects of both impact evaluation, in that it considered the actual benefits gained by the recipients of the program, and process evaluation, in that it broke the system down into its components and determined how all the details worked together. But it was primarily a cost–benefit analysis. The costs of the program were measured fairly simply in terms of the dollars it cost to administer. The benefits, however, were much more difficult to measure and to evaluate. One of the simplest benefit measurements was the number of treatment hours the clients received. More difficult to assess were the types of mental illness that are diagnosed and the medication prescribed. If one patient receives a serious diagnosis and strong medication, and another receives a milder diagnosis and a few office visits, which patient got the greater benefit? It is almost impossible to give a final answer to that question.

Quantitative versus Qualitative Research

This book is about quantitative research, not research in general. **Quantitative research** is research that involves measuring quantities of things, usually numerical quantities. **Qualitative research**, which this book is not about, involves assessing the quality of things. For instance, if one were studying the special education program in a certain school district, qualitative research might explore how the students, teachers, and parents feel about and react to their experiences with the program, while quantitative research might assess the progress of the children academically, psychologically, and socially.

This book focuses on quantitative research, which means that issues of measurement are of primary importance. Less emphasis is given to exploring the personal, individual meanings of experiences to the people who lived them. This does not mean, though, that meaning and feelings have no place in quantitative research. The quantitative approach to research does not deny or ignore personal experiences. It merely insists that these experiences be quantified, measured on some scale, before they can be scientifically studied. Within this framework, a dazzling variety of questions can be addressed. The chapters to come will give you a small glimpse at this variety, and explain why there is more variety in the world than any book like this can possibly show.

First, we will take a side excursion into the philosophy of science, to learn how science can help our research be systematic. Then we can move more directly into the territory of research itself.

SUMMARY

A. Research can be defined as a systematic approach to answering questions. This book describes some of the systems used in research to answer questions.

B. The purposes of research generally fall into four broad categories.

1. Descriptive research simply measures the current state of some system, without addressing issues of how to explain, predict, or change it.
2. Exploratory research represents the first few forays into a new area of study, before the researchers have a very clear idea of what the appropriate questions are. Exploratory research is rich in complex information and is often used to form more structured theories later on.
3. Theoretical research involves the systematic testing of specific theories. Theoretical research is necessary for developing a deep understanding of why things happen as they do.
4. Applied research is aimed at making a real-world decision. When it is designed to assess the effectiveness of a program, it is called evaluation research.
   a. Summative evaluations look at the current effectiveness of a program, while formative evaluations make recommendations for improvement in the future. Impact evaluations focus on the total effectiveness of the program, while process evaluations look at the details of how it operates. Cost–benefit analysis attempts to compare all the costs and the benefits of a program, which is often extremely difficult.
   b. Some special difficulties are likely whenever a researcher is involved in applied research. The researcher often lacks control over the situation. The people involved in the situation may react favorably or unfavorably to the research, and they may attempt to bias the results. There is usually some disagreement as to what factors need to be measured, how they should be measured, and what the final results mean.
C. This book is about quantitative research, which involves the measurement of quantities, usually in numbers. This excludes qualitative research, which is focused on the individual meanings of experiences to the people who lived them.

CHECKPOINT

Check your understanding of the material in this chapter:

- What is our preliminary definition of research?

- What are the three major categories of research discussed so far? What are their special purposes? What are their major difficulties?

- What is the difference between summative evaluation and formative evaluation?

- What is the difference between impact evaluation and process evaluation?

- What is cost–benefit analysis? Why is it particularly difficult to do?

- What is the difference between quantitative research and qualitative research?

EXERCISES

1.1   Think of a situation in your own area of interest in which you might perform descriptive research. What aspects of the situation would you choose to measure? How might you choose to measure them?

1.2   Think of a situation in your own area of interest in which you might perform exploratory research. What sorts of questions might this research address?

1.3   Think of a situation in your own area of interest in which you might perform theoretical research. Do you think this research might be important? Why or why not?

1.4   Think of a situation in your own area of interest in which you might perform applied or evaluation research. What special problems might you run into with this research?

1.5   Look back at the research you described in writing after reading the Introduction. Which of the categories (descriptive, exploratory, theoretical, or applied) do you think it belongs to? Why? Think of a different research project that addresses the same question but falls into a different category. Which category does it belong to? Why?

1.6   This chapter describes qualitative research briefly, as contrasted with quantitative research, the subject of this book. Do you believe that qualitative research is something you would like to learn more about? Do you think it might be applicable to a particular research question that interests you? Look back at the research you described in writing after reading the Introduction. Is that research qualitative, quantitative, or both? Why do you say that?

Chapter 2

The Nature of Science

Questions to Consider as You Read

- What is science?

- What do scientists try to do?

- Where does knowledge come from? How do we know what we know?

- Why do some people say that you should believe only the things you can figure out logically for yourself?

- Why do some people say that you should believe only the things you can actually observe for yourself?

- In what ways is scientific thinking better than other types of thinking?

- What sorts of questions cannot be answered with scientific thinking?

- How does a scientist go about testing a theory?

- What kinds of statements can be valid scientific theories, and what kinds cannot?

This book is addressed to behavioral scientists. What makes someone a behavioral scientist? For that matter, what makes someone any kind of scientist? The stereotype of a scientist, the image that comes immediately to mind when most of us hear that word, is usually a physicist or a chemist, easily recognizable by virtue of the complex mathematical equations scribbled on the blackboard or the test tubes bubbling away in the background. Is this what it means to be scientific? If so, how can the study of people be scientific?

To answer these questions, we need to know something about what science is. Science is not defined by the equipment a person uses or by the activities a person performs. Science is defined by the things a person is trying to accomplish and the kinds of thinking done to accomplish them. Using the tools of scientific thinking is one way we can make our approach to questions systematic, so that we are doing research instead of just idle thinking.

Misunderstandings about the nature of science are widespread. Even a high quality children's television show such as "Sesame Street" can demonstrate confusion. Oscar the Grouch, having observed on many occasions that people have their umbrellas out when it rains, conducts an experiment to see whether opening your umbrella can cause it to rain. He has drawn an interesting theory from a series of observations, and he goes about testing it in a systematic way, just as a good scientist should. However, other more "sensible" characters ridicule him for entertaining such a silly idea, giving the impression that it is foolish to test ideas that do not make sense according to our understanding of the world. Just because a theory seems silly, it is not necessarily wrong. Good scientists question everything, test everything.

Science is one particular way of finding out about the world, and this includes the world of people, their actions and their feelings. The best way to understand this is to look at what scientists try to do and the sorts of thinking they use along the way.

Goals of Science

Every scientist is interested in finding out about something, understanding it. Behavioral scientists are interested in finding out about people: their pasts, their presents, their futures. How do children learn arithmetic? What sort of person makes the best police officer? Is there any way to avoid World War III? Whatever a scientist wants to find out about, there are four basic goals that can contribute to that understanding.

Description

The first step toward understanding anything is to describe it, to answer the question, "What happened?" To describe something is to observe it and record what happens. Descriptive research obviously addresses this goal of science, but the other types of research usually involve description, also. Behavioral scientists use **description** when they watch people and record what they do and what happens to them. Some descriptions are personal and subjective, describing what something felt like to the people who went through it. These are part of qualitative research and as such are beyond this book. Others are objective and controlled, allowing us to measure and evaluate the experience, and will be discussed in the chapters that follow. Both types of description are important, and both are useful for different purposes, though this book has chosen to focus on only one type.

Consider the important social issue of racial prejudice and discrimination. Clearly observing and describing a phenomenon is the first step in studying it. For example, Duncan (1976) showed white people videotapes of one man shoving another man. When a white man shoved a black man, the observers described the action as "horsing around," but when a black man shoved a white man, they described the incident as "violent." This is an objective, systematic way of describing discrimination in the way people see each other.

Prediction

After one has observed and described a situation, one may notice certain regularities in the observations, and start to answer the question, "What will happen next?" **Prediction** involves saying things about what is going to happen before actually observing it. If two things consistently go together, it makes sense to try to use one of them to predict the other. Correlational research, as discussed in Chapter 6, is particularly useful for this, though many other types of research involve prediction as well. For example, people who conduct direct mail campaigns to sell products or to raise money for political causes have noticed that people from certain social classes are more likely to respond positively to their letters than others. Then they can target their mailings to those likely customers, by using existing mailing lists or ZIP codes. They may not know or even care what makes those people better prospects, but they can predict that they will be.

To return to the example of racial prejudice, it has been observed that prejudice requires that there be two groups of people, Us and Them. In fact, discrimination will often occur when people are divided into two groups, no matter how temporary or trivial the conditions that divide them. Tajfel (1982) demonstrated this clearly. A group of boys were shown some slides that contained a random display of dots, presented so briefly there was not enough time to count the dots. Some of the boys consistently overestimated the number of dots on the slides, and others consistently underestimated the number. One of the boys would then be given a small sum of money and told to distribute it any way he chose among the other boys. He would demonstrate his prejudice by giving more of the money to the boys who were similar to himself in either overestimating or underestimating the number of dots on the slide.

Two things have been observed to go together here: the presence of a factor that divided the boys into two groups, and discrimination between the groups. We are now in a position to be able to predict that any time people can be divided into groups, they will tend to behave better toward those who are members of their own group and to discriminate against those who are members of the other group.

Explanation

The third goal of science, beyond describing what occurs or predicting what will occur, is to explain something, answering the question, "Why did it happen that way?" To explain something is to give a coherent set of reasons why a particular thing happened as it did and not any other way. **Explanation** involves finding out the causes of events, the laws that determine what happens. Theoretical research is particularly useful for testing explanations.

Why do people discriminate against those who are different from themselves? There are many possible explanations. One comes from sociobiology (Wilson, 1975). According to the theory of evolution, all living things have been selected to behave in ways that increase the chances that their genes will be passed on to the next generation. For humans, one thing this would mean is that we would be biologically biased toward those who are related to us, and biased against those who are not related. This would easily generalize to a bias against those who are different from us in any way.

Another explanation for prejudice is called the "just world phenomenon" (Lerner, 1980). When we see bad things happen to other people, it creates anxiety in us to think that they might happen to us, too. A way of defending ourselves against this fear is to decide that the unfortunate group got what they deserved. Thus the members of the dominant group tell themselves that the members of the subordinate group have problems because they are not capable of doing any better. Before the Civil War, there was a widespread belief that blacks were an inferior form of human being, incapable of taking care of themselves if not under the control of a white master. This belief was comfortable to the whites, because believing anything else threatened their economic dependence on the black slave. It was easy to ignore the fact that the blacks had survived quite well in Africa for thousands of years without the help of whites.

How much truth there is in these explanations for racial prejudice is an open question. We do not yet understand the phenomenon well enough to be sure just why it happens. But each of these explanations, and others as well, is an attempt to say why people behave in this way under these conditions.

Control

The final goal of science is control, answering the question, "How can I make something happen?" To **control** something is to make things tend to happen in a certain way. This is where many people become decidedly against the idea of applying the scientific method to human beings. We do not want some fanatic in a white coat controlling our behavior! But scientists who attempt to control behavior do not want to determine exactly what each person does at each moment. It is probably impossible to do that, anyway. Control can mean many things, most of which you would not find objectionable. (Perhaps it would help to think of "modifying" behavior, rather than "controlling" it.) Helping to get your favorite political candidate elected is controlling people's behavior. Putting disadvantaged children in special classes where they can learn to read is controlling people's behavior. Working to curb government spending and reduce the federal deficit is controlling people's behavior. And, to continue our example, finding ways to reduce racial prejudice and discrimination is controlling people's behavior. Theoretical research, which studies causes, and applied research, which evaluates treatments, are both useful when attempting to control or modify a situation.

Sherif (1966) performed a classic demonstration on the control of prejudice. He studied two groups of boys attending a Boy Scout camp one summer. The groups were first put in competitive situations, playing such team games as capture the flag for team prizes. As we can predict from the study by Tajfel (1982) mentioned before, the boys became prejudiced toward members of their own group and against members of the other group. Soon the two groups could hardly come in contact without shouting, name-calling, and scuffling. Then, however, Sherif set up a number of situations in which the boys had to cooperate to achieve some common goal. The water supply in the camp broke down, and they all had to work together to get it going again. They wished to rent a movie, but it took their combined contributions to raise enough money. The camp truck stalled when they were going to get supplies, and they all pushed it to get it started. After working together like this, the boys showed less prejudice, and soon some boys had friends in the other group. Sherif has demonstrated a technique for controlling prejudice that can be applied to a number of situations.

Behavioral scientists are people who want to answer questions about people. They want to know what happened to them, what will happen, why it happened, and how to make it happen (or not happen) again. How do they go about answering these questions? Scientists approach their goals by observing people and thinking in a particular way about what they observe.

Ways of Knowing

Think of all the things you know or you believe. The world is round. Germs cause disease. Cats have whiskers. Snow is cold. Money does not grow on trees. The phone always rings when you are in the shower. Real men do not do dishes. Socialism is evil. Communism is evil. Capitalism is evil. The list of facts and opinions each of us holds is nearly boundless. How do we know these things? Where does our knowledge come from?

This is one of the great, classic issues of philosophy, which means that over the years many brilliant minds have pondered the question of where we get our knowledge. It seems as though the answer should be very simple. Knowledge comes from seeing the world and thinking about it. But, when you start to analyze it closely, you find the answer is not so simple after all. Seeing what kinds of things? Can you see diseases, or socialism? How do you know that somewhere there does not exist a tree that grows money, or a real man who does dishes? And what kinds of thinking are involved? You have never seen a leprechaun, and you have never seen an atom, yet it is far more likely that you believe in atoms than that you believe in leprechauns. Why? What is the reasoning process that permits you to believe some things and not others?

Most of the time, most of the things we believe are probably true. That is, most of them are things other people would agree with, and things that allow us to function well in the real world. This is really somewhat surprising, when you think of all the chances we have for misinformation. Consider a song from the musical *You're a Good Man, Charlie Brown*. Lucy has taken responsibility for teaching her little brother Linus about the world, and she regales him with many fascinating statements: sparrows grow up to be eagles, and on Thanksgiving we eat them; fir trees give us fur for coats (and wool in the wintertime); bugs make the grass grow by tugging on the blades; snow comes up out of the ground like flowers. The song is humorous because the beliefs are so outrageous. But why? How do we know the world is not exactly as Lucy describes it? There are fundamentally three different ways we can find out about the world, three different sources of beliefs and knowledge.

Traditionalism or Authority

Most knowledge, of course, is transmitted from person to person through education. This way of knowing is called *traditionalism* or *authority*, because knowledge is passed to you through your society's traditions or though authority figures telling you what to believe. You probably believe the world is round because you have always been told so, and everyone acts as though it is, and this belief seems to cause them no particular problems. But only a few astronauts have ever actually seen this property for themselves. Based on your own personal experience with the parts of the world you have been in, it certainly does not look round. So a lot of what we know we have been told, and we generally cannot afford the time and the energy to doubt everything we hear. Fortunately for us, however, many people throughout history have doubted many of the things they were told, and in challenging accepted beliefs were able to change our understanding of our world. Without this doubt, we would all be sitting around campfires, scratching fleabites and gnawing half-cooked deer bones.

There is nothing wrong in accepting most of what you learn. Most of it is probably true, in any case. But you must always keep in mind that some of it might be wrong. Each of these ideas had to come from some place originally, and ideas do not come with warranties. Where did the knowledge come from originally?

Rationalism

One source of original knowledge is one's own brain and reasoning processes. This is **rationalism**: figuring things out through logical, rational thought. Many of the great philosophers used this sort of reasoning. In 1641 Descartes wrote a famous treatise representing his attempt to find out what knowledge he could prove to himself through pure logic (Descartes, 1641/1955). He began with the most basic sort of question: What am I? He concluded that he was a thing that thought. In this way he proved that he himself existed. (*Something* was wondering what was real. Whatever it was, it was him.) Descartes was unwilling to believe things just because he saw them or heard them or even touched them. Sensory experiences might not be real. For instance, he said, it seems to me that I am awake as I write this, but I can remember many occasions when I had the same impression while dreaming. Perhaps, he reasoned, I am dreaming right now, and everything that I experience is only an illusion. If this were true, he concluded, then the only things he could believe were things he could prove to himself through logic.

Socrates was another famous practitioner of rationalism. He addressed himself to problems of the physical and social world, such as how people think and how best to run a society. The answers he gave to these questions were based on his reasoning about them in the privacy of his study and discussing them with other philosophers. According to Plato, who recorded the discussions, Socrates said that anyone who would get hold of the truth would have to approach it through "intelligence alone, not adding sight to intelligence, or dragging in any other sense along with reasoning, but using the intelligence uncontaminated alone by itself. . ." (Plato, 427–347 BC/1956, p. 469). This is the rationalist credo: reasoning alone can find the answers to important questions, because observation may not be correct. Seeing may be a lie; only thinking is believing.

Rationalism is not restricted to brilliant thinkers. Some of the popular psychology, self-help, advice, and how-to books on the market are basically rationalistic. Some child-care books, for example, have been written by people who have firm beliefs about what children are like, despite the lack of any real experience with them. They have logically, rationally figured out what sorts of things parents ought to do, based on their logical, rational ideas about children. If their ideas happen to be right—that is, if they happen to correspond in important ways with what real children are like—their suggestions will be helpful. If not, they can cause more harm than good.

The central tool of rationalism is deductive reasoning. **Deduction** means reasoning from general principles to specific conclusions. If used properly, deduction allows you to have absolute logical certainty in the truth of your conclusions. The simplest example of deductive reasoning, called a **syllogism**, begins with a general principle and a specific assumption, and draws a conclusion that must be correct if the initial assumptions are correct. For example, if one accepts as true assumptions the statements "All required courses are boring" and "This is a required course," then through deduction one can conclude, "This course is boring." Another example would be to begin, as Descartes did, with "Anything that thinks must exist" and "I think," and conclude, "I exist." Deductive reasoning such as this allows the logical certainty of the assumptions to lead to the logical certainty of the conclusions.

However, your conclusions are not necessarily true if your assumptions are not true. In the examples above, if it is not true that all required courses are boring, or if not everything that thinks exists, then the conclusions just given may be false. Deduction can help you reason logically from your assumptions, but the whole foundation of deductive reasoning rests on the accuracy of your assumptions.

The value of rationalism as a way to find out about the world depends on many things, including the quality of thinking of the rationalizer. People with clear thoughts, who rigorously question their assumptions and observe proper rules of logic, will probably go far. People with fuzzy thoughts, who assume things more or less because they wish they were true, will have good ideas only by chance. The value of rationalism also depends on what sort of world the thinker is trying to understand. When exploring a world that is not available to our normal senses, such as the world of spirits or of God, rationalism or authority are probably the only answers. But when the things you want to find out about are available to your senses, when they are things you can see and hear and touch, then rationalism is probably not the most effective way to explore them.

Empiricism

The other major source of knowledge is one's experience with the world. This is **empiricism**: deciding about how the world works by observing events and drawing conclusions from them. Empiricism differs from rationalism in that it is based on actual observations of actual events. A rationalist might conclude that heavier objects must fall faster than light ones; an empiricist would drop a heavier object and a lighter one from a tower and time them as they fall. A rationalist might deduce that people who are paid directly for the work that they do will like their work more than people whose pay is unrelated to the quality of their work. An empiricist might observe people's actual reactions and discover that most times just the opposite happens: if two people are paid the same amount of money, but one's salary depends on the work done while the other is paid the same regardless of work done, the one paid the flat rate will find the work more pleasant (Pinder, 1976). Empirical knowledge is based on real-world observations, not logical reasoning.

Science, as you have probably guessed, is essentially empirical. This does not mean that scientists do not use logical, rational thought, because they do. It also does not mean that every piece of information believed by any scientist is ultimately based on actual observation. It is frequently impossible to observe interesting phenomena (when was the last time you actually saw another person's memory?), and scientists often build theories that describe events that no one has observed. But if there is a conflict, a scientist will generally give more weight to an observed event than to a logical argument. When scientists are discussing some issue, you will often hear one of them say, "That's an empirical question," which means, "Why are we sitting around *talking* about it? Let's go out and *look.*"

There are many advantages to empirical knowledge, as compared to rational knowledge. When dealing with complex situations, logical reasoning will often be able to argue equally well for any possible answer. Sometimes, in fact, people hold two beliefs that are absolutely contradictory but are both based on logical reasoning. First they say, "Absence makes the heart grow fonder," because when you are away from people you love, you realize how much you miss them. Then they say, "Out of sight, out of mind," because when you are away from people you love, you forget how much they mean to you. Which is true? Perhaps both are true, under different conditions. Which conditions? When is one true, and when the other? To answer questions like these, you would need to observe different people who are separated from loved ones for different reasons, under different circumstances, and see what happens. In other words, you would need to engage in empirical thinking.

Rationalism also fails when the faulty use of deductive reasoning leads to false conclusions. Sometimes this failure can have serious social consequences. Many times a generalization is true sometimes or often without being true in every instance. For example, it is true that women in general have better verbal skills than men. This can easily lead people to reasoning like this: "Women are better with language than men. Mary is a woman. John is a man. Therefore, Mary is better with language than John." This seems to be an unassailable example of deductive reasoning, but in fact it is wrong. The reasoning would be correct only if the first assumption were "All women are better with language than all men," which is not a true statement. It would be more accurate to say, "The average woman is better with language than the average man"; this assumption, however, does not allow you to conclude that Mary is better than John. There is a strong tendency for people to generalize from a group to an individual, which is one likely source of prejudice and stereotyping. Things that are true on the average, however, are not always true in particular cases. Rationalism allows such logical errors to go unchecked because it is difficult to find the flaws in one's own assumptions. Empiricism, which checks beliefs against actual observations, includes a system for discovering when one's beliefs are mistaken.

It is important to remember that empiricism has drawbacks as well as advantages. Many times observations can be inaccurate for one reason or another. Important principles such as Newton's law of gravity could not be derived solely from observations on earth, because factors such as the earth's rotation, air resistance, and friction complicate the issue. Some questions involve things that cannot be observed at all, directly or indirectly, and so cannot be studied empirically. An example of this is one of the key questions surrounding the abortion issue. Specialists in embryology can testify about how developed the human fetus is at various points before birth. But when concerned citizens ask them point blank, "When is it a human being?" the embryologists back off, claiming that this is not a question science can answer. The response often seems like mealy-mouthed, wishy-washy evasiveness, or like a lack of caring about the issues involved. In fact, it is neither. These people are exactly right. The question of what makes someone a human being is not one that can be answered through observation. It is not an empirical question. Therefore, science simply cannot provide the solution, and a scientist who admits this is merely being honest. We must answer that question for ourselves individually, through rational thinking, and not expect our answer to be proved scientifically. Questions such as whether God exists, whether ESP works only when it is not being observed systematically, and whether the soul continues to exist after death are not empirical questions and so cannot be answered through the scientific method.

Unscientific Empiricism
Scientific thinking is empirical, but not all empirical thinking is scien-

tific. Just because an idea is based on observations does not make it accurate. We have many ideas about people, ourselves and others, that are wrong because they are based on casual, informal reasoning. We observe a few people in a few situations and draw general conclusions about people. Sometimes our conclusions may be right. Other times, they are wrong. With this kind of informal reasoning, it is impossible to know which ideas are right. As an example, it seems only reasonable that children who were very strongly attached to their parents and cried loudly when they left the room while they were infants will be shyer and more reluctant to explore new situations than children who were more independent and less concerned when their parents left. In fact, securely attached infants developed into confident, mature, enthusiastic 2- to 4-year-olds (Sroufe, Fox, & Pancake, 1983). Casual thinking has led us astray in this case.

Casual thinking leads to problems in other cases, too. Superstition is one example. Think of a compulsive gambler. Why did I win tonight? It must be my green socks. So the gambler wears the green socks every night, but loses. On the night of the next big win, an old woman is at the table. Aha, the gambler thinks, the green socks *and* an old woman. And so it goes. The gambler collects many separate observations and draws generalizations from them.

Another case of faulty conclusions from casual thinking is our tendency to draw false generalizations from specific observations. When you have had contact with one or a few members of a group, there is a tendency to think that all members of the group are similar to the ones you have met. Many social stereotypes are born this way. If you met a hot-tempered redhead, a jolly fat person, or an unfeeling scientist, you are likely to think that all redheads are hot-tempered, all fat people are jolly, and all scientists are unfeeling (see Figure 2-1). We are moderately good at describing what people do, not quite as good at predicting what they will do in the future, and not very good at all at explaining why they do what they do, because of our reliance on casual, unsystematic reasoning.

Falsificationism

A different, more scientific type of empirical thinking that avoids the problems inherent in casual reasoning was developed by Karl Popper (1965). **Falsificationism** is a system in which the emphasis is shifted from proving beliefs to be *true* to proving them to be *false*, by attempting to find observations that disagree with the belief. In this system it is perfectly all right for your beliefs to come from faulty observations. This works because falsificationism concentrates not on producing true beliefs but on testing beliefs after they are created. Because the falsificationist approach has no way to prove a belief, in this approach there can *never* be a belief that is accepted as true. In falsificationism,

"She's all I know about Bryn Mawr, and all I have to know."

Figure 2-1 An example of the casual thinking error of drawing a false conclusion from a specific observation. Surely all students at Bryn Mawr College are not like this one.

beliefs are always on probation, subject to constant testing, which should serve in the long run to remove any incorrect belief.

This is not a natural way of thinking. Most of us do not go through life considering that all our beliefs might be wrong and wondering how we might prove them false. We as human beings have a strong tendency to look for evidence that our beliefs are *true* rather than the other way around (see Bower, 1991, for a summary of some recent research on this). Consider the following example, modified from one developed by Wason and Johnson-Laird (1972):

There are four cards on the table in front of you, as shown in Figure 2-2. These cards are from a special deck, and they all have letters on one side and numbers on the other. I have made a statement about this deck: "Every card that has a vowel on one side has an even number on the other." Your job is to decide whether my statement is true of the cards in front of you, turning over the *fewest* possible cards in the process. Which cards will you turn over?

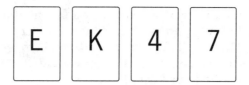

Figure 2-2 Decide which card or cards you would have to turn over to test the statement "Every card that has a vowel on one side has an even number on the other." (Based on Wason & Johnson–Laird, 1972.)

Before you go on, take a moment to think about it, and then write the letters or numbers of the cards you would turn over here:

————————   ————————   ————————   ————————

If you are like most people, you choose to turn over the E and the 4. You choose these cards because the statement mentions them indirectly, as vowels and even numbers, and you are attempting to check whether the statement is true. However, this is not the right choice. There are two cards you should turn over, but you have not chosen exactly the right two. Think again, this time concentrating on the idea of trying to prove the statement false. Does this give you another idea? The correct choices are given at the end of the chapter.

How Falsification Works

Falsificationism is the backbone of modern science. Remember Oscar the Grouch putting up umbrellas in the bright sunshine to test the idea that umbrellas make it rain? I said that he was being truly scientific, because he was using the falsificationist approach. He was testing his theory by trying to prove it wrong. When, in fact, it did not rain, Oscar behaved just as a scientist should, by rejecting his theory as disproven by the facts. Next we will look in more detail at the falsificationist approach.

Falsifiable Statements

At the heart of the falsificationist approach (to mix my anatomical metaphors somewhat) is the falsifiable statement. A statement is **falsifiable** if there is some logically possible, imaginable set of observations that would prove the statement false. If the statement or belief could never, under any imaginable circumstances, be proven false, then it can never be tested, and falsificationism cannot operate. Remember, in this approach there is no barrier to prevent false beliefs from arising. The only defense against them is to test them all and gradually weed out the false ones. Without the ability to test a belief, we cannot say whether it is true or false.

When we say that there must be some set of observations that would prove the statement false, it does not matter whether those observations are actually likely to occur in the real world. If the statement happens to be true, then observations that would prove it false obviously will not occur. But there must be some logically possible, imaginable observations one could look for in trying to prove the statement false, or the statement is not falsifiable.

Let us consider some examples. The law of gravity predicts that any solid object, heavier than air, will fall if released a few feet off the ground. This is a falsifiable statement, because one can imagine picking up a rock, letting it go, and having it just stay there, floating in the air. This is not likely to happen, because the law of gravity is very nearly a true theory, at least about events near the surface of the earth. But it is possible to imagine it happening, so the theory is falsifiable.

Some beliefs are not falsifiable, because it is impossible to imagine *any* set of events that would prove them false. There are basically three different types of unfalsifiable statement. Some statements are unfalsifiable because they include all the possible conditions inside themselves. I call these **inclusive statements**. An example of this type of statement is "Either it will rain tomorrow, or it will not." No matter what happens, this statement cannot be shown to be false, because both possibilities are included. Another type of unfalsifiable statement I call a **definitional statement** because it is based on the definitions of the words and cannot be false by definition—for example, "All women are female." There cannot possibly be a woman who is not female, because being female is part of the definition of the word "woman." A third type of unfalsifiable statement, which I call a **vapor statement**, is simply so vague that it makes no specific predictions. One such statement is "It might rain soon." Sure, it might. Then again, it might not. And just how soon is "soon," anyway? There would be no way to prove that something this vague is false.

Lest you think that unfalsifiable statements are problems only for philosophers of science, rest assured that there are examples in daily life of each of these types. People who think that a statement or theory is important and meaningful simply because they can think of no contradiction are easily impressed by fancy examples of unfalsifiable statements. A scientist, however, tries to think of some possible way the statement could be false. If there is no such possibility, the statement is scientifically meaningless.

Take the inclusive statement that contains all possibilities. There is a belief system called "scientific creationism," a system many people would like to see taught in school along with, or in place of, the theory of evolution. Most scientists object strongly to this use of the term "scientific." The proponents of creationism may consider this to be simple chauvinism, due to the scientists' idea that only the things they believe in can be called scientific. Perhaps in some cases this is true, but most of the time the scientists object to calling creationism "scientific" because the statements of creationism are unfalsifiable. Absolutely anything that we find or fail to find in the fossil record can be explained by creationists, because God can do anything. It is this argument that scientists raise against creationism, and it is the strongest argument there is for saying that something is not scientific. In a collection of essays called *Hen's Teeth and Horse's Toes* (1983), Stephen Jay Gould, a well-known expert in evolutionary science, said this:

> "Scientific creationism" is a self-contradictory, nonsense phrase precisely because it cannot be falsified. I can envision observations and experiments that would disprove any evolutionary theory I know, but I cannot imagine what potential data could lead creationists to abandon their beliefs. Unbeatable systems are dogma, not science.[1]

It is important to remember that a scientific, falsifiable belief may easily be false, and that an unscientific, unfalsifiable belief may easily be true. Science is not a sure path to truth, nor is it the only way to get there. But if a belief cannot be falsified by any imaginable set of observations, then it cannot be a scientific theory, no matter how strongly it is believed, or how true it may be.

An example of a definitional statement, an unfalsifiable statement based on a definition, was offered by a Soviet diplomat several years ago, after a prominent Communist Party member defected to the United States. The diplomat said that the defector had obviously been living a lie, joining the party but not really believing in it, because, he said, "no true Communist would ever defect." This is not a falsifiable statement. Anyone in the world, no matter what or who, could defect, and the diplomat would be able to say that such persons could not have been true Communists in the first place, because not defecting is part of his definition of being a true Communist. There is no way to prove his statement false. This means, according to falsificationism, that the statement cannot be scientifically tested and is therefore meaningless from a scientific point of view.

Examples of statements that are unfalsifiable due to vagueness are common in horoscopes. In the astrology column of my local paper on a randomly chosen date I find at least 10 examples of such vapor

---

[1]From *Hen's Teeth and Horse's Toes* by Stephen Jay Gould, pp. 256–257 by permission of W. W. Norton & Company, Inc. Copyright © 1983 by Stephen Jay Gould.

statements, including the following: "You have an opportunity to accomplish something truly great." (Of course, you may not recognize the opportunity, or you may not succeed.) "Someone may admire you but be too timid to show his or her feelings." (You may never figure out who this person is.) "Romance could be unpredictable." (Then again, it might not.) "Expensive gifts are not necessary." (But any particular inexpensive gift might not be appreciated.) And, my personal favorite, "Other people have their problems, too." At the end of the day, many people look back on these "predictions" and, because nothing happened that contradicted them, exclaim that they came true and become more convinced that there is something to astrology after all. It is difficult to imagine any sort of day these statements would not fit. They are unfalsifiable.

Falsification and Confirmation

Prisons, generally speaking, are places of great violence. Most people assume that the inmates' attacks on their guards, their environments, and each other are caused by their violent nature, which, after all, is what got them into the prison in the first place. Some people, however, have developed a new theory that explains this behavior as being *caused* by the restrictive, inhumane settings of the prisons (Farbstein, 1986; Nelson, 1986). This is a testable, falsifiable theory, because one can build a prison in which there are fewer barriers and more freedom of action for the inmates. In fact, several prisons have now been built on the newer model. The inmates play cards or checkers, watch whatever they want on TV, or just relax on comfortable upholstered furniture. There are no bars separating the officers from the prisoners, but there are doors on the cells to provide privacy, and carpets on the floors and curtains on the windows. Even when they house some of the most serious offenders in the criminal justice system, in major cities such as Detroit, New York, and San Diego, the new prisons have drastically reduced incidents of violence directed at property, officers, or other inmates (Nelson, 1986).

Having seen the success of the new prisons, you might be tempted to conclude that we have proven that the new theory of the causes of prison violence is true. Remember, however, that we said that in falsificationism no theory is considered to be true. When an attempt is made to falsify a theory, and a situation is set up to test a prediction derived from the theory, there are two possible results. If the outcome contradicts the prediction of the theory, then the theory is falsified and it cannot be considered to be true in that situation. If, however, the results uphold the prediction of the theory, this does not mean it is true. We say that a theory is **confirmed** when an attempt made to falsify it fails. Repeated attempts to falsify a theory under many different conditions, all of which lead to confirmation of the theory, may make the individual scientists believe the theory is true, but this can never be proven. There is always the chance that the next attempt will succeed in falsifying the theory. Someone might some day discover, for example, that a chemical used in manufacturing the comfortable upholstery and carpeting of the new jails happened to get into the atmosphere and produced a tranquilizing effect on people who breathed it. This might account for the reduced violence, rather than the freer environment. It is not likely that this is true, but something like it cannot be ruled out completely.

Actually, the situation is more complex than this. The outcome of an attempt to falsify a theory may result in something that neither confirms nor falsifies a theory, but only creates confusion. It is also possible that a negative result, one that falsifies a theory, might be due to an error of measurement, and the theory is in fact true. All these possibilities are part of why science is not a steady, straightforward march to the truth. It depends in large measure on the individual scientists who participate in it, with all their human strengths and weaknesses. This interaction of human nature with scientific practice is discussed more thoroughly in Chapter 12.

SUMMARY

A. Science has four goals toward which scientists may work.
  1. Describing just what happens in some interesting situation.
  2. Predicting what will happen in the future based on something in the present.
  3. Explaining why things happen in a particular way rather that some other way.
  4. Controlling or modifying what happens in the future.
B. Our knowledge of the world comes from many sources, mainly other people. However, each idea came originally from one of two different sources.
  1. Rationalism is an approach to knowledge that maintains that the only way to truth is through pure logical, rational thought, figuring out what it must be.
  2. Empiricism is another approach that maintains that actual observations of what happens in the real world are essential to finding out the truth.
    a. Many kinds of empirical reasoning are casual and unscientific. For instance, human beings tend to draw general conclusions from a few specific observations without considering the exceptions.
    b. A modern, scientific empirical approach is falsificationism, which maintains that no theory can ever be proved true; rather, scientists must always try to prove theories false.

C. Falsificationism is not a natural way of thinking, so it is crucial to understand how it works.

   1. The key idea is the falsifiable statement, a belief that could be proved false by some imaginable observation. If nothing you could imagine would prove the theory false, then it is unfalsifiable, and useless as a scientific theory.

   2. Science consists of repeated attempts to falsify theories. If the theory is falsified, then it is modified or replaced. If the attempt to falsify it fails, the theory is confirmed. This does not mean that it is true, merely that it has not yet been falsified.

─────────────────── **CHECKPOINT** ───────────────────

Check your understanding of the material in this chapter:

- Define rationalism, empiricism, and falsificationism.

- In what ways do these different types of reasoning affect the scientific process?

- What makes scientific reasoning different from other types of empirical reasoning?

- What makes a statement falsifiable? Why is it important that a scientific theory be falsifiable?

- According to the falsificationist approach to science, how are theories generated? How are they tested? Can theories be proven true or false?

- What exactly does it mean to say that a theory is confirmed?

─────────────────── **EXERCISES** ───────────────────

2.1 In your career, what things about people will you probably want to describe? To predict? To explain? To control?

2.2 What are some beliefs that you hold that were developed through rationalistic thinking?

2.3 What are some beliefs that you hold that were developed through empirical thinking?

2.4 When you make decisions in your professional field, what are some of the assumptions that you make (or will probably make) about people?

2.5 Can you make up your own examples of falsifiable and nonfalsifiable statements?

2.6 Find an example of scientific writing in your field, either a scientific journal article or a book, and read it carefully to find some of the assumptions the author makes that are not explicitly described. For instance, perhaps the author believes that theories of certain types are more valuable than others or that certain explanations for behavior are very unlikely. Do the same for this textbook. Do you agree or disagree with these hidden assumptions? Why?

ANSWER
To the Card-Choice Problem in Figure 2.2 You should turn over the E and the 7. These are the only two cards that might prove the vowel–even number statement false. The statement predicts that there will be an even number on the back of the E, and a consonant on the back of the 7. The statement does not predict what will be on the back of a card with a consonant, so turning over the K tells you nothing. Turning over the 4 is also not useful. If there is a vowel on the back, this fits the statement. If there is a consonant on the back, this also fits, since the statement makes no claim about cards with consonants. There is no way to decide whether the statement is true, based on this card.

Chapter 3

The Ethics of Research

Questions to Consider as You Read

- What sorts of rules govern the ethical behavior of researchers?
- Why are these rules often difficult to apply to actual situations?
- What sorts of activities raise ethical questions about a piece of research?
- Would it make a difference if you got people's permission before doing them harm?
- How would you define an invasion of privacy? Anonymity? Confidentiality?
- Is it ethical to deceive research participants? If so, when?
- What methods may researchers use to persuade people to participate in research? What methods may they *not* use?
- How are the rights of research animals protected?
- When evaluating the harm a piece of research might do, what sorts of things are taken into account?
- What committees exist to help researchers make ethical decisions?
- What committees exist to evaluate the ethics of research that has already been conducted?
- What penalties can be applied to researchers who conduct unethical research?

Systems of morals, beliefs about what is right and wrong that are held in common by a group of people, are called **ethics**. For instance, the belief that unprovoked murder is wrong is part of the ethics of most societies. When discussing the ethics of research, we are discussing the system of beliefs that scientists hold in common about what is morally right and morally wrong for researchers to do while conducting research.

One of the frustrations for students in a course such as this is that there are seldom any clear-cut answers to what seem to be simple questions. When is research ethical and when is it unethical? Can a researcher legitimately deceive the people who participate in the research? Observe them without their awareness or permission? Expose them to possible danger? The only honest answer is "It depends." The purpose of this chapter is to make you aware of what "it depends" on, so that you can make ethically appropriate judgments about any research in which you become involved. For more information, consult a book about ethics in behavioral research, such as Kimmel (1980).

Ethically Questionable Activities

The activities in this section are called "ethically questionable" for very good reasons. They are not necessarily wrong, but neither are they always right. They should raise questions in a researcher's mind, however. These activities have the potential to make a piece of research unethical, but whether it really is unethical depends on many factors. In a later section we will cover what those factors are and how to take them into account.

While all these issues represent potential ethical problems for a piece of research, the details of how a particular piece of research is done will determine whether the problem is a real one. So it is not enough to ask "What are the problems with this research?" The researcher must ask "How serious is each of these problems?" The answer may range from a very minor problem, one that no one would take seriously, to a problem so large that no one could possibly allow the research to be conducted. And, as usual, honest people may disagree on just how serious a particular problem is.

The list of ethical problems given here is loosely based on the ethical guidelines of the American Psychological Association (1982), but most professional organizations, including the American Sociological Association and the American Political Science Association, have similar sets of guidelines, and the discussion here is generally compatible with them.

Physical and Mental Harm

You must try to avoid exposing your research participants to any physical or mental harm. This obviously means you cannot give people electric shocks intense enough to cause burns. It also means you should not give them medications without their knowledge or ask them to walk across busy highways at rush hour. Such risks of physical harm are fairly obvious, and a researcher is not likely to inflict them unknowingly or without taking precautions to minimize them. The risks of mental harm, however, are more subtle and may not even be apparent to the researcher. You should avoid causing people stress, fear, or anxiety. Researchers should not make the participants depressed or let them think they have done badly or failed at some task. This is particularly difficult to ensure because what one person sees as stressful may be fun to another person. For instance, much behavioral science research is conducted by academics, people who teach college for a living. These people are obviously comfortable speaking before a group. However, many other people find speaking in front of a group very stressful. So a researcher may innocently design a study that involves having the participants speak in front of a group, never thinking about the fact that some participants might find this experience terrifying. The researcher might be inflicting unnecessary mental harm on the participants. The situation can be more complex even than this, because you can probably find some people who would find any given situation terrifying and some who would find it fun. How many people would have to experience stress, and how stressful would participation have to be, before the research was unethical? There are simply no clear-cut answers.

Back in the 1950s, there was much less concern about mental harm to one's participants than there is now. To give just one example, Zeller (1950) wanted to show that the stress caused by individual failure would cause people to forget material learned just before the failure. He taught a group of college students a list of meaningless syllables and then had them do a task (tapping a group of wooden blocks in a particular order) that seemed easy but was actually very difficult, telling them that it was a good measure of general mental abilities. When the students did not perform well, Zeller feigned concern over their "very poor performance," and as the session wore on he told them they were performing at an 8-year-old level, that he had never tested anyone who did so poorly, and that they could never hope to get through college. Then the students were dismissed and asked to come back three days later for more testing. At the second session they were tested on their memory for the nonsense lists, then performed the block-tapping task again. This time they were told how fabulously well they were doing and what superior students they were. Three days later they came back for one more test on the nonsense lists. Zeller's point was that the students' memory for the lists was much worse at the first test, after the failure experience, than at the second test, after their success. However, Zeller mentions that several students (we do not know how many) never came back at all for the second and third sessions, so they faded from view still thinking their performance was hopelessly awful. Even the students who completed the experiment were never told its true nature, or that the "results" were faked both times. Clearly this research caused the students considerable distress (that was its whole point), with no effort whatsoever to measure or reduce that distress. There is no way at all research like this could be performed today.

One study that brought this ethical issue to public awareness was conducted by Stanley Milgram in 1963. He was concerned about the blind obedience of much of the population of Germany during World War II to the atrocious, genocidal orders of the Nazi regime. To study obedience in a laboratory, Milgram placed volunteers in the situation of receiving orders from a legitimate authority figure (Milgram himself, of the Yale Department of Psychology, complete with laboratory coat) to administer to another volunteer electric shocks that ranged up to 450 volts. If shock of this level had actually been administered to anyone, there would clearly have been a risk (more of a certainty) of physical harm, but actually the shocks were faked and the other "volunteer" was in fact a **confederate**. A confederate works with a researcher but appears to be unrelated, assuming a role to see how the participans respond.

The participants in the study experienced considerable stress. Most of them (about two thirds in the original study) did obey Milgram's authority: that is, they believed that they had administered the full shock to the "volunteer." These people were shaking, crying, and pleading with Milgram to let them stop, but they did it. After the study, when they were told exactly what had really happened and could shake the hand of the uninjured "volunteer," many of them felt deeply ashamed that they had gone along with the experiment, even though no one was hurt. As part of his research plan, Milgram provided his participants with psychological counseling after the study, including follow-ups years later if needed.

The ethical challenges to Milgram's study have revolved largely around its obvious potential for mental harm to the participants. No one denies that the potential is there, or that the participants experienced very painful emotional reactions to the study. The defenders of Milgram's research claim that the research has produced enormous benefits for all of society, benefits that could not have been achieved in any other way, and that the long-term follow–ups showed no negative aftereffects in those who participated. From research like Milgram's, we know that many, perhaps most, cases of systematic atrocity are conducted not by individuals who are abnormal in some way, but by normal, average people caught in abnormal, atrocious situations. Most of the people who were tried for war crimes—the torture and murder of millions of people in concentration camps—claimed that they were "only following orders," and this research indicates that this may well be the truth. If we want to prevent future situations like this, we must first understand them, and Milgram's research can help us do so. Surely, his supporters argue, understanding and preventing future holocausts is important enough to risk the temporary discomfort of a few research participants who were, after all, free to leave at any time. There is no clear answer to this ethical dilemma.

Like all the activities in this chapter, risk of harm is relative. That is, some risks are minor, some major, and many fall somewhere in between. Most research, of course, will not involve any substantial risk at all. The degree of risk will vary from situation to situation and from individual to individual. Asking someone who is sensitive about his age to fill in his date of birth on a questionnaire might cause him some stress, but it will probably be pretty minor, and such a question would not make the research unethical. Interviewing victims of violent crimes about their feelings might traumatize some, but it might help others express and let go of their anger or fear. In each and every study, it will take careful thinking, and perhaps directly asking the first few participants what they think, to decide just how much risk there is of physical or mental harm.

Whenever there is any substantial risk of physical or mental harm to the people in a study, it is important to make them aware of this risk ahead of time. Some of the ethical burden on the researcher is reduced if the participants know what risks exist and still agree to participate. **Informed consent** exists when the participants are told at the beginning what all the risks are and give their consent to the procedure. The greater the risks, the more important informed consent is, and the more detailed the informed consent documents, although, as we will see in Chapter 8, a participant who knows too much about the details of the research might not respond in a natural way. (An example of a simple informed consent form that I used in my own research appears in Figure 3-1.) It is important to remember, however, that giving informed consent does not commit the participant to completing the research. Anyone who participates in research should have the right to quit at any time for any reason, and it is the researcher's obligation to make sure that the participant knows this and understands it.

Date_____

I, _____, agree voluntarily to participate in an experiment on the perception of moving visual forms. I understand that I can quit the experiment at any time for any reason. This research is conducted by and under the control of the Psychology Department of Cornell University,and any problems or complaints can be brought to the Chair of that department, Dr. Leo Meltzer. I understand that the researcher may not discuss with me the purpose of the experiment or my responses, but that a report of the experiment will be sent to me as soon as available if I wish it. All result will be confidential, and will be reported only as averages and not identified by individual participants.

Researcher: Celia C. Reaves
                Department of Psychology
                Uris Hall, Cornell University

Signed:_____

Figure 3-1 Sample informed consent form; this simple form was used in a series of experiments on visual preception.

Observing Hidden Behaviors

Research in the behavioral sciences frequently requires that we observe behaviors that under other circumstances the participants might consider to be hidden or private. **Covert research** is research whose existence is hidden from those being observed, as compared with **overt research**, which exists when the participants know what is being observed and why. Covert research can cause ethical problems not only with respect to illegal or sexual behavior, but everyday behaviors as well. Many people would be upset to learn that researchers had been observing what they ate, how late or how early they went to bed, what television shows they watched, or what tones of voice they used to talk to their kids or their spouses. The researcher must take care to minimize the harm that might come to these people because of the observation of such private behaviors. In an ethical sense, the behavior belongs to the behaver, who has a right to control who observes the behavior and what use is made of that observation, even when the behavior is illegal. Researchers are not agents of the law or the courts, but of science and society as a whole. The responsibility of research restricts the scientist's freedom to both observe what people want to hide and to use those observations.

On the other hand, like all citizens, researchers have an ethical obligation to protect the rights of others, including protecting them from illegal behavior. It is useful here to draw a distinction between past and future criminal actions. Most researchers agree that if anonymity has been promised, it is wrong to reveal knowledge of a criminal action that a research participant admitted. If the participant indicates a serious plan to commit a crime in the future, most researchers agree that the researcher would have an obligation to try to prevent the crime or to warn the intended victims. However, in actual situations the ethical considerations may be confusing indeed.

Invasion of Privacy

An **invasion of privacy** occurs when someone observes a behavior or an object that the person involved can reasonably expect will not be observed at all, or at least will not be observed by the researcher. Peeking through the windows of a house, wiring the house for sound, or going through items in the house when people are not home would all be invasions of privacy if the residents had not given permission for these activities. The key here is that the observation occurs in a situation the individual would not normally expect to entail such an observation. Secretly using a hidden camera to watch people eat dinner in their kitchen is a clear invasion of privacy; watching the same person eat dinner from the next table in a public restaurant is probably not. If your observation in the restaurant is extremely detailed, counting the number of bites per minute or estimating exactly how much of each dish was eaten, this might still constitute an invasion of privacy, because the diner would not normally expect to be under such close scrutiny. However, because the diner is presumably aware that very curious, nosy people exist, and that such people might watch others eat in restaurants, this invasion of privacy is really quite minor.

A good example of the ambiguity of observations made in public places is a study by Middlemist, Knowles, and Matter (1976) on how people react to violations of their personal space. Most people realize that when someone else, particularly a stranger, comes too close to us, we feel uncomfortable. For instance, if a stranger walks into a practically empty bus terminal and sits down on the same bench with you, you will probably feel tense. Behavioral scientists would like to show that such violations of our space cause actual, physical stress, that can be measured with scientific instruments. The problem is, it is very difficult to attach scientific instruments to people wandering around in the real world without their becoming aware of it, and if people are aware of the research then the "violation" is not the same at all. (If you know about the experiment, it will not bother you very much when a stranger sits next to you.)

Middlemist, Knowles, and Matter found a way to measure physical stress in a real-world situation without the participant's awareness, by measuring how long it takes a man to get his flow of urine going at the urinal in a public rest room. Stress tightens most of the muscles in the body, including those that must relax to let the urine out, so stress makes it more difficult to release the flow of urine. The investigators manipulated the situation so that uninformed participants entering the rest room would always use the urinal closest to one stall, in which a male researcher was watching through a periscope that gave a view of the participant's lower torso, but not his face. The researcher used a stopwatch to time how long it took the urine to start under three conditions: no one else using a urinal, a confederate using the urinal farther from the participant, or a confederate using the urinal closer to the participant. They found that the urine came fastest when no one else was visible, somewhat slower when someone else was using a distant urinal, and slower still when someone else was using a neighboring urinal, indicating that nearness to a stranger increased stress.

The study by Middlemist, Knowles, and Matter (1976) is an excellent example of finding an imaginative way to operationalize a difficult variable (see Chapter 4), but ethically it is questionable. On the one hand, the urinals in a public rest room make no pretense of offering complete privacy. Other men using the rest room can watch what is happening, although good manners usually prevent close observations (just as in the example of the diners in a restaurant). A man who wants to make sure that no one sees what he is doing can use a more private stall. And, of course, the observations are completely anonymous, with the researcher unable to identify the participants at the time of the research, much less later. On the other hand, using a periscope to peer directly at a man's "lower torso" while he is urinating is not the kind of observation that a man in a rest room might expect. While public rest rooms are public, they are not as public as, say, a shopping mall or a busy street. Detailed observations in a rest room constitute a violation of privacy, at least to some degree.

Of course, if the individual involved knows in advance that the observations will be made, and gives permission to make them, there is no invasion of privacy. Informed consent is again important as a way of reducing the ethical questions in the research. When Ross Parke (1981) was interested in how fathers interact with their children, he observed father–child interactions with the full knowledge and consent of the people involved. In such situations there can be no invasion of privacy. When observing private behaviors, informed consent is sometimes given in writing, but often the situation is such that the participants obviously knew of and permitted the observation. It is unlikely that an angry father would later claim to be unaware that the researcher was sitting in his living room taking notes as he changed the baby's diaper.

Loss of Anonymity and Confidentiality

Even when the participant knows that the researcher is watching, and agrees to this, there can still be a problem if the researcher uses the observations in a way the participant does not like. **Confidentiality** exists when the person knows that the observer can identify who has done a behavior, but expects that the observer will not pass the information on to anyone else. **Anonymity** exists when the person expects that no one, including the observer, will know who has done the behavior. To clarify this distinction, imagine you have called the police to report a crime that you observed. That call would be confidential if you identified yourself but requested that your name never be revealed to anyone else. It would be anonymous if you hung up without giving your name, so even the police did not know who you were. In both cases the individual is never identified to others, but with anonymous behavior the individual is not identified even to the observer. Anonymity is also considered to exist if the observer knows that a certain group of people gave a certain group of responses, but does not know which responses came from which people, as when a survey is taken of the people in, say, a church, but there are no names on individual responses. The study by Middlemist, Knowles, and Matter (1976) of urination in the rest room is anonymous, since the observer could not see the faces of the men.

In behavioral research, most observations are so innocent that the participant would not care how the information was used. It probably would not bother you much if a researcher reported you by name as someone who likes to eat Mexican food. Sometimes, though, it can be a problem, as when researchers interview people about illegal activities that they have committed. The participants may agree to give the information to the researcher on the condition that it never be reported to law enforcement agencies, and indeed never reported at all in such a way that the people involved can be identified. If that agreement is broken, because the information is given in the wrong form to the wrong people, this ethical requirement has been violated and the participant potentially damaged.

Most research results are reported anonymously. That is, what are reported are averages, without identifying the specific behaviors of any individuals. The full names of the participants are almost never revealed. However, just hiding the participants' names might not be enough to protect their anonymity. For instance, if you conduct research on the members of a specific organization and identify the organization in your report, people who know the members will know that the research is about them. Thus you will need to hide the specific location, size, and name of the organization to shield its members.

Informed consent is as important in dealing with issues of anonymity and confidentiality as it is in other ethical areas. If the behavior being studied is particularly sensitive or secret, the researcher will usually give the participant a written statement of exactly what information will be reported, how, and to whom, along with information about who to complain to if the participant believes these conditions have been violated. This gives the participant more confidence in the safety of the information given to the researcher.

Issues of confidentiality occasionally cause ethical dilemmas for people conducting behavioral research. For instance, researchers at the Mental Research Institute in California were doing a survey of the reactions of military personnel stationed away from their families (reported by Fisher, 1988). The researchers had promised the participants that they would not give any information about the specific people in their study to anyone in the military. However, one of the survey responses indicated that the man who had submitted it felt depressed and suicidal and did not know where to turn. The researchers knew it would be wrong to violate their promise of anonymity but felt they had to do something to help this man. They finally contacted him directly at his post overseas, without alerting anyone else in the military, and found that he had gotten help on his own and was coping better.

In another example, the confidentiality principle ran into conflict with the principle of informed consent (reported by Landers, 1988). A graduate student wanted to do research on adolescents who visited a local family planning clinic. Because the proposed participants were minors, the researchers needed permission not from the adolescents themselves but from their parents. However, the clinic did not require the parents' permission to treat the teenagers, and the researcher suspected that many of them did not want their parents to know they went there, so getting parental permission could have violated their confidentiality. Because the researcher was a member of the American Psychological Association, she asked for advice from the APA's officer for research ethics. After some deliberation it was decided that, since the law allowed the clinic to treat the adolescents as adults in granting treatment without parental consent, the researcher could do the same, getting informed consent from the teens themselves. This is another case in which even complete knowledge of the ethical principles as outlined in this chapter is not enough to allow an easy decision of an ethical question.

There is, however, one point on which almost all ethical authorities agree. If a researcher has promised a participant confidentiality, and there is no reason to break that promise to protect either the participant or another person, the researcher must keep that promise. Even if a court discovers that you have evidence about who committed a crime and subpoenas your records, you must not produce those records, even if it means going to jail for contempt of court. It is for this reason that most people who conduct sensitive research do not keep records that identify individuals unless it is absolutely necessary. Even in their field notes, the researchers use false names, code numbers, or other devices to keep track of what information came from whom without revealing identities. These researchers also cultivate a remarkable ability to forget very quickly the names of their participants.

Deception

Deception is anything that deliberately causes people to believe something that is not true, or to be unaware of something that would be important to them if they knew it. Thus deception can be *active*, as in telling a deliberate lie, or *passive*, as in not mentioning something you do not want someone else to know about. Both types of deception can be ethically wrong, although most people take active deception more seriously than passive deception.

To a certain extent, all research on human beings involves deception. As Chapter 8 will show, it is important that the participants not know exactly what the researcher expects a particular person to do in a particular situation. In hiding this information from the participant, the researcher is engaging in passive deception. However, most professionals consider this to be such a minor degree of deception that it is of no concern. Those who are particularly careful of ethical issues may in fact tell their participants that the expected results of the experiment are being hidden from them in order not to affect their behavior and, after the experiment is over, will tell the participants what was expected. In most behavioral research, this is the only type of deception that occurs, and therefore most behavioral research has no ethical problem with deception. However, there are exceptions.

The issue of deception is one of the most controversial ethical issues in the behavioral sciences. One reason for this is that informed consent, by definition, cannot eliminate the problem. If the participant is deceived about the research, then whatever consent the participant gives cannot be fully informed. Yet the participant might not agree to participate at all if full information were given. This makes ethical issues difficult to settle. However, if the researcher is sufficiently motivated to make the research as ethical as possible, informed consent can be used to drastically reduce the problem of deception.

One excellent example of a study that uses informed consent to reduce the problems of deception was done by Ceci and Peters (1984) to determine how confidentiality affects the letters of reference that professors give their students who are applying to graduate school. They had student confederates ask several professors to write letters of reference for them, but the letters were phonies and were analyzed by the experimenters. Some of the letters were confidential, in that they were marked CONFIDENTIAL across the top and the professors mailed them directly to the colleges; others were not confidential and were picked up by the students themselves. All the letters used exactly the same rating questionnaire, differing only in the college letterhead at the top of the page. Ceci and Peters found that professors gave significantly higher ratings to the same student in nonconfidential letters, presumably because they considered the feelings of the student who might be reading the letter.

Clearly this research involved deception, because the professors thought that the letters they were writing would have an effect on the students' future careers. Ceci and Peters handled this problem by approaching the students' faculty advisers months ahead of time and asking for their participation in a study on how people evaluate other people. They were told that if they agreed, they would be deceived at some time in the next few months, because deception was necessary to the research, and that they would hear nothing more about the study until it was completed. Of the 16 faculty members they approached, only four refused to participate, and these instructors were of course not used in the study. The remainder were informed of the details of the study as soon as all the letters were completed. By thus filling their participants in, Ceci and Peters removed most of the ethical objections that might be raised to this sort of research. Because the letters were written months after the initial informed consent was given, because the informed consent was given to the professors' colleagues while the letters were requested by their students, and because these professors were used to being asked to write letters of recommendation for their students at this time of year, it seems unlikely that the informed consent could have affected the way in which the faculty members wrote their letters.

How is a researcher to decide whether the deception used in a particular study is ethically justified? Behavioral scientists have developed guidelines describing how deception can and cannot be used in research. The guidelines described here are loosely based on those published by the American Psychological Association (1982). The study by Milgram (1963) discussed earlier serves as an example to illustrate these guidelines.

Deception should not be used unnecessarily. If there is any way to get the information desired without deceiving anyone, then that way must be used, even if it is more expensive or time-consuming. Because Milgram's research was about the conditions under which people will commit acts that would harm other people, but Milgram did not really want to harm anyone, it is difficult to imagine a way to get this information without using deception.

Another guideline is that the research must be important. It is not justified to deceive someone seriously just to settle some minor theoretical dispute of interest only to a few scholars. However, it might be justified if the question being studied were of vital importance to all of society. This is one of the major justifications of Milgram's research, because preventing events like the slaughter of 12 million people is certainly an important social goal.

The participants should be fully informed about the true nature of the research as soon as this is possible. **Debriefing** is the term used for the process of explaining the true situation at the end of the experiment to a participant who has been deceived. The more elaborate the deception, the more elaborate the debriefing needs to be. There are two guidelines related to debriefing. First, it should be reasonable to think that the participants will find the deception acceptable when it is explained to them. If it seems likely that they will suffer feelings of resentment, embarrassment, or anger at the researchers when the deception is explained, the research should not be conducted at all. Second, most authorities on ethics agree that a participant who believes after being debriefed that the research was ethically wrong, who feels betrayed by the deception, has the right to demand that the researcher not use any information gathered from that participant, as well as the right to complain to higher authorities. This is in line with the principle that the participant's behavior belongs to the participant and can be removed by the participant.

Finally, the researchers are completely responsible for finding out whether there has been any harm done to the participants as a result of being deceived and for removing any harm that they find or suspect. Of course, in most research where the deception consists simply of not telling the participant exactly what results are anticipated, there is virtually no possible harm to worry about. However, the researchers cannot simply say, "Well, we didn't notice any problems." They must carefully evaluate what harmful effects there might be, examine the participants to find out whether any of these effects occurred, and actively provide whatever services are necessary for undoing any damage that might be there. This is why Milgram provided his participants with psychological counseling and why he asked them whether they felt the research was worth it.

Guidelines such as these are fairly well accepted in the behavioral sciences as providing an ethical framework for the use of deception in research. You should know, however, that there are many researchers who feel strongly that they are not strict enough. For instance, Diana Baumrind is outspoken in her campaign to eliminate most uses of deception in the area of psychology. She and others like her believe that the use of deception, even as governed by the guidelines given above, causes harm that cannot easily be measured to the participants, the researchers, the behavioral sciences, and society as a whole. Baumrind summarizes her position by saying that "the use of intentional deception in the research setting is unethical, imprudent, and unwarranted scientifically" (1985, p. 165). Before using deception in research, or condoning the use of deception by others, you should become aware of the arguments against it so that you can make an informed, concerned decision.

Coercion

Human research participants are free to decide whether to participate in the research, and they may change their minds and quit if they choose. **Coercion** is any action on the part of the researcher that would tend to make people do something when they do not really want to. Note that part of this definition requires that the research be something that the participant really does not want to do, and so there can be little coercion when the research experience is short and painless, or even pleasant. Coercion comes into question only when the research is something the people involved would not do if they were not pressured into it.

As with all the ethical principles, it is difficult to decide just what is coercive and what is not. A researcher may explain to the participants what benefits are expected from the research, and indeed this is usually expected. At what point is such an explanation really a sermon designed to make people feel guilty if they refuse? Researchers often offer to pay participants for their help, and this is considered to be ethical, particularly when the research is time-consuming or difficult. However, suppose your research involves studying how people react to life below the poverty level? If you offer people qualified to participate $25 for an hour of their time, how many of them are likely to refuse? They might feel compelled to participate for the sake of the money, even if they find the research frightening or unpleasant. In this case, is the offer of money coercing them to do something they really do not want to do? Does that make it unethical?

The question of coercion is particularly tricky when the researcher has some sort of power over the participants. It is fairly easy to see that this problem comes up in researching, for instance, prison inmates. The researcher would naturally have permission of prison authorities before beginning, and those authorities would usually announce that the research has their approval. How many inmates would believe that refusal to participate would be interpreted as lack of cooperation by a future parole board? They might easily think that they had to volunteer for the sake of getting out sooner.

The same is true of researching employees of a corporation, members of the armed services, and students in a classroom. In fact, it is a standard practice in many colleges to require that students in introductory courses in the behavioral sciences, particularly psychology, participate in research conducted by faculty members and graduate students. This practice is considered to be unethical by many. Professional guidelines now require that students be offered an alternative way of fulfilling that course requirement if they prefer not to participate in the research, perhaps by serving as a research assistant or writing a research paper. However, faculty members who consider the introductory class to be a captive pool of research subjects will downplay these alternatives or make them so difficult that almost no one considers them seriously. This is unfair coercion of research participants and is unethical.

One controversial aspect of coercion applies to the military. According to one school of thought, service people have entered into a contract with the military that obligates them to carry out any legal orders given to them by their superior officers. Therefore, there is no need to get permission from them; they gave blanket permission when they enlisted. Whatever research the government wishes to do on military personnel is allowed. Another school of thought holds that service people have the same rights as anyone else, including the right not to participate in research. This sort of question can become important when considering the sort of research the military is interested in conducting. Unlike college students or corporate vice presidents, military personnel are expected to function well under extreme conditions. Therefore, the military wants to test behavior under those conditions. Baddeley (1972) reports on research on how stress affects memory for details and complex procedures, in which military personnel were convinced that they were in immediate life-threatening emergencies: airplanes about to crash into the ocean, sites of dangerous atomic radiation, incoming shells with live ammunition. Partipants were asked to fill out forms ("We have to be able to show the insurance companies that we trained you properly, so it wasn't our fault you were killed") or repair a broken field radio so they could get help. The researchers compared their memory and their performance under these emergency conditions with normal levels and showed that stress caused substantial reductions in both memory and performance. At least, in this research the personnel were told all about the experiment as soon as it was over.

Informed consent can do much to reduce the problem of coercion. To be useful, the informed consent must specify clearly that participation is voluntary and that the participant can stop at any time without penalty. If a researcher has promised money to a participant who began the study in good faith, the researcher should pay the money even if the participant decides not to continue. The researcher also has an obligation to pay attention to how the participant is acting and, if it appears that the participant really does not want to continue, the researcher should mention again that it is permissible to stop at any time. In other words, the researcher has a responsibility to make sure the people involved really want to be involved, no matter what they say.

Psychology has uncovered a fact of human nature that makes it particularly difficult to apply the rule that people can stop participating in research at any time. If you will recall Milgram's electric shock study, you may remember that the participants were emotionally distressed through much of the research and even begged Milgram to stop. All he said was "The experiment requires that you continue," and continue they did. This was true even though they had signed a consent form that clearly stated they could terminate the experiment at any time.

Once people have agreed to participate in any piece of research, they feel almost compelled to continue, no matter what. This was demonstrated in the laboratory by Martin Orne (1962). He carefully created the most boring, meaningless task he could think of: adding hundreds of numbers on a sheet of paper, then tearing the paper up into small pieces and throwing it away and going on to the next sheet of additions. He wanted to find out what you needed to do to get people to stick with this task for hours. What he found was that all you needed to do was ask them. Once they agreed to do it, they continued until, after 5 1/2 hours, the *experimenters* got tired of it and told them to stop. It is something of a miracle that anyone in Milgram's study ever refused to administer any of the "shocks" to the confederates. One way of looking at Milgram's results, instead of complaining that two-thirds of the people obeyed Milgram's orders, is to rejoice that one-third of them managed to find the strength to stop.

What all this means for the researcher is that you must not put your faith in people's intellectual comprehension of a statement that they are free to terminate their participation at any time. Be sensitive to the fact that the research itself puts heavy pressure on the participants. It is your obligation as the researcher to counteract that pressure by noticing any reluctance of the participants and encouraging them to stop if they want to, and to stop the experiment yourself if you believe that a participant is being harmed by it. You are responsible for your participants, and it is your duty to protect them from any possible damage your study could do to them, even if they fail to take steps to protect themselves.

Plagiarism

A scientist's reputation, and very career, rests on the ideas the scientist has. Stealing someone's ideas, or the reports a scientist writes, without giving that person proper credit is stealing one of the most valuable things a scientist has. When scientists portray as their own research or ideas that came from others, it is a grave violation of research ethics.

Violations of this ethical rule generally take two forms. One is for a researcher to put an idea into a research report without giving full reference credit to the source of the idea. Even ideas that come to you in private letters or telephone calls should be given credit, in ways described in Chapter 11 on writing a research report. Scientists cannot, and should not, control who discusses their ideas or how they are discussed, but all scientists deserve credit for their ideas themselves.

This rule also is violated when someone in a position of authority publishes work done by someone under that authority, taking credit for the work. For instance, a student's research project may be published by a faculty adviser under the adviser's name, thereby stealing the student's work. This issue, like all ethical issues, can sometimes become blurry. For instance, if the work was done under the supervision of and in consultation with the adviser, so that the adviser contributed substantially to the design of the project, it is reasonable for the adviser's name to appear. However, it is almost never reasonable for the student's name to be completely removed, if the student had any meaningful role in designing, conducting, or reporting results of the research. And when the only contribution of the adviser was to provide laboratory space and then step aside, there is little justification for the adviser's name to appear at all.

A famous example of this sort of misuse of an adviser's role was the case of Anthony Hewish and Jocelyn Bell (described in Broad and Wade, 1982). Bell was a graduate student in radio astronomy, conducting a research program on how radio waves produced by the sun affect light from distant stars. She was looking for small radio "twinkles" among hundreds of other radio signals. In addition to the radio twinkles she was looking for, Bell found a total of four stars that produced extremely regular radio pulses; these she reported in an appendix to her doctoral thesis. However, a paper on the discovery of pulsars was published in *Nature* with Hewish's name (Hewish, Bell, Pilkington, Scott, & Collins, 1967), under the argument that Bell was his student and using his equipment. In 1974, when the Nobel Prize in astronomy was was given to Hewish alone for the discovery, other astronomers familiar with Bell's contribution were scandalized.

Fabricating Data

If science is to progress toward the truth, it must be based on truthful reporting of observations. When a scientist alters or makes up those observations, not only can it set back scientific progress, but it can cause active harm to people who are treated according to the incorrect ideas those false data give us.

A famous early example of fabricated data was provided in the case of Sir Cyril Burt, an English psychologist who was knighted for his work on the determinants of intelligence (see Hearnshaw, 1979). Burt reported decades of work with twins, separated at birth and raised in different homes, that showed that intelligence was determined mostly by a person's genetic inheritance and very little by the environment in which the person was raised. However, it eventually came out that most, if not all, of his data were false. Not only did he make up many of his test scores, he even made up many of the twins he supposedly studied.

A more recent example is the controversy surrounding work done by Sobell and Sobell (1973) on treating alcoholism through behavior therapy. They claimed that they were successful in teaching alcoholics to control their drinking (drinking in moderation and only in appropriate situations) and reported follow-up studies showing that the new behaviors lasted at least two years. Other researchers, notably Pendery, Maltzman, and West (1982), followed up on the same subjects ten years later, and claimed that the successes were greatly exaggerated if not falsified. The Sobells were investigated by a committee on charges that they did not actually conduct all the follow-up examinations they claimed and that they falsified the data reported on their patients. The investigative committee found the investigators innocent of all the charges, but they were still subjected to suspicion by many people in their field. Peele, in discussing the episode in 1983, claimed that the controversy was really much more political than scientific.

The Ethics of Animal Research

Most researchers believe that the issues of privacy, anonymity, and deception do not apply to animals. As far as we know, nonhuman animals have no concerns about being observed without their knowledge or consent. This leaves two basic issues that do affect animals: the infliction of harm, both physical and mental, and coercion.

Physical harm to animals is most prevalent in biomedical research, but even in the behavioral sciences, animals are sometimes physically harmed. Research animals in the behavioral sciences have been subjected to starvation, electric shock, brain surgery, and other dangerous situations, to study the effects of these variables. Mental harm to research animals is even more common. Some mental harm is deliberately created as part of an experiment, for example, to study stress or overcrowding. In addition, it is often argued that simply living in small, sterile laboratory cages, being fed and exercised by machines, creates mental harm for the research animals.

The problem is complicated because research animals obviously cannot give informed consent to participate in the research, which makes them vulnerable to coercion. The animals simply have no choice as to whether they will participate in the research. This puts even greater ethical burdens on the researchers to protect the rights of the animals, because the animals are helpless to protect their own rights. I recall a movie about a Hollywood stuntman involving a stunt in which the actor and a small dog fell many stories onto a large air bag. A representative of the American Society for the Prevention of Cruelty to Animals (ASPCA) was on the set to see that the live dog was replaced at the last instant by a stuffed model, so that the dog could avoid the dangerous fall. "You don't care if I get hurt," the stuntman observed. "You made the decision that you wanted to do this," the ASPCA representative replied. "The dog didn't."

Along similar lines, there is a national organization specifically created to protect the rights of animals used in research. The American Association for Accreditation of Laboratory Animal Care (AAALAC) examines the treatment of animals in various research laboratories and refuses accreditation to any laboratory that treats animals in an unethical way. Its concerns include the amount of space the animals have, how much contact they are allowed with others of their species, their access to facilities for exercise and instinctive behaviors such as digging or climbing, cleanliness and nutrition, and anything else that could affect the well-being of the animals. Without accreditation from this kind of body, a research laboratory would not get much in the way of government funds to conduct research. The protection of such an organization is the best substitute for informed consent for laboratory animals.

Because mental and physical harm to research animals can occur, deliberately or through neglect, and because research animals cannot knowingly accept these risks or complain if their rights are violated, there is a widespread debate on the ethics of animal research. On one side is the extreme antiresearch position, as expressed by Goodman (1982), that no research should be conducted using animals unless the research will benefit the animals themselves. By this position, animals could be used to study, say, rabies, if the results are used to protect animals from this deadly disease. However, using animals to study AIDS, cancer, or anything else for the benefit of *humans* would be a violation of the rights of the animals. Animal rights activists claim that killing a rat, frightening a baboon, or performing experimental surgery on a cat is just as wrong as doing any of these things to a person who has not given permission and does not understand what is happening.

On the other side of the debate are the beliefs that people are more important than animals and that not only is it permissible to use animals to relieve human suffering, but it would be cruel and immoral not to do so (Driscoll & Bateson, 1988). If people are suffering from an illness with no cure, is it not right to make a few animals suffer from it also in the hope that a cure can be found, so that neither animals nor people will have to suffer from it in the future? To say no, it seems, is to say that the well-being of the animals is more important than the well-being of the people. Everyone, however, agrees that the health and welfare of research animals should be protected as far as humanly possible, that research should not be conducted with live animals if it is not necessary, and that no harm should be inflicted on them that is avoidable.

Evaluating Ethical Issues

After you have thought carefully about all the ethical questions raised by the research you plan to do, you must decide whether the research should be done as planned, modified to make it more acceptable, or not be done at all. How do you make this decision? This chapter has emphasized that there are no clear answers to ethical questions, and this is no exception. Making ethical decisions is always a matter of personal judgment, not following rules or applying formulas. However, there are techniques for making these decisions, and they are the subject of this section.

Cost-Benefit Analysis

As a general rule, ethical decisions are made on the basis of a **cost–benefit analysis**, which measures the probable or possible costs or damage that the research might do against the probable or possible benefits or good that it might do. Unfortunately, many, perhaps most, of the costs and benefits of behavioral research are subjective, emotional, personal factors that are difficult to measure and to compare. Nevertheless, this comparison must be done to decide whether a study should be conducted.

Consider again the study by Milgram I have been using as an example. The costs of that research include most obviously the stress and trauma caused for the participants, particularly those who believed they were administering electric shocks of 450 volts to an innocent volunteer. This trauma can be divided into two parts: the anguish they felt when they administered the shock, and the memory of themselves as someone who would do such a thing under the right (or wrong) circumstances. There is also the stress to the experimenter, who must cause these unhappy situations and may feel some guilt about it. The obvious benefits of the research include a better understanding of the causes of human cruelty and the hope of being able to reduce its occurrence. How do you compare these? Is the increase in understanding worth the pain to the participants? This is the essence of the ethical controversy over this or indeed any research.

The full picture, however, is even more complex. Part of the issue is just thinking of the things that should be counted as costs and benefits of the research. One of the points made by critics of the use of deception, such as Baumrind (1985), is that long-term costs of intentional deception are rarely considered. After people have participated in deceptive research, they may be more likely to disbelieve what researchers tell them in the future, even when the research is not deceptive. This could shift into a distrust of behavioral scientists and behavioral science, which is clearly not a result behavioral scientists want. Also, once researchers have accepted the use of deception in research, it could undermine their commitment to truth and honesty, which is destructive to the researchers as individuals and to their profession. If any of these effects actually occur as a result of the use of deception in research, they are costs of the research and should be considered in the cost–benefit analysis. However, researchers almost never do so, because these costs are so vague and ill-defined, and may not exist at all.

When evaluating the ethics of a piece of research, what is most important is to consider alternatives. The researcher should give much thought to the question of whether there is any other way to answer the research questions without ethical problems. For instance, consider again the Middlemist, Knowles, and Matter (1976) study in the men's room. The urinals in the rest room that was used had no standing water in them, which is why the investigators used the periscope arrangement to watch men urinating. However, with more effort they might have located a rest room with the necessary physical arrangement that included standing water. Then they could have watched the men's feet to see when they were in position and listened to hear when the urine started flowing. Most people feel that listening to a man urinating in a public rest room is more acceptable than watching. Whenever you are contemplating doing any research, you should discuss it as much as possible with as many people as possible, both professional colleagues and friends and acquaintances, to get suggestions about alternative ways to study the same question.

Ethics Oversight Committees

Oversight committees are committees that watch over the activities of people, and **ethics oversight committees** watch over the ethics of research done by members of some organization. There are generally two types: ethics committees associated with professional organizations and those associated with research facilities. Most professional organizations whose members conduct research with human or animal participants have ethics oversight committees, which will investigate claims of unethical behavior and will expel members who prove to have engaged in unethical practices. Also, any organization that conducts research funded by the United States government, as are almost all research facilities, is required to maintain an ethics review board that must approve ahead of time all research conducted by its members or under its affiliation. Thus the institutional ethics committee must approve research before it is conducted, and the professional ethics committee can evaluate research afterward if there is any challenge to its ethics. Both types of committee were created because of the increased awareness of the importance of ethical questions in the late 1960s and early 1970s.

One problem associated with such ethics committees is that they pass judgment on research after it is already designed or even conducted. The institutional review committees may make recommendations on how to modify research that has been turned down, but it would be better if these suggestions happened earlier, while the research was still in its formative stages and the researcher had not invested as much in the detailed research design. A more useful tool is becoming available, at least to certain types of researchers. For example, the American Psychological Association has an Ethics Office that can give informal advice over the telephone to members who are faced with ethical dilemmas. While the Ethics Office of the APA has no official powers, it can help a researcher decide how to proceed if there are conflicting ethical requirements. Using resources like the APA's Ethics Office is part of the advice given above to discuss your research before you conduct it with as many people as possible, to help get ideas for better ways to do it. No matter how brilliant you are, there is a better chance of many people coming up with a solution to a problem than one person.

Responding to Unethical Research

Almost all the behavioral research you will ever hear about or come in contact with is completely ethical. However, there is always the slight chance that some overly enthusiastic researcher will push the limits a little, and you may be involved. If you believe that someone has conducted or is conducting unethical research, you have a moral obligation to try to stop it. The first thing to do is to discuss the issue with the researcher involved. It might well be that you do not fully understand the research, and your questions might be resolved. Or the researcher may accept your criticisms and work with you to find some less objectionable way to conduct the research. Or it might be one of those fuzzy ethical questions on which honest people can disagree, and while you firmly believe the research is unethical the researcher believes equally firmly that it is not. Then you must decide whether to continue to press the matter.

If you decide to go further, you begin working up the ladder of authority from the researcher. For instance, in a college environment, the researcher will generally be a member of an academic department, and you should go to the department chair. If the researcher is a member of a professional organization, you can contact the ethics officer for that organization. If the research was funded by a grant, you can contact the organization that provided the grant. If the research involves animals, there are various animal rights organizations that would be interested in your opinion that the animals are being treated unethically. As you work your way through these responsible institutions, you will almost certainly be able to resolve the issue.

Before you go out to attack someone who seems to have conducted unethical research, remember that there are no clear answers to most ethical questions. If you discuss your concern at all the levels suggested above, and everyone you talk to believes that the research as conducted was ethical, you are probably dealing with one of these unclear questions. This is not to say that your ethical judement is wrong in this case, but it means that their judgment is not necessarily wrong either. If you feel strongly enough to continue the fight until the end, it is your right to do so. However, do not make the mistake of assuming that those who disagree with you are heartless, uncaring, unethical people. They are probably honest in their disagreement with your position.

A Reminder to Students

As part of this course, and perhaps other courses you take, you may be required to conduct research with human beings or animals. Whenever you do so, you are obligated to consider all the ethical issues discussed in this chapter. Just because research is "only for class" does not mean that you do not have to worry about harming participants, invading their privacy, or deceiving them. It is important that you explain to your teacher exactly what you plan to do before you do it and specifically ask whether the teacher believes the proposed research is ethical. There probably will be no ethical problems, because most research has none, but you must think about it to make sure. If there were ethical questions that you wrestled with in designing your research, discuss them with the teacher beforehand and also mention them in your research report, telling what questions you dealt with and why you resolved them as you did.

You must remember that as the person conducting the research, you are responsible for making sure that it is conducted in an ethical manner. If a piece of research makes you feel uncomfortable, even if it has been approved by the teacher, DO NOT DO IT. If something you believe is unethical is required for the course, discuss it with your teacher. Do not attack the teacher as an unethical monster; it is quite likely that the teacher never considered the research in that way before, or in fact might honestly disagree with you. After all, professional scientists often disagree on ethical issues. Try to suggest alternative research you believe would be acceptable. If after this discussion you are still required to do something you do not feel is right, take it up with the department chair or the academic dean. As long as you are sincerely concerned about ethical issues, and not just trying to get out of work, you are almost certain to see the issue resolved in a way that will satisfy you.

We are each of us responsible for what we do and how it affects others. For scientists, this responsibility is even greater. Science is a thrilling activity, and it carries with it the requirement that we think as clearly about the consequences of our actions to other people as we do about our theories and our research. Even comic book scientists realize this. England's Doctor Who once said, "We purchase our right to experiment at the cost of total responsibility." When you perform research, or when you discuss with others research they are performing, you have a moral obligation to consider the ethical implications of the research for the participants, the researchers, and society as a whole.

SUMMARY

A. Ethically questionable activities are those that might be problems if they are serious enough. Researchers must carefully evaluate any study containing problems like these.

   1. Causing physical or mental harm to the participants, including emotional distress. Obtaining informed consent from the participants before the study can reduce the ethical problems of harm.

   2. Observing hidden behaviors. Informed consent can reduce or eliminate these ethical problems.

      a. Invading participants' privacy, by observing behavior that they would expect not to be observed.

      b. Violating anonymity or confidentiality, by revealing information about participants that might harm them.

   3. Deceiving the participants, causing them to believe things that are not true. It is difficult, but not impossible, to use informed consent to reduce the ethical problems with deception. Some people believe deception to be widely misused in the behavioral sciences.

   4. Coercing or forcing people to participate. Sometimes there is unfair situational pressure to participate, as when the researcher is in a position of power over the participant, or when participants who have begun are reluctant to stop even if the research task is unpleasant. Researchers must protect their participants from these pressures.

   5. Using research ideas or actual research produced by others without giving them proper credit. A scientist's ideas may be cited by others and discussed in any way, but failure to give credit is plagiarism.

   6. Fabricating or concealing data. The accuracy of science rests on the truthful reporting of observations.

B. While some believe that animals should not be used in research unless the work will benefit the animals themselves, most scientists accept the use of animals to study important issues of concern to humans when it is difficult or impossible to use humans. Research animals should never be harmed unnecessarily, and their health and well-being must be protected.

C. Having identified the ethical questions raised by a piece of research, the researcher must evaluate whether the research should be performed.

1. Cost–benefit analysis compares the damage done by the research with the benefits it can produce. One complaint about the ethics of behavioral research is that few researchers consider long-term, hidden ethical problems as costs of their research.

2. Ethical oversight committees of various types exist to evaluate ethical issues. Institutional review boards must approve any research to be conducted within an institution before it is performed. Professional ethics committees evaluate claims of unethical conduct and can expel members who have behaved unethically. Recently, committees have been formed in some professional organizations to help researchers resolve ethical dilemmas while planning their research.

3. If you believe a research project is unethical, you should first discuss it with the researcher. If you get no satisfaction there, you can go over the researcher's head. Remember that ethical issues are not clear-cut, and honest people may disagree with your opinion.

D. Students are often expected to conduct research as a course requirement. Make sure that ethical considerations are an important part of your preparation to conduct that research. Discuss any ethical questions with your teacher, who shares responsibility for your actions. However, as the person doing the research, you have the ultimate responsibility for what you do. You should refuse to conduct any research you believe is unethical. It is generally possible to work out an alternative.

CHECKPOINT

Check your understanding of the material in this chapter:

- What are the six major kinds of ethically questionable activity?

- What is informed consent? How can it reduce the ethical problems of harm to the participants?

- When is an observation an invasion of privacy?

- What is the difference between anonymity and confidentiality?

- What sorts of deception are there?

- Why is it particularly difficult to use informed consent to reduce the ethical problems of deception?

- What is the distinction between persuasion and coercion?

- What fact of human nature makes coercion difficult to avoid without special care on the part of the researcher?

- What rights do animal participants in research have, as compared with human participants?

- Who protects the rights of animal participants?

- How do researchers decide ethical issues?

- What costs do critics of the ethics of research say usually are not taken into consideration?

EXERCISES

3.1 What sorts of ethical questions do you think might arise in your particular area of interest? How might you deal with them?

3.2 How might you use animals in research in your area of interest? What steps would you take to ensure their rights?

3.3 What different ethical committees exist in your college, department, or institution? What do they do?

3.4 If a piece of unethical research has already been conducted, is it ethical to use the results of that research? Would it be unethical to discard the results, thereby making the participants' involvement worthless?

3.5 An experiment in which participants believed they were giving other people electric shocks (Migram, 1963), was much discussed in this chapter. If you were on the ethics review board that had to pass judgment on this experiment, would you permit it to take place? Why or why not? How might it be improved?

3.6 The research by Middlemist, Knowles, and Matter (1976) on stress and urination in a public rest room was discussed in relation to several of the ethical issues raised in this chapter. If you were on the ethics review board that had to pass judgment on this experiment, would you permit it to take place? Why or why not? How might it be improved?

Part 2

Making and Using Measurements

Now that Part 1 has established a general idea of what research is for and what researchers must consider, we can look at some specific ideas in the research process. This section considers some important topics related to measurement.

Chapter 4 deals with measurement from a theoretical perspective. In this chapter we will look at what one is actually doing when measuring something, and what a measurement really is. We will find out what measurements can and cannot tell us about the things we are measuring.

Chapter 5 examines some specific measurement issues. It discusses sampling (deciding what to measure), measurement techniques behavioral scientists often use, and how a group of measurements can be described once they have been collected.

Chapter 6 discusses correlational research, a type of research that involves measuring not only individual variables but also the relationship between variables. These measurements can then be used to predict the future.

Once we have discussed measurements—how they are done and what they are for—we can look more closely at experimental research in Part 3.

Chapter 4

The Theory of Measurement

Questions to Consider as You Read

- What does it mean to measure something?
- How can you measure something you cannot see, such as honesty?
- Do measurements always have to be numbers?
- What kinds of factors affect a measurement?
- How can scientists deal with a topic such as honesty, if we cannot all agree on what it is?
- What makes one measurement better than another?
- What is a reliable measurement? A valid measurement?
- Why might you want to give the same measurement over again in the same situation?
- Why might you want to give a measurement to a group of people when you know what the result should be?
- Why do we need statistics?
- How can we describe the measurements we make?

Last night, in playing Trivial Pursuit, I was presented with the following question: "How many flights of stairs would you have to climb to expend the energy used during sexual intercourse?" No, I will not tell you the answer. Right now, I am much more interested in the question. Besides, I got it wrong.

When you hear a question like this one, what is your reaction? Does the question seem entirely sensible, or does it seem a little bit odd? If you had to answer it correctly or lose your turn, would you feel that this was reasonable, or unfair? If unfair, why? My own reaction was something like "Good grief. It depends on how you measure it, doesn't it?" (For another example, see Figure 4-1.) And that is why the question is relevant to this chapter. Here we will learn what it means to measure something, and why some measurements are better than others.

What Is a Measurement?

The concept of measurement is intuitively simple. If you want to measure how long a table is, you just hold a ruler up to it and read off the length in inches or centimeters or whatever unit you like. But if you are doing research, trying to find the answers to difficult questions in a scientific way, you need a better understanding of what you are really doing when you lay the ruler up against the table.

When you measure something, there are two concepts involved: the thing you are measuring and the measurement you produce. The thing you are measuring is some property of an object or event: its size, duration, pleasantness, strength, or any of a number of other properties. The measurement you come up with is some kind of label, often a number, that relates somehow to one of these properties, such that knowing the label is to know something about one of the properties of the object or event. To measure something is to find out which label relates to the particular thing you are measuring. So we can define a **measurement** as a relationship between a system of labels and a property of an empirical object or event. A few examples will make this idea clearer.

A ruler is a device that specifies a relationship between the particular property we call length and a system of labels that in this case consists of a number and a unit. Thus the length of the table on which I am typing

Reprinted by permission of UFS, Inc.

Figure 4-1 An example of a questionable measurement.

is about 48 inches, or about 140 centimeters. The ruler specifies the relationship between a particular label (such as "48 inches") and a property ("length"), so if you know the label you know the length of the table. The table has many other properties I could measure. Examples include its height (26 inches), its weight (20 pounds), its color (medium brown), its shape (rectangular), and its composition (wood). Note that not all the properties of the table are represented by numbers. Some of the labels are simply words for properties such as shape and color. To measure something does not necessarily mean to give it a number. It just means to give it some sort of label that relates to a property.

Or consider the Trivial Pursuit example that opened the chapter. To answer the question, one would have to measure how much energy is used in sexual intercourse. Thus the property being measured is "energy," and the empirical event is "sexual intercourse." There are many different measurements that can be applied to the property of energy, but the one that was probably used in this case was "calories." Thus someone, somewhere, used a measurement system to come up with a number of calories that represented the amount of energy used in sexual intercourse. The same system could be used to find the number of calories used in climbing stairs, and then the relationship between the two would give the answer to the question. This may seem quite different from holding a ruler against a table, but the basic idea is the same. A system of measurement is used that specifies the relationship between a property of an event or object and a label.

We would not need to go to all this trouble to understand the nature of measurement if everything could be measured in relatively straightforward ways. But science is not always so simple. How do you measure honesty? Mental health? Child abuse? Criminal tendencies? Fear of technology? Political unrest? Sexuality? These are not just matters of holding rulers up against things. Nevertheless, they are still matters of specifying relationships between labels and some properties of objects or events.

Constructs and Observations

Very often the particular property you wish to measure is something you cannot observe directly. Take, for example, the property of honesty. You would need the psychological equivalent of a ruler that you could hold up to an applicant and read off the label that corresponds to how much honesty the person has. Naturally enough, it is not that simple, because, in one sense, there is no such thing as honesty.

You may have seen people behaving in ways you consider to be honest or dishonest, you may have had thoughts or ideas you consider to be honest or dishonest, but you have never experienced pure honesty itself. Suppose you see two people pick up wallets they find lying in the street, and one person goes to a lot of trouble to return the wallet while the other person pockets it without a second thought. Seeing a difference in the behavior of these two people, you say the difference is that one person is more honest than the other. But the word "honest" really does not mean very much. You could just as easily say that one person has more "substance X" than the other one has. You cannot point to honesty, only to behaviors that you believe demonstrate honesty.

Your idea of honesty is constructed out of things you have been taught and things you have seen, so we call a property like honesty a construct. **Constructs** are abstract properties of things that cannot be directly observed. (Constructs are sometimes called **conceptual variables** or **theoretical variables**, because they deal with concepts and theories, not with concrete observations.) Most of the important ideas in behavioral science are constructs, because so many of the important things about people cannot actually be seen, but can only be constructed out of our knowledge of what people are like and our observations of how people behave in different situations. Each of us has an individual idea of what sorts of behavior indicate honesty, what sorts of events indicate child abuse, or what sorts of situations indicate political unrest, and from these individual ideas we construct words for these things. But what do they really mean?

Research is empirical, which means that it is based on observations, as was discussed in Chapter 2. Constructs are abstract, which means that they themselves cannot be observed. So how can research be applied to constructs? Constructs are constructed out of observations in the first place, which means that the observations are related to the constructs in some meaningful way. We use our empirical observations to provide information about the invisible constructs. This adds another layer to the measurement process. When measuring a concrete property, such as length, we can directly measure the property itself. When measuring an abstract property, such as the construct of "honesty," we must measure the empirical observations that relate to the construct. That is, we cannot directly measure honesty. We must measure the behaviors that we believe are related to honesty. The idea of measurement has gotten a little more complicated.

Variables and Variability

Scientists and mathematicians often speak of variables. Indeed, much of this book deals with variables of one kind or another. In its simplest definition, a variable is anything that can vary. When a certain property is measured in different objects under different conditions, it might or might not give the same answer each time. If, under all conceivable circumstances, a particular type of measurement would always yield exactly the same result, then what is being measured is not a variable. If, on the other hand, you might get different answers, you are in fact measuring a variable. That is, a **variable** is any property that, when measured in different objects under different conditions, might yield different measurements.

With a definition this broad, we can only expect to encounter a great many different kinds of variables. The examples above of properties to be measured (length, height, weight, color, pleasantness, honesty, mental health, child abuse, criminal tendencies, fear of technology, political unrest, sexuality) are all variables. So is almost any other property you can think of, because it is very difficult to think of any property of anything that could not conceivably vary.

We refer to the properties of things as variables to emphasize the concept of variability in measurement. **Variability** is the name for these differences in the measurements of a property, and **sources of variability** are the many possible factors that can cause these differences. Variability is one of the most important concepts in research, because it has such a large effect on what our measurements really mean.

To return to the honesty example, let us suppose for the moment that our construct of "honesty" has a real meaning. That is, we will assume that deep down inside each person is a certain amount of something we can call "honesty," that this amount does not change much as time goes by, and that it has important effects on the kinds of things that person will be willing to do. Now let us imagine that we have developed a measuring system that will give us a number for each person on a scale of 1 to 10, where higher numbers mean more honesty. What will our numbers actually mean?

Any time you measure a construct, your result depends on many things besides the construct you are trying to measure. A particular measurement of honesty might depend on the true value of the person's honesty, but it might also depend on the person's intelligence or political attitudes, the weather, or just random chance. The many things besides the construct that can affect a measurement are divided into two groups. First, the measurement may be responding to irrelevant values, constructs that are different from the construct of interest. This would be the case, for instance, if the measurement were affected by a person's intelligence. Second, the measurement may simply be affected by

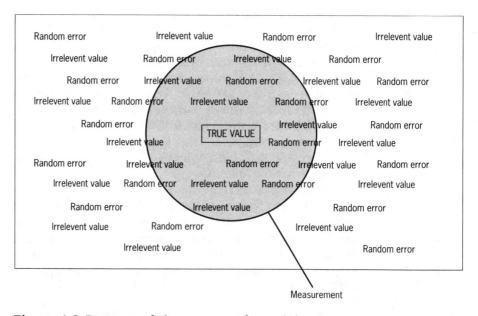

Measurement

Figure 4-2 Diagram of the sources of variability in a measurement. The measurement depends not only on the true value being measured, but also on the values of other irrelevant constructs and on a certain amount of random error.

random error, factors that do not depend systematically on anything but just happen. This can be expressed in an equation (and in a picture in Figure 4-2):

true value + irrelevant values + random error → measurement

For instance, the grade a teacher assigns a student might depend on the student's knowledge of the material (the true value the teacher wants to measure), on how much the teacher likes the student or whether the student is related to the president of the college (irrelevant values of other constructs), and on how many multiple-choice questions the student happened to misread on the final exam (random error). To understand what any measurement means, you need to be able to evaluate each of these sources of variability. You will find as we go along that most of the research methods that have been developed by scientists can be considered to be ways of dealing with one or more of these sources of variability.

This general discussion is all very well, you say, but it does not tell me how I actually go about measuring something. If I want to measure the honesty of job applicants at my company, what do I do? How does it help me to know about constructs and sources of variability?

If you keep this information in mind, it will tell you what measurements are and are not, what they can and cannot do. Perhaps you will remember to be skeptical of any measurement, your own or someone else's, that claims to measure some hidden construct. You now know better. It may measure an observation that is *related* to the construct, and it may be more or less affected by the various sources of variability; but the measurement is *not* the construct. A child's score on an IQ test is not the child's intelligence. A culture's cohesiveness score is not the relationship among its people. A city's crime rate is not how safe it is. Measurements can tell us about things, but they are not the things themselves.

Operational Definitions

When researching something, and measuring variables such as honesty, a researcher must make decisions about how measurements will be obtained. An **operational definition** is a specification of exactly what steps, or operations, are conducted to arrive at a particular measurement. The operational definition specifies the particular empirical observations that will be collected in trying to measure a particular construct. When we specify an operational definition for a variable, we say that we have operationalized the variable. Thus when scientists talk about operationalizing things, they are discussing how to go about measuring them.

If you left a five-dollar bill in the reception area of the company and noted whether an applicant turned it in at the desk, this would be one operational definition of the construct of honesty. Or, for another example, suppose you gave applicants an "intelligence test" that required them to define words such as "tergiversate" and "badinage." (Go ahead, look them up.) Then the applicants scored their own papers and reported the scores. You could assume that anyone who claimed a high score on this test must have fudged the score and probably has little honesty. Or, for yet another example, you could investigate the pasts of the various applicants and ask them during an interview for information you already have. If their answers agreed with what the investigator turned up, the applicants would be considered to be honest. These are three different operational definitions of honesty, and they might well all give different results. (Actually, a real operational definition would give more details than the brief descriptions here. The location of the money in the reception area, the exact words on the "intelligence test," and the precise questions asked in the interviews would all have to be specified for the operational definition to be complete.)

Operational definitions are very important in science, behavioral science in particular. They allow everyone to know exactly what is being discussed. Because constructs are abstract and invisible, what I mean by the word "honesty" may not be the same as what you mean. You and I might never agree on how honest a person is, because we might be using different kinds of observations to make our decisions. The term "honesty" is **subjective**, because different observers are likely to give different responses to a situation. Is President Bush honest? How about former President Nixon? Mother Theresa? General H. Norman Schwarzkopf? You will get different answers from different people. Operational definitions, on the other hand, are **objective**, because everyone can agree on what happened. We will all agree on whether the money was turned in, on what score the subject reported on the "intelligence test," on what answers the applicant gave in the interview. Of course, we may still disagree on what these observations mean, but at least we will be disagreeing on the same terms.

Much of the skill of a researcher in the behavioral sciences is in the ability to come up with good operational definitions. Before you can study anything, you need to develop a way to measure it, and because some measurements are better than others (see next section), the operational definitions you select will be very important to the success of your research.

Because of the limitations inherent in any operational definition, the best way to measure any complex construct is to use several different operational definitions together. A conscientious personnel director should probably use all three operational definitions of honesty before deciding whether an applicant is honest. **Converging operations** are several different operational definitions that all apply to, or converge on, the same construct. If you have lots of converging operations, all very different from one another, and all agree in their measurement of the construct, you can have a lot of confidence in the measurement.

Levels of Measurement

The symbols in the set used in any given measurement system can be related to one another in a number of different ways. For example, in some systems one symbol represents more of the property being measured than another symbol does, as the symbol "10 inches" represents more length than the symbol "5 inches" does. In other systems, one symbol represents a different example of the property, but neither more of it nor less of it. Thus the symbol "rectangle" represents a shape different from the symbol "circle," but neither the rectangle nor the circle has "more" shape than the other. The **level of measurement** of a measurement system tells us how the different symbols in the system are related. (Some authors use the term "scaling" to refer to these differences, but this term also has another meaning in the context of measurement, so I prefer not to use it here.) There are four different levels of measurement: the nominal, ordinal, equal interval, and ratio levels.

Nominal Measurements

The word "nominal" comes from the Latin *nominalis*, meaning "of a name." **Nominal measurements** use symbols that are names for examples of a property, names that put each object into a category but do not contain any information about the amount of the property. The property of shape is a nominal mesurement; it is represented by names for shapes of different kinds (rectangle, square, circle, triangle), names that do not mean that one kind of shape has "more" shape than another does. The objects being measured are placed into categories that are simply different from one another: in nominal measurements, questions of "more" or "less" have no meaning.

Many important variables used by behavioral scientists are measured at the nominal level. Common examples include sex (male or female), religion (Protestant, Catholic, Jewish, etc.), and political affiliation (Democrat, Republican, Independent, etc.). In each case, people can be put into categories, but there is no expectation that one category has "more" sex, "more" religion, or "more" political affiliation. The category names are simply names, and they can be arranged in any order without disturbing their meaning. Numbers may be used as category names—for instance, when entering data into a computer. However, they do not represent amounts, so while it is possible to use these numbers in arithmetical calculations, the result means nothing. One example of this was a computerized spreadsheet I once used to calculate the average test scores for a large number of students. Each student's ID number was entered into the spreadsheet, and by mistake I calculated the average of the ID numbers instead of the average of the test scores. An "average ID number' has absolutely no meaning, because the ID numbers are not really numbers at all, they are only category labels in a nominal measurement system. Even television humor can reflect the silliness of this mistake. In one episode of "Get Smart," Agent 86 was depressed because a new guy, Agent 43, was making him look bad. His girl friend, Agent 99, consoled him by saying, "You're worth two Forty-Threes, Eighty-Six."

It might seem that nominal measurements have no place in a book on quantitative research, because these measurements are not quantitative at all. It is true that qualitative research relies much more heavily on nominal measurement than quantitative research, but nominal measurements are important in quantitative research as well. This is because, although each measurement can tell us nothing about quantity, a collection of measurements can. It is possible to count the number of observations that fell into each category, and the frequencies that are produced are definitely quantitative.

Ordinal Measurements

The word "ordinal" refers to the order of things, arranged from first to last. An **ordinal measurement** specifies the order of the items being measured, without specifying how far apart they are. Ordinal measurements give us information about the amount of a property an item has, but only relative to the other items. That is, you will know that one item has more than another item, but not how much more.

A standard example of an ordinal measurement is the standings of competitors. When you are told that the Bone City Skeletons are in first place and the Ghoulton Goblins are second, you know something about how much success each team has, because you know that the Skeletons have more than the Goblins. But from this information alone you do not know whether the Goblins are out by a half game or ten games.

The symbols used in ordinal measurements are often numbers, but not necessarily. Regardless of whether numbers are used, the symbols can be arranged in some natural order, corresponding to the relative amounts of a property they represent. However, it is still not meaningful to multiply or divide the numbers in ordinal scales, and addition and subtraction must be applied carefully, because these operations assume that the distances between the categories are equal. These numbers are not arbitrary labels, as they were in nominal measurements, but they also do not represent how much of a property an item has. They are instead simply ranks, specifying which item was first, which second, and so on.

Ordinal measurements are also very common in the behavioral sciences. Societies are rated by how cohesive they are. Crimes are categorized as felonies or misdemeanors. Economic conditions are labeled depression, recession, growth, or inflation. Rating things on a scale of 10 is a familiar ordinal measure. And in your everyday experience as a student, you receive measurements on an ordinal scale every time a test or paper is graded. Letter grades give relative information as to the quality of the work (an "A" paper is better than a "B" paper), but there is no reason to believe that the difference in quality between an "A" and a "B" is the same as the difference in quality between a "C" and a "D." Thus this measurement specifies the order of the items, but not their actual quality.

Equal Interval Measurements

The name of the third level of measurement is self-explanatory. An **equal interval measurement** is one in which the categories are ordered by the amount of a property they have, and the intervals between the categories are equal everywhere. (Sometimes scientists leave out the "equal," and call these simply "interval measurements.") Temperature, as measured on the Fahrenheit scale, is an equal interval measurement, because the difference between 5°F and 6°F is the same as the difference between 92°F and 93°F. Because the distances between categories is the same everywhere in an equal interval measurement, it is meaningful to add and subtract these numbers, and to compute averages. However, you still cannot meaningfully multiply or divide them because the scale has no true zero point so the actual numbers are arbitrary. For instance, it makes no sense to say that a temperature of 10°F is twice as hot as a temperature of 5°F, because there is nothing special about the temperature of zero on the Fahrenheit scale. In the Celsius temperature scale, the same temperatures are about -12°C and -15°C, and one is obviously not twice the other. The reason is that these two scales differ not only in the size of the degree, but in the zero point, which in the Celsius scale is at the freezing point of water (32°F). Because equal interval measurements have arbitrary zero points, they may easily have negative values.

Sometimes in the behavioral sciences there is confusion over whether something is really an ordinal measurement or an equal interval measurement. Part of the problem is that it depends on what you are using your measurement to represent. Take, for example, family income. In one sense, the difference between $8000 per year and $9000 per year is the same as the difference between $108,000 per year and $109,000 per year. After all, $1000 is $1000, right? But if you are using your observations of family income as part of your operational definition of an abstract construct such as "affluence," then the intervals are far from equal. A family whose income goes from $8000 to $9000 will experience a definite change in their affluence, while a family whose income goes from $108,000 to $109,000 probably will not. So in deciding whether a measurement is ordinal or equal interval, you must consider the purpose of your measurement.

Ratio Measurements

A ratio is one thing divided by another thing, and a ratio measurement is the only level of measurement in which you can divide the numbers you obtain. A **ratio measurement** is an equal interval measurement that also has a true zero value: the number zero means that you have absolutely none of the property and cannot possibly have any less. (Note that any ratio measurement is also an equal interval measurement. If the intervals are unequal, then the measurement is ordinal, and it cannot be ratio.) Temperature on the Fahrenheit scale is not a ratio measurement, because a temperature of 0°F does not represent absolutely no heat, and negative temperatures are possible. There is a temperature scale called the Kelvin scale, in which 0 degrees means absolute zero. An object whose temperature was 0° K has no heat whatsoever, and objects cannot have negative temperatures on the Kelvin scale. Thus the Kelvin scale is a ratio measurement of temperature.

Ratio measurements are very rare in the behavioral sciences, particularly if one takes into account what constructs they are being used to measure. Take, for example, a measurement of city size. It is easy to understand this as a ratio measurement, because the intervals are equal (the difference between a population of 10,000 and 10,001 is the same as the difference between a population of 20,000 and 20,001) and because there is a true zero (a population of zero means that there are absolutely no people in the city, and there can never be less than zero people). However, if you are using city size as an operational definition of a construct such as crowding, it is probably an ordinal measurement, neither equal interval nor ratio. As another example, age in years is a candidate for a ratio variable, but if it is being used as an operational definition of maturity, then the intervals are not likely to be equal and it is really ordinal.

I should note that my position on this issue is not accepted by all scientists. Most researchers consider measurements such as the time someone takes to complete a task, the number of times something happens, or the number of errors a person makes to be ratio measurements. Others, of which I am one, are skeptical, because these measurements represent underlying constructs in which the intervals might not be equal, and if the intervals are not equal then it cannot be a ratio scale.

For instance, consider the measurement of the time it takes for a child to complete a vocabulary test. Is this a ratio measurement? Some would say yes, but I would ask whether perhaps the last few items might not be more difficult than others, so that the intervals are not equal. And anyway, if it is impossible for anyone to complete the test in no time at all, is the zero point of the scale truly meaningful? This is simply one of those issues on which rational people can disagree, and as a researcher you will have to make your own decisions.

In practice, the difference between equal interval and ratio measurements is not very important unless you wish to compute ratios. If you intend to make statements such as "city A is twice as crowded as city B," you must use a ratio measurement of crowding. As far as I know, no such ratio measurement exists. Most of the mathematical procedures that scientists use work equally well with equal interval and ratio measurements.

How Good Is the Measurement?

Not all measurements are created equal. Two major considerations determine how well a particular measurement reflects a property of an item. These factors correspond to the sources of variability mentioned earlier. A good measurement will depend mostly on the true value of the property being measured, and not much on irrelevant values or on random error. Measurements that are affected strongly by these other sources of variability are not as good.

Reliability

If you were on the jury in a murder trial, you would not be very impressed by a witness who told a different story every time. Such a witness would be considered unreliable. In the same way, a measurement that gives a different answer every time is not a very good measurement. A measurement has high **reliability** if it gives the same result every time the same property is measured in the same way. Reliability means repeatability, consistency. No measurement is perfectly reliable, so you will never get exactly the same result every single time, but the more similar the results are, the more reliable the measurement is.

An unreliable measurement is strongly affected by the random error source of variability. You may not know just what it is that is causing the result to vary; it might be the weather, the time of day, someone's mood, the color of the walls, or anything at all. When random error has such a large effect on a measurement, it is impossible to figure out just what the true value being measured is.

There are many different techniques that can be used to determine how reliable a measurement is. The most obvious is **test–retest reliability**: you simply measure the same thing more than once and compare the measurements. Sometimes the test–retest technique cannot be used. For instance, consider a multiple-choice test as a measurement of how much you know about the material in a course. You might be expected to improve when you take a test over, so test–retest measures of the reliability of this test are not useful. Instead, you could use **split-half reliability**, in which you randomly divide the test in half, and compare the scores on half the items with the score on the other half. For instance, with a 30-question test, you could compare the score on the 15 odd-numbered items with the 15 even-numbered items. If the test is reliable, you should get roughly the same scores on both halves. A variation on this idea is **alternate form reliability**, in which the items on a long test are divided into two or more separate tests. If people tend to get the same score on the different forms of the test, these alternate forms are said to be reliable.

Another common type of reliability is **interrater reliability**, in which the judgments of two or more different observers are compared. For instance, one issue of great concern to mental health professionals is the reliability of our diagnostic systems. A great deal of energy has been spent over the past several years developing a set of procedures specifying just how professionals should classify their clients into diagnostic categories (in other words, developing a set of operational definitions for the measurement of mental disorder). The concern stemmed from a number of studies showing that the same patients received different diagnoses from different professionals more than 50 percent of the time (Schmidt & Fonda, 1956). This meant that the interrater reliability of this measurement of psychological disorder was very poor.

Validity

Just as a murder witness can be completely consistent and still be lying, a measurement can be completely reliable and still not be any good. A reliable measure is not much affected by random error, but it may still be affected by another undesirable source of variability, the values of irrelevant constructs. A measurement has **validity** when it reflects the construct you intended to measure, not other irrelevant constructs. For instance, I once wrote a multiple-choice test item to determine whether students knew that jet lag is worse when flying from west to east than it is when flying from east to west. The item asked which trip would produce the worst jet lag: (a) Paris to New York, (b) Moscow to London, (c) Los Angeles to Tokyo, or (d) Paris to Moscow. It turned out that most students got this question wrong, not because they were confused about jet lag, but because they were confused about geography. Knowledge of geography was an irrelevant construct that had a large effect on this measurement, so the measurement was invalid. Instructors detect this sort of problem through item analysis, which examines the relationship between the probability that a person will get an item correct and the person's score on the entire test. If this relationship is strong, then those who know the material the best tend to get the item right, which means it is probably measuring knowledge of the material. If the relationship is backward, those who know the most tend to get it wrong, indicating a serious validity problem with the item.

It is much easier to tell whether a witness's testimony is consistent than whether it is truthful, without knowing the truth in advance. In the same way, determining the validity of a measurement is harder than determining its reliability, because you would have to have some independent idea of what the construct is that you are trying to measure. If it were easy for you to know what the construct really was, you would not need the measure. There are several different types of validity, corresponding to several different techniques that can be used to help determine how valid a measurement is. Ideally, you should use as many of them as possible to be sure of the validity of a measure. Let us see how they might apply to the various operational definitions of honesty developed earlier in the chapter.

Face Validity

Face validity simply entails deciding whether something looks valid on the face of it. You would ask people who are not particularly expert on the construct you are studying to look at your measurement and tell whether it seems to be valid to them. For example, the honesty measure that involved returning the "lost" money had a great deal of face value, while the "intelligence test" measure had less face value. As you might expect, face validity is not always a good indicator of the true validity of a measurement.

Criterion Validity

A measure of **criterion validity** is one in which the result of the measurement is compared with a criterion that is related to the construct but is separate from the measure itself. That is, you will have an external way of determining what the construct is, and you compare your measurement to that criterion. There are two different types of criterion validity, depending on whether the external criterion is available at the same time as the measurement or in the future. In **concurrent validity**, the external criterion is available at the same time. For instance, you might give an honesty measure to two different groups of people, one who might be expected to be highly honest (religious leaders, perhaps), and one who might be expected to be less honest (convicted felons, for example). If the measure really reflected honesty, you would expect the scores of one group to be higher than the other. In **predictive validity**, the external criterion is some future behavior that depends on the construct. For instance, you might give the honesty test to a large group of job applicants, and then five years later find out who stole the most from the company. If the score on the measure is related to their later behavior, the item has predictive validity. This is an excellent measure of validity, but because you must wait to test the predictions, it takes time to apply.

Content Validity

It would be difficult to claim that any of the operational definitions given truly measure honesty, because the concept of honesty includes many different kinds of behavior. Keeping someone else's wallet is very different from omitting income from an income tax return. A measure that has **content validity** will include all the different aspects of the construct. If your final exam for any course included questions only on one chapter of the text, it would not have content validity. Only a test that covered all the content could be considered to be valid.

For everyday constructs like honesty, those most people are familiar with, there is little difference between content validity and face validity. However, when experts in a field have developed theoretical constructs from their research, the distinction becomes greater. Something has face validity if most ordinary people would agree that it measures what it is supposed to measure. It has content validity if most experts on the construct being measured would agree that all the important theoretical aspects of the construct are addressed by the measurement. For instance, an important topic in the area of social psychology is **locus of control**, a person's belief about who or what controls important events in life. A person who believes that we each control what happens to us, that we can take credit for our successes and blame for our failings, has an internal locus of control. Someone who believes that what happens to us is largely controlled by someone or something outside ourselves, such as luck or God or the government or international conspiracies, has an external locus of control. If social psychologists asked everyday people whether a certain questionnaire was a valid measure of locus of control, they would not get many useful answers. Other experts, however, could discuss whether all the important aspects of this construct were addressed in the questionnaire—that is, whether the instrument had content validity.

Construct Validity

If a measure of a construct is valid, it should coincide with results of previous measurements of that construct. A measure has **construct validity** if is it related in sensible ways to measures of other variables that are related to the construct being measured. You would expect a measure of honesty to be related to measures of related concepts, including religiosity, dependability, and legality. If you find that scores on your honesty measure have nothing to do with number of convictions for robbery or theft, there is something wrong with your measure. To determine construct validity, then, you must compare your measurement with accepted measurements of related constructs and show that the relationships are as you would expect.

Describing Measurements

When you measure only one thing, it is not too difficult to tell people the result. My table is 48 inches long. But suppose you want to know about tables in general, not just my particular table. If you measure a group of things and get a group of different numbers, how can you report this result? One obvious way is to give people a list of all the measurements you obtained (table A was 48 inches long; table B, 42 inches; table C, 49 inches, etc.). This is not very useful. It is difficult from this haphazard list of measurements to get a clear idea of the group of numbers as a whole. How long is a typical table? Are they all similar, or all different? To answer these questions, we use statistics.

A **statistic** is a number that you calculate by applying a mathematical procedure to a group of other numbers. While some statistics are based on very complex formulas, many others are very simple. Later in this book (Chapter 10) we will discuss statistics that scientists use to help make decisions. Right now, we look at statistics that are used to help us get a sense of what a group of measurements is like. **Descriptive statistics** are statistics that describe a property of a group of measurements. Therefore, descriptive statistics are themselves measurements, because they are symbols that correspond to some property of some object or event.

When discussing statistics, we use a letter to refer to a score in the group, because we are talking about abstract examples of scores, not specific ones. The examples below use the letter X.

Describing Frequencies

If the measurement you wish to describe is a nominal measurement, the only meaningful numbers that are available are **frequencies**, which are the numbers of items that fell into each category of your measurement scheme. A **frequency distribution**, all the frequencies of all the categories collected together, can be described in various ways. A **frequency table** is just a list of the frequencies (f) of all the categories. For instance, Table 4-1 is a frequency table showing the frequency distribution of the terms college students use to describe the best and the worst teachers

Table 4-1 Frequency Distribution of Descriptors Given for Best and Worst College Teachers

| | Type of Descriptor | | | | | |
| | Personal | | Classroom | | Interpersonal | |
Evaluation	f	%	f	%	f	%
Best	86	42	58	28	60	29
Worst	37	23	85	53	38	24

Based on Waters, Kemp, & Pucci (1988).

they had in college (Waters, Kemp, & Pucci, 1988). The students' terms were classified into three categories: personal characteristics (describing the teacher personally, such as enthusiastic, funny, likable; no personality, superior, mean), classroom characteristics (describing what went on in class, such as organized, open to questions, fair; boring, often late), and interpersonal characteristics (describing the relationship between the teacher and students, such as helpful outside of class, cares about students; hard to talk to, unfriendly). It is difficult to compare the frequencies directly, because more words overall were used to describe the best teachers than the worst teachers, but it appears that the students used more personal and interpersonal terms to describe their best teachers and more classroom terms to describe their worst teachers. The frequency distribution can also be converted to a chart or graph, as described in Appendix B.

It is often clearer to convert frequencies into percentages. The word "percent" comes from the Latin for "out of one hundred" ("cent" stands for hundred, just as one cent is one-hundredth of a dollar). A **percentage** tells you what proportion of your cases out of 100 fell into each category; it is the frequency for a single category divided by the total number of observations, multiplied by 100. The percentages for each of the categories in the statistical analysis report are also given in Table 4-1. Converting frequencies to percentages allows direct comparison of groups with different numbers and lets us see in this case that more personal terms were indeed used to describe the best teachers and more classroom terms to describe the worst teachers. The percentage of interpersonal terms was about the same for both.

Describing Central Tendency

If a measurement is on a level other than nominal, it reflects the amount of a property the item has. In that case, you would like to know something about the central tendency of your measurements. The **central tendency** of a distribution tells you where the center of your distribution tends to be, and therefore tells you how much of the property a typical item has. There are three common measures of central tendency: mean, median, and mode.

The **mean** is the mathematically expected value of a group of numbers; it is computed by adding all the numbers and dividing by the total number of observations. When people use the word "average," they are usually referring to the mean. The symbol M stands for the mean of a group of scores. The formula for the mean is:

$$M = \frac{\Sigma(X)}{N}$$

where the Greek letter Σ (sigma) means "the sum of" and the letter N means the number of observations. In reading this formula, you would say, "M equals the sum of X, divided by N." Table 4-2 shows the calculation of the mean of a group of scores on an exam that I gave last year. It shows that the mean of these scores is 76, indicating that 76 is a typical or central score on this exam.

Because the mean involves adding all the measurements, it is meaningful only for equal interval measurements. For ordinal measurements, a different measure of central tendency is used. The **median** is the middle of a group of scores, the number that has half the scores above it and half the scores below it. To find the median, you must arrange all the scores in order from highest to lowest. If there is an odd number of scores, the median is simply the value of the middle score. If there is an even number, you compute the mean of the two middle numbers (that is, you add them together and divide by 2). Table 4-2 also gives the median for the group of exam scores.

The final measure of central tendency is not as useful as the other two, but it is the only one that can be applied to nominal measurements. The **mode** is the most common score, the measurement that occurred most frequently in the group. If two different scores, not next to each other, are tied for the highest number of scores, then the group is **bimodal**, which means that it has two modes. The mode of the exam scores in Table 4-2 is shown.

Describing Variability

In addition to knowing what a typical score of a group would be, it is useful to know how similar or different the scores are. Are all the measurements very close together, or are they spread all over the map? Earlier we defined variability as the differences in the measurements of

Table 4-2 Three Descriptives of the Central Tendency of a Sample of Exam Scores

Exam Scores	Calculation of Mean, Median, and Mode
83	$Mean = \dfrac{\Sigma X}{n} = \dfrac{912}{12} = 76.0$
72	
76	
91	*Median*: Arrange the scores in order: 56, 64, 68, 72,
56	72, 75, 76, 78, 83, 84, 91, 93
68	
84	There is an even number of scores, so find the middle
93	two and average them: $\dfrac{75+76}{2} = 75.5$
75	
78	*Mode*: Take the most common score: 72
64	
72	
$\Sigma X = 912$	

a property. If there is a lot of variability, the scores will be very different; if there is little, they will be more similar (see Figure 4-3). Three different measures of variability are commonly used: the variance, the standard deviation, and the range.

The variance of a group of scores is computed by subtracting each score from the mean, squaring all these differences (that is, multiplying them by themselves) to make them all positive, adding them, and dividing by the number of scores minus 1. The difference between a score and its mean is called a **deviation**, because it measures how far it is from the typical value. This is almost like computing a mean: add up everything and divide by the number of items added. Because the things being added are squared numbers, the variance is often called the **mean square** and is abbreviated *MS*:

$$MS = \frac{\Sigma(X - M)^2}{N - 1}$$

(The sum is divided by $N - 1$ rather than N because for mathematical reasons, this makes it a better estimate of the actual variability in the

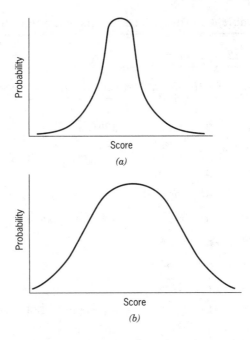

Figure 4-3 Distributions of scores displaying different variabilities. The distribution at the top has very little variability, so the scores are close together. The distribution at the bottom has a larger variability, so the scores spread out a lot.

population of numbers from which our sample was taken.) This gives a mean, or typical, value for the squared deviations in our measurement. The variance of a set of exam scores is given in Table 4-3.

One problem with the variance is that it is a typical *squared* deviation. That is, it is typical of what you get when you multiply all the deviations by themselves, but not typical of the deviations themselves. To get a typical *nonsquared* deviation, it is only necessary to take the square root of the variance. This gives us the **standard deviation** of a group of scores, which is in some sense the typical difference between the scores and their mean:

$$s.d. = \sqrt{MS}$$

Table 4-3 gives the standard deviation of a set of exam scores.

The standard deviation is not meaningful when applied to measurements on the ordinal level because it involves adding scores. For ordinal measurements, or whenever the standard deviation is not necessary, a much simpler measure of variability can be used. The **range** is the difference between the lowest score and the highest score; it is computed

Table 4-3 Three Descriptions of the Variability of a Sample of Exam Scores

Exam Scores			
X	X - M	(X - M)²	Calculating Variance, Standard Deviation, and Range
83	7	49	Variance: $\dfrac{\Sigma(X-M)^2}{N-1} = \dfrac{1272}{11} = 115.6$
72	-4	16	
76	0	0	
91	15	225	
56	-20	400	Standard deviation: $\sqrt{\text{variance}} = \sqrt{115.6} = 10.75$
68	-8	64	
84	8	64	
93	17	289	
75	-1	1	Range: (93 - 56) + 1 = 37 + 1 + 38
78	2	4	
64	-12	144	
72	-4	16	
912 = ΣX		1272 = Σ(X - M)²	

by finding the highest score and subtracting the lowest score from it. (It is actually a little more complex than this, because if the true value of what you are measuring were just a little higher than the highest score or just a little lower than the lowest score, your numbers would look just the same. For this reason, to be accurate you would have to add in one of the smallest units you are measuring, to represent the half-unit extra at the top and the half-unit at the bottom. So if all your measures are whole numbers, add 1 to get the range. If all your measures are given to the nearest hundredth, then add 0.01 to your range.) When a range is reported, the highest and lowest scores are usually also reported. Table 4-3 gives the range of the exam scores.

One problem with the range is that it will naturally grow with sample size; this is because as you take more and more measurements, you are more and more likely to get very high and very low scores. This means that it is meaningful to compare the ranges of two different sets of scores only if they contain the same number of scores. For this reason, the sample size is usually reported along with a range.

Now that we have begun to discuss what it means to measure something, what makes some measurements better than others, and how to describe our measurements, we are ready to discuss some particular measurement techniques that are commonly used in the behavioral sciences. This is the subject of the next chapter.

SUMMARY

A. A measurement is a relationship between a set of symbols and some property of an object or event.

   1. A construct is an abstract property that cannot be directly observed. We measure observations that we believe are related to the construct.

   2. A variable is any property that might give different results when measured repeatedly. There are different sources of variability: the true value of the property you wish to measure, irrelevant values of properties you are not interested in, and random error.

   3. An operational definition specifies the steps used to measure something, describing the relationship between the construct and the observations used to measure it.

B. Measurement systems measure things on different levels.

   1. Nominal measurements put things in categories, without specifying which has "more" or "less."

   2. Ordinal measurements can be arranged in order, so that one has more of the property than another, but the distances between them are not equal.

   3. Equal interval measurements have equal distances between the categories, but no special zero value.

   4. Ratio measurements have equal intervals between the categories and also a true zero point with absolutely none of the property, making ratios of scores meaningful.

C. Two factors affect the quality of a measurement.

   1. The reliability of a measure is its consistency. Test–retest reliability involves performing the same measurement twice and comparing the two results. Split-half and alternate form reliability involve splitting one measurement into two halves and comparing them. Interrater reliability involves comparing the judgements of two different observers.

   2. The validity of a measurement indicates how well it measures what it was intended to measure. Measuring validity requires some way of knowing what the true value is.

   a. Face validity exists when the measure looks on the face of it as though it measures the right thing.

    b. Criterion validity involves comparing the measurement against some standard of what it should be. Criteria that are available in the present time give concurrent validity, and future behavior that reflects the construct gives predictive validity.

    c. Content validity involves covering all different aspects of the construct, not just part of it.

    d. Construct validity involves having a sensible relationship with other related variables, based on our understanding of the construct involved.

D. If a group of measurements have been collected, different techniques can be used to describe those measurements.

    1. Nominal measurements are described in frequency tables, giving the number of examples of each category, sometimes as percentages.

    2. The central tendency is the typical value of a group of numbers. The mean, which applies only to equal interval or ratio measures, is computed by adding all the numbers and dividing by the number of values. For ordinal measurements, we can use the median, which is the number that has half the scores above it and half below it. The mode is simply the most common score in the group and can apply to nominal measures.

    3. The variability of a group of numbers describes how spread out the numbers are. The variance is the typical squared deviation from the mean. The standard deviation is the square root of the variance. The range, which applies to ordinal measurements, is the difference between the highest and the lowest score in the group, plus one measurement unit.

CHECKPOINT

Check your understanding of the material in this chapter:

- What is the definition of a measurement?

- What is a construct? How do observations relate to constructs?

- What is a variable? What are the different sources of variability that can affect a measurement?

- What is an operational definition? Why are operational definitions so important?

- What is a nominal measurement? An ordinal measurement? An equal interval measurement? A ratio measurement?

- When is a measurement reliable? When is it valid?

- What are the three different types of reliability? Think of an example of each.

- What are the four major types of validity? Think of an example of each.

- What is a statistic? What is a descriptive statistic?

- How are frequencies described?

- What is central tendency? What are the three different ways of describing it?

- What is variability? What are the three different ways of describing it?

EXERCISES

4.1 Think of two different constructs that are important in your own area of interest. Give two different operational definitions for each one.

4.2 In your area of interest, think of two different examples each of a nominal measurement, an ordinal measurement, and an equal interval measurement.

4.3 Calculate various descriptive statistics from some interesting samples of numbers. For instance, find the mean and standard deviation of the sizes of the checks you have written for the past few months, or rate your friends on their taste in clothing and compute the median and the range of your ratings.

4.4 Find an example of some research you are interested in. From this research, find at least two examples of measurement. For each example, give the construct and the operational definition, and discuss the quality of the measurements. That is, how reliable are they? How valid? Did the researcher present any measurements of reliability or validity? Were they good measurements? How do you think the operational definitions might be improved?

Chapter 5

Issues in Measurement

Questions to Consider as You Read

- What do scientists mean when they talk about populations? About samples?

- Why can it be difficult to draw general conclusions from a specific set of measurements?

- What is wrong with simply selecting whatever examples of a population are the easiest to measure?

- What are the different ways of constructing useful samples from a population?

- In designing questions for a questionnaire, what are some of the problems you must avoid?

- What is the difference between an interview and a survey? How do interviews differ from each other?

- What is an unobtrusive measurement? What are its advantages?

- Why are archives of data useful? What problems are encountered using them?

- Why do researchers study advertisements, songs, speeches, and other messages people produce?

- What can researchers learn by studying the traces a behavior leaves behind?

- Why do researchers use hidden recordings? What problems are associated with this practice?

The number of different operational definitions that behavioral scientists could use to measure important constructs is limited only by our imagination. The past hundred years or so have seen the development of several general types of measurement techniques that have proven useful in a wide variety of research circumstances. In this chapter, we look at some of these common techniques and explore their strengths and their weaknesses. Remember, though, that this listing is not complete. It could not be, because creative scientists are constantly thinking of new ways to measure the things that interest them.

What to Measure

Before measuring something, you need to decide just which examples you are going to measure. If you wanted to know about the heights of tables, you would probably want to measure not just the tables in your own house, but those in other places as well. Which ones would you choose? It depends on what you plan to do with the measurements you collect.

Sampling and Generalizability

One way to find out about the heights of tables would be to measure the height of every single table in the world. A **population** consists of every member of a particular group, and you could measure every member of the population. Given that you would probably like to do something with your life other than measure tables, you are unlikely to choose that option. Instead, you will select some tables out of the billions that exist. A **sample** is the smaller group of examples chosen from the population that you actually measure. **Sampling techniques** are procedures for deciding which examples of a population will be in your sample.

As is often the case, these definitions are a little bit slippery. A researcher has a lot of flexibility in just how to define a population. For research on the mental abilities of the elderly, for example, the population might be defined as all human beings over a particular age, or all men or all women over that age, or all Americans over that age, or all black Americans over that age, or all Americans living in institutions for the elderly, or whatever else defines the group of people the researcher wants to study.

Researchers very often wish to draw conclusions that apply to a whole population, not just to the sample of people actually observed. Researchers make **generalizations** when they take measurements from a sample and apply the results to the population in general. As you might guess, this does not always work very well. If you sampled elderly people living in institutions, it would not be accurate to apply your findings to all elderly people. Relatively few old people live in institutions, and those who do are probably older and sicker than those who do not. A sample is **representative** when it is similar in all measured respects to the population it is being used to represent, and therefore it is safe to generalize from that sample to that population. Representativeness is a relationship between a sample and a population, and therefore a sample may be representative of one population without being representative of another population. For instance, a sample may be representative of the institutionalized elderly without being representative of elderly people in general.

The most famous example of the importance of representativeness in generalizing from a sample to a population happened in 1948. George Gallup, a skillful assessor of public opinion, had correctly called the winner in the preceding three presidential elections. He based his predictions on the responses of a number of voters before the election and generalizing from the views of this sample to the entire American electorate. In 1948 Gallup and nearly all other political pollsters predicted that New York Governor Thomas Dewey would win. The conclusion seemed so certain that several newspapers actually published early editions on the day after the election proclaiming Dewey as the next president. In fact, there has never been a President Dewey; Harry Truman was elected instead. While a variety of factors caused this error, one of them was Gallup's failure to use a sample that was representative of his population (Babbie, 1986). Later in this chapter we will look at the reason why his sampling techniques, so successful before, failed in 1948.

If you want to generalize from a sample to a population, you obviously need to know whether that sample is representative of that population. The critical factor is the method used to select the sample out of the population. Sampling techniques differ in the representativeness of the sample they provide. They also differ in other ways, and different techniques may be used to produce representative samples. The technique used depends on the particular circumstances of the research.

Types of Samples

Sampling techniques can be classified into two general categories: probability sampling and nonprobability sampling. If each member of the population has an equal opportunity to take part in the sample, it is a probability sample; if not, it is a nonprobability sample. Because nonprobability samples are somewhat simpler, we will look at them first.

Nonprobability Sampling

Nonprobability sampling techniques do not provide every member of the population an equal probability of being selected for the sample. Nonprobability samples are generally not representative and cannot safely be used to generalize to the entire population.

The simplest form of nonprobability sampling is **haphazard** or **convenience sampling**, which consists of simply observing the members of the population that happen to be handy. This type of sampling is sometimes used by marketing research firms, when they survey people in shopping malls and supermarkets. The people they select look friendly, making eye contact and smiling, they are not in too much of a hurry, not leading small children, and so on. In other words, they are convenient. People will sometimes say that this technique involves selecting people "at random," but this is incorrect. Random sampling is something quite different. We will discuss it below.

Sometimes a convenience sample is chosen by the participants rather than the experimenters. A sample is **self-selected** (or **self-selecting**) when the people in the sample are simply those who volunteered to take part. Such a sample is certainly convenient, but it is hardly representative. It is quite likely that there is some systematic difference between those who chose to be in the study and those who did not.

A slightly more sophisticated nonprobability sampling technique requires that you know something about the makeup of the population. That is, you must be able to state that the population consists of a certain percentage of this kind of person, a certain percentage of that kind of person, and so on. You can then conduct **quota sampling**, in which you make sure that your sample has the same percentage of each type of person as the population, but you select the actual examples for your sample in any convenient way. Thus, a marketing research firm may know that the people who shop for a particular product are 80 percent women and 20 percent men. They can still select people in a shopping mall who look easy to approach, but they will make sure that they interview 80 percent women and 20 percent men. This type of sample is slightly more representative than a simple convenience sample. It is still not safe to generalize from a quota sample, however, because for one thing, the particular men and women you select to interview might not be typical. For another, you might be wrong about the makeup of your population. This is what happened to George Gallup in 1948. He was basing his quotas on the results of the 1940 census, specifying the number of people in each economic class, how many urban, how many rural, and so on. But World War II and the resulting industrial boom had caused major shifts in the American population between 1940 and 1948.

Gallup's quotas no longer reflected his population, and as a result his sample was not representative (Babbie, 1986).

In general, if it is important to be able to generalize accurately from your sample to your population, you should not use nonprobability sampling techniques because they do not ensure that your sample will be representative of your population.

Probability Sampling

Probability sampling techniques are those that give every member of the population a known probability of being selected for the sample. These techniques are also often referred to as **random sampling techniques**, which is why it is not appropriate to refer to haphazard samples as randomly selected. In general, probability samples are representative of the populations from which they are drawn. This does not mean that the results you get from measuring a probability sample will be identical to those you would get from measuring the entire population. But with probability samples, it is possible to figure out mathematically just how different the population is likely to be from the sample. Thus, if you want to be sure that your measurements are accurate to, say 1 percent, probability sampling allows you to select your sample in such a way that this is true.

The most basic probability sample is a **simple random sample**, in which you randomly select members one at a time out of the entire population, just as you might select cards at random from a well-shuffled deck. This technique gives every member of the population an equal chance of being chosen, but it can be applied only to a well-defined, finite population for which you have a list. If your population is, for instance, all the students at your college, this rule might not be too hard to apply; if it is all elderly people, however, it will not be so easy. Once you have such a list, you can select members of your sample by any random method: the use of a table of random numbers, which is carefully constructed so that it is impossible to predict the next number from knowing the numbers that came before (such a table is found in Appendix D), or a computerized random selection procedure; rolling dice, or even drawing cards, can be used for small populations. It is not appropriate to take the first names on the list, or the last, or those of people who live closer to you. If you do something like this, all you have is a convenience sample. A mathematically random procedure is necessary to obtain a random sample.

If you have a list of all members of a population, it is generally easier to use **systematic sampling**, in which you begin by selecting a member of the list at random, and then systematically select items every so many items from the last one. For example, suppose your sample will be one-hundredth of your population. You would use simple random selection to choose a starting member out of the first hundred on your list, then take the item that is 100 farther down the list, then the one that is 100 after that, and so on. It is still a random sample, because it is a random choice that determines who will and who will not be in the sample, but only one random choice determines all the members in the sample. After that one choice, all the experimenter has to do is count. You can think of this as systematically separating the population into a number of different samples, say 100 them, and then randomly choosing one of those samples. Because this procedure requires only one random choice, and this choice is out of only 100 possibilities instead of out of the whole population, this technique is easier to apply than simple random selection, and it usually gives identical results. The major danger of systematic sampling occurs if the list is arranged in some meaningful order and that order has a cycle that matches the cycle of the systematic sampling. For instance, suppose you were studying the residents of a home for the elderly and the names were listed by room numbers. If you elected every tenth name from the list, and there were 10 rooms on each wing of each floor (or 20, or 5), you might always get the person living nearest the nurses' station, or across from the elevator or whatever. You can never be sure that such consistency will not bias your study. So whenever you use systematic sampling, you must be very careful that there is no possible relationship between the order of the list and the system you are using to sample.

Two other important techniques are not alternatives to simple or systematic sampling; rather, they are approaches that can be used along with either of those techniques. **Stratified sampling techniques** involve dividing the population into subgroups, or strata, that have something in common, then selecting from among those subgroups. For instance, you might divide your population by sex, race, age, educational level, or all these at the same time. This part of the process is very much like quota sampling, but in quota sampling you take a convenience sample from each subgroup, whereas with stratified sampling you take a probability sample. The number of elements selected randomly from each subgroup will depend on that subgroup's proportion in the whole population. Stratified sampling can produce a more representative sample than simple or systematic sampling because it ensures that the subgroups will be represented properly in your sample.

In this technique, a subgroup that is very small as a proportion of the whole can be oversampled; that is, the number of people from that subgroup in the sample can be larger than its size in the population. This allows a more accurate reading of the variable in that particular subgroup. The result can then be scaled back down when it is combined with the other parts of the sample. For instance, when standardizing IQ test scores it is common to use a proportion of moderately to severely retarded people in the sample that is larger than the proportion in the population. This allows the test results to be more accurately computed for that subgroup. If the size of the subgroup in the sample were proportional, it would be so small the results might not be accurate.

The last technique can be used when it is difficult to develop a complete list of a population that is naturally divided into smaller subgroups or clusters. In **cluster sampling**, you first select a random sample of clusters and then select a random sample of members within those clusters. For example, you might be able to get a list of all the homes for the elderly that are licensed to operate in each state and then randomly select, say, 25 of these homes. Then you could either measure everyone in each of those homes or randomly select, say, 10 residents from each home, giving you a total sample of 250 people. This is much simpler than trying to obtain the names of the residents in every home in the country and randomly selecting names from that enormous list. This simplicity is purchased with some loss of accuracy in your sample. This loss can be estimated mathematically, and a somewhat larger sample may be needed to get the degree of accuracy you desire; even with the larger sample, however, cluster sampling is still easier than simple random sampling. Not only is the selection process easier, but the data collection is also easier, because you will have to visit only those 25 homes to speak with the people in your sample. If you selected 250 people at random from all the residents in the country, you would probably have to visit 250 different homes.

Multistage cluster sampling applies the same technique over and over in different stages. For instance, if you wanted a larger sample, you might randomly select 25 counties out of all the counties in the country, then select three homes in each county, then select two floors or wings in each home, and then select five residents from each wing or floor, for a total of 25 x 3 x 2 x 5 = 750 people in your sample. As a rule of thumb, it is useful to divide your population into clusters whenever the clusters have some sort of natural identity, so that people in the same cluster are more similar than people in different clusters. Using arbitrary clusters, such as a "cluster" of all people with five letters in their first name, is not advisable.

Sample Size

A probability sample, as described above, is necessary if your sample is to be representative of your population. But even a probability sample might not be representative, if it is not large enough. How large is large enough? Unfortunately, it depends on how variable the population is and on the size of the effect you are looking for, neither of which you can really know ahead of time. The more the measurements differ from one another, the larger the sample will have to be to represent it accurately. (See Figure 5-1.) Also, the smaller the effect you want to find, the larger the sample must be to pick that effect out from the random variability.

"And don't waste your time canvassing the whole building, young man. We all think alike."

Drawing by Stevenson; © 1960, 1988. The New Yorker Magazine, Inc.

Figure 5-1 The greater the variability, the larger the sample that is needed. If they all truly do think alike, then variability is zero, and a sample size of one is enough.

It is possible to deal with both these effects. For instance, after your sample is complete and the variability of the measurements can be computed (see Chapter 4), it is mathematically possible to calculate the sample's accuracy. This is what reporters mean when they say that the error in the survey is such-and-such a percent. If a survey with an error of 3 percent says that 45 percent of the people surveyed gave a particular answer, you can be reasonably sure that the number of people in the entire population who would have given that answer is somewhere between 42 percent and 48 percent.

In an experiment, if a reliable effect is not found, it is possible to do an analysis that will determine the largest effect that could have occurred without being seen, to make sure the problem is not just that the sample was too small. Such calculations, however, are possible only if the sample was selected by a probability technique. If you are willing to decide ahead of time how accurate you want your sample to be (that is, how large an effect you want to be able to find), you can use tables such as Table D-6 in Appendix D to determine how large the sample needs to be. That table assumes that you want to be 95 percent sure that the number of people in your sample who fell into a particular category is within a certain percentage of the true proportion in the population. Suppose, for instance, you are trying to find out how many students at your school approve of a new ruling. If there are 2000 students at the school, and you want to be 95 percent sure that your answer is within 5 percent of the true proportion, simply look in the entry for a population of 2000 and an error of 5 percent: you will need to ask 330 students. In looking at this table, you will see that a surprisingly small sample is needed to arrive at a good estimate of a large population. If our population size is multiplied by 5, we only need to add 40 people to our sample.

Cross-Sectional versus Longitudinal Techniques

Measurements of how something is affected by the passage of time involve another factor in deciding what to measure. There are two different ways to assess how things change with time. The one you use depends on many things.

Cross-sectional techniques involve measure many different things of different ages all at the same time (see Figure 5-2). If you find a difference between the older things and the younger things, the discrepancy might be due to age. For instance, researchers used this technique to measure how people's mental abilities changed as they grew old (Schaie & Geiwitz, 1982). They measured the mental abilities of a large number of people of different ages and looked at how each person's mental abilities related to the individual's age at the time of the study. It appeared that mental abilities reached a peak at around age 35, declined slowly until age 55 or so, and then dropped off dramatically. These results appear as the lower line in Figure 5-3.

Longitudinal techniques measure the same things in the same people over and over throughout a long period of time (see Figure 5-2).

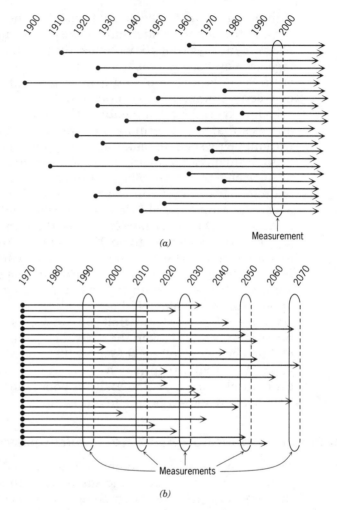

Figure 5-2 Cross-sectional research (A) measures different people of different ages all at the same time. Longitudinal research (B) measures the same people over and over at different ages at different times.

Then you can see how each thing changes as time passes. Schaie and Geiwitz (1982) also applied this technique to the issue of mental abilities in the elderly, by finding people who took intelligence tests as college freshmen in the 1920s. Using these scores as a base, they retested the same individuals over a long period of time. They found that mental abilities increased up to age 55, and then dropped off only slightly until age 70. Their results appear as the upper line in Figure 5-3.

As Figure 5-3 shows, cross-sectional and longitudinal research may give different answers to the same question. Which is correct? It is

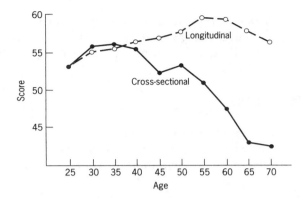

Figure 5-3 In measuring how people's intellectual abilities vary as they grow older, cross-sectional research (lower curve) gives different results from longitudinal research (upper curve). Neither type of research is perfect, but scientists generally consider longitudinal research more accurate. (From Schaie & Geiwitz, 1982. Copyright 1982 by the American Psychological Association. Reprinted by permission.)

impossible to be certain. It is easy, however, to understand how the results of cross-sectional research can be wrong. In 1968, when the study was published, someone older than 35 lived through the Great Depression, while a younger person had not. An individual older than 50 had lived through World War I. Thus the older and the younger people in the cross-sectional study were doubtless exposed to very different conditions of nutrition, health care, and education. These so-called **cohort effects** reflect the differences due to the history that members of any given set of cohorts have lived through together. It is not the age of members of the older group that accounts for the differences; rather, it is the difference between the experiences common to the older and younger groups.

On the other hand, there is a problem with the results of the longitudinal study as well. People die as they grow older. The people who were tested in 1920 included some who died before they reached age 50. Since people with higher test scores are more likely to survive to later measurements (Schaie & Hertzog, 1986), then the sample of 50-year-olds will be biased. This could account for the results that were found: it is not that people get smarter as they get older; rather, more of the smarter people live to get older.

In general, longitudinal research is preferred over cross-sectional research. However, it is much more difficult to do. The research takes a long time, and it is often difficult or impossible to find the same people again and again. If you cannot find them, because they have died or moved, then you have to worry that those you can find are somehow not typical. But if you can do longitudinal research, it is likely to be a more accurate way to determine the effects of time.

Types of Measures

The techniques behavioral scientists use to measure the variables they study are infinitely varied, but they can be classified loosely into several categories. We will look at some of the most common categories here.

Behavioral Measures

The best way to learn how people act is to watch them and see what they do. This is called **behavioral measurement**, because the behavior itself is being observed directly. For instance, to learn whether people prefer caffeinated to decaffeinated coffee, you could send out questionnaires (survey method), ring doorbells and ask people (interview method), or look at the amount of time devoted to each beverage in television commercials (content analysis method). However, the most accurate way is probably to stop people on the way out of the grocery store and check their bags to see what type they bought. This is a behavioral method, because it involves direct observation of the behavior in question.

For instance, suppose you ask people whether watching movies with violent fights in them makes them tend to act more violently themselves. Most people probably will say no. However, Berkowitz and Green (1967) showed experimentally that people who watched a fight scene from a film delivered more electrical shocks to another person (actually a confederate, who was not shocked) than people who watched a nonviolent scene about a track race. By observing actual behavior, the investigators were able to uncover an effect of violence in media that was hidden from the people involved.

When behavioral measurement is possible, it offers the simplest, most accurate way to learn about behavior. Little justification or explanation is needed to understand what a measurement means or why the researchers think it is valuable. However, interesting behavior is not always directly observable. Even when it is observable, if it seems clear that people are aware of their own behavior and are willing to tell others about it, then other measurement techniques are as good as or better than behavioral measurements. For instance, when studying private or illegal behavior, one might be able to get more information from sensitively conducted interviews than from trying to observe the actual behaviors themselves. Or, at the other extreme, one can probably get a pretty accurate idea of the kind of coffee people drink just by asking them, without resorting to poking through grocery bags. So behavioral methods should be used when the behavior either is very easy to observe directly or is something people might not be aware of themselves.

Surveys

A **survey** is a set of standard questions asked of a sample of people, whose answers are collected and combined to represent the answers of an entire population. Common surveys include public opinion polls, election polls, and marketing surveys. A survey is a good way to find out about a large number of people, as long as the information you want is fairly well defined ahead of time.

Questionnaire Design

Before you can begin asking questions, you must think clearly about what you want to learn and make sure the questions you ask will give useful answers. It is not uncommon for researchers to spend an enormous amount of time and effort collecting answers to a survey questionnaire, only to find out that the data will not quite answer their most important questions.

Begin by writing down, in one sentence, the main question you want answered. Try to be as specific as possible, but use just one sentence. Then break this material down into the smaller questions you would have to answer to get the answer to the big question, making each question as clear and precise as you can. For instance, a good main question might be "How do prison inmates feel about the criminal justice system?" This is really several smaller questions: "How do they feel about their interactions with police officers? With lawyers? With prison officials? With other inmates?" Make sure the list includes every question that you need to have answered in order to answer the main question. It is very helpful to talk this list over with other people to make sure it is complete and precise.

Next you must make sure you will be asking the right people. It will do you no good to ask, say, college students what the real cost of a college education is. They may know what *they* are paying, but they probably will not know about money coming from other sources, such as government grants. To get that information, you would have to ask college officials. You must also allow for the fact that people may not be able to tell you accurately what they have experienced; some college students might not remember how much tuition they pay. Even when asked a simple factual question, people may respond incorrectly (see Figure 5-4; also Plumb, 1986; Bradburn, Rips, & Shevell, 1987).

Then you must write the actual questions you will ask of your **respondents**, the people who respond to a survey. If you do it right, this step should take time. Write the best questions you can, then put them aside and think about them. Show them to other people, often called the

"How many children?"   "Eleven."

Drawing by Stevenson; © 1960, 1988. The New Yorker Magazine, Inc.

Figure 5-4 No survey responses should be considered perfectly accurate. Even when asked what seems to be a simple, factual question, the respondents may have unexpected difficulties.

"jury" because they put your questionnaire on trial. Give your questionnaire to a few respondents and ask them what they are thinking as they answer the questions. Go over each question carefully and try to imagine how it might be interpreted other than the way you intended. Pretest your questionnaire by conducting a pilot study, on a small group of people similar to your intended sample. Most of the problems that researchers have with questionnaires are due to misleading, confusing, ambiguous, or biased questions. Table 5-1 gives a few factors to consider when designing survey questions with some possible solutions.

With all these different things to think about, you can see why it is important to pretest your questionnaire before giving it to the actual respondents. It is easier to correct problems that you identify ahead of time.

You will also have to make decisions about the answer format for your questions. The answers you can collect are basically of two different types. **Fixed-response questions** offer the respondent a number of possible answers, and the respondent must choose one. **Open-ended questions** allow the respondent to give any answer at all. Some questions combine fixed-response and open-ended types, for instance, by adding an "other" category. If the researcher cannot identify in advance all the possible answers to a question, a fixed-response question might put the respondent into a situation of having no right answer to choose, or, occasionally, of being faced with more than one right answer.

Table 5-1 Some Things To Be Concerned About in Writing Survey Questions[a]

Vague or general questions
  a. What radio station do you like?
  b. What radio station is your car radio tuned to right now?

Biased questions
  a. Are you in favor of a strong America?
  b. Should we have sent our military to the Persian Gulf?

Ambiguous questions
  a. Are you married?
  b. What is your marital status? (Never married, divorced, separated, widowed, now married.)

"Double-barreled" questions
  a. Are you in favor of manned space flights to the moon or other planets?
  b. Are you in favor of manned space flights to the moon? To other planets?

Questions that presuppose answers
  a. Do you think you have a reading problem? How long have you had a reading problem?
  b. Do you think you have a reading problem? If yes, how long have you had this problem?

Memory questions
  a. What do you usually eat for breakfast?
  b. What did you eat for breakfast this morning?

Sensitive questions
  a. Do you eat a healthy diet?
  b. Which of these foods do you eat often: (give a list).
    NOTE: For sophisticated techniques to deal with very sensitive issues, see Bourke (1984).

Question order
  a. Has anyone in your neighborhood ever been the victim of a violent crime? How important to you is the issue of law and order in a political campaign?
  b. Same questions, but in reverse order.

[a] Item a illustrates the problem; item *b* gives a solution.

In early stages of research, therefore, open-ended questions are to be preferred. However, open-ended questions have problems of their own. They are more difficult to answer, and demand more patience and commitment from the respondent. They are also more difficult for the researcher to analyze later. Typically, researchers who are beginning a research project will conduct a relatively small number of open-ended surveys first, to get a good sense of the sorts of answers people give, and then conduct a fixed-response survey with a large, representative sample.

Survey Administration

Surveys can be administered in person or over the telephone, by asking questions and recording answers, or by mail, allowing the respondents to record their own answers. The problems are similar in all cases. The survey must be administered to the right people, the questions must be asked properly, and the answers must be recorded correctly.

When the representativeness of a survey sample is important, care must be taken that the people who actually contact the respondents follow the rules of the probability sample. If, for instance, a certain address has been randomly selected, and the surveyor is to talk to the female head of household at the selected address, the surveyor must talk only to that person, the prime source. If the female head of household is not at home, or if the household has only a single male head, the interviewer cannot give the survey in that household at that time; the interviewer may *not* survey the male head of household or the teenage daughter or the next-door neighbor or anyone else, unless that is the specific plan of the study. In large-scale studies, where a number of interviewers are hired to conduct the surveys, it is important for those running the show to make sure that the instructions are followed exactly.

It is also important that all the interviewers ask the questions in the same way, and that all answers be recorded in the same way. The accuracy of a survey can be reduced if one interviewer records "Gee, I don't know, I guess so," as a "yes" and another one records the same answer as "don't know."

Finally, there is the problem of what to do about nonrespondents, people who will not answer the survey questions. This problem is particularly common with mail surveys, which often have response rates under 10 percent because people are more likely to forget or mislay a survey that comes in the mail. It is easy to select a representative sample of people that is large enough to ensure sufficient data even without the nonrespondents. However, if the number of nonrespondents is too large, your sample will no longer be representative, because the people who did respond will no longer be randomly chosen. It has instead become a self-selected sample. There is probably some consistent difference between those who responded and those who did not, so your sample will be representative only of the type of people who responded to the survey. As a broad rule of thumb, you can be fairly confident if more than two-thirds of your initial sample reply, and you cannot be confident at all if fewer than half reply. Remember that these are general guidelines, based on experience with surveys, not mathematical prescriptions based on statistical analysis. The only sure thing is that the higher the response rate, the better.

Interviews

An **interview** consists of one person asking another person questions and recording the respondent's answers. When the interviewer is asking a standard set of fixed questions, the interview is also a survey. Sometimes, however, the questions are not standardized, and the interviewer has much more freedom about what to ask and how to ask it.

Types of Interview

Interview methods vary generally along a continuum, depending on how much freedom the interviewer has in asking questions. **Structured interviews** involve a fairly specific set of questions to be asked in a certain order, while **unstructured interviews** will typically specify only a general area of interest and allow the interviewer to explore that area in any effective way. Because this is a continuum, interviews are not entirely either structured or unstructured, but some interviews have more structure than others.

Structured interviews, like surveys with fixed-response questions, are best when the researcher has already developed a fairly clear idea of the area to be studied. Unstructured interviews, on the other hand, are most useful when the area is new and the researcher is trying to get an idea of how it works. A researcher will frequently begin studying an issue with unstructured interviews, then shift to more and more structured interviews as a clearer understanding of the issue is gained. For instance, consider Cressey's (1953) analysis of the causes of embezzlement. This researcher interviewed a large number of men who had been convicted and jailed for embezzling money from a position of trust.

Initially Cressey just asked the respondents to explain in their own way why they had decided to take money that did not belong to them. Gradually, based on what the men told him, he built up a hypothesis about the causes of embezzlement. People take money that is trusted to them, he said, when three conditions are met. First, they must have a serious financial problem that they cannot discuss with other people. For instance, some of the embezzlers had run up large gambling debts that their families did not know about, and others had set up completely separate households for mistresses and illegitimate children. Second, these people must realize that their financial problems could be solved by taking the money in their control. And third, they must convince themselves that their act of embezzlement is just a technical violation, that certain ways of taking the money are not really wrong but are expected in their line of work, or that the irregularity is just temporary and the money will be paid back before anyone misses it. Rationalizations like these blurred the embezzlers' knowledge of right and wrong.

Having developed this hypothesis, Cressey switched to more structured interviews and asked another large group of embezzlers specific

Table 5-2 Duties of an Interviewer in a Structured Interview

Selecting the respondents, according to the sampling procedures established for the research.

Making the respondents comfortable and willing to answer questions fully and accurately.

Asking all the questions exactly as they are specified, without changing the wording or the order.

Recording all the responses exactly as they are given, without biasing them in any way.

Probing for more complete or analyzable answers if necessary through neutral probes, such as "Why is that?" or "In what way?"

questions about why they took the money when they did and why they did not do it at an earlier point in their careers. These questions were specifically designed to test whether the hypothesis fit every case of embezzling—that is, that no one embezzles money unless all three factors are present. For this type of testing of an idea that is already formed, more structured interviews are better.

Interview Techniques

Most surveys are conducted using telephone interviews, rather than the fact-to-face kind, for several reasons. First, they are cheaper to conduct, and it is easier to get a respondent to agree to talk on the telephone than to let a stranger into the house. In addition, there is less interviewer bias, because many characteristics of the respondent are hidden (for instance, age, race, appearance). Finally, it is easier for the survey administrators to control who an interviewer calls than who an interviewer visits. Still, a telephone interviewer must be careful in following the appropriate techniques.

First of all, the interviewer should take care to make the most favorable impression possible on the respondent. Interviewers should be polite and friendly; they should display interest in a respondent's feelings and opinions without seeming pushy. For face-to-face interviews it is generally best to dress and groom in ways similar to the respondents. Presenting yourself well not only makes it more likely that respondents will take the time to answer your questions accurately, but it will also make the experience a more pleasant one for the respondents. Researchers of any type owe it to their research participants to make them as comfortable as possible, in return for their cooperation in the researcher's study.

Second, an interviewer must be familiar with the subject of the interview, as well as all the technical aspects of conducting the interview.

Care must be taken that the information gathered through the interview is not damaged by a mistake made by the interviewer. Table 5-2 lists some of the interviewer's duties in a structured interview. For unstructured interviews, the major duties include making respondents comfortable and recording both the questions asked and the responses exactly. Many researchers use tape recorders to record unstructured interviews, with the respondents' permission, of course.

Unobtrusive Research

Unobtrusive research techniques are those that collect data without in any way affecting the people who are being observed. The major strength of these techniques is that the observation will not change the behavior being observed. As discussed in more detail in Chapter 12, people tend to act differently when they know that others are studying what they do. With unobtrusive research, this is not a problem.

Archival Research

Archival research uses data collected by other people for other purposes and made available to researchers in general. Many large data bases are available on computer networks; your college library probably can help you access them, though there may be a fee. Data also are collected by various branches of the government, including data on the census, the economy, education, and criminal activity. Researchers often use these figures to investigate phenomena that affect large numbers of people. For instance, Johnson, Petersen, and Wells (1982) used data collected by the National Commission on Marijuana and Drug Abuse, comparing the data on people arrested on drug charges with data on people who reported drug use in a survey. This enabled the investigators to estimate the probability of being arrested for using marijuana in three different jurisdictions, and then to discuss the problem of selective law enforcement. It was concluded that the different jurisdictions do differ in their arrest probability, partly because drug use occurs in different circumstances in different areas, and partly because the arresting officers differentially suspect different types of people.

There are, of course, problems with archival data. Large amounts of data on vast numbers of people cannot be collected with complete accuracy, or reported with promptness. For instance, the Uniform Crime Reports collected by the FBI may provide useful information on activities that are recorded as crimes by law enforcement officers. However, the large number of such events that are never reported or are for any reason dismissed as noncrimes by the police will not be reflected in the reports. Similarly, census data necessarily offer a more accurate representation of the employed, affluent, educated people in our country than the jobless, poor, and illiterate. In addition, census data are generally around eight years out of date. The researcher who attempts to use archival data such as these must be cautious. Remember, the figures published in such archives are not the same as the variables you might be trying to measure. They are merely operational definitions of those variables, and in some cases not very good ones. This is especially true if you are using these figures to represent some other variable.

Suppose you wanted to use the FBI's crime statistics to draw conclusions about the degree of alienation present in different sections of American society. These figures are already dubious in their relationship to the actual amount of crime that occurs. When you use them to measure another variable like alienation, you add another layer of dubiousness. All this is not to say that the data collected by large agencies are useless; the researcher who uses them, however, has a responsibility to carefully consider how valid they really are. Converging operations can also be very useful in archival research, because the use of measurements of many different kinds can help to overcome the limitations of any one measure.

Content Analysis

Content analysis is the systematic analysis of the content or meaning of a recorded message, be it written, oral, or visual. In content analysis, the researcher typically is trying to measure some aspect of a person or culture by carefully counting the number of times certain ideas appear in the messages that person or culture produces. Because it requires contact only with the message, not with the producer of the message, content analysis is frequently used for historical comparisons. While we cannot interview or survey people who lived in the past, we can analyze the messages they have left behind. Content analysis is similar to archival research in that the researcher does not have much control over the materials to be analyzed but must make do with whatever messages are available. It differs from archival research in that only the raw message is available; the data themselves are produced by the researcher.

Researchers have used content analysis in many interesting ways. For instance, the lyrics of popular songs played on radio stations during the 1950s and 1960s show a decrease in romance and commitment with an increase in emphasis on establishing one's identity (Carey, 1969). Popular books and music from different periods in history have allowed a measurement of the strength of the needs for achievement, affiliation, and power at different times (McClelland, 1961). Examination of the inaugural addresses of U.S. presidents has shown that chief executives who reflect their times in need for achievement, affiliation, and power are most popular at the time of their election, but those who differ from their time are more likely to be successful presidents (Winter, 1987). Another use for content analysis is in developing a survey. Open-ended questions can be used in a preliminary version, and then content analysis of the responses can help researchers develop fixed-response questions that offer the respondents reasonable choices.

Like archival research, content analysis presents problems in interpretation, because the operational definitions of the constructs are so far removed from the constructs themselves. The chain from a person feeling the need for achievement, through a whole society's need for achievement and the effects this has on authors and hymn writers, to the count of words and phrases in the books and hymns they wrote, is a fairly tenuous one. Once again, the researcher who uses this method must be alert for problems in the interpretation of the data, and converging operations can be helpful in reducing the difficulties.

Trace Measures

Whereas content analysis uses the messages people leave behind, **trace measures** use evidence of the actual behavior being studied. If a researcher interested in courtship gets data from the lyrics of songs, as Carey (1969) did, that is content analysis; if the researcher counts the tire tracks on Lovers' Lane on Sunday morning, that is a trace measure.

Trace measures supply some of the most interesting examples of operational definitions in social psychology. A most famous example compared the popularity of various exhibits in the Museum of Science and Industry in Chicago by studying the amount of wear on the floor near the exhibits. This and other classic examples of trace measures, and indeed unobtrusive measures of all types, are reported in Webb, Campbell, Schwartz, and Sechrest (1966). It is also said that advertisers pay attention to how much the water pressure in city water mains drops during the commercial breaks in various shows. A large drop indicates that lots of people are watching that show, and advertisers are then willing to pay more to advertise on it. (Of course, if the viewers are drawing down the water pressure, they are probably not actually watching the commercials, but this does not seem to concern the advertisers.)

Because trace measures are based on the traces of actual behaviors, they are frequently better measures than archival or content measures. The chain of reasoning between worn floor tiles and public interest in an exhibit is not as questionable as that between hymns and a national need for achievement. Even trace measures, though, are not perfect reflections of the actual behaviors themselves, and they should be interpreted carefully. Also, relatively few behaviors of interest to scientists leave behind traces that the scientists can measure. Thus trace measures are often not possible.

Hidden Observations

The last type of unobtrusive research uses **hidden observations**, which are observations or recordings that are made without the participant's awareness. These range from an observer sitting on a bench in a public place, jotting down the number of people who walk by, to hidden microphones or cameras set up in more private places. Hidden observations raise more ethical questions than other forms of unobtrusive research because they may involve violating the participant's privacy, which is, as we saw in Chapter 3, an important ethical consideration. Directly observing a behavior, rather than messages or data about it or traces it leaves behind, is more personal and therefore more disturbing, particularly if the behavior is one people might expect to be private.

The most acceptable hidden observations involve public, nonembarrassing behavior. Wohlstein and McPhail (1979) have used films of people taken in crowded, public situations such as sporting events to draw conclusions about mass behavior. It is ethically even better if the behavior can be recorded not on film, but by an observer who makes notes about how many people are doing what at which times. The advantage of this is that the people observed cannot be identified later, which protects their privacy even more. The disadvantages are that no observer can accurately record everything that happens, and the record cannot be examined later to look for information that may have been missed the first time. This is yet another example of how ethical considerations must be played off against the quality of data collected in almost any behavioral science research.

Systematic Observations

Of course, all scientific observations are systematic to some degree. However, there is a particular type of technique called **systematic observation**, which involves recording very specific, well-defined observations, usually of naturally occurring behaviors, in very specific, well-defined ways. It is more systematic than the types of observation that might occur when doing exploratory research, because the behaviors are so well specified. However, it is not like the observations that probably would occur in laboratory experiments, because those are not spontaneous, naturally occurring behaviors.

In systematic observations, the events to be recorded are specified ahead of time to a degree of detail that makes it likely that all observers will record the same behaviors in the same way. For instance, a well-designed systematic observation of nursery school children could not say that researchers were going to count instances of children "being friends." If one child watches another playing with the blocks, is that friendship? If two children are building a tower with the blocks, but are arguing about it, is that friendship? The behaviors must be specified so clearly that there can be little doubt over what should and should not be recorded. For instance, you might have a category that included two children making eye contact without physical violence, another category for cooperative behavior consisting of two children working together toward the same goal, regardless of whether they argue, and so on.

As an example, consider the research by Wawra (1989) on vigilance in humans. This investigator applied a kind of observation usually used with animals to a large number (more than 1200) of humans while they were eating in a student dining hall. Speaking into a tape recorder, Wawra took note of the number of people seated at a table: she recorded the beginning and end of every period when the people looked up from their food but not at another person at the same table. This is called vigilance behavior, because when animals exhibit it, we assume that they are checking for predators sneaking up through the grass. Just like grazing antelopes, humans in large groups spend less time scanning for danger than humans in small groups, presumably because each one feels protected by all the others who are on the lookout.

This example used **continuous sampling**, because each group was watched continuously, and every incidence of the target behavior was recorded. Continuous sampling provides the most complete data of any form of systematic observation, because the observer is recording all the time. It is also the most difficult to achieve, because the observer can never take a break. Another problem with continuous sampling is that it cannot be used if there are lots of different subjects to be observed at the same time. Wawra (1989) watched only one group at a time, and in fact watched only those who were facing toward her. If she had wanted to observe all the people in the dining hall at the same time, continuous sampling would not have been possible.

When continuous sampling is inappropriate, some form of time sampling can be used instead. In **time-point sampling**, the observer records a sort of snapshot of the situation at specific predertermined time intervals, and records nothing the rest of the time. Sometimes the time intervals are determined randomly, but more often the sampling is done at the end of a set time period. For instance, Wawra could have chosen to record how many people are engaged in vigilance scanning at the end of every 5 minutes. **Time-interval sampling**, on the other hand, has the observer recording whether a behavior occurs during a certain time interval, and then nothing at all until the interval begins again. For instance, Wawra could have recorded whether anyone looked up from the dining table during a certain 10-second interval, and then waited 50 seconds for the next interval to begin. In Wawra's situation, neither of these methods would have worked particularly well. However, other research situations make them very useful.

LaFrance (1979) used time-point sampling in a study of synchrony of posture between college students and professors. A college class was videotaped, and the researchers watching the tape literally froze the frame every 6 minutes, to compare the postures of the students with that of the professor. It was shown that students whose posture was similar at any moment in time to the professor's posture were more likely to give the professor high ratings than students whose posture was very different. This is time-point sampling because the observations were made at certain specific points in time, not recording whether the behavior changed or how long it lasted, but only what the situation was like at that particular moment.

On the other hand, Guida (1987) used time-interval sampling in a scale he developed to measure how much academic anxiety is felt by elementary school children. He observed each of the children in a classroom at six 30-second intervals during a session. Each 30-second observation was divided into 5-second intervals, and each interval was recorded according to whether the student showed certain behaviors characteristic of academic anxiety: excessive passivity (sitting head down, no eye contact), acting out (talking out of turn, getting out of seat inappropriately), physical symptoms (headache, stomachache), and so on. By counting the number of behaviors recorded in the entire session, a score was given to each child that measured how much anxiety the child was feeling during the session. This is time-interval sampling because the behavior was recorded according to whether it happened during a specific time interval, rather than at a specific moment. A behavior that occurred at the beginning of the interval would count the same as one that occurred at the end, or one that was already going on when the interval started and lasted until it finished.

Systematic observations are useful any time the researcher wants detailed, objective measurements of the behaviors on display in a situation that is occurring naturally, in its natural setting, without disturbing it. Such observations can be useful in studying the behaviors of families (Grotevant & Carlson, 1987), crowds (Wohlstein & McPhail, 1979), or people waiting to see the dentist (Barash, 1974).

SUMMARY

A. First a researcher must decide which things to measure.

    1. Instead of measuring the entire population, the researcher will usually select a smaller sample to be analyzed. A representative sample is one that produces measurements similar to those on the entire population, so we can generalize from the sample to the population.

    2. There are two major sampling techniques.

        a. Nonprobability samples (every member of the population does not have an equal chance of being chosen) in general are not representative. The haphazard or convenience sample consists of whatever examples are handy. The quota sample is one in which the researcher uses information on the composition of the population to select the sample.

   b. Probability samples (every member of the population has an equal chance of being chosen) in general are representative samples. It is possible to compute just how representative this type of sample is. Random sample types include the simple random sample, the systematic sample, the stratified sample, and the cluster sample.

3. The larger the probability sample, the more representative of the population it will be. It is possible to calculate the sample size that will give the desired accuracy for a particular study.

4. There are two ways to measure change over time. Cross-sectional research involves measuring a number of items of different ages all at the same time. Longitudinal research involves measuring the same items over and over through a long period of time. This technique is more difficult but generally is preferred.

B. Most of the measurements that behavioral scientists use can be classified into five general categories.

   1. Behavioral measurements are direct observations of the behavior being studied; these are to be preferred if people themselves might not be aware of their behavior.

   2. Surveys are sets of specific questions asked of a large number of people.

      a. Problems can occur if the questions are not well written. The answers may be open-ended, allowing the respondents to give any answer they wish, or of the fixed-response type, requiring the respondent to select from a predetermined set of possible answers.

      b. All the people who are collecting responses to the survey must follow the procedures carefully or the result may not be accurate. Response rate is important, because if too few people respond, the responses may not be representative.

   3. Interviews involve one person talking to another person and recording what is said.

      a. Interviews range from the highly structured, in which the interviewer asks questions from a list, to the highly unstructured, in which the interviewer makes no attempt to guide the conversation.

      b. The interviewer must not only follow the proper procedures but also establish a feeling of trust and honesty with the interviewee.

   4. Unobtrusive measures do not affect the situation being measured.

   a. Archival research uses data collected by other agencies.
   b. Content analysis uses messages recorded by people.
   c. Trace analysis uses the marks left by the behavior.
   d. Hidden observations secretly record the actual behaviors, causing possible ethical questions.

  5. Systematic observations are measures in which well-defined natural behaviors are recorded in specific ways, either continuously, at specific points in time, or over specific time intervals.

CHECKPOINT

Check your understanding of the material in this chapter:

- What does it mean to say that a sample is representative of a population? What does this allow the researcher to do?

- What are the types of nonprobability sample? What is the major problem with nonprobability sampling?

- What are the types of probability sample? What is the major advantage of probability sampling?

- What are the steps involved in systematic sampling? In stratified sampling? In cluster sampling?

- What is the difference between cross-sectional and longitudinal research? Which type of research is generally preferred? Why?

- What are some of the concerns that must be considered in designing a questionnaire?

- Why is response rate important? What response rates are generally acceptable?

- You should be able to define and give the advantages and disadvantages of the major instrumentalities of measurement: behavioral measures, surveys, interviews, unobtrusive research, archival research, content analysis, trace measures, hidden observations, systematic observations.

EXERCISES

5.1 Consider some population of interest in your area. How might you construct a probability sample from this population? What type would you choose? How large would it be?

5.2 Think of a research question in your area of interest and discuss how it could be addressed with a structured interview and with an unstructured interview. What sorts of question might you include in each type of interview? What sorts of information might you get?

5.3 Using the same research question or a different one, write some survey questions to address the issue, taking care that they are well designed.

5.4 Think of how examples of each of the unobtrusive measures might be applied in your area of interest.

5.5 Design a systematic observation procedure to measure a variable you find interesting.

5.6 Select one of the questions above and elaborate on your answer, turning it into a fairly detailed plan for measuring a particular social variable, describing both the construct to be measured and the precise operational definition used to measure it. Discuss the strengths and weaknesses of your measurement plan.

Chapter 6

Measuring and Using Correlations

Questions to Consider as You Read

- What purposes does correlational research serve?
- When is correlational research unsuitable?
- What kinds of relationship can correlations measure?
- If you can predict what will happen, does that mean that you can explain or understand it?
- What are correlation coefficients?
- What are scatterplots? Why are they useful?
- What is a crucial principle to remember about correlations?

The measurements discussed so far measure one variable at a time. In this chapter we consider correlations, which measure relationships between two variables. Before a correlation can be measured, each variable must be measured separately, so all the considerations in Chapter 4 and 5 still apply. Correlational research is a descriptive type of research because it tells what something is like rather than how it came to be that way or how to change it into something else. It is also predictive research, because it helps us make guesses about what we will find in another place or at another time. Correlational research is a very common type of research, and very useful, as long as you remember what it can and cannot do.

What Is Correlational Research?

Correlational research is used to measure a relationship between two different variables. Once you know the relationship between the two variables, you can use one variable to predict the other. This is why correlational research is both descriptive and predictive; it describes a relationship, then uses that relationship to predict something. Let us look at both these processes in more detail.

Finding Relationships

A **correlation** is a "co-relation," a relation between two variables. (Most correlational research is concerned with relationships that are linear, or at least **monotonic**, such that when one variable goes up the other consistently goes up or goes down, but never reverses itself. There are ways to get around this limitation, but they are beyond this book.) To find that relation, you must measure both variables together, over and over again in different situations. For instance, consider the relation between the amount of violent crime in a city and the temperature. Information on the average daily temperature is kept by the National Weather Service, and information on the number of violent crimes each day can be found in criminal justice records. These numbers can be arranged in pairs, with two numbers for each day: a temperature and a crime rate (see Table 6-1). Once a large number of such pairs has been accumulated, the relation between them can be examined. The Federal

Table 6-1 Pairs of Observations To Be Used in Calculating Correlation (Fictional Data)

Temperature	Crime Rate
57	125
82	175
42	112
35	97
87	164
76	143
61	138
58	162
49	126
69	165

Bureau of Justice Statistics (1983) has suggested that violent crime is more likely to occur on days when the temperature is very high, so that one high number in a pair goes with another high number, and one low number goes with another low number. This is one example of the sort of relationship that a correlation can uncover. (However, others disagree that there is any such relationship between temperature and violence; see Cheatwood, 1988.)

The relationships between variables can differ in several ways. For example, a relationship is not an all-or-nothing thing. Some relationships are stronger than others. One of the factors a correlation measures is the strength of the relationship between two variables.

Relationships also can vary in the direction of relationship. It is possible to have very strong relationships between two sets of variables that are exactly the opposite. One relationship we call positive, the other negative. A **positive correlation** exists when one variable gets larger and the other variable also gets larger. The top two diagrams in Figure 6-1 show positive relationships, which are recognizable by their tendency to go from lower left to upper right. The relationship between temperature and crime rate mentioned above is a positive relationship:

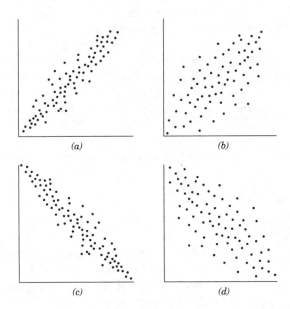

Figure 6-1 Diagrams of various possible relationships between variables. These **scatterplots** have one variable on the horizontal axis, increasing to the right, and the other variable on the vertical axis, increasing upward. Relationship (A) is strongly positive; (B) is weakly positive; (C) is strongly negative; (D) is weakly negative.

as temperature goes up the crime rate also goes up. A **negative correlation** exists when one variable gets larger and the other variable gets smaller. The bottom two diagrams in Figure 6-1 show negative relationships, which are recognizable by their tendency to go from upper left to lower right. For example, Wells and Rankin (1988), who studied several different kinds of delinquent behavior in a group of teenagers, measured different ways the parents treated these children. One parenting behavior they measured was punishment consistency, or how likely the parents were to punish the child's misbehavior every time it occurred, rather than punishing it sometimes and ignoring it at other times. Another parenting behavior was punitiveness, which is a measure of how severely and frequently the parents punished their children. The investigators found that there was a positive correlation between punitiveness and delinquency; that is, as parents were more vigorous in punishing their children, the children were more likely to be delinquent. But there was a negative correlation between punishment consistency and delinquency: as punishment consistency went up, delinquency went down.

The strength and the direction of a relationship are entirely different. That is, you can have a strong positive relationship, a strong negative relationship, a weak positive relationship, or a weak negative relationship. And remember, "strong" and "weak" are not absolute terms. Relationships can vary from totally nonexistent to absolutely perfect, or anything in between. So remember, if you read about a positive correlation, this does not mean that the correlation is definite or strong, only that it is in the positive direction. Similarly, a negative correlation is not necessarily weak or trivial. In fact, it is easy to change a positive relationship into a negative one, or vice versa, just by redefining the variables. If one measured the "gentleness" of a parent's treatment, rather than its punitiveness (really the same thing, only backward), then the relationship between gentleness and delinquency would be negative, but it would be just as strong as the relationship between punitiveness and delinquency.

Making Predictions

Once you know the relationship between two variables, you can use either one to predict the other. With the two examples above, you can predict the crime rate if you know the temperature, and you can predict a child's delinquency if you know the parents' consistency. It does not matter whether a relationship is positive or negative, because the directions work equally well for making predictions. It does, however, make a difference how strong the relationship is. In fact, one way of defining the strength of a relationship is: strong relationships allow better predictions. Suppose you know the relationship between two people, and you see one of them at a party. What is the chance that the other will be there, too? If they are the closest of lovers, the chance is very good. If they are the worst possible enemies, the chance is very bad. Either way, your prediction will be fairly strong. However, if they have a weak relationship, either mild friendship or mild dislike, your prediction is likely to be wrong. It is the strength of the relationship that allows you to make the prediction. (Which is why predicting who will be good college roommates from preadmission questionnaires is so hard; see Figure 6-2.)

Making predictions is one of the main reasons for doing correlational research. In one of the examples discussed in Chapter 4, the idea was to predict one variable, future honesty on the job, from another variable, an honesty test that could be given before hiring. For such a prediction to be useful, a personnel director would need to know that there was at least a moderate correlation between these two variables. Similarly, colleges and universities with limited admissions use several variables, including high school grades, standardized test scores, and recommendations from teachers, to predict future success in college. The National Weather Service uses hundreds of variables to try to predict the weather. These are all examples of the use of correlations to make predictions.

Figure 6-2 What sorts of information did the computer use to predict that these two would be good roommates? Probably the answers to a questionnaire both students filled out when they were accepted. It appears that the correlation between the answers to those questions and the individuals' compatibility as roommates is not as high as we might hope.

When making predictions, the technique used is actually a regression, rather than a correlation. These two ideas are closely related but not the same. A correlation is a measure of the strength and direction of the relationship between two variables. A **regression equation** is the mathematical formula that will best allow you to predict one of the variables from the other. To say this another way, a correlation *measures* a relationship, while with a regression equation you *use* a relationship to make a prediction. The stronger the correlation, the more accurate the regression equation will be. One difference between correlations and regressions is that a correlation is the same no matter which variable you take first; as long as you are consistent, you can reverse the numbers in your pairs and you will get the same answer with a correlation. A correlation of height and weight will be the same no matter whether you consider height first or weight first in your computations.

A regression equation however, is different if you reverse your variables. This is because you are using one of the variables to predict the other, not the other way around. Consider a simple example. If a typical person's weight in pounds was roughly double the person's height in inches, someone who was 5'6" (66 inches) tall would weigh about 132 pounds. (Of course, the real relationship between height and weight is not nearly this simple.) In that case, the regression equation to predict weight from height would be to double it, while the equation to predict height from weight would be to halve it. To take a real example, the formula to "predict" temperature in Fahrenheit from temperature in Celsius is to multiply by 1.8 and add 32, while the reverse equation is to subtract 32 and then multiply by .56. In this chapter, when I talk about using a correlation to predict one variable from another, what I mean is that the correlation indicates the relationship; it is then necessary to compute a regression equation to do the actual prediction.

It is quite possible to make very good predictions of one variable from another without having the slightest idea of why those two variables are related. For instance, people frequently complain that schools should not be allowed to use standardized intelligence tests in planning a student's education because the scores may be biased or unfair, because the tests do not really measure a person's worth as a human being, or because we really have no idea just what IQ tests are measuring, anyway. All these arguments might be valid, but they miss the point. IQ test scores are the best predictor of elementary school success that we have (McNemar, 1942). Even if we do not know why this is so, we can still use one of the variables to predict the other.

As another example, the engineering school my father attended was trying to develop a test to identify the applicants most likely to succeed as engineers. A preliminary version was administered to my father's entire graduating class. The school kept the records of the test scores but made no immediate use of them. Over the years, however, the school kept track of the students' success as engineers. By finding a relationship between the test questions and later success as an engineer, the school could then use the test to predict success. (That is, the test's predictive validity could be determined; see the discussion in Chapter 4.)

Again, it makes no difference whether the relationship makes any sense to an observer. In fact, the only question my father can remember from the test is "Do you enjoy walking barefoot through soft mud?" If it turns out that there is a correlation between the answer to this question and success as an engineer, then you can use the answer to predict success, even if you do not understand why.

Bower (1990b) reports on a study about a correlation between the level of anxiety experienced by a pregnant woman and her likelihood of giving birth prematurely or of having a low birth weight baby. It was found that even when the mother's medical risks have been taken into account, there is still a correlation between anxiety and birth complications. This is important, as the authors of the original study point out, because it can allow physicians to predict just a little better which mothers are likely to need special care as their due date approaches, so they can recommend more frequent visits to the doctor, or have special equipment available when the women go into labor.

However, the relationship between two variables is not fixed and unchanging. Just because there was a correlation at one time in one situation does not mean that this correlation can be used to make predictions safely at all times in all situations. A perfectly valid correlation can break down for many reasons. For instance, consider the correlation between temperature and crime rate. I suspect that the correlation would not be the same in a very hot climate. In fact, the relationship might well reverse, so that crime is more likely when it is cool enough for people to have the energy to invest in violence. The study of maternal anxiety and childbirth problems was conducted with low income mothers, primarily Hispanic, and the authors were careful to say that it might not apply to more affluent mothers or to mothers of another ethnic background. In general, you must be careful when applying a correlation that was measured in one group of people to people in another group. The variables might not be related in the same way in the new group.

Sometimes the changes from one group to another are not obvious, but they are still important. A classic example has to do with what is called "restricted range." A correlation that is strong in a group of people who vary a lot on one of the variables might not be as good a predictor in a group of people who are very similar on that variable. Consider a fairly obvious correlation, the one between height and weight. In general, taller people weigh more, although we all know of exceptions. However, if we take a roomful of people who are all between 5'4" and 5'8", we are likely to find that the correlation does not hold very much any more. We have restricted the range of the height variable to the point that it is no longer a good predictor.

To take a more serious example, consider the use of standardized tests to predict school performance. As already mentioned, IQ scores predict elementary grades fairly well (McNemar, 1942). Scores on the SAT tests commonly used for college admission predict college grades somewhat, but not very well (Linn, 1982). The standardized test for graduate school, the GRE, does a very poor job of predicting grades for graduate students. In fact, I was once told by the graduate adviser at the graduate school to which I had applied that a high score on the GRE might be considered a mark against me, and he was only half joking. Is this because the GRE test is not as good as the other standardized tests? Possibly, but a more likely explanation is the restricted range problem (see Figure 6-3). Almost all children go to school and take IQ tests, so the range of IQ on those tests is not very limited. The people on the low end of the range, however, are less likely to go to college, so the range of school abilities is somewhat restricted for the SAT scores. And only the most scholastically able students go to graduate school, restricting the range even further, until the variable simply does not predict very well any more.

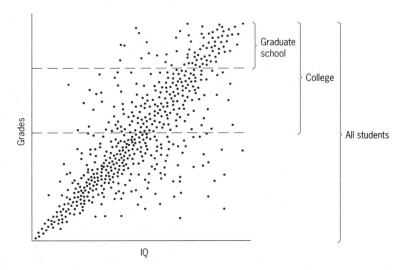

Figure 6.3 The restricted range problem. Suppose the correlation between IQ score and scholastic success looks like this. When considering everyone who goes to school (A), the positive relationship is obvious. When considering only those who go to college (B), the relationship is not as strong. When considering only those who got to graduate school (C), the relationship disappears almost entirely. Without enough variability in either variable, the correlation weakens.

The restricted range problem can cause serious dilemmas for people who use tests to screen applicants for education or employment. Some people argue that standardized test scores should not be used for black applicants because these measurements do not predict future performance very well for this group (that is, they have low predictive validity for blacks: see Chapter 4). Others argue that this is because there are fewer black applicants, since there are fewer blacks in the population at large, and that this restricts the range of their scores, making the test a poor predictor. To make the test more accurate, they say, the scores of the black applicants must be combined with the scores of the white applicants, thereby increasing the range. This, however, goes against decades of affirmative action programs. This dilemma has not yet approached a resolution.

The problem of restricted range is just one example of the general problem of applying a correlation to a population different from the one used to measure it. Anyone using correlations to make predictions must be very careful to minimize these differences, or the predictions will be of little value. A personnel director should not try to use an honesty test devised on a prison population to screen job applicants, unless most of the applicants happen to be prison inmates.

What Correlation Is Not

If there is one rule that any researcher is expected to know, this is it: *correlation is not causation.* If you can truly understand this rule, and know how it applies, and remember to apply it all the time, it will save you from a large number of mistakes.

To begin with, we need to know what causation means. Something *causes* something else when the first makes the second happen, or makes it happen in a particular way rather than in some other way. In other words, changing the first thing will necessarily change the second thing. The first thing is the **cause**, and the change in the second thing is the effect, from which we can conclude that causes must come before effects. Gravity makes things fall down; if you changed how gravity worked, things would not fall, or would fall differently. Thus, gravity causes falling. This represents the philosophy called **determinism** because it says that one thing (gravity) determines another thing (falling). The word **causation** refers to a special type of relationship between variables, a relationship in which one of the variables has a direct, definite, deterministic effect on the other variable.

Knowing what causation means (it is discussed in more depth in Chapter 7), we next must ask what it has to do with correlation. Obviously, if two things are causally related (that is, if one causes the other), then, all else being equal, they will tend to be correlated. As humans, we sometimes take one extra step and think that when we find a correlation, we have therefore learned that one of those things causes the other. After all, why else would they be correlated? This is a mistake: *correlation is not causation.* Relationships of many different types are possible between variables, and most of them are not casual.

Everyone has favorite humorous examples of correlations that are obviously not causal. Let me share two with you. First, there is probably a small but real negative relationship between the number of people who pass out on the streets on any given day and the hardness of the pavement in those same streets. Why is this? Could it be that all those people falling down batter the pavement and make it soft (passing out causing soft pavement)? Or could it be that soft pavement gives off fumes that makes people dizzy (soft pavement causing passing out)? Probably neither. Most likely, it is high temperatures that both soften the pavement and make people pass out. For a second example, there is probably a fairly strong positive relationship between the number of churches in any given town and the number of bars in the same town. Perhaps church goers feel guilty over their sins and patronize bars to cheer up (churches causing bars). Or perhaps people who drink a lot in bars feel guilty, and they go to church for forgiveness (bars causing churches). On the other hand, it is more likely to be simply the number of people in a town that determines both the number of churches and the number of bars.

In both these examples, a correlation between two variables was not causal, because there was a third variable that affected the first two. If that third variable was not measured, and if you never thought of it, you might be fooled into thinking that the correlation meant that one of the variables caused the other. Of course, it is impossible to be sure you have thought of every possible variable that might conceivably affect the two variables in the correlation, so with any correlation you must assume that there might be such a variable. This is why *correlation is not causation.* You cannot trust the idea that one variable causes another unless you have ruled out every possible candidate for the third variable, and you cannot do this simply by measuring things (although some techniques will work under certain circumstances; see Chambers, 1986). If you actually controlled the values of one of the variables, instead of just measuring it, then you would be doing an experiment, as discussed in the next two chapters, not a correlation at all. The defining characteristic of a correlational study is not that it uses correlation coefficients, but that the things being correlated are simply measured, not controlled.

The trouble with humorous examples of noncausal correlations is that because they are so bizarre, no one takes them seriously. Who could actually think that churches caused bars? But when the causal connection seems reasonable, the problem is a serious one. For example, Bower (1990a) reports some research by Lane and others on a negative relationship between psychological defensiveness and mental disorders.

Psychological defensiveness is a tendency to deny responsibility for the bad things that happen to you. Psychological defensiveness would have you believing that, for instance, you failed a test because it was too tricky or you were coming down with a cold, rather than because you failed to study. The researchers found that people who are psychologically healthy show more defensiveness than people who are psychologically depressed. The conclusion they draw is that it is psychologically healthy to see yourself in a good light and psychologically depressing to blame yourself for your failures. However, this report prompted a reply (Premo, 1990) that it is just as likely that the depression caused a lack of defensiveness as the other way around. Premo's argument is that people with psychiatric diagnoses are likely to have undergone some form of psychotherapy, which probably included learning to face up to one's faults and accepting responsibility for one's own life. It might be the success of this therapy that the original study was detecting, not a benefit of defensiveness.

Or recall the study about parental behavior and juvenile delinquency (Wells & Rankin, 1988). The investigators found very strong relationships between certain things the parents did and how likely their children were to become delinquent. Does this mean that the parents' actions caused the children's delinquency? If a parent is very vigorous in punishing a child, will that child become a delinquent? Perhaps, but perhaps it works the other way around—for example, a parent trying to control a rebellious, antisocial teenager might well resort to very strong punishment to try to bring the teenager's behavior back into line.

Consider again the study summarized by Bower (1990b) of anxiety during pregnancy and premature birth, in which it was reported that financial problems constituted one of the major sources of anxiety in the women who were studied. It is conceivable that these financial problems interfered with the mother's diet, the number of times she could visit a doctor, or her ability to buy vitamins or other medications, and these medical factors could have been a third variable that accounted for the relationship.

To take another important example of the difference between correlation and causation, consider the relationship between smoking and illness, such as lung cancer and heart disease. Virtually the entire medical profession, and probably most other people as well, believe that there is a direct, causal relationship: smoking causes illness. I believe this, too. Nevertheless, the tobacco industry maintains that it has never been proven that smoking causes illness in humans, and they are absolutely right. All the research that has been done either has used animals or has been correlational research. Researchers have measured the amount of smoking and the amount of illness in thousands of people, finding a strong correlation. They have measured and controlled for as many third variables as possible, including stress, diet, overall health, age, and sex, and the correlation persists. But it is still a correlation, and *correlation is not causation.* Of course, rational people may choose to look at the quantity of evidence that has been collected and decide that the only sensible thing to do is quit smoking. Even researchers funded by the Council for Tobacco Research, sponsored by the tobacco industry, believe that smoking is addictive, that it causes lung cancer, and that second-hand smoke is harmful ("Tobacco Researchers," 1991), Still, it must be admitted that the causal connection between smoking and illness has never been proven in humans, though it has been in lab animals. (See the next chapter for a discussion of how it would be possible, under some circumstances, to go about proving this connection.)

Correlations, then, are useful for finding out whether two variables are related and for using that relationship to predict one variable from the other. These are very useful things to be able to do if you need to predict something. However, the correlation cannot tell you *why* the variables are related. You can use it, but you cannot understand or explain it. Trying to do that is like trying to use a screwdriver to hammer nails; you are asking a useful tool to do something it simply is not built to do. The key to remember, of course, is that *correlation is not causation.*

Expressing Correlations

A correlation expresses the relationship between two variables, based on a list of pairs of numbers that measure the two variables in different situations. But how do you get from a list of measurement pairs to an understanding of the relationship? How do you describe or express what the relationship is? It is not very precise to say that a relationship is "strong" or "weak." Scientists use two methods to describe relationships, one numerical and one visual.

Correlation Coefficients

The numerical way to express a correlation is by calculating a statistic called a correlation coefficient. Remember from Chapter 4 that a statistic is a single number, calculated from a group of numbers, that summarizes some information about that group of numbers. A **correlation coefficient** is a statistic, calculated on pairs of numbers, that describes the relationship between members of the pairs. The actual calculation of a correlation coefficient is not particularly difficult, but it is tedious. The method for calculating the most common correlation coefficient is given in Appendix C. This section describes what such statistics mean.

You already know that correlations can be positive or negative, and that both positive and negative correlations can range from extremely weak to extremely strong. Correlation coefficients describe both aspects

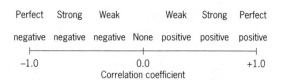

Figure 6-4 A correlation coefficient is a statistic that describes the reltaionship between two variables. It varies from -1.0 to +1.0. The sign of of the coefficient indicates the direction of the relationship, and the distance from zero indicates the strength of the relationship.

of the relationship between variables. Reasonably enough, positive and negative relationships are described by positive and negative numbers. That is, a positive correlation coefficient describes a relationship in which an increase in one variable goes along with an increase in the other variable, and a negative correlation coefficient describes a relationship in which an increase in one variable goes along with a decrease in the other variable. A correlation coefficient of zero means that there is absolutely no relation between the variables, so that knowing one of them will not help you in predicting the other. As the relation between the two variables gets stronger, the correlation coefficient moves further from zero, in either the positive or the negative direction. All correlation coefficients fall between +1.00 and -1.00, where +1.00 means a perfect positive relationship and -1.00 means a perfect negative relationship. Thus a correlation of -0.20 would indicate a fairly weak negative relationship, a correlation of +0.70 would indicate a fairly strong positive relationship, and so on, depending on the exact situation (see Figure 6-4). It is traditional to leave off the zeros before the decimal point, and to omit the + sign from positive relationships. Thus the two correlations above would be written as -.20 and .70, respectively.

In interpreting a correlation coefficient, you first look at how far it is from zero. A coefficient of .02 (either positive or negative) is not worth very much. It is so close to zero that it indicates no practical relationship at all. On the other hand, a correlation of .93 (again, either positive or negative) almost certainly means something, because it is so far from zero. How strong a correlation must be to represent a real, important relationship varies from situation to situation. For one thing, the meaning of the coefficient depends in part on how many pairs of numbers were observed. If you look only at a short, very fat person and a tall, very thin person, you would get a correlation of -1.00 between height and weight, but it would not mean very much at all. (In Appendix C we discuss the procedure for taking sample size into account when evaluating a correlation.) In addition, different fields of behavioral science have different standards with respect to the size of a "strong" correlation. In some areas, anything over .60 is considered very strong; in other areas, no one is impressed unless it is at least .80. You will have to talk to experts in your area of study, and read published reports in that area, to get a good idea of what the standards are for correlation coefficients. (There is a way, given in most statistics books and discussed in Appendix C, to find out whether a particular coefficient is likely to be just a coincidence.)

The second step in interpreting a correlation coefficient is to look at its sign. This will let you predict how one variable changes when the other changes by telling you whether the relationship is positive or negative. Remember, the direction of a correlation is easily changed by renaming the variables. If there is a positive correlation between worker satisfaction and company productivity, then there is a negative correlation of the same strength between worker *dis*satisfaction and company productivity. To know what a positive or negative correlation is really saying, you must interpret carefully the meanings of the variables.

Scatterplots

The visual way to express a correlation is with a type of graph called a **scatterplot**, in which one variable is plotted along one axis and the other

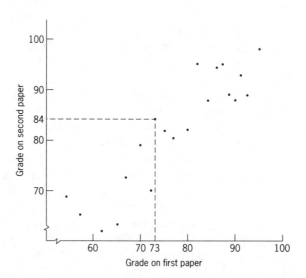

Figure 6-5 Scatterplot of the grades on the first and second papers of the semester. The dotted lines show how the point for one student was plotted: a 73 on the first paper and an 84 on the second. The correlation coefficient is .61.

variable plotted along the other axis, with each pair of measurements represented by a single dot. For example, Figure 6-5 is a scatterplot of the grades I gave one semester to 20 students on their first and second research reports. The grades on the first report are measured along the bottom, and the grades on the second report are measured up the side, with lower values near the bottom left corner. (It is traditional in this sort of plot to put the variable you are likely to use to predict with on the bottom, or X axis (called the **abscissa**), and the variable you are likely to try to predict up the side, or Y axis (called the **ordinate**). Because I am more likely to use the first score to predict the second score, I measure the first score along the abscissa at the bottom and the second on the ordinate up the side. (For more on using the axes in graphs, see Appendix B.)

In the scatterplot of Figure 6-4, each student is represented by a dot. (To place the dot for each student, go across the bottom to that student's grade on the first paper and follow a vertical line up from that grade. Then go up the side to that student's grade on the second paper, follow a horizontal line over from that grade, and put a dot at the point where the two lines intersect. The vertical and horizontal lines that you follow are shown on the graph for one of the dots.) You can see that the scores tend to go from the bottom left corner to the upper right corner. Plots that slope this way have positive correlations, because it means that when one variable is getting larger (farther to the right, for instance), the other is also getting larger (up toward the top). The correlation coefficient for these data is .61, which is a fairly strong positive correlation. This is not surprising, because a third variable, each student's writing ability, is likely to have a sizable effect on the grades on both papers.

I asked 18 of my students how many hours they worked per week, on the average, at a paying job during the semester. Figure 6-6 is a scatterplot of the relation between the reported hours worked (on the horizontal axis) and the students' grades in the course (on the vertical axis). As you can see, these points tend to go from the upper left of the graph to the lower right, which indicates a negative correlation, with larger values on one variable corresponding to lower values on the other variable. In fact, the correlation coefficient for these data is -.56, a moderately strong negative correlation. This means that the more hours a student works, the lower that student's grades tend to be. Does this imply that a student who wants better grades should quit working? Possibly, but remember: *correlation is not causation.* It could be that some unmeasured third variable is causing this relationship, and the number of hours worked in fact has no effect on grades by itself.

Finally, I asked 15 students to estimate how many hours each week they spent studying for the course (including readings, homework, preparing papers, and studying for exams). The relationship between hours studying and final course grade is shown in Figure 6-7. Does the scatterplot tend to go from upper left to lower right, or from lower left to

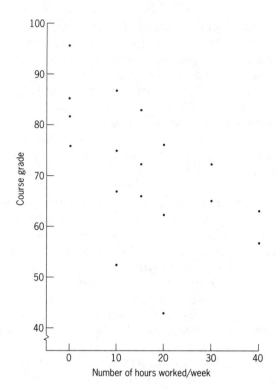

Figure 6-6 Scatterplot of students' grades versus the number of hours worked per week. The correlation coefficient for these data is -.56.

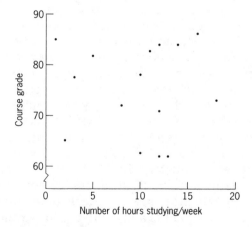

Figure 6-7 Scatterplot of students' grades versus the number of hours spent studying per week. The correlation coefficient for these data is -.01.

upper right? It seems to go neither way. The points are scattered in a rough circle, with no clear slant at all. This kind of plot indicates no relationship between the two variables, and the correlation coefficient for these data is -.01, very close to zero. (The fact that this coefficient is negative means nothing much, because it is so small. A tiny variation in the data could easily have made it turn positive. All it indicates is that the plot is very slightly higher on the left side than on the right side.)

A zero correlation such as this means that studying has no effect at all on grades, right? Wrong. If *correlation is not causation*, then it is also true that *no correlation is not no causation*. Suppose, for instance, that studying produced a definite improvement in grades, but each student studied just enough to compensate for his or her own weaknesses in the course. In that case, the effects of intelligence, motivation, preparation, and all the other factors that might affect the student's weaknesses would cancel out the observed effect of studying, producing just this sort of zero correlation. From these data you can conclude that knowing how much a student studies will not allow you to predict that student's grades, but you cannot conclude that studying has no effect on grades.

So far, this discussion has implied that there is only one kind of correlation coefficient, but that is not true. The coefficient that has been used so far is the most common one. It is called the **Pearson product–moment correlation**, and it is abbreviated *r*. When someone gives an unspecified correlation, it is probably the Pearson *r*. However, there are other coefficients that are useful in certain cases. In particular, the Pearson *r* has the limitation that it is best applied to equal interval or ratio scale data (see Chapter 4). If the intervals between numbers on either one of the two variables is likely to vary, the Pearson *r* becomes a rather weak measurement of their relationship, and you will want to use a different coefficient, such as the **Spearman rho** (ρ). If you are ever in a position to need this coefficient, consult an expert or a book on nonparametric statistics (see Chapter 10). Calculating these special correlation coefficients is not particularly difficult, but there is not space in this book to discuss them.

Another problem with the Pearson *r* is that it can find only straight-line relationships between variables. If the variables are related along a curved line, all the Pearson can do is find the best-fitting straight line, which may not be a very good fit. For example, I taught a course in which the students' grades were based on the scores of 13 weekly quizzes. If students wished, they could take each of the quizzes over to improve their grades. At the end of the semester I counted the number of retests each student chose to take and compared it to the student's grade in the course. The data for 25 students are shown in a scatterplot in Figure 6-8, with number of retests on the bottom and grade on the side. You can see that the relationship is actually very strong, but it rises to a peak and then drops off again.

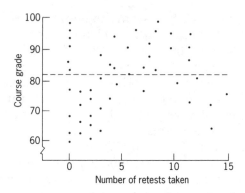

Figure 6-8 Scatterplot of students' grades versus the number of retests taken in the semester. The usual sort of Pearson product–moment correlation calculated on these data would be forced to use the straight line shown as its best fit, which would produce a fairly weak correlation. Other correlations would be better able to fit data like these (curved).

At the beginning of the chapter I raised the caution that most correlation coefficients can evaluate only linear or monotonic (always rising or always falling) relationships. These correlations would not deal well with the inverse-U relationship shown in Figure 6-8. A researcher who simply calculated the Pearson correlation for these numbers without checking the scatterplot would find a weak relationship, because this statistic would have to use the straight line shown as a dotted line on the figure. After looking at the scatterplot, the researcher would probably decide to use a different type of correlation, one that could look for a curved line instead of a straight line. Such correlations are available, but it is beyond the scope of this book to discuss them all.

In the rest of this chapter, and indeed in the rest of this book, I will use the usual Pearson product–moment correlation unless I specify otherwise. This follows the common procedure of most behavioral scientists.

There are other reasons for always drawing a scatterplot when you compute a correlation. It is easy for special situations to mask real relationships so that they disappear or even reverse. To take a fictional example, the research course I teach has students from different behavioral science majors. Some of these students are psychology majors; others are criminal justice majors. Let us suppose that I gave these two groups of students a test of psychological knowledge, and I also asked them to conduct a mock interrogation of an actor pretending to be a criminal suspect and rated the competence of each student in the interrogation. The results I got might look like those shown in Figure 6-9. A correlation coefficient calculated on these data would show a

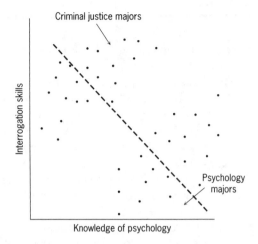

Figure 6-9 Hypothetical scatterplot of students' skills at interrogating criminal suspects versus their knowledge of psychology, with two groups of students indicated by academic major. The overall correlation coefficient is negative, as indicated by the dotted line, although the correlation within each group is positive.

negative correlation, corresponding to the dotted line drawn on the scatterplot. This would imply that the more you know about psychology, the worse you are at interrogating criminal suspects. But looking at the scatterplot, you see that this is not true. For both criminal justice majors and psychology majors, the more they knew about psychology, the better they were at interrogating suspects. This positive correlation is completely obscured by the fact that psychology majors know a lot more about psychology than criminal justice majors, and that criminal justice majors know a lot more about how to treat suspects than psychology majors. Looking at the scatterplot of your correlation can help prevent this sort of mistake.

It is important to interpret a correlation properly, which is why scatterplots are so useful. They can help you see how one variable is related to another. However, you must still remember that *correlation is not causation*, and avoid the temptation to conclude that one of the variables directly affects the other one or that changes in one cause changes in the other. Correlations are very useful tools for finding relationships, or for predicting one variable from another. If they fail to determine causation, that is because it is not their job. A screwdriver is not very useful if you want to drive nails or smooth a piece of wood, but that does not mean there is something wrong with it. Keep in mind what a correlation is for, and it can be an important part of your research toolbox.

SUMMARY

A. Correlational research is research that deals with the relationships between variables.

   1. One purpose of correlational research is to find the relationships that exist. These relationships may be stronger or weaker, and they may be positive or negative.

   2. Another purpose of correlational research is to use those relationships to predict one variable from the other variable.

   3. It is critical to remember that *correlation is not causation.* That is, just because two variables are correlated does not in any way mean that one of them has a direct, causal effect on the other one.

B. There are two ways to express a correlation.

   1. Correlation coefficients are statistics calculated on pairs of numbers, measurements of two variables, that describe the relationship between the variables. They vary from -1.0 to +1.0, with a correlation of zero indicating no relationship and correlations of +1.0 or -1.0 indicating perfect relationships.

   2. Scatterplots are graphs that allow you to visualize the relationship between two variables. These diagrams can help you interpret correlation coefficients.

CHECKPOINT

Check your understanding of the material in this chapter:

- What are the two major functions of correlational research?

- Explain the expression, *correlation is not causation.*

- What is a correlation coefficient? What different types are there?

- What does a correlation coefficient of .62 mean? -.78? -.04? .49?

- What is a scatterplot? Why are such diagrams important?

EXERCISES

6.1 Can you think of an example in your own area of interest where you might use correlational research?

6.2 Make up any ten pairs of numbers and draw a scatterplot of them. Or use the numbers in Table 6-1.

6.3 Find an example in the popular press (newspapers, magazines, etc.) of a correlation that is mistakenly used to imply causation.

6.4 Find an example of correlational research in your area of interest. What relationship does the research describe? What might this research allow you to predict? Discuss why it cannot demonstrate that one variable causes the other. What other explanations might there be for the relationship?

Part 3

Experimental Methods

The preceding sections established some basic concepts any researcher should know. Now we look more closely at a particular type of research, experimental research.

As Chapter 7 will show, experimental research is the tool specifically created to determine what causes particular events. This chapter also introduces the basic terms and concepts necessary to an understanding of the experimental process.

Chapter 8 goes into more detail about the central idea of experimental research, the control of extraneous variables. Without this control, research is not truly experimental.

Chapter 9 describes quasi-experimental research, a compromise between a true experiment and the realities of the world. When experiments are not possible, quasi-experimental research can rule out some, but not all, of the possible causes for events.

With these chapters, plus the preceding ones, the student will have learned enough to understand and participate in the research process. However, the study of research is not yet done. Part 4 discusses what to do with results after they have been obtained, and how scientific research fits in with society at large.

Chapter 7

Fundamental Ideas in Experimental Methods

Questions to Consider as You Read

- What is experimental research?

- What can experimental research demonstrate that other kinds of research cannot?

- What are the special techniques needed to perform good experimental research?

- What are the special problems that must be avoided in performing experimental research?

- How are experimental techniques especially related to the concept of falsificationism as described in Chapter 2?

- What different kinds of variable are present in any experimental situation?

- Why is it so important to be concerned about all the possible variables?

- What variations on the experimental design allow for more complex research situations?

Imagine a high school principal interested in the problem of drug use by students. The principal could use various measurement techniques, as discussed in Chapters 4 and 5, to assess the amount of drug usage and the types of drugs being used. Through correlational research, the principal could find various factors in the students' personalities, families, friends, and so on that are related to increased use of drugs. However, if the principal were interested in showing that drug use interferes with education, or in finding something that could be done to reduce the problem, simply measuring variables and relations between variables would not suffice. In that case, the only sort of research that is capable of accomplishing the principal's goals is experimental research.

Goals of Experimental Research

In Chapter 2 we discussed four goals of science: description, prediction, explanation, and control. Experimental research is the only type of research that can address the last two goals, explanation and control. We can *explain* behavior by finding out what caused it, what made it be the way it is. And we can *control* behavior once we know what causes it, by changing those causes. Let us consider an example. Suppose you were interested in elderly people who have lost much of the responsibility for what happens to them. They may be institutionalized, or they may have moved in with their adult children, but either way they no longer control as much of their lives as they once did. Sometimes these people seem to "give up," becoming ill and withdrawn.

Does a degree of personal responsibility in their lives make people healthier? If you found a group of people who had varying levels of responsibility in their lives and measured their health, a positive correlation might allow you to predict that a person with more responsibility will be healthier than one with less, but it would not not be an experiment, and you could not show whether the responsibility actually caused the person to be healthier. It is easily possible that healthier people take on more responsibility because they feel more up to it. To show that a person's improved health was caused in part by feelings of responsibility, you would have to do a true experiment. Then this explanation could be used to improve people's health by giving them more responsibility, thus changing or controlling their health.

Causation

The special thing about experimental research, as opposed to observational research, is that it can allow the researcher to draw conclusions about the *causes* of behavior. Chapter 6 made the point that correlation, the measure of a relationship, does not necessarily indicate causation. Just because two things are related does not mean that one of them directly affects the other. But if a scientist wants to explain or control a phenomenon, a cause must be discovered. An experiment can reveal whether one factor directly affects another factor and thus can demonstrate some degree of causation. This is why the experiment is such an important tool for a scientist.

What is causation? The term was briefly discussed in Chapter 6, but a more detailed analysis is appropriate here. When something *causes* something else, it has a direct, definite effect on the thing caused, even with all else equal, so that changing the first thing will have some effect on the second thing. A key idea here is in the phrase "all else equal." We cannot establish that one thing causes another thing unless we can rule out any other possible source for the change in the second thing. For instance, about 20 years ago there was a popular belief in the power of the shape of a pyramid to heal, preserve, or strengthen almost anything. Several of my friends heard that you should water your houseplants with water that first sat under a wire pyramid shape for several hours, because the pyramid would "strengthen" the water so it would grow healthier plants. My friends tried it and claimed that their plants were indeed healthier afterward. Assuming for the moment that these perceptions were accurate and the plants really were healthier, there is another explanation. Leaving tap water to sit out for several hours will allow it to come to room temperature, and also will allow any chlorine or fluorine dissolved in it to dissipate. Room temperature, nonchlorinated, nonfluoridated water is better for houseplants than cold, chlorinated, fluoridated water. Letting the water sit out will generally produce healthier plants, with or without the pyramid. Because there is another reason for the change in the second variable (the health of the plants), its suggested cause (the pyramid) has not been proven.

To show causation, then, we must have three things. First, we must show that the potential effect did not come before the potential cause. If it did, we know that it could not have been a result of that cause, because causes must come before effects. Second, we must show that changing the first thing was related to a change in the second thing. This is simple enough to show with a correlation. Third, we must show that there is nothing else that might have caused the change in the second thing. This is what correlation cannot do, and this is why we need experimental research if we wish to determine the causes for events. Consider the case of the connection between cigarette smoking and illness. In Chapter 6 I explained that all the research on smoking done so far with humans has been correlational research and therefore cannot prove that smoking *causes* illness in humans. Only experimental research can prove that smoking is a cause of human illness, because only experimental research can prove causation.

Ruling out all the other things that could have caused the effect we see is one of the main ideas of experimentation. A good experiment will eliminate all the **rival hypotheses**, the alternative explanations for what could have caused the effect besides the thing we say caused it. In the pyramid example, the effect of letting water sit out is a rival hypothesis, because it is an explanation for a factor other than the pyramid that could have made the plants healthier. In all three chapters of Part 3, we focus much of our attention on how researchers go about eliminating rival hypotheses.

Experimental Overview

While every experiment is different, it is possible to get a general sense of experimental research through looking at a diagram of a very simple experiment (Figure 7-1). The several stages shown, which are part of any true experiment, are discussed in more detail in this chapter and the next, but a brief overview is appropriate here.

The first stage is sampling, as discussed in Chapter 5. In fact, very few experiments are conducted on representative samples. The reasoning is that the results of the experiment are not going to be used to draw conclusions about the behavior of the population but, rather, to show how two variables can be related. If the relationship exists in the experiment, then regardless of whether the sample is representative, the relationship holds for the people in the experiment. Experimenters are less interested in whether the result holds for people in general than in whether it can be shown to hold for anyone at all.

The second step is to divide the sample into two (or more) groups. In an experiment, this is usually but not always done through random assignment, as discussed in the next chapter. The third step is to manipulate the two groups according to the experimental plan, and the fourth is to measure the results in both groups. In our example on health and responsibility, one would have to select a sample of elderly people, divide them into two groups, give more responsibility to one group than to the other, and measure the level of health in both groups. This is the skeleton of a basic experiment. The rest of this chapter, and the next, will put flesh on it.

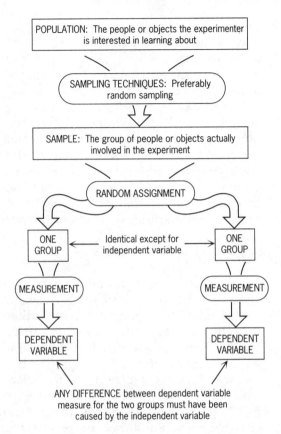

Figure 7-1 Simplified diamgram of a true experiment, showing the steps invovled in selecting the participants, assigning them to groups, and measuring the results.

Types of Variables

The concept of a variable as something whose value changes and can be estimated was introduced in Chapter 4. In any given situation there are probably infinitely many variables that could be measured if one were so inclined. As I type these words, I could measure how many letters I type per minute or how well written the passages are. The list of possible variables in this situation includes the height of my chair off the floor, my weight and how hungry I am, the temperature of the air and the color of the walls, my political orientation and my attitudes on abortion, and many more things than I could possibly list. Obviously some of these potential variables are more important in some contexts than others are. When conducting experimental research, we focus our attention on some key variables, removing all the rest. The trick to conducting good experimental research is in knowing how to treat the key variables and how to eliminate the other ones.

To return to our original example, if you were interested in the effects of responsibility on a person's health, two variables you obviously would have to measure are how much personal responsibility a person has (the potential cause) and how healthy the person is (the potential effect). Other interesting or important variables to measure might be the person's age, the types of things for which the person is responsible, and the person's health before accepting the responsibilities. The effects of environmental pollution, time of year, and the person's hair color probably are not related to this issue. The potential variables in any experimental situation can be divided into three general categories: independent variables, dependent variables, and extraneous variables.

Independent Variables

In an experiment, **independent variables** are the variables whose effects on something else you are trying to evaluate, and they are independently controlled by the experimenter. In the diagram of the experiment in Figure 7-1, the independent variable is the only difference between the two groups, and in our example, responsibility is an independent variable. While many experiments have more than one independent variable, for now we will concentrate on the simplified case in which there is only one. Later in the chapter we will discuss more complex situations and what to do when the experimenter wants to study the effects of more than one possible cause and how multiple variables interact.

Any experiment contains at least two groups of individuals (or sometimes groups of scores) that have different levels of the independent variable. The word **level** refers to a specific, predetermined amount or type of independent variable. Different levels of the independent variable are what make the groups different. The independent variable is the thing that the experimenter controls, and its levels are the values it is given, which are different for the different groups. In an experiment on the effects of rewards on a child's behavior, rewards are the independent variable, controlled by the experimenter. The different kinds of reward used in different groups of children are its levels. In an experiment on the effects of responsibility on health, responsibility is the independent variable, and the specific amounts of responsibility given to the groups of people (higher in one group, lower in the other) are its levels. In summary, the independent variable refers to the entire experiment, while a particular level of the independent variable refers to only one group.

Langer and Rodin (1976) conducted an experiment on responsibility and health of the type we have been discussing. They manipulated people's feelings of responsibility in the context of a nursing home for the elderly. Some residents, chosen ahead of time by the experimenters, were given decisions to make, such as how to arrange the furniture in their rooms, whether to watch a movie and on which night to attend, and whether to accept a plant and take care of it. Other residents were told that their furniture was already arranged in the best way, that they were scheduled to see a movie on a certain night, and that the nurses would take care of plants that were given to the residents. The researchers randomly selected who would and who would not get to make these decisions, which means they were manipulating the independent variable.

Sometimes one group is called the **control group** because the people in it experience a level of the independent variable that either is zero or is what they would be expected to have if they were not in the experiment. The controls, therefore, are expected to react as they would if they were not in the experiment (also, see Figure 7-2). People without much personal responsibility over their own lives would be in the control group in our study, because they have something close to a zero level of the independent variable. The **experimental group** is the group (or groups) whose level of the independent variable is higher than the control group or different from what they would have had on their own. Therefore their reactions are expected to differ from what whey would have been if the participants had not been in the experiment. In Langer and Rodin's (1976) study, people with more personal responsibility were in the experimental group, because they were given a higher level of the independent variable.

CONTROL GROUP   OUT OF CONTROL GROUP.

Reprinted with permission from *The Spread of Terror*, P. S. Mueller, Bonus Books, Chicago, 1986.

Figure 7-2 This is not really what is meant by "control group." The control group is a group that is included for comparison, a group that differs from the experimental group only in the independent variable.

Often neither group's level of the independent variable can be considered to be a "normal" or a "zero" level, so neither group is considered a control group. The critical thing is that the levels must be different for the different groups. A difference in the responses of the two groups demonstrates an effect of the independent variable, because the two groups start out equivalent in every way except with respect to the independent variable. (Chapter 8 explains how you can be sure that the groups really are equivalent.)

The independent variable is called independent because in an experiment the researcher manipulates the independent variable so that it is independent of any other effects. That is, the experimenter controls the level the independent variable will have for any particular person or particular group. This factor of control is crucial to what makes a research enterprise an experiment. Only by manipulating the independent variable can the experimenter create two groups that are truly equivalent.

Some variables can almost never be independent variables, because the experimenter cannot determine them completely. It is not ethical, for instance, to do experimental research on the effects of child abuse on later personality development. To do so would require putting each child into one of two groups and deliberately deciding that some children would be abused. This is why there has been no experimental research on the smoking–illness link in humans. A truly experimental researcher would have to take a group of people and decide independently who would smoke and who would not, thereby manipulating the independent variable. This grouping would have to be rigidly enforced for many years, not allowing the smokers to quit or the nonsmokers to start up, to see whether the habit made a difference to the smokers' health. Such research is of course not ethical, especially since there is so much reason to believe that the forced smoking would cause serious harm to the participants. It is similarly not usually possible to determine the sex of the participants, their intelligence, or their age. This means that most of the time true experimental research on these variables is not possible. The independent variable must be controlled by the experimenter if it is to be truly an independent variable.

Dependent Variables

Where there is a cause, there must be an effect. **Dependent variables** are the variables the researcher thinks might be affected by or dependent on the independent variable. In other words, while independent variables measure the potential causes, changes in the dependent variables measure the potential effects. In Figure 7-1 the dependent variable is measured in each group, and in our example, the researchers want to know whether responsibility affects a person's overall health. The potential effect, the variable that might be dependent on the independent variable, involves health. Therefore, in our example, health is the dependent variable. Once again, we will consider first the simple case in which there is only one dependent variable, discussing experiments with more than one dependent variable later.

In an experiment, the experimenter must manipulate the independent variable. This is not true of the dependent variable. The experimenter does not manipulate it, but instead measures it to see how it is affected by the independent variable. If the values of the dependent variable in the control and the experimental groups are different, this shows that the people reacted differently to their different levels of the independent variable. This shows that the independent variable had an effect on the dependent variable.

In our example, Langer and Rodin (1976) were interested in people's overall health, including its physical, mental, and emotional aspects. They measured overall health by asking the nurses on duty and the residents themselves to fill out questionnaires on how active, involved, happy, and medically healthy they were, and from this questionnaire they derived a measure of overall health for each resident. They concluded that people who were given responsibilities were healthier overall than those who were not, because they became more involved in activities and were happier and medically healthier, both in their own judgment and in the judgment of the nurses. Thus this experiment showed that some control over one's life, some personal responsibility, can cause one to have better overall health. Overall health can be explained, at least a little, as an effect of having control over some portions of life.

Extraneous Variables

In a simple experiment there is one independent variable and one dependent variable. As we noted before, however, it is impossible to list all the possible variables in any situation, including an experiment. **Extraneous variables** are all the other potential variables in the experiment besides the independent and dependent variables. In our example, there are some extraneous variables, such as the initial health, sex, age, and social status of the participants, that might reasonably be considered to be relevant to the central issue, the effect of responsibility on health. Others, such as the participants' hair color and the price of tea in China, are less likely to be relevant, although it is impossible to rule them out completely. All extraneous factors must be dealt with, directly or indirectly, or they can ruin the entire experiment. (The most common way of dealing with an extraneous variable is through random assignment: see Chapter 8.) It is not uncommon for scientists designing an experiment to spend much more time thinking about all the factors they are *not* really interested in than on the factors they are. Fortunately, extraneous factors can be classified into three general categories, making it easier to understand what they might be like.

Subject Variables

Subject variables are any extraneous variables that describe relatively stable qualities of the people who are participating in the research. Eye color, number of letters in surname, and length of big toe are all subject variables, though they have very little interest for anyone. Age, sex, race, political and religious affiliations, intelligence, social class, and family background are subject variables that are somewhat more interesting. In our example on responsibility and health, some subject variables that might be important include the participants' (initial) health, age, and sex, and whether the skills necessary to take responsibility are present. There are no doubt many other relevant subject variables in this study.

Experimenter Variables

Experimenter variables are any extraneous variables that describe properties of the people conducting the research. The experimenters' sex, clothing, appearance, behavior, and so on are all examples of experimenter variables. While it is easy to understand that a well-dressed, polite male and a sloppy, nasty female will get different responses, there are other experimenter variables that are less obvious, and therefore more dangerous. These experimenter variables are called **experimenter expectancy effects**, or **experimenter bias**: ways in which the researcher's expectations about what is going to happen in an experiment affect the outcome of the experiment. A researcher usually has some ideas about how the study will turn out and therefore has expectations about how the participants are likely to act in each situation. These expectations can profoundly affect the way the participants actually do act and therefore can affect the dependent variable.

One of the most powerful demonstrations of the strength of the expectancy effects was done by Rosenthal and Fode (1961). Participants acting as administrators were given photographs of people and asked to get ratings from several others on how successful the people in the photos had been recently, on a scale of -10 to +10. The administrators read instructions from a printed sheet to the people giving the ratings and were not allowed to say anything beyond what was written in the instructions. All the administrators had identical photographs and identical instructions; they were told ahead of time, however, to expect different average ratings from the raters. Half of them were told that the photos got an average rating of +5; the other half were told the average was -5. This set up expectancies on the part of the administrators. Although in this experiment the administrators were not actually the experimenters (someone else set up this experiment), they acted as experimenters act, and any effect their expectancies had on the results would be similar to the effects experimenters might have on their own experiments. When the actual ratings given to the photographs were compared, they were found to be strongly affected by the average the administrator was expecting to achieve, demonstrating how easily an experimenter's expectations can affect the results of an experiment. (Can you identify the independent and dependent variables in this experiment?)

Without actually telling the participants what to do, the administrators in this study affected their behavior. One can imagine an administrator who expects a +5 average raising an eyebrow at a rater who gives a photo a -3, while an administrator who expects a -5 would simply nod. However, when the rater gives a photo a +4, the one expecting the +5 average would nod, while the one expecting a -5 might frown. These sorts of nonverbal signals might easily affect how the raters responded to the photos. An experimenter's expectations can affect the participants' behavior any time the experimenter has specific expectations about what the participant will do in a specific situation and there is any contact between the experimenter and the participant, even if the experimenter tries not to affect the results. Obviously, as we shall see in the next chapter, the solution is either to isolate the experimenter from the participant or to arrange for the experimenter to have no specific expectations.

Situational Variables

Situational variables are any extraneous variables that describe qualities of the context of the experiment. A person who reacts differently in public and in private is demonstrating a situational variable. Temperature, crowding, the color of the walls, and the time of day are all situational variables. Hunger, fatigue, stress, and the effects of drugs are also considered to be situational variables. Even though these factors represent processes that occur inside the subject, they are not considered to be subject variables because they are not permanent parts of the person, but vary depending on the situation.

Confounding Variables

Sometimes, one or more of the extraneous variables (subject, experimenter, or situational) can become a confounding variable. A **confounding variable** (sometimes called a **confound** for short) is any variable, not one of the independent variables, that is systematically different in the two groups in an experiment. In our example, the hair color or height of the participants would be confounds if you have most of the redheads or the tall people in one group. If the variable in question is balanced equally in the two groups, it cannot be a confounding variable.

The experimenter must avoid confounding variables at almost any cost. In fact, if there are any confounding variables present, the results of the study are unclear, and any conclusions about the effect of the independent variable are suspect. The reasoning is simple. Earlier in the chapter it was explained that any difference in the dependent variable between the groups in an experiment must have been caused by the independent variable, because the groups start out equivalent *except for the independent variable*. But if there is a confounding variable present, our assumption of equivalence is false. A false assumption, of course, can easily lead to a false conclusion. If a variable can affect the dependent variable, and if it is systematically different in the two groups, then the confounding variable, rather than the independent variable, may be the cause of the difference in the dependent variable. This is the source of rival hypotheses—the alternative explanations that can account for what we observe without the independent variable. As we said earlier, rival hypotheses can destroy an experiment's value, and an experimenter must try to eliminate them in any way possible. This means that to make sense of an experimental result, experimenters must eliminate all confounding variables.

Consider for example a famous study by Brady (1958) on the causes of ulcers in "executive" monkeys. Basically the study linked several pairs of monkeys up to wires that gave them occasional painful electric shocks, producing stress. Both monkeys in each pair got identical shocks. One of the monkeys in a pair, the "executive" monkey, had some control over the shocks. If he moved a bar with his hand often enough, he could avoid the shocks for himself and his companion. If he fell behind, both monkeys were shocked. Brady found an effect of responsibility on ulcers; the "executive" monkeys had more ulcers than the passive monkeys, which seemed to explain why hard-driving business executives tend to get ulcers. All that responsibility, not only for yourself but for others, too, increases your stress.

However, other research has consistently shown that having control over the things that threaten you generally *reduces* the amount of stress you experience (Weiss, 1972). It began to seem that the passive monkey should have been under more stress and should have had more ulcers. Upon closer examination of the original experiment, a possible confound was discovered. The monkeys were selected for the two groups by pairing them up and putting them in a situation that forced them to make responses to avoid shocks. The monkey in each pair that made more responses was selected to be the "executive" monkey, presumably because it was easier to train this animal to press the bar in the experiment. This meant that the more reactive, excitable monkeys became the "executives" (Weiss, 1972). Thus we have a subject variable that has become a confounding variable: the monkey's personality. Personality can certainly have an effect on how likely the monkey is to develop ulcers (Mikhail, 1969). In Brady's study, personality was systematically related to the way the monkeys were divided into groups. The "executive" monkeys had more ulcers: but perhaps this was because of their nervous personalities, not because of their heavy responsibilities.

This shows why confounds present such serious problems for an experiment. Every confounding variable represents a rival hypothesis, making it impossible to be sure that any observed difference between the two groups in an experiment was caused by the levels of the independent variable. In the study by Brady (1958), the major hypothesis was that the difference in ulcers was caused by the monkeys' responsibilities. The rival hypothesis, made possible by the confounding variable, was that the difference was caused by the monkeys' personalities.

Now we can see why it is so important for an experimenter to have control over the independent variable in an experiment. If the researcher simply lets the two groups form as they will, the groups may differ on any number of variables that could affect the dependent variable. Researchers ran into this problem in evaluating the effectiveness of Head Start, a preschool nutrition and education program designed to help prepare disadvantaged inner-city children for school. The obvious way to find out how well Head Start works is to open the program to all disadvantaged children, and then see how they do in comparison to children who did not enroll in the program. However, in this situation the researchers are not manipulating the independent variable. If the Head Start children do better than the others, it may be due to the program, but there are a number of confounding variables that also could account for the difference. To take only one possibility, the parents of the children who did attend the program may have been more concerned about education than parents who did not sign up their children. It is easy to imagine that a difference in parental attitudes toward school could account for the difference in school performance, even without Head Start.

Once an experiment has been conducted and all the dependent variables measured in the various groups, the size of the causal effect is estimated. The first step is usually to compute the mean (or average) of the dependent variables, or the frequency of some event, in the various groups (see Chapter 4). Brady (1958) computed the frequency of ulcers for the two groups of monkeys, "executive" and "nonexecutive." In the Head Start program, a variety of dependent variables were computed for Head Start and non-Head Start children, including average intelligence, average school grades, and frequency of various school problems such as truancy or academic retention. It is highly unlikely that all the means would be identical in all the groups, even in the absence of any real effect of the independent variable. Therefore, the researcher must decide whether the differences that are found between the various means are large enough to represent a real effect, or whether they just represent random chance. Chapter 10 discusses the basic processes involved in making this decision.

Doing good experimental research obviously hinges on the careful handling of extraneous variables to prevent the appearance of any confounding variables. The ability to recognize and eliminate potential confounds is the mark of a successful experimenter. To do this well involves learning a new way of thinking, first deciding what cause–effect relationship is under study, and then trying to think of all the possible rival hypotheses, all the factors that might confound the issue. We have come back to the central idea of falsificationism, as discussed in Chapter 2. Once a scientist has developed a theory, the next step is to try to think of all possible ways to prove it false, by finding other hypotheses that can account for the observed effects. It is not enough to show that an effect *might* have been due to the independent variable. One must show that it could not have been due to anything else, at least to within a certain level of uncertainty, as we will discuss in Chapter 10. The next chapter, on the control of extraneous variables, shows how to do this.

More Complex Designs

So far, almost all our examples have involved only two groups of participants, differing only in their level of a single independent variable, and resulting in the measurement of only one dependent variable. This is the simplest kind of experiment, and in fact a great many important experiments reported in the scientific literature are exactly like this. However, more complex situations sometimes call for more complex designs. It is time to make good on the promise to discuss experimental designs slightly more complicated than the basic two-group experiments covered so far.

Dealing With Three or More Groups

A great many published experiments have more than two levels of an independent variable. Longo, Clum, and Yaeger (1988) were interested in the idea that stress and tension seem to trigger outbreaks of genital herpes in people afflicted with the herpes virus. If this is true, they reasoned, then learning to control stress and tension might reduce the outbreaks. From a number of herpes sufferers who had signed up for group sessions to deal with the problem, the investigators randomly selected some to participate in training in stress management and relaxation techniques, while another group were put on a waiting list and received no treatment. However, the researchers did more than compare the relaxation treatment with no treatment. They also controlled for the experience of being involved in a group of other people with the same problem by having still other sufferers placed in a group where they could discuss how herpes affected their lives and how they had learned to deal with it. What they found was that the support group experienced a slight benefit, compared to no treatment, but the relaxation group experienced a much larger benefit by learning to control their stress. (Can you identify the independent and dependent variables in this experiment?) This experiment contained three different groups, with three different levels of the independent variable (what are they?), but still only one independent variable.

Factorial Designs

A **factorial design** is an experimental design that involves the simultaneous manipulation of more than one independent variable, in such a way that each level of each independent variable is combined with each level of every other independent variable (see Table 7-1). The different independent variables are usually called **factors**, which is why the design is called a factorial design. This kind of study allows the researcher to determine not only the effect of each factor on the dependent variable, but how they interact with each other as well.

Table 7-1 Diagrams of Factorial Designs

Abstract example of a factorial design

	Independent Variable A	
Independent Variable B	*Level 1*	*Level 2*
Level 1	Group 1 (A1/B1)	Group 2 (A2/B1)
Level 2	Group 3 (A1/B2)	Group 4 (A2/B2)

The Chaiken and Pliner (1987) study on perceptions of men and women who eat small and large meals.[a]

	Meal Size	
Sex	*Small*	*Large*
Male	3.12	3.17
Female	3.56	2.65

[a]Numbers in cells are the targets' perceived average concern about their appearance.

As an example, consider a study on perceptions of eating habits in which Chaiken and Pliner (1987) asked a group of college students to make judgments about a person described to them. The subject of the description was either male or female and said to have eaten either small or large meals over several days. This study involves two different independent variables: sex and eating habits. (As an aside, you might have noticed that sex is one of the things I said cannot generally be a true independent variable, because the researcher cannot actually control the person's sex. In this study, however, sex could be controlled, because the subject of the judgments was not a real person but was just a description of a person. Because the researchers had complete control over whether the "person" described would be male or female, sex was a true independent variable.)

Each of the independent variables has two different levels: male or female for the sex variable, and small meals or large meals for the eating habits variable. The study is factorial because there are two independent variables and each level of one variable is combined with every level of the other variable. That is, there are men who eat small meals, men who eat large meals, women who eat small meals, and women who eat large meals. Table 7-1 presents a diagram of the variables of this study, with the mean ratings measured. The results are shown in a graph in Figure 7-3.

In a factorial design, two different kinds of effect can be examined. First, there are **main effects**, the direct causal effects of one independent variable on the dependent variable that occur with all else equal. These are just like the effects found in any experiment. In factorial designs, these are called main effects to distinguish them from the other type of effect, which we will discuss in a moment. The main effect tells something about how the dependent variable will change as a result of a certain change in the independent variable, even if you know nothing else about the situation. Because there is more than one independent variable in a factorial design, there is also more than one possible main effect. In our example, both the individual's sex and his or her eating habits could have simple main effects on the judgments made by the college students. Chaiken and Pliner (1987) found a main effect of meal size on the judgments; thus you could predict the judgments, at least a little, just by knowing how much food the individual ate.

To find the main effects of two independent variables, you could simply do two basic one-factor experiments and not bother with factorial designs. However, factorial designs can uncover something that one-factor designs cannot. Only a factorial design can expose **interaction effects**, which are effects that can be described only by considering how two or more independent variables modify each other's effects on the dependent variable. That is, when there is an interaction effect, you can explain how one independent variable affects the dependent variable only when you take the other independent variable into account. In the

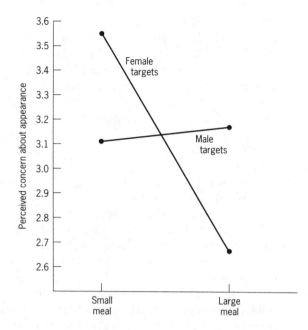

Figure 7-3 Results of the study by Chaiken and Pliner (1987) on how meal size affects perceived concern about appearance. There is no effect of meal size for men, but there is an effect for women, and also an interaction between sex and meal size.

example of the college students' judgments, the researchers found an interaction between meal size and sex (see Figure 7-3). The size of the meals the individuals ate did make a difference in how they were judged, but only when the individuals were women. Women who ate small meals were perceived as more concerned about their appearance than women who ate larger meals. However, meal size had no effect on how men were judged. This is an example of an interaction effect, because you can describe how one independent variable (meal size) affected the dependent variable only when you take the other independent variable (sex) into account. The interaction works both ways; you can describe the effect of sex only when you take meal size into account, because the judgments of women differed from those of men, depending on what they ate.

Let us take another example. Many things affect how much we like other people, even when we first meet them and know very little about them. Aronson (1969) studied the effects of two of these factors. He had people observe actors who either were or were not generally competent at what they were doing, and then had the actors either make or not make a small, dumb mistake (spilling their coffee). (Can you identify the two independent variables in this study, and also identify their levels?)

The observers then made judgments about how likable each actor was. In general, the more competent people were judged to be more likable, which is not surprising. What was surprising was the interaction between competence and blundering (see Figure 7-4). Superior people who made mistakes were more likable than those who did not, perhaps because it made them seem more "human." Average people, however, were liked even less if they made mistakes, perhaps because such errors made them seem inept. This is an interaction effect, because the effect of the mistake depends on how competent the person seems to be, overall.

The fact that factorial designs have more than one independent variable makes a new confusion possible. Sometimes people get mixed up about what is an independent variable and what is a *level* of a variable. In discussing our last example, I have heard students claim that there are *four* independent variables: high competence, incompetence, blunders, and no blunders. Of course, this is wrong; highly competent and incompetent are two levels of the same variable, competence, while blunder and no blunder are two levels of the same variable, fallibility. How can you tell the difference? The key is in the measurement process. Remember, when you measure something, you are attaching a

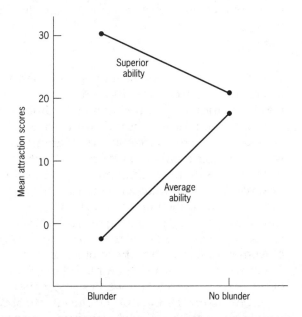

Figure 7-4 Results of the study by Aronson (1969) on the interaction effect between competence and fallibility. In general, competent people are better liked than incompetent people, but making a mistake increases the likability of competent people, while it decreases the likability of incompetent people.

label to a quality the thing has (see Chapter 4). The name of the quality, which every such thing has in some way, is the variable. Everyone has a level of competence, either high or low; everyone has a certain degree of fallibility, either making blunders or not. The label that is assigned to a particular value of the variable in a particular instance is the level of the variable. Thus the variable is something all participants in the study have to some degree, no matter what group they are in; the levels of the variable are its values in particular instances, and these will be different in the different groups.

Multivariate Designs

A **multivariate design** is a plan for an experiment that contains more than one dependent variable. That is, the researcher wants to see how the independent variable or variables affect more than one thing. For instance, in the study of the effect of stress reduction techniques on outbreaks of genital herpes discussed earlier (Longo, Clum, & Yaeger, 1988), the researchers measured the number, length, and severity of outbreaks in people who had or did not have training in stress reduction. Stress reduction training was found to lead to lessening in all three measures, while participation in the social support group reduced only the number of attacks without affecting their severity or their duration. This was a multivariate study, because it measured three dependent variables.

For another example, consider research conducted on the effect of sugar on juvenile delinquents (Weiss, 1990). It is widely believed that sugar causes people, particularly children, to become wilder and harder to control, and that sugar should be eliminated from the diets of children with behavior problems. The researchers in this study conducted an experiment to find out the true effect of sugar on high school students and juvenile delinquents. All the subjects were given breakfasts with sweet cereals, but half the cereals were sweetened with sugar and half with the artificial sweetener aspartame. Then the investigators measured dozens of variables, including concentration, memory, hyperactivity, mood, and behavior variables. Instead of finding that sugar made the youths wilder, they found that sugar had no effect on the nondelinquent participants—but it *improved* the behavior of the delinquents.

Why, then, do so many people believe that eating sugar causes behavior problems? The researchers speculate that there is a real correlation between sugar consumption and wild behavior in children in general. However, their study raises the possibility that it is the behavior problem that causes the sugar consumption, rather than the other way around. Perhaps some children are unconsciously using the sugar to help them control their own behavior. (This is yet another example of why it is dangerous to use even a well-documented correlation to make decisions about causality, as discussed in Chapter 7.)

It is entirely possible for a particular piece of research to be both factorial and multivariate. In fact, the study by Chaiken and Pliner (1987) about the effects of sex and eating habits on people's judgments was both factorial and multivariate. In addition to the two independent variables discussed previously, the study had six dependent variables, because the students made judgments about how masculine and how feminine the individuals were, about how well they expressed their feelings or how much effect they had on their own environment, about how good looking they were, and about how concerned they were about their appearance. In this study, the pattern of results was generally different for the different dependent variables. For masculinity, femininity, expressiveness, and concern for appearance, the pattern is as described before: meal size affects how we see women but not how we see men. For instrumentality (effectiveness in controlling one's environment), meal size had no effect on how the individuals were perceived, though men were seen as more instrumental than women overall. For appearance, there were main effects of both variables, with women considered to be better looking than the men and people who ate small meals considered to be better looking than people who ate large meals, but there was no interaction effect. This shows that a multivariate study can give different results for its different dependent variables. It is then up to the researcher and the research consumer to figure out what it all means.

When discussing factorial research designs, I explained that factorial designs can give you information unobtainable from a number of separate single-factor studies, specifically information about the interactions of the independent variables. Multivariate studies have no corresponding advantage over studies with single dependent variables. When analyzing the results of a multivariate study, it is common sense and reason that tell you how the dependent variables are related to each other, not some built-in aspect of the research. Thus the study of meal size and sex does not tell us much about the relationship between perceptions of attractiveness and instrumentality: it tells us only that the sexes react differently to meal sizes. However, if the different dependent variables are converging operations, supposedly measuring the same construct (see Chapter 4) as the various behavior measures on the teenage sugar eaters did, then they ought to be correlated with each other.

Multivariate research nevertheless offers some advantages compared to single-variable research. First, there is an economic advantage. By measuring the two variables simultaneously, multivariate research makes it possible to effectively conduct two studies at once with the same participants and virtually the same costs in money and time. Second, there is the great difficulty of to conducting two separate studies that are exactly the same except for the dependent variables. If, for instance, if Weiss (1990) had measured only one behavioral variable in teenagers given and not given sugar, then conducted the study again and measured another variable, and so on, each individual study would have been unimpressive because it showed the effect in only one variable. Perhaps sugar makes children wilder in all ways except that one. And, because the same participants could not be used again in the next study without automatically being older, it would be hard to show that the effect held in many different variables at the same time. The only way to do this is to measure all those variables at the same time, by doing a multivariate study. So although multivariate designs do not allow researchers to measure interactions among dependent variables, they do allow comparisons of how the participants respond in the same situation. This makes multivariate designs another set of useful tools in the experimental arsenal, enabling us to find out more about the causes of the events we want to understand.

Experimental techniques are the best suited for finding out the causes of behavior, but they must be used carefully. This chapter has given only a general idea of what an experiment is like. The next chapter elaborates on how the promise of causality is to be achieved.

SUMMARY

A. Experimental research is best suited to understanding and explaining events. It is the only type of research that can consistently tell us about what causes what.

B. Causation is a key concept in experimentation. To demonstrate that one thing causes another, we must show that (a) changing the first thing produces a change in the second thing, and (b) there is no other possible cause for the change in the second thing, ruling out all rival explanations.

C. The steps that are part of any true experiment include selecting the sample to be used, dividing it into groups, manipulating the groups, and measuring the results.

D. In any experimental situation, there are an infinite number of possible variables. We divide them up into categories.

   1. Independent variables are controlled by the experimenter, who decides who will have what levels of the variable. An independent variable is a possible cause that is being explored in the research.

   2. Dependent variables are not controlled but are rather measured to see what effect the independent variable has. A change in the dependent variable is the effect that the researcher is looking for.

3. Extraneous variables are all the other variables present in the situation. Most of them are of no interest to the researcher, but must still be taken into account.
   a. Subject variables are relatively stable properties of the participants in the research.
   b. Experimenter variables are properties of the people conducting the research. Especially important are experimenter expectancy effects, in which the experimenters' expectations about how the subjects are likely to act have an unintended effect on how the subjects really do act.
   c. Situational variables are properties of the situation in which the research is conducted, including physical characteristics of the setting, the social atmosphere, and the demands that are placed on the participants.
4. Confounding variables are extraneous variables that are systematically associated with the different groups in the experiment. Because the independent variable is no longer the only consistent difference between the groups, there are rival explanations for the effect. It is critical to eliminate any possible confounding variables from an experiment.

E. Some experimental designs are used for more complex situations.
1. When an independent variable has more than two levels, there will be more than two groups in the experiment. This allows for more complex comparisons between groups.
2. Factorial designs involve more than one independent variable, organized so that every level of each independent variable is combined with every level of each other independent variable. It is possible to measure the main effect of each independent variable, all else being equal, and also interaction effects, which can be described only by taking two or more independent variables into account, because the effect of one variable depends on the other variable.
3. Multivariate designs involve more than one dependent variable. It is not possible to measure an interaction between two dependent variables, but it is possible to observe how both act in the same situation. A particular study can be both multivariate and factorial.

CHECKPOINT

Check your understanding of the material in this chapter:

- What is the major advantage of experimental research, as compared to descriptive research?

- What do we mean when we say that one thing causes something else? How can we demonstrate causality?

- What is an independent variable? A dependent variable? An extraneous variable?

- What is the difference between a control group and an experimental group?

- What are the three types of extraneous variable? Give some examples of each type.

- When does an extraneous variable become a confounding variable? Why are confounding variables so damaging for an experiment?

- What is a rival hypothesis? What causes a rival hypothesis?

- Why is it so important for an experimenter to control the independent variable in an experiment?

- In what situations do experimenters use factorial designs? What can factorial designs show that simpler designs cannot?

- In what situations do experimenters use multivariate designs?

EXERCISES

7.1 In a study of the effect of celebrity endorsements on sales of a product, what would be the independent variable? What would be the dependent variable?

7.2 In a study of how a child's self-image is affected by attending nursery school, what would be the independent variable? What would be the dependent variable?

7.3 Think of a simple experiment in your own area of interest. What would be the independent variable? What would be the dependent variable? What levels of the independent variable would be used? What extraneous variables might be of importance?

7.4 Find some examples of experimental research in your area of interest. Which are simple experiments? Which are factorial? Which are multivariate? Identify the independent and dependent variables in each experiment.

7.5 Dr. Research conducted a study to determine which of two college algebra textbooks was better. He found four colleges using book A, which featured a rigorous, theoretical approach and was chosen mostly by engineering schools, and five using book B, which had a more intuitive, practical approach and was used mostly by small liberal arts colleges. He gave all students who had finished a course with either book a standardized algebra exam and found that the students using book A scored much higher than those using book B. Dr. Research concluded that book A was a better textbook. What are the independent and dependent variables in this study? What variable is a confounding variable? Why is it a confounding variable? What rival hypothesis does it create, to suggest that Dr. Research's conclusion might be wrong?

Chapter 8

The Control of Extraneous Variables

Questions to Consider as You Read

- How can you be sure that two different groups of people are really the same except for the independent variable?

- What are some types of extraneous variable for which researchers must control?

- How can subject variables such as personality and age be controlled?

- What are some of the different types of groups that experiments can use? What are their advantages and disadvantages?

- How can experimenters deal with the ways in which their participants react to being in different groups of the experiment?

- Will people react differently just because they expect to react differently?

- Will people feel cheated if they know other people in the study are getting what seems like special treatment?

- Will people respond differently to different experimenters?

- Are people affected by the experimenter's expectations about how they will respond in the experiment?

- How can experimenters deal with all these questions to conduct a good, well-controlled experiment?

Chapter 7 emphasized how important it is in an experiment that all the groups or conditions, as defined by the different levels of the independent variables, start out equivalent in every way except respecting the independent variables. You will recall that anything other than the independent variables that is consistently different in the groups is a confounding variable and provides a rival hypothesis. Rival hypotheses make it impossible to be sure that the independent variables are causing any observed differences in the dependent variable. However, Chapter 7 never told you exactly how you go about making sure that the groups are equivalent. Thiat is what we discuss in this chapter.

It is a little confusing to learn that you must control extraneous variables, after it has been explained that independent variables are the ones controlled by the researcher. However, extraneous variables must be controlled, also, or perhaps "controlled for" is a better phrase. You cannot simply ignore extraneous variables, because they might become confounding variables and contaminate your experiment. You must control them in the sense of making sure that they do not become consistently different between the conditions in your study. This chapter shows you how to achieve such control.

The Nature of Equivalence

If you are very alert, you might have noticed that I have never said that the groups in an experiment must be "identical" or "equal" or "the same" in every way except the independent variables. I have used the word "equivalent" consistently. "Equivalent" means not "exactly the same," but "equal in value or meaning." Loosely speaking, it means "roughly the same." When we say that two conditions are **equivalent** in some way, we mean that they are not consistently or meaningfully different in that way, even though they may not be exactly the same.

The use of the term "equivalent" is important because two different groups of anything, particularly people, can never be exactly the same. So instead of trying to make the groups identical, we just try to make them equivalent, using the techniques described in this chapter. When the groups are equivalent, we know that any differences that are present between them are just random, coincidental differences that had no particular reason for existing. This does not mean that they do not exist, or even that they might not accidentally turn out to be large once in a while. But they are still random, and generally they are small.

Once we have allowed a little bit of difference between our two conditions, does that invalidate our experiment? How can we be sure that the small, supposedly unimportant differences between two equivalent groups are not the true cause of any observed differences in the dependent variable? The answer, I'm afraid, is that we can never be completely sure. We can, however, find out just how sure we can be, by using statistical analyses like those described in Chapter 10. These tools allow us to figure out how likely it is that some unknown, accidental, random fluctuation of unknown factors might have caused the result we find in our dependent variable. As long as we are careful to control our extraneous variables, so that they have no systematic relationship to our groups, then the groups are equivalent, and we can do a statistical analysis to tell us how much confidence we can place in our results.

This emphasizes again the importance of controlling extraneous variables. If they are not controlled, if they systematically affect one group more than another, then they are confounding variables and can easily provide rival hypotheses for our results. They also invalidate our statistical analyses. Remember, those analyses apply only to processes that are random. If the coin that I am flipping is secretly a biased coin, one that tends to flip one way more than another way, then all bets are off. There is no way to predict how likely a certain pattern of results is without knowing just how it is biased. In the same way, the statistical analyses all assume that any factors besides the independent variables operate randomly, and if this is not true then the estimates of how reliable our results are become meaningless. So not only are there problems with the experiment, but the statistical analyses will not reveal them.

Having convinced you that it is important to control all the extraneous variables in an experiment, we now go on to finding out how to do that. Extraneous variables of different types are controlled through different techniques.

Simple Subject Variables

Subject variables are the most pervasive and potentially troublesome variables in the behavioral sciences, because the subjects in behavioral science research are always living organisms, usually people. Living organisms differ from each other in a very large number of ways, and we do not even know what all those ways are. This creates a large chance that unless all subject variables are carefully controlled, an extraneous one will become a confounding variable.

Random Assignment

The most important technique for controlling subject variables is random assignment. It can control for all possible simple subject variables, without the researcher even knowing what they might be. (Please note that this is different from the random sampling and random selection techniques discussed in Chapter 5. Random sampling determines who will participate in your research; random assignment determines which conditions your participants will experience.) **Random assignment** refers to any procedure that randomly determines which participants in an experiment will experience which groups or conditions. In other words, with random assignment it is randomly decided who will receive which level of the independent variables. Think back to the study on the executive monkeys (Brady, 1958), mentioned in Chapter 7. I said that the monkeys' personalities constituted a confounding variable in that study because in each pair of monkeys, the more reactive, excitable monkey was chosen to become the "executive." Brady should have randomly decided which monkey in each pair would work the bar. Then the monkeys' personalities would not have been systematically related to the group they were in, and the study would not have been confounded.

Any procedure that gives random results can be used in random assignments. If there are just two groups, as in Brady's study, simply flipping a coin is fine. With more groups you can roll dice, cut cards, or use the tables of random numbers printed in the back of most statistics books. (Table D-1 in Appendix D contains hundreds of random numbers.) Some random number generators run on computers, but you have to be very careful with these programs, which use complicated mathematical procedures to take one number and give you another: for example, multiply by 387, subtract 1439, take the square root, throw away the first ten digits of the answer, and the next three digits are the random number. The numbers are not related to each other in any obvious way, but they *are* related by this mathematical procedure, so the "random" numbers may not be as random as they should be. Some simple computer "random number generators" produce sequences in which, say, a 5 is more likely to be followed by a 9 than by a 1. This sort of bias might possibly affect your research.

Do not let anything except random chance decide who is assigned to which condition. Do not let your participants decide which group to join. Do not make the decisions yourself, "arbitrarily," because who knows what factors might affect a human being's arbitrary judgment? Do not put all the first to arrive in one group and all the last to arrive in the other, because then membership in a group would be associated with the personality trait of punctuality. Go out of your way to make sure that a mechanical, truly random procedure is controlling who goes into which group. And avoid the temptation to "fix" a random assignment that seems wrong for some reason. If you think that you have too many of one kind of person in one group, do *not* shuffle names around to make the groups "better." If you do that, you are introducing nonrandom human judgment, and the assignment is no longer random.

At this point students usually raise the question, what if you get a "bad" random assignment? What if a simple flip of the coin puts all the males in one group, or all the left-handed people, or all the homicidal maniacs? There are two reasons not to worry about this. First, the statistical analyses I mentioned before will allow you to compute how likely it is that such a statistical fluke has happened, and therefore how much you can trust the results (see Chapter 10 for more detail on this). Second, the chances of such a coincidental bias occurring become extremely small as the number of people in each group increases. If you have a small number of people, say two men and two women, the chances of having all the men in one group is pretty good, only one out of two. If you have eight men and eight women, the odds of all the men getting into the same group goes down to one out of 128. With 15 men and 15 women, the odds are only one out of 16,384. So as long as you have a reasonable number of participants in each group, the chances of getting a really bad random assignment are too small to be worth worrying about, and anyway the statistical analyses will take this anomaly into account for you.

As we shall see, random assignment is not the only way to control for subject variables, but it is by far the most common and the easiest to use. For this reason, because controlling subject variables is so important in behavioral sciences research, having random assignment of subjects to groups or conditions has become synonymous with having a true experiment. In fact, most researchers have a gut reaction that anything with random assignment is an experiment, and anything without random assignment is not. There is some truth to this reaction, in that without random assignment it is more difficult to control for subject variables, and therefore more likely that the study is confounded and cannot be used to demonstrate causality. However, random assignment is not the only method for controlling for subject variables, and even with random assignment there are other variables that need to be controlled. Therefore it is not quite true that random assignment is the defining characteristic of an experiment.

Related versus Independent Groups

Selecting groups as defined above will produce **independent groups**, groups in which no score in one group has any special relationship to any score in any other group. The scores in the two groups have nothing in common except that they are all in the same experiment. There is another way of organizing groups in an experiment. When **related groups** are used, each score in one group is connected in a special way with one score in each other group. This gives us certain advantages and certain disadvantages compared to independent groups.

Types of Related Groups

There are two different situations that produce related groups. With **matched groups designs**, there are different people in the two groups, but each person in one group is matched with a person in another group on the grounds of great similarity on a variable that seems important. (These are sometimes called **yoked designs**, and the two related scores in the different conditions are said to be **yoked**, referring to the device farmers used to use to link a team of two oxen for pulling a plow.) For instance, suppose you were doing an experiment on the effects of a certain curriculum on children learning to read. Assuming that a child's intelligence could have a big effect, you might match each child who is using the target curriculum with a child who has a very similar intelligence score using the control curriculum. This is usually done by arranging all the children in the experiment in order by the matching variable, intelligence in this case. Then you take the top two scores (or three if you have three different conditions, and so on). These two children will be matched, and will be in different groups. It is important to use a random procedure, such as flipping a coin, to decide which of the pair will be in which group, to avoid any consistent differences between the groups. Repeat the procedure with the next two children, and the next two, and so on until all the children have been assigned to groups. The scores of the two matched students on the dependent variable, such as reading, will be associated in a special way, which makes this a related groups design.

The other type of related group design is the **within-subjects design**, in which each participant experiences more than one level of the independent variable, and therefore the change in the dependent variable must be found within the subjects, rather than by comparing one subject with another. A score in one group would be related to a score in another group because both scores came from the same person. In this design, each participant acts as his or her own control, with matched scores coming from the same individual (the "perfect match"), and therefore this is a matched design that controls for every possible subject variable. For instance, in taste tests such as the Pepsi Challenge each participant typically tastes all the different foods or drinks being compared. One person's rating of Coke would be related to the same person's rating of Pepsi, making this a related groups design. (By the way, this is the only experimental design that does not use random assignment of subjects to conditions, because each subject is in *all* conditions.)

Within-subjects designs create a new problem that must be dealt with. **Order effects** are extraneous variables involving the order in which the participant experiences the conditions; these effects exist, of course, only when the participants experience more than one condition. If everyone tasted Pepsi before they tasted Coke, it might be that everyone rated Pepsi higher just because they were thirstier when they drank it, or rated Coke higher just because it was different from their first drink. What is required is **counterbalancing**, which is a system of controlling for the effects of order by allowing all the conditions to appear equally often in each ordinal position, and allowing each condition to follow each other condition equally often. One way to do this is to present all possible orders, with an equal number of participants experiencing each order. This is easy when there is a very small number of conditions, but it quickly becomes impossible. If there were eight different conditions, there would be more than 40,000 possible orders. To control for order effects when there is a large number of conditions, you can choose a different random order for each participant. As long as the number of participants is larger than the number of conditions, there will be no systematic relationship between the order and the dependent variable, and the experimental design will be valid.

Reduction of Variability

By using related groups rather than independent groups, we reduce some of the variability in the experiment. Simply put, the **reduction of variability** means that the scores under different conditions are a little more similar to each other than they would be in independent groups designs. For instance, in matched designs you are comparing scores between people who were not selected at random, but people who are known to be similar on some important variable. In our example, you are comparing reading scores of children who have similar intelligence levels. This means that you can be even more certain that any differences you see are due to the reading curriculum being used, not to differences in the children's intelligence. In within-subjects designs, you are comparing scores obtained from the same individual, so you know that all the subject variables are the same in both conditions. Reducing variability increases the **power** of the experiment, making the experiment more sensitive to differences that are caused by the independent variable.

The advantage of variability reduction is, however, offset by some disadvantages. Otherwise no one would ever do independent groups designs. Within-subjects designs are subject to the problems of order effects; in addition, it is often impossible to expose the same person to more than one experimental condition. For instance, you could not compare the results of two different reading curricula on the same child because a child learns to read only once. With matched groups designs, there is a different problem, one that is somewhat technical. Substantially reducing the variability does make the experiment more powerful, but in matched groups designs this is offset by a reduction in the number of independent observations. Since the groups are not independent, the number of independent observations is related to the number of people in each group, not the number of people in the whole experiment. So if you took thirty children and matched them into two groups, the number of independent observations would be fifteen, not thirty. For mathematical reasons, a smaller number of independent observations makes for a weaker experiment. So it is worthwhile to use match groups only if you can be sure that this research design will reduce the variability enough to compensate for the reduction in the number of independent observations. This is the case if you know that the matching variable is strongly correlated with the dependent variable. For instance, if intelligence is strongly correlated with learning to read, it might be worth matching on that variable. But it is not a good idea to match your scores if you just suspect or wonder whether the matching variable is important. Do it only if you can be sure.

Reactivity Effects

Reactivity effects are not precisely subject variables because they deal with how the subjects react to the various conditions of the experiment. That is, reactivity effects are really interactions between subject variables and the independent variable. It is important to control for them, because they will obscure other actions of the independent variable. However, simply randomizing the assignment of subjects to conditions will *not* control for reactivity effects, because the conditions of the experiment differ by definition in the different groups. There are several different types of reactivity effect, and they require different methods of control.

Placebo Effects

In Chapter 7, experimenter expectations were mentioned as an example of extraneous variables. However, the experimenter is not the only person in the experiment who can have expectations about what will happen. The participants may expect that a certain treatment will make them feel better, that a certain technique will help them perform better, or that one task will be easier for them than another. Any such expectations will tend to have powerful effects on how the participants actually behave, perhaps more powerful than the effects of the independent variable itself. These expectations are one type of **placebo effect**.

The term "placebo" (pronounced "plah-SEE-bo") comes into behavioral science from the medical profession. It was discovered hundreds of years ago that medicines that had absolutely no chemical effects sometimes produced striking results in patients who believed in them. This is how quack doctors and patent medicine men made their livings. If you convinced enough people that your Miracle Snake Oil would cure their ills, it probably would work for some of them, even if contained nothing but sugar water and food coloring. The word "placebo," which means "I will please," indicates that doctors sometimes prescribed medicines they knew to be useless just to keep the patients happy, and sometimes the trick worked. The placebo effect is a reactivity effect, because it is a difference in how the participants react to the different conditions applied in the experiment.

In the behavioral sciences, the term is not as clear-cut as it is in medicine because most of the variables we are interested in have no chemical, medical function (see Critelli & Neumann, 1984 for a comprehensive discussion of the meaning of the placebo in psychology). For instance, imagine a number of troubled teenagers who are divided into two groups, half of which receive a specific treatment to try to help them fit into society while the other half participate in weekly group discussion sessions on vague topics. It is not unusual for both groups to show substantial improvement. Just being part of the study, getting special attention from officials, and believing that whatever experiemental condition they are in can help them, is enough to cause improvement in many people. In a famous study, described in detail in Chapter 9, it was shown that being part of a research program on improving the productivity of an assembly line made the workers feel important and respected, and any change whatsoever as part of the study caused improvements in productivity for just this reason.

Please note that the improvement produced by attention and expectation is a real improvement. The workers on the assembly line really did improve their productivity. However, if you want to claim that your program is particularly effective, you must show that it is better than the other treatments available. To do this you need to compare it to another treatment that offers the general benefits of attention and expectation but lacks the special value of your program. This leads us finally to a definition of the placebo in the behavioral sciences. A **placebo** is a condition that provides the general benefits of most programs, particularly the participants' expectations of improvement, without providing the specific treatment that is being tested in the experiment.

To control for the placebo effect, we provide a control group that is given the general benefits of most standard treatments without the specific benefits of the new treatment, and see whether the experimental group performs better than the control. For example, in the study discussed in Chapter 7 about the use of stress reduction in the control of genital herpes (Longo, Clum, & Yaeger, 1988), the researchers were interested in the specific effects on participants of learning to relax, to manage their stressful situations, and generally to remove some of the pressure from their lives. To show that this program was effective, they needed a control group for purposes of comparison, a placebo control that provided the general benefits of group therapy without the specific relaxation treatment of the new program. That is why the investigators compared their program with a typical group support program including discussions about life with herpes and how the members have had to deal with the problem. Because all the benefits of this group support treatment were available to the people in the control group, the reduction in the severity and duration of herpes outbreaks in the stress reduction group had to be due to special benefits of that treatment.

For another example, consider research on the effectiveness of audio cassette tapes with "subliminal" messages, hidden suggestions that are supposed to effect some change in the listener. People can buy tapes with hidden messages to improve their memory or their self-image, help them quit smoking or lose weight, or change their sleeping habits or their relationships. A group of researchers (reported in Bower, 1990c) examined how effective these tapes really are. It was important to control for placebo effects, because people who believe that the tapes will help them will often show some improvement no matter what. Therefore the researchers used tapes that sounded the same but supposedly had two different messages, some to improve the listener's memory and some to improve the listener's self-esteem (feelings of worth and importance). They left half the tapes as they were and switched the labels on the other half, so that some tapes were labeled for memory improvement but were really to improve self-esteem, and vice versa. The people who used the tapes were tested for their memory abilities and their self-esteem both before and after listening to the tapes. Most of the listeners reported that the tapes helped. However, their reported improvement was related to the label on the tape, not the tape's actual content. That is, if the tape was a memory tape, labeled for self-esteem, the listener reported improvement in self-esteem but not in memory. And despite the listeners' reports, the actual changes in both memory and self-esteem, as measured by the before and after tests, were unrelated to the tape the listener used. In fact, the researchers reported some results indicating that many of the subliminal tapes on the market actually contain no hidden messages at all. Their conclusion is that the reported success of these tapes with some users is entirely due to the placebo effect.

Control Group Effects

Control group effects is a term that I have created to cover a variety of effects dealing with how participants react to being placed in the control group in an experiment. Imagine that the professor of one of your courses announces that she is developing a tutoring program to help students do better. To give the new program a fair test, she will randomly divide the class in half. One group will have a scheduled half-hour meeting with a tutor once a week, plus access to walk-in tutoring at many other times, copies of past tests to examine, printed study guides, and tapes of lectures. The control group will receive none of these. How would you feel if you were assigned to the control group? How might you react?

In a situation such as this, participants in the control group will almost certainly react, but it is impossible to predict exactly how. One possibility is **demoralization**, which makes people just give up, feeling that they could never compete without the extra help. Another possibility is **overachievement**, also called **overcompensation**, which makes people try extra hard to overcome their unfavorable situation. Either reaction will complicate the experiment, making it very difficult for the professor to be sure whether the new program is helpful. Suppose both groups do equally well in the course. Perhaps the program is no good. Or perhaps it did improve the grades of the experimental group, but the control group worked extra hard and made up the difference. On the other hand, suppose the experimental group does better in the course. Perhaps the program helped them. Or perhaps it did not and the experimental group did just as they otherwise would have but outscored the control group because the latter gave up and quit working. When control group effects like these appear in an experiment, they make it impossible to draw any firm conclusions about the meaning of the results of the experiment.

In more general terms, control group effects are any effects that cause the people in the control group to modify their behavior from what it would have been if the experiment were not happening. For example, consider the problem discussed in Chapter 7 of evaluating the effectiveness of the Head Start program. If the program is open to all applicants, then there is the problem of comparing disadvantaged children whose parents signed them up with those whose parents did not. As we saw, this creates a confounded experiment because parental interest in education would differ in the two groups of children. This problem could be eliminated by holding a lottery to decide which of the applicants would be admitted to the program, thereby assuring random assignment of the children to the two groups. However, this procedure could trigger control group effects if the disappointed parents of children denied the program work extra hard to enrich their home environment, or if the children themselves felt excluded and handicapped when they entered school.

The way to eliminate control group effects is to prevent the participants from comparing their situation with that of the people in the experimental group, usually by not telling them that there are other people who are given a different treatment. In the study by Longo, Clum, and Yaeger (1988), neither the herpes sufferers who got the traditional group discussion treatment nor those who were wait-listed and got no treatment were informed that there were other patients who were assigned to a new, experimental treatment program. What the participants are unaware of cannot affect their behavior. Designs like this are called **blind designs**, because the subjects cannot see, or are blind to, which condition they are in and what is expected of them. Blind designs can control not only for various control group effects but also for any effect of the subjects' beliefs about how the experiment will affect them, because in blind designs the beliefs will be the same for both groups.

Response Style Effects

Have you ever, since you became an adult, knowingly told a lie? If you are a normal human being, the true answer is almost certain to be yes. But if a potential employer asks you that question in a job interview, you are likely to say no (thereby proving that the answer is yes). Most of us want to look good, to give the right answers, to make others think well of us. Behavioral scientists use the term **response style** to refer to a person's tendency to respond in a certain way to a question, no matter what the correct answer is. Wanting to look good is one kind of response style. Another is liking to be positive; thus some people will answer most yes/no questions with a yes. Others like to startle people, and will give the most shocking answer to any question. Any consistent tendency to respond in a certain way regardless of the real answer to the question is a response style bias.

Response style, like any other extraneous variable, becomes a problem only if it affects one group differently from another. If you want to know how people feel about abortion and you word your questions so that all the "yes" answers fit a pro-choice opinion and all the "no" answers fit an anti-abortion opinion, then you have a problem with people who prefer to answer any question "yes"; but if the answers are mixed up so that half go one way and half go the other, you avoid this source of possible bias. In fact, careful public opinion surveys often ask the same question in both positive and negative ways at different parts of the questionnaire just to balance out this effect. For instance, toward the beginning you may be asked, "Do you think America should spend more money on national defense?" and later on you may see "Do you think America is already spending enough money on national defense?" If you are someone who just likes to say no, your answers will cancel out on these questions and will not affect one group of responses more than the other.

For instance, suppose you have a theory that certain specific foods, including corn and tomatoes, are very bad for a person's long-term health. (There is, as far as I know, absolutely no reason to think this idea is true.) You could develop an educational program designed to change people's diets to avoid these foods. A group of people who sign up for a nutrition lecture at a community club could be divided randomly into two groups. One group would get the usual lecture about reducing saturated fats and increasing fiber, while the other group would be lectured on the dangers of corn and tomatoes. Suppose that a month later you call up everyone in both groups and ask how many times in the past week each person had eaten corn or tomatoes. Even if the lecture had no effect at all on how the people eat, some who heard the experimental lecture might report eating less of the "dangerous" vegetables, just because they think it is the right thing to say. The people in the other group might be just as anxious to give the right answers, but they have a different idea of what the right answers are, since they never heard a lecturer claim that corn or tomatoes are unhealthy. Because the participants' response style is known to affect the two groups differently, this experiment is confounded and no clear conclusions can be drawn. (Some of the participants might have a different response style—for instance, preferring to answer "no" to any question— but this particular bias would affect both groups the same way and would not confound the results.)

As a general rule, the best way to anticipate response style effects, or indeed any subject effects, that might affect your experiment is to put yourself into the mind of your participants. If you saw this study from their point of view, how might you act? What might you do? If you can think of these things ahead of time, you have a chance of dealing with them. For instance, in the example about eating habits, you could turn to some measure of actual behavior, rather than verbal answers. You might consider going through the participants' garbage for corn cobs and spaghetti sauce jars. Or you could hide a camera in the kitchen light to record the food on the table each evening. These methods pose ethical and other problems, but they would avoid the issue of response style.

Experimenter Variables

In the physical sciences, the individual experimenter is important in that the experiments must be well designed, and laboratory techniques must be meticulously followed. However, the experimenter is not likely to have a direct effect on the results of the experiment. When measuring the atomic weight of a substance, it makes little difference whether the researcher is male or female, pleasant or crabby, old or young. For the careful worker, it does not matter whether the researcher would like the answer to be larger or smaller. Even so, with critical observations, such as early naked-eye astronomy, different observers often disagreed on such details as the precise position of a celestial body at a certain moment in time. Behavioral scientists, however, work with people or animals, and in such investigations it can matter a great deal what kind of person the researcher is and what results the researcher would like to find. These variables must be controlled, or they can contaminate the experiment.

Simple Experimenter Variables

By simple experimenter variables, I mean properties of the experimenter that do not vary much from time to time. The experimenter's age, personality, appearance, behavioral style, and so on are all examples. It is easy to imagine that you might respond differently as a research participant to a crabby old woman and to a pleasant young man. Experimenter variables like these can be powerful extraneous variables, and they must be prevented from becoming confounding variables.

As with any other simple variable, the secret to preventing experimenter variables from becoming confounds is to make sure that they are not systematically related to the different conditions of the experiment. In many experiments there is only one experimenter who collects all the data, so the experimenter variables are constant for all groups. If the experimenter variables are constant throughout the experiment, they cannot be related to any observed differences in the dependent variable and cannot provide a rival explanation for these differences. However, if more than one experimenter is collecting the data, care must be taken to ensure that there is no relationship between which experimenter collected the data and the group from which the data were collected. For instance, if you are comparing how Alzheimer's disease patients react to two different memory training techniques, you must make sure that both experimenters collect data from patients in both groups. Either ensure that half the data in each group is collected by each experimenter, or randomly decide which experimenter will collect data from each patient. With either of these solutions, there is no relationship between the experimenter and the experimental group, so there is no confounding.

Many beginners in research tend to ignore the experimenter as a blank screen on which the participants' responses are projected, but these variables can really be very important. A professor of mine once discussed a study he conducted but never published because of problems that were identified later. He and a colleague were studying real-life memory processes, like remembering where you left your car keys or what you wanted to get at the grocery store. They had developed a questionnaire they hoped would classify people according to how good their everyday memories were. When they gave the questionnaire to a large number of college students, they were excited to find that most people could be classified into those whose memories were clearly superior and those whose memories were terrible. When they looked closer, they found that almost all those with "superior" memories had been questioned by one researcher, while almost all those with "terrible" memories had been questioned by the other. The differences were due not so much to the students' memories, but to the differences between the two researchers. The last I heard, they were working on a questionnaire that the participants would fill out all by themselves, with no experimenter present at all, to control the experimenter variables. (Why is it correct to describe the original questionnaire as a low validity measurement of memory, based on the definition of validity given in Chapter 4?)

Experimenter Expectations

Experimenter expectation effects, like subject reactivity effects, are more complex than simple variables. They cannot be controlled simply by making sure that the same experimenter collects all the data. We discussed earlier how the participant's expectations about what is likely to happen can affect the way the participant behaves. It is just as true that the researcher's expectations can affect the way the participant behaves. In the study by Rosenthal and Fode (1961: see Chapter 7), in which administrators asked others for their ratings of how successful people were, based on their photographs, the administrators elicited different responses, depending on what kind of results they expected to get. In that study there was no confounding, because the expectations of the administrators constituted the independent variable, not an extraneous variable. However, in most research the experimenter's expectations are said to be an extraneous variable which, if not controlled, can confound the experiment.

In dealing with the expectations of the participants, we simply prevent them from forming any expectations of how they are expected to behave, but experimenters cannot be prevented from forming expectations. Researchers are, after all, human beings, and they will have definite ideas of how a study "ought" to come out, no matter how much they try to guard against this mindset. So how can experimenter expectations be controlled? The answer is, it makes no difference how the experimenter expects the *study* to come out, as long as there are no definite expectations about how a particular individual *participant* ought to behave at any given moment. The only way to achieve such an experimental environment is to make sure that the person who collects the data is not aware of which group any participant has been assigned to, and therefore is not aware of how a particular participant ought to react. Such studies are called **double blind**, because not only is the participant unaware of what is expected, but even the researcher has no idea how this participant "should" respond.

Double-blind studies were developed by the medical profession for the testing of new drug treatments. Suppose you have developed a new drug to relieve symptoms of the common cold. To test it on human patients, you would need to divide them randomly into two groups, one to receive your new drug and one to receive a placebo, a substance with no medicinal value. (Actually, you would probably need three groups, one to receive a standard treatment such as antihistamines and decongestants, but we will ignore this complication for now.) The placebo and the new drug would look exactly alike, or at least similar. For instance, they might both be capsules from numbered packages, such that the technician knows who got number 1 and who got number 2, but neither the technician nor any participant knows which is the placebo. That way the placebo effect will apply equally to both groups and will not confound the experiment. Once each day during the experiment, the participants would check in with the clinic and have their symptoms monitored. Their temperature and pulse would be measured, and they would be asked a number of questions about how they had felt during the past day. Then they would be given the medication for the next day. Imagine the interviewer asking, "How have you been feeling?" and the patient replying, "All right, I guess." An interviewer who knew this patient had received the new wonder drug might be tempted to say, "Not too bad, huh?" and record a fairly positive response. If, on the other hand, the interviewer knew this patient has gotten the placebo, there might be a temptation to say, "Not too well, huh?" and record a fairly negative response. So the interviewer must be blind to each patient's experimental condition. All the interviewer knows is that Mr. Jones gets capsule number 1 and Ms. Smith gets capsule number 2, but no one who has any contact with the patients knows which one is which. This experiment is double-blind; neither the participants nor the researchers with whom they have contact know how the medications have been allotted. After the experiment is over, the collected data will be turned over to the experimenter, who has never met the participants but does know that the placebo was in capsules numbered 1, and the data can be analyzed safely from any confounding from expectations.

Similar procedures are necessary in behavioral sciences research to prevent confounding from the experimenter's expectations. For instance, consider an experiment done by Darley and Batson (1973) on the factors that affect whether someone in trouble will receive help from passersby. These investigators had a group of students travel, one at a time, from one building to another on campus, passing through a narrow alley on the way. Some of the students were told that they were late and thus were in a big hurry. Some, told simply to go right over, were in a moderate hurry. Some were told that the people in the other building were not quite ready yet, so they were in no hurry at all. Everyone saw a figure huddled in a corner of the alley, moaning from time to time.

Did people stop to help the victim, or at least report his plight to someone else? It depended on how much they were hurrying. Nearly two-thirds of those in no hurry, about half of those in a moderate hurry, and only one in ten of those in a big hurry helped the victim. An important aspect of this study is that neither the victim, an experimental confederate whose job was to huddle and moan convincingly, nor the people in the other building, to whom some of the subjects reported the problem, knew which participants were in how much of a hurry. This meant that the victim would not moan louder at the unhurried participants, and the people in the other building would not be tempted to ask, "Anything happen on the way over?" Thus expectations about how the study would turn out could have no consistently different effect on the responses of the different groups.

Only by controlling extraneous variables can researchers conduct a true experiment, one that eliminates all rival hypotheses and allows us to draw conclusions about whether the independent variables have caused the results we see in the dependent variables. Experimenters who are clever at thinking of all the possible confounding variables and ways to control for them are those who produce the best experiments. It takes a certain skill at falsificationist thinking, one that can be developed through practice. If you are interested in questions of cause and effect and want to find clear answers, you will have to learn this skill as you continue your education.

SUMMARY

A. Since it is impossible for two groups to be exactly the same, experiments use groups that are equivalent, which means that there are no consistent, systematic differences between them at the outset. Then any differences between them are due to random chance and can be taken into account statistically.

B. Simple subject variables are fairly durable properties of the participants in the study.

    1. Simple subject variables are usually controlled through random assignment. This assures equivalent groups.

    2. Random assignment produces independent groups. In related groups designs, each measurement in one group has a special relationship with some specific measurement in another group.

        a. Matched groups designs have different people in each group, but each person in one group is related to a person in each other group who is very similar on some important variable. Within-subjects designs use all the same people under each condition in the experiment. In within-subjects designs, order effects become important.

  b. Related groups designs have the advantage of reducing some of the unwanted variability. This makes the experiment more sensitive in one respect, but less sensitive insofar as the number of independent mesurements is reduced. So related groups designs should be used only when it is clear that the variability will be substantially reduced.

C. Reactivity effects are interactions between subject variables and the various conditions of the experiment.

  1. The placebo effect has to do with how attention and expectation affect people. Placebo controls involve giving the control group a treatment that provides the general benefits of most common treatments without the special benefits of the new experimental treatment.

  2. Control group effects reflect how the subject reacts to being denied the treatment given to the experimental group. Subjects can react with demoralization (giving up) or overcompensation (trying extra hard). Blind designs, in which the participants do not know what group they are in or even that there are other groups getting other treatments, can be used to control for these effects.

  3. Response style effects are tendencies to respond to questions in certain ways, regardless of the true answer. One solution is to balance the questions so that one type of answer is not related to the meaning of the response. Another is to observe actual behavior, rather than asking questions.

D. Obviously the experimenter can have a large effect on what happens in the experiment.

  1. Simple experimenter variables such as age and sex can affect how the subject responds. Either keep the experimenter constant for the entire experiment, or make sure that there is no systematic relationship between the experimenter collecting the data and the groups in the experiment.

  2. The experimenter's expectations for how the subjects will respond can affect how they do respond. The solution is a double-blind design, in which neither the subjects nor anyone who has contact with the subjects knows which subjects are in which groups, and therefore which subjects should respond in which ways.

CHECKPOINT

Check your understanding of the material in this chapter:

- Why is it so important that extraneous variables be controlled?

- What does it mean to say that two groups are equivalent?

- What purposes do statistical analyses serve?

- What is random assignment? How does it differ from random selection or random sampling? What does it accomplish?

- What are independent groups? What technique produces independent groups? What are related groups? What are their advantages and disadvantages? When should they be used?

- What are matched groups? How are they produced? How does research using matched groups differ from work having within-subjects designs?

- What special extraneous variables must be controlled in within-subjects designs? How can they be controlled?

- What is meant by reactivity effects? How are they different from simple subject variables?

- What are placebo effects? What are control group effects? What are response style effects? What are simple experimenter variables? How can these different effects be controlled?

- What are blind designs? Double blind designs? Why are these designs used?

EXERCISES

8.1 List some examples of the extraneous variables that might be important in research in your area of interest. Identify each of them (simple subject variable, reactivity effect, etc.).

8.2 Identify some of the ways the variables given above could be controlled.

8.3 Find an example of experimental research in your area of interest. What extraneous variables were controlled in that experiment? What techniques were used to control them?

8.4 Think of a simple experiment you might consider doing in your area of interest. What extraneous variables would you need to control? How might you go about controlling them?

8.5 A psychologist believes that hyperactive children are able to concentrate better when there is soft music playing than when the room is quiet. To test this, the psychologist spent 15 minutes talking alone with each of several hyperactive children. For half the children (chosen randomly), there was music playing;

for the other half, there was not. At the end of each 15-minute conversation, the psychologist rated how well the child paid attention, on a scale from 1 to 7. As predicted, the children got better scores when the music was playing. What are the independent and dependent variables in this study? What variable is a confounding variable? What rival hypothesis does this confound create? How might this variable be controlled?

Chapter 9

Quasi-Experimental Research

Questions to Consider as You Read

- Why is it sometimes not possible to conduct a true experiment?

- What can you do if you want to know what causes something to happen but cannot perform a true experiment for some reason?

- Why is a true experiment sometimes not the best way to study a question about the causes of events?

- What is a quasi-experiment? How is it different from a true experiment?

- Under what conditions are quasi-experiments conducted?

- Might you at any time conduct a quasi-experiment in your own field of interest?

- What is the simplest, most basic type of quasi-experiment?

- What basic problems associated with quasi-experiments must concern researchers?

- What are some of the ways of varying the basic design of a quasi-experiment to apply to different circumstances?

- How can research be done with single individuals or single measurement groups?

In earlier chapters, we have seen that experimental research controls extraneous variables to eliminate rival explanations and uncover the causes of events, while nonexperimental research does not control extraneous variables and makes no attempt to uncover the causes of events. Quasi-experimental research falls between these two extremes. It is what you can do when you want to examine the causes of events but it is impossible or unethical to do a true experiment. The prefix "quasi-" comes from the Latin for "as if," and in English it means "giving the appearance of." A quasi-experiment, therefore, is something that looks like an experiment but really is not.

Partial Control of Extraneous Variables

A good experiment will eliminate all rival explanations, or at least all the ones the experimenter can imagine. This requires that the experimenter control all possible extraneous variables. However, a lot of research, particularly research on important social issues, is done under conditions that make it impossible for researchers to control all the extraneous variables. **Field research**, for example, is conducted in the real world, under real circumstances, without manipulating the situation. Other research is conducted under partial control, where the experimenter manipulates the situation to a certain extent but cannot control every variable. Either way, a true experiment is impossible, but the researcher still wants to find out what causes events.

What can a researcher do? **Quasi-experimental research** is a compromise, research that controls some of the extraneous variables but not all of them, so that it eliminates some but not all of the possible rival hypotheses. A skillful researcher will design a quasi-experiment that controls the extraneous variables that are most likely to provide rival explanations for the results and leave uncontrolled those that seem less likely to be a problem. The results remain open to challenge, but this approach is better than nothing.

For instance, I have said earlier that no true experimental research has been done on the link between smoking and illness in humans. A true experiment would require dividing a group of volunteers in half in some random way and forcing half of them to smoke for a number of years while preventing the other half from smoking for the same period. While research like this is possible, it is certainly unethical and is not likely to be performed. Correlational research, however, can say only that smoking and certain health problems seem to go together; it cannot indicate why. Quasi-experimental research on smoking and health could rule out some of the possible causes of the ill health of smokers, making it more likely that the cigarettes themselves are to blame. For instance, researchers have pointed out that when it was unfashionable for women to smoke, women were relatively free of lung disease, compared to men. However, as the number of women smokers has increased, their incidence of lung disease has begun to rise (Devesa, Blot, & Fraumeni, 1989). By comparing women and men in this way, the researchers can rule out effects such as changes in diet, which might be the cause of the women's poorer health. After all, women and men eat pretty much the same things. But other effects cannot be ruled out by this research. For instance, women have entered the work world in much greater numbers recently. Perhaps the stress of holding a paying job contributes to the rising incidence of lung disease. Quasi-experimental designs can rule out some rival explanations, but not all of them.

Researchers perform quasi-experimental research for two main reasons. The first, as in the example above, has to do with ethics or sometimes just possibility. There are a great many situations in which you simply cannot do true experiments. You cannot randomly assign women to marry men who do or do not beat them to see how they react. You cannot control the information a jury receives when deliberating in a real criminal trial. You cannot randomly determine which students attend which universities to find out how a college's political climate affects student attitudes. You cannot control which individuals will be exposed to a major disaster like a nuclear plant meltdown. Interest in how people behave in situations like these cannot be pursued through true experiments. Researchers who still want to study the causes of events must resort to quasi-experimental research.

Another reason for doing quasi-experimental research is something that has been called "external validity." The kind of control that is required for a true experiment is usually achieved in a laboratory setting. The situation captures the essence of the independent and dependent variables under study, but it does not capture the flavor of real life. For instance, consider the experiment mentioned in Chapter 7 on how our impressions of people are affected by the amount they eat (Chaiken & Pliner, 1987). This well-controlled experiment effectively isolated the effects of eating habits from the millions of other things that affect our judgments of other people. But how often in real life have you been asked to rate attractiveness or concern about appearance on the basis of written descriptions of people? **External validity** refers to the degree of similarity between the research situation and the real-life, normal, natural situation it mimics. In comparison, **internal validity** offers a measure of how well the experiment is designed to eliminate rival hypotheses. A study with a high degree of internal validity gives confidence that, within its own situation, the independent variable caused the changes in the dependent variable. A study with a high degree of external validity gives confidence that the results of the study are related to the real world outside the research. Doing research in real-life, natural situations frequently requires quasi-experimental research, which has lower internal validity than experiments, because the extraneous variables simply cannot be controlled without making the situation artificial. To deal with this problem, many researchers perform both internally valid true experiments in laboratory situations and externally valid quasi-experiments in natural situations. If they get the same pattern of results in both situations, they can have more confidence that their results are not only rigorous but also meaningful in real life.

Of course, the best of both worlds would be to create a well-controlled true experiment that could be conducted in a natural setting. That is what Darley and Batson (1973) did in their research on the effect of being in a hurry on helping others, mentioned in Chapter 8. Although the study was well-controlled, eliminating all the rival hypotheses that anyone has thought of, it was very natural from the participants' point of view: they knew that they were taking part in an experiment, but they did not know what it was about, and when they were confronted with someone who appeared to need help, they had to make a very real decision about how to react. This type of research is the sign of a skillful scientist, but it is not always possible. Many times true experiments are impossible, or so artificial as to make their results of questionable value. In those situations a quasi-experiment is the only alternative. And quasi-experiments can be a useful addition to experimental research when the results can be supported in a more natural setting.

The Basic Before–After Design

The other day I took a pain reliever for a sinus headache. A little later, my husband asked if the pills had helped, but all I could say was that I felt better than I had before I took them. Did this mean that the pills made the headache go away, or was it something else? It is difficult to say. This is a casual, unscientific version of the before–after design, a basic type of quasi-experimental design. This does not mean that it is the best or the most common design. It is basic in the sense that the other designs can be considered to be variations on the theme of the before–after design.

The Basic Design

The **before–after design** involves measuring the dependent variable, changing the independent variable, and then measuring again. Sometimes this is called the **pretest–posttest design** because there is a test (a measurement of the dependent variable) both before (pre-) and after (post-) the change in the independent variable. In this example, the independent variable is the headache pills, and the dependent variable is the headache. Therefore the before–after design involves measuring the headache, taking the pills, and then measuring the headache again. Any change in the dependent variable from one measurement to the other might be due to the change in the independent variable. Of course, because this is a quasi-experimental rather than an experimental design, there might be other reasons for the change in the dependent variable as well.

Consider a more scientific version of my casual experiment. I could ask several people who have sinus headaches to rate their headaches, perhaps on a scale of 10. Then I could give them all the pain reliever, and an hour later ask them to rate their headaches again. If I find that most of them rate their headaches as less painful after taking the pills, I might be tempted to think that the pills made their headaches better. By now, I hope you can think of some reasons for criticizing this conclusion. Many alternative explanations easily could account for people's headaches getting better, regardless of whether they took those headache pills. This is why the basic before–after design by itself is not an experimental design.

The Basic Problems

The number of possible extraneous variables that might provide alternative explanations in a quasi-experiment is much too large to list in this or any other book. However, there are a number of categories of variables that frequently turn up as problems in behavioral science research, and the researcher must be very careful to account for them. Every book will have its own list of such variables, because there is no definite way to categorize all possible variables, but the ones I have chosen to list are among the most common. Please remember that there are potential problem variables that are not included in this or any other list of trouble spots. It is the responsibility of the researcher to be as diligent as possible in trying to think of all problems that might have occurred in research, eliminating them wherever possible, and admitting them where they cannot be avoided.

In addition to all the problems discussed in Chapter 7 on experiments, any quasi-experiment is susceptible to the problems listed in this section. These problems are given here because a true experiment is usually (though not always) immune to them. So these are the special problems that must concern quasi-experimental researchers in addition to the problems experimental researchers have to worry about.

History Effects

Suppose in my headache research I gave each of my participants their headache pills right at dinner time. Here we have a rival hypothesis because it is entirely likely that eating dinner might by itself make the headache go away. This is an example of a **history effect**, which is a common event that all the people in a group experienced. For another example, suppose you developed a lecture on the dangers of nuclear energy. You might measure attitudes toward nuclear energy in a group of people, then give them your lecture. A month later you could measure attitudes again and look for a change. But if the first measurement had been on April 15, 1986, and the second on May 15, 1986, it would be difficult to know how much their attitudes were due to your lecture and how much to the news of the Chernobyl disaster in the Soviet Union. A common event or experience outside your experiment could easily have altered the measurement.

Maturation Effects

Maturation effects are sometimes confused with history effects because both have to do with changes over time. But while history effects are caused by events that happen outside the experiment, **maturation effects** are changes caused simply by the fact that the participants are getting older. Such changes can occur in the short run, as when results are altered because a participant has become fatigued or bored or irritated with a questionnaire. Usually, though, the term refers to changes due to increased maturity, and this type of effect takes time to work, hence it is unlikely to influence a one-hour study on headache pills.

Suppose you wanted to see how historical events affect people's attitudes toward nuclear energy. You might have measured the attitudes of a group of people many years ago, before the accidents at Three-Mile Island and Chernobyl. You could measure the attitudes of the same people now, to see whether they had changed. But you would have to remember that the people in your sample have grown many years older in the meantime. Perhaps growing older by itself changes a person's attitudes toward nuclear energy, as it can change attitudes toward so many other things. Any study that examines the same people over an extended period of time, especially when the initial measurements are made on children, must compensate for the fact that people change as they grow, no matter what you do to them.

Testing Effects

The before–after design requires that the dependent variable be measured twice. However, some measurements by their very nature can be done only once. For instance, you might measure a person's attitudes toward nuclear energy by asking for donations to an antinuclear organization. It would not make sense to do this twice in a fairly short period of time, though, because people are unlikely to give twice to the same cause, no matter what their attitude. This is an example of a **testing effect**, in which the very act of measuring the dependent variable once changes the value you get on the second measurement. Such an effect makes it difficult to know whether any change you observe in the dependent variable is due to the independent variable or to the testing effect. Another example of a testing effect is practice. Having taken a multiple choice test once, for instance, you might be motivated to think about how the test was constructed and how to second-guess the answers the next time, even if you have not learned anything about the course material in the meantime.

Instrumentation Effects

Instrumentation effects (sometimes called instrument decay) refer to the possibility that the effectiveness of the technique you use to measure the dependent variable might change between one measurement and the next. If the measurement technique involves a physical device, such as a ruler or a polygraph, the instrument might have been damaged or its proper calibration might have been destroyed. Even with measurement devices such as questionnaires or behavioral observations, however, the meaning of the measurement can change over time. An attitude survey developed in the 1950s would probably have to be rewritten before it could meaningfully be given in the 1990s. Words and expressions change their meanings, and the way people interpret the items on the questionnaire may change. For instance, the responses to a survey of attitudes of racial prejudice taken in 1950 and today might be very different, even if people's attitudes had not changed, just because it is no longer socially acceptable to admit to racial prejudice. The meaning of the measurement has changed.

Mortality Effects

The word "mortality," like "mortuary" and "mortal," stems from the Latin word for death. This label comes to us from medicine and biology, where experimental animals sometimes die unexpectedly during the course of the research. Of course, participants in behavioral science research seldom die during a project, but they may drop out of the experiment for other reasons, and the term is still used. **Mortality effects** can occur whenever a number of participants drop out of the study between one measurement and another, particularly if the people who drop out are systematically different from those who do not. Suppose in my hypothetical sinus headache research I gave the pills to people and an hour later called on the phone to ask how they felt. Many of them reported feeling about the same, but many of them were not home. What might this mean? Probably the ones who felt better were the ones who left the house, and those who did not stayed home. My second measurement would be biased because some of the people in the study dropped out.

Regression Toward the Mean

Regression toward the mean refers to the mathematical tendency for an extreme measurement of any variable to be followed by a second measurement that is closer to the mean, or average, or expected value for that measurement. This effect is sometimes called statistical regression, and it sometimes seems complicated, but the idea is really very simple. Any time you measure anything, and the measurement you get is very far from the usual measurement, if you measure the same thing again, you are likely to get a measurement closer to normal the second time (see Figure 9-1). Remember from Chapter 4 that any measurement contains error, both random and systematic. Therefore neither your first nor your second measurement will be exactly what it "should" be to reflect the construct you are measuring, and the measurements almost certainly will not be the same, even if

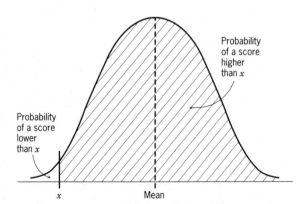

Figure 9-1 Measuring the same variable twice can produce regression toward the mean if the first score is extreme. In this probability distribution, the height of the curve at any point shows how likely that score is in the population, which means that the area under the curve between any two points is equal to the probability of getting a measurement between those two scores. If the measurement is extreme, say at the point marked *X*, it is much more likely that the next measurement will be closer to the mean, somewhere in the large shaded area rather than the small unshaded area to the left of the *X*.

absolutely nothing has changed. Usually random error will make the second measurement higher than the first as often as it makes it lower, but when the first measurement is extreme, this is not true. The second measurement, just because of random error, is likely to be closer to the mean. It is like the common condolence after a series of bad breaks: "There's nowhere to go but up." Suppose you normally score about 85 percent on the weekly quizzes in your history class, but one terrific week you score 98 percent. Is it more likely that the score on the following week will be higher or lower than 98 percent? Of course, it is more likely that it be lower, because the 98 percent is an extreme, unusual score for you. This effect can be a problem any time you select a group of measurements that are extreme, or far from average.

Imagine in my nonexperimental search for the truth about headache pills that I ask a hundred people to rate how their heads feel on a scale of 10, and give the pain relievers to the ten people with the worst headaches. An hour later, is it likely that their heads will feel worse or better, even if the pills have no effect at all? Since most of the people most of the time feel about average, you could predict that the measurement an hour later will be closer to normal—that is, feeling better—even without the pills. This is regression toward the mean.

Variations on the Theme

All the quasi-experimental research designs to come can be looked at as variations on the basic theme of the before–after design. Each of them can eliminate or avoid some of the problems listed above, but none of them can avoid every pitfall. There are so many designs because they all have different strengths and weaknesses and are useful in different situations. There are no "right" and "wrong" designs. You choose the design that best fits your situation, the one that eliminates the most likely problems, just as you would select the right tool from a toolbox. Best of all, of course, if you are seriously interested in an issue, you may do different kinds of research with different designs, in the hope that a consistent picture will emerge. The more different signs that point in the same direction, the more sure you can be that is the right direction to go.

When comparing and contrasting different ideas, it is often helpful to show them as patterns or diagrams. Figure 9-2 shows the diagram of a before–after design. It is simple, as the before–after design is simple, but it will be worthwhile to study it for a moment to get an understanding of the system I use to diagram these designs. That will make it easier to understand the more complex diagrams of the more complex designs to follow.

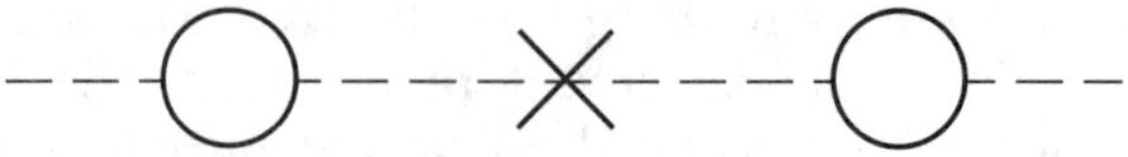

Figure 9-2 Diagram of the basic before–after design. In these diagrams, time goes from left to right, the symbol 0 stands for an observation (measurement of the dependent variable), and the X stands for the treatment (change in the independent variable).

Simple Variations on the Before–After Design

The designs covered in this section elaborate on the basic before–after design, but the changes are not terribly dramatic. Eeach one controls for some but not all of the extraneous variables just discussed.

Static Group Comparisons

One obvious characteristic of true experiments that is missing from the basic before–after design is the control group. When deciding whether a change in the independent variable caused a change in the dependent variable, it helps to have available another group of people who did not experience the same change in the independent variable, for purposes of comparison. In **static group comparisons**, the researcher finds two groups of people who differ in the level of the independent variable to which they were exposed and compares their measurements on the dependent variable. This design is diagrammed in Figure 9-3. There are two groups of people, and the dependent variable is measured in both, but only one has experienced the change in the independent variable. A difference between the two observations might be due to the change in the independent variable.

For example, suppose I called a group of known sinus headache sufferers, determined which ones had taken headache tablets in the past few hours, and then asked everyone—those who had and those who had not taken the pills—to rate their headaches. If those who had taken tablets claimed better feeling heads than the others, I might decide that the headache pills helped. This illustrates one of the main problems with static group comparisons. Because I did not make any observations of the headaches before the people took the pills, it is very hard to decide that the pills made any difference. There is no reason to assume that the groups were the same at the beginning. The groups may not be equivalent, because they were not assigned through any random procedure. Most probably, those who had taken pills recently had headaches to begin with, while those who did not take pills felt fine. This design is also subject to problems from instrumentation effects, because someone

Figure 9-3 Diagram of the static group comparison. Each row represents a separate group of participants: one receives the treatment, one does not.

who recently had a blinding headache might rate a mild throb as pretty good, while someone who recently felt great might rate the same mild throb as pretty bad. There can also be problems related to experimental mortality, if, for instance, most of the people who had not taken any pills went out for the evening and were unreachable.

Static group comparisons have been used to address some very controversial issues. For instance, Bailey (1975) examined the effectiveness of capital punishment as a deterrent to the commission of murder by comparing the murder rates in states with and without capital punishment in 1967 and 1968. It was found that the murder rate was substantially higher in states with capital punishment than it was in states with no capital punishment. Why has this research not resulted in the immediate repeal of all capital punishment laws? As a static group comparison design, it is subject to widely divergent interpretations. For instance, it could be argued that capital punishment existed only in states with high murder rates, where lawmakers and voters felt it was needed to control the high levels of violence, while it was not needed in states with low murder rates. In other words, the two comparison groups were not similar enough to make the comparison valid. This does not mean that the research is useless, because it was an attempt to find one effect of a treatment (capital punishment) that failed, indicating that the effect is not strong enough to show up in this measurement. If capital punishment laws had an extremely strong deterrent effect on murder, they would tend to compensate for the (possibly) higher initial murder rates in states with capital punishment laws, so that those states would not be likely to show substantially higher murder rates after the institution of the death penalty. The research is suggestive, and indicates that the deterrent effect, if any, is not as strong as some of the proponents of capital punishment had hoped.

Before–After Nonequivalent Groups Designs

The **before–after nonequivalent groups design** is basically the same as the static group comparison, except that both groups are measured both before and after the change in the independent variable (see the diagram in Figure 9-4). Bailey (1975) addressed some of the arguments against his research by showing that murder rates did not go down in states that adopted new capital punishment laws compared with states that did not adopt them, and did not go up in states that repealed existing capital punishment laws compared with states that kept them. A before–after nonequivalent groups design might involve measuring headaches in a group of people, letting participants decide whether to take headache pills, then measuring headaches again.

The advantage of a before–after nonequivalent groups design is that you can make better comparisons of the two groups to see how similar they are before the change in the independent variable affects one of them. This allows you to have a little more confidence in the comparison, even though the groups are not equivalent. Sometimes the comparison group allows you to make conclusions completely different from those you might have made if you had looked only at a single group. Abney and Hutcheson (1981) measured the attitudes toward government of black and white citizens of Atlanta, Georgia, both before and after the election of Maynard Jackson, Jr., as the city's first black mayor. They found that whites showed a decline in their confidence in and trust of government officials, while blacks showed no change in their attitudes.

However, Abney and Hutcheson went on to compare the attitudes found in Atlanta with the attitudes of people across the country as measured by a national survey (see Figure 9-5). They found that Americans in general, and white Atlantans in specific, all showed a decline in trust in government during the years of the study. Without the comparisons, it might have been concluded either that electing a black mayor had no effect on blacks at all or that it caused real problems for whites. With this comparison, it is apparent that the election of a black mayor in Atlanta helped the blacks in that city hold on to some of their confidence in government officials in a way that whites, or Americans in general, did not.

The disadvantage of the before–after nonequivalent groups design is that you have to worry about testing effects that are not a problem with

Figure 9-4 Diagram of a before–after nonequivalent groups design. Groups are not assigned randomly.

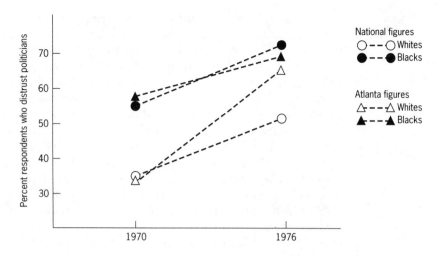

Figure 9-5 Results of the surveys of the public opinion of office holders, nationally and in Atlanta, before and after the election of Atlanta's first black mayor, Maynard Jackson, Jr., in 1973. (Abney & Hutcheson, 1981).

static group comparisons. Simple testing effects can be expected to affect both groups equally and therefore are not a problem. However, suppose that the experience of the people in Atlanta consisting of the media attention and the political novelty of their election of a black mayor caused them to think about some of the questions they had been asked on the first survey, and to develop ideas on the issue of political trust different from those they would otherwise have had. When this new political awareness showed up on the second test, researchers might have failed to attribute it partly to the questions on the first test. The term **pretest sensitization** is used whenever the experience of the pretest has sensitized the participants to notice or experience things differently.

Simulated Before–After Designs

Imagine that you have a large group of people who are about to undergo some experience, say training on how to deal with an emergency at a nuclear power plant. Imagine also that you have a way to measure their ability to deal with such an emergency, but the test can be used only once. For instance, you might have a way to simulate an emergency and observe people's reactions, but once a particular worker has experienced the simulated emergency, the element of surprise is gone and the worker cannot be observed in the same way again. How can you find out whether the training helped?

In this situation a simple before–after design is no good, because it requires that the people be tested both before and after, which is impossible if they can be tested only once. A static group comparison is no good, because everyone is going to be exposed to the training, so there will be no group of unexposed people available for comparison. A before–after nonequivalent groups design is no good for both these reasons. There is one design, however, that can be used: the **simulated before–after design**, in which you randomly select half the people to be tested before and half to be tested after the change in the independent variable (see Figure 9-6). This design is not a true experiment, but it does use random assignment of subjects to conditions. Because the selection of who will be tested first and who second is random, you may assume that there are no consistent differences between them, so the before–after measurements can be meaningfully compared. If there is a difference, you can be confident that it was not due to some difference between the people you chose for each group.

The simulated before–after design is not a true experiment because there are still extraneous variables that might have affected the result. Variables that have to do with time are particularly problematic for this design. If there might have been some event outside the study that affected the result, such as a major corporate crackdown on safety issues, then history is a possible confounding variable. If the time span of the research is long enough, maturation of the subjects is a possibility. Mortality effects must also be considered. It is likely that any workers who have a tendency toward carelessness would be convinced by the training that the nuclear power industry was not for them and would switch to another line of work. In that case, the "before" measurement would contain a mix of careful and careless workers, but the "after" measurement would contain only the careful ones. This might indicate that the training was effective in increasing overall safety (weeding out the careless people is certainly a useful thing to do), but not necessarily effective in changing the actions of individual workers who remain in the plant.

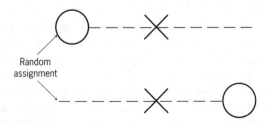

Figure 9-6 Diagram of a simulated before–after design. Participants are assigned randomly to the two groups.

Expanded Variations on the Before–After Design

The simple variations on the before–after design, as discussed so far, involve measuring one or two groups of people one or two times. The expanded variations, discussed here, involve many more observations in many different situations. This provides much more information, making it easier to draw meaningful conclusions. However, it also makes the studies somewhat more difficult to conduct or to interpret. Usually the increase in information more than offsets the increase in difficulty, but, as usual, the decisions must be made by the researcher for each situation.

Interrupted Time-Series Designs

One of the problems associated with the basic before–after design is that it uses only one measurement before and one measurement after the change in the independent variable, which provides a very small amount of information. Suppose the headache pills take an hour and a half to work, but I measure only after an hour? Or suppose people's heads always feel better as time goes on? The **interrupted time-series designs** are just like the basic before-after designs, except that they involve many observations over an extended period of time, both before and after the change in the independent variable (see Figure 9-7). That is, they involve a time series, or a series of measurements over time, that is interrupted by the change in the independent variable. This can show whether there was an abrupt change in the dependent variable at or just after the time of the change in the independent variable. Such an abrupt response would not prove beyond doubt that the change in the independent variable caused the change in the dependent variable, but it would make it more likely.

McAlister, Perry, Killen, Slinkard, and Maccoby (1980) used an interrupted time-series design as part of their research on helping teenagers choose not to begin smoking. They developed a program that used high school students to provide seventh and eighth graders with ways to resist peer pressure to smoke. For instance, the high school students had the youngsters practice ways to answer things their peers

Figure 9-7 Diagram of an interrupted time-series design. The repeated measurements of the dependent variable are graphed to permit you to look for a change at the time of the treatment.

might say, such as responding to being called a chicken by saying, "I'd be a real chicken if I smoked just to impress you." The investigators, who measured how many students in the younger group smoked over a period of time during and after the program was in operation, found that the percentage of students who smoked rose steadily from the beginning of seventh grade, when the program started, until about the middle of eighth grade, and then dropped off again. It seems as though the education program helped reverse a trend toward more and more students smoking as they got older.

The interrupted time-series design is open to problems from both history and maturation variables. It might be that the tendency for students to smoke would reach a natural peak about the middle of eighth grade and then drop off on its own, even without any special program, just because of the maturity of the kids. Or it might be that some locally famous person, someone they looked up to, got heart disease or lung cancer at the same time as the study and blamed it on smoking, which would naturally have caused the smoking rate to drop. By itself, the interrupted time-series design cannot eliminate problems associated with history and maturation variables.

Multiple Time-Series Designs

We mentioned that the basic before–after design could be improved by finding a comparison group as similar as possible to the group being studied and noting whether the group showed the same changes in the dependent variable without experiencing the change in the independent variable. The interrupted time-series design can be improved in the same way. **Multiple time-series designs** involve collecting a series of measurements over time from more than one similar group, only one of which has received the change in the independent variable (see Figure 9-8). This way one can compare the changes over time that occur when the independent variable is changed with the changes that occur in another group when the independent variable is not changed. Of course, the two groups are only similar, not equivalent, because the people are not

Figure 9-8 Diagram of a multiple time-series study, with two nonequivalent groups, one with and one without the treatment.

randomly assigned to the two groups. (If they *were* randomly assigned to the two groups, what sort of study would this be?)

The study that McAlister, Perry, Killen, Slinkard, and Maccoby (1980) actually performed on the smoking prevention program was a multiple time-series design. They found a nearby junior high school at which the students and parents matched those in the school with the new program with respect to students' rate of smoking at the beginning of seventh grade and parents' rate of smoking, and they measured how the student smoking behavior changed over time without any new program being introduced. Although the smoking rates in the two schools started out the same, the school with the smoking program showed a smaller increase in smoking rate; the difference became quite large by the end of the program after the eighth grade and persisted into high school.

Results like these make a more convincing case for the effectiveness of the program than the results from one school by itself, but all rival explanations still cannot be ruled out. It is possible that there is a consistent difference between the students in the two schools, or in their experiences during those three years, that had nothing to do with the new program but might affect their smoking rate. For instance, someone very important to the young people in one of the towns, a favorite teacher for instance, might have come down with a smoking-related illness, which might have had a large effect on the youngsters in that town. However, if several studies like this are done in different situations, in different parts of the country, by different researchers, and they all get similar results, then even the most skeptical scientist will begin to believe that there is something about the program that helps teenagers avoid smoking.

Regression–Discontinuity Designs

Many times researchers want to know whether a treatment is effective in changing a dependent variable, but because of the situation, the treatment is confounded with another variable that is known to affect the dependent variable. (In this book, "treatment" usually means a change in the independent variable that is supposed to change the dependent variable.) For instance, suppose you wanted to evaluate a program that provided school children from disadvantaged homes in your town with breakfast and an extra hour of special attention before school, in an attempt to improve their performance in school. The obvious route would be to randomly assign children to the program and then look for differences in a true experiment. However, in the real world this is not often possible. If money is available for such a program, and if the proponents think that it will help the disadvantaged children (and why else would they be involved?), they probably feel it would be wrong to deny the program to some needy children just for research purposes.

Most likely, all the children from poor, uneducated families will get the program, while children from middle-class, educated families will not. This makes it hard to use the designs we have discussed so far, because there is no similar group to which the children in the program can be compared. Because socioeconomic status (meaning the family's financial and educational standing in society) is correlated with the dependent variable of school performance, and it is systematically different between the treatment and the no-treatment groups, the study is obviously confounded. This correlated variable is called a **predictor variable**, because it is being used to predict which children are likely to do poorly in school (the dependent variable) and therefore need the program.

The solution in situations like this is a **regression–discontinuity design**, in which the predictor variable is used to predict what the dependent variable would be for the treatment group if the treatment had no effect, whereupon the researcher looks for changes from this predicted level. A regression–discontinuity design involves three steps. First the predictor variable is measured in all the participants. In our example it is the children's socioeconomic status, but it could be any variable that predicts the future levels of the dependent variable. Because one good predictor of a variable is the variable itself, the current value of the dependent variable can be used as a predictor variable. For instance, the children's current school grades could be used to predict their future school grades.

After the predictor variable has been measured, a cutoff is established: all the participants whose scores on the predictor variable are on one side of the cutoff get the treatment, and none of the participants on the other side get the treatment. In our example, the cutoff is the level of socioeconomic status below which children are eligible for the program. In this type of research it is important that the cutoff be strictly held. Slippage (whereby some children just above the cutoff are allowed in anyway, while some children just below the cutoff are not) must be minimized because it would blur the results. These two steps are diagrammed in Figure 9-9.

The third step is to measure the dependent variable after the treatment is administered and draw a scatterplot, with the predictor variable along the horizontal axis and the dependent variable along the vertical axis. Each participant is represented by a point showing the individual's measured level of the predictor variable at the start of the study and of the dependent variable at the end of the study. Find the point on the horizontal axis that corresponds to the cutoff level of the predictor variable, and draw a vertical line at that point. Every point to one side of this line is in the treatment group, while every point to the other side of the line is in the no-treatment group. If the predictor variable is truly a good predictor for the dependent variable, the result should be a fairly smooth graph on either side of the cutoff line, representing the regres-

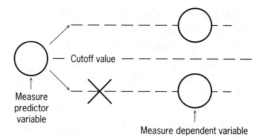

Figure 9-9 Diagram of a regression–discontinuity design. First the predictor variable is measured in all participants, then they are divided into two groups on the basis of the predictor score. One group gets the treatment, the other does not. If the treatment has an effect, a plot of the dependent variable versus the predictor variable will show a discontinuity at the cutoff level of the predictor.

sion or prediction of one variable from the other. If the program made no difference, this regression would continue smoothly right through the cutoff line. However, if the program made a difference, there would be a jump or discontinuity in the regression line at the cutoff line. Hence the name, regression–discontinuity design. Figure 9-10 shows some graphs of different results you might get from this sort of study.

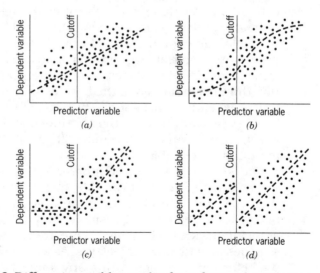

Figure 9-10 Different possible results from fictional regression–discontinuity studies. In these examples, the treatment was given to those who scored below the cutoff, those to the left of the vertical cutoff line on the plots. The dotted lines are the regression lines showing the relationship between the dependent and predictor variables. Patterns A and B show no effect of the treatment. Patterns C and D do show treatment effects.

Regression–discontinuity design is not much used, partly because there is no statistical or objective criterion for what results mean an effective program. The researchers must look at the graph and make a value judgment about whether there is or is not a real discontinuity. To convince others, they are reduced to publishing the graph and saying, "Well, doesn't it look like a discontinuity to you?" Scientists prefer more reliable ways of making their decisions and justifying them, as we shall see in Chapter 10. However, there are situations in which no other design will do, and regression–discontinuity is the only choice.

Single-Subject Designs

Most of the research discussed in this book involves many participants. However, **single-subject designs** offer a type of quantitative research that uses only one subject. Please note that in this type of research, "subject" does not always mean "person." Single-subject research may involve many people or many animals, or whatever the research uses. However, it involves only one subject as far as measurement of the dependent variable goes. The subject may be an entire department in a college, but in single-subject research that department will be treated as a single unit, not as a group of people. If the dependent variable is, say, grade point average, then it will be measured as a single grade point average for all the courses offered by that department. Anything can be a subject in single-subject research, but it will be treated and measured as a single unit, not a combination of participants.

Single-subject research is fairly simple to conduct, because it is not necessary to collect large groups of people and make sure that they are treated equally. It tends to be used more for illustration and demonstration than for proof, along the lines of showing that sometimes, at least, that independent variable can have an effect on that dependent variable. People who want to show that the independent variable often or usually affects the dependent variable will probably need to do research with more than one subject.

The simplest way to conduct a study with a single subject is to measure the dependent variable, change the independent variable, and then measure the dependent variable again. This is simply a basic before–after design with a single subject, and it has all the problems associated with that design. There are two ways to improve the before–after design with one subject, just as we have seen many ways to improve the before–after design with many subjects.

Reversal Designs

Most single-subject research uses **reversal designs**. A reversal design; in which the treatment is alternately provided to the subject and then removed, thereby reversing the treatment (see Figure 9-11). This is often referred to as an ABA design: A stands for baseline periods with no treatment and B stands for treatment periods, so ABA indicates baseline followed by treatment followed by baseline again. (If there is another reversal, and treatment is added again, it is an ABAB design, and so on.) In reversal designs, the pattern of the dependent variable is measured for a period of time before, during, and after the treatment, to look for patterns. This is similar to an interrupted time-series design, except that the treatment is alternately given and removed.

For instance, Ayllon and Roberts (1974) reported on an attempt to use classroom rewards and punishments to improve the reading performance of a group of five students in a particularly disruptive fifth grade class. This type of technique is called behavior modification. The investigators began by carefully measuring the dependent variable, reading performance, for a period of time without making any changes in the classroom situation. This is called a **baseline** measurement, in which the base or beginning level of the dependent variable is measured before there are any changes. Baseline measurements are very important because they provide a standard for comparison with to see whether the treatment has any effect. The students' baseline performance on reading tasks, such as vocabulary and comprehension tests, was 40 to 60 percent (see Figure 9-12).

After getting a stable baseline measurement, the researchers began the treatment period. They gave the whole class, including the five target students, points each day for good performance on the reading tasks. The students could turn in the points for rewards such as extra recess time or having a letter sent home to parents about their good work. The students' performance on the reading task is shown in Figure 9-12. Then the researchers reversed the treatment, no longer giving the points or the rewards, and the reading performance dropped back to what it had been before. Then the design was reversed again, reinstating the point system, and the students' performance went back to the higher level. Based on this pattern of results, the researchers concluded that the treatment was effective in increasing the children's reading performance. (By the way, what constitutes the "subject" in this single-subject design?)

A◯◯◯B◯◯◯A◯◯◯

Figure 9-11 Diagram of a reversal design with one independent variable: A indicates the beginning of a baseline period, with no treatment; B indicates the beginning of a treatment period. This is an ABA design, with one reversal back to a second baseline period.

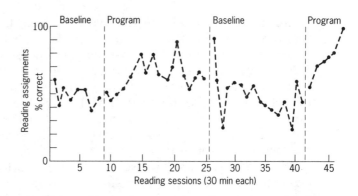

Figure 9-12 Results of a study of how the reading performance of five students was affected by a behavior modification program (Ayllon and Roberts, 1974). This reversal design shows that the program has a positive effect on reading.

Strictly speaking, a single reversal, in an ABA design, is sufficient for single-subject research; most such research, however, has at least two reversals—an ABAB design. The example above is like this, since treatment was given, then removed, then given again. When time and money are available, researchers will often flip back and forth over and over, and each time the dependent variable changes to match the treatment condition, more confidence can be had in the relationship. Also, when the treatment improves the dependent variable, as in the foregoing example, researchers will typically end the study with a treatment condition, thereby leaving their participants better off than they were before.

The Importance of Reversal

Once upon a time, Roethlisberger and Dickson (1939) conducted a very famous series of studies at a General Electric plant in Chicago. The subjects worked under assembly-line conditions, wiring equipment for telephone service. The researchers and the company were interested in many things, including finding out whether any changes in plant conditions would improve the employees' work productivity. First the investigators carefully measured productivity for a time without changing any of the conditions, to get a baseline. Then they would make one change, and continue to measure productivity, looking for a corresponding change. For instance, upon increasing the lighting in the workroom, they found that productivity improved. Then they increased the lighting still more, and productivity improved again. They really seemed to be onto something!

The researchers then reversed the design, reducing the lighting back to its original levels—and the workers' productivity improved. Careful study of this situation revealed that practically any change in any aspect of the workers' environment, no matter what, increased productivity, at least in the short term. The reason, it turned out, is that the attention paid to the workers as part of the study was more important than any of the changes. Whenever something changed, they were reminded that their company was scientifically trying to find the best working environment for them, and this knowledge made them work harder. They were also asked repeatedly for their evaluation of the changes, causing them to feel listened to and respected, which also made them work harder. Because of the careful work done at General Electric's Hawthorne plant, the **Hawthorne effect** has become a general term to describe changes in the behavior of the people, usually for the better, which occur simply because the subjects were in a research study.

This research points out the importance of reversal. If Roethlisberger and Dickson had not reversed their design, they might have concluded that better lighting improved the workers' productivity. Only by removing the treatment and seeing a return of the dependent variable to baseline levels can we be confident that it was the treatment itself that caused the dependent variable to change. If the treatment causes the change in the dependent variable, then the changes ought to appear only during the treatment periods, not during the baseline periods. Another way of looking at it is to notice that without reversal, this is simply a before–after design with only one subject, hence highly unreliable.

In single-subject research the only comparison you can make is with the same subject under other conditions. The more times you make that comparison, the more confidence you can have in your results. Every time you reverse the conditions between treatment and no treatment, you provide another comparison, making your case stronger.

Reversal with Multiple Variables

Reversal designs are simple when there is only one independent variable. You turn it on, then off, then on again, and so on. However, what if you wish to study two independent variables? What if Ayllon and Roberts, for instance, had wanted to study the effects on students' behavior of the behavior modification program *and* a new curriculum? There are two ways to go about this. The simplest is to do two separate reversal studies. First you would turn one variable, say behavior modification, on and off, and decide whether it has made a difference. Then you would turn the other variable, say curriculum, on and off, and decide whether it has made a difference.

The problem with this simple approach is that it will not tell you how the two independent variables interact. Recall the discussion in Chapter 7 on factorial experiments, in which I said that factorial studies are better than separate studies on multiple variables because the former will find the interactions between the variables. It is seldom enough to know how the variables work one at a time, because in real life variables do not come at us one at a time. A teacher, for instance, must make decisions about behavioral techniques *and* curriculum at the same time. Therefore you must vary the two variables together. However, one rule of research in general is to change only one thing at a time, so you can evaluate the effect of that one change by itself. How can you vary both variables while changing only one thing at a time?

In the simplest multiple-variable case, we can use A to represent the baseline condition, B to represent one treatment, C to represent the other treatment, and BC to represent both treatments at the same time. Then our design could be represented as follows:

A, B, A, B, BC, B, BC, C, BC, C, A, C, A

This design looks complicated, but it is really simple. It starts out as an ABAB design. Then only one thing is changed: the other treatment is added, giving the BC condition. This is reversed and then reversed again, just as was done in the ABAB design, ending that pattern with BC. Then one thing is changed again: the first treatment is removed, giving the C condition. Reverse, then reverse again, back to C. Finally the treatment is removed, returning to the baseline condition. Reverse twice, and you are done. We can now compare each treatment alone with the baseline condition and with their combination.

Let us take a fictional example. Suppose I want to teach my 5-year-old son to put his toys away at the end of each day. (That much of the example is not fictional!) I have two techniques that I think might work. One is to nag him each night until the toys are put away. The other is to give the boy a token, perhaps a plastic star, each night that he puts his toys away, telling him that every Saturday he can turn in his stars for rewards. If he has only a few stars, he gets a small reward, perhaps an extra cookie after lunch. If he has lots of stars, he gets a larger reward, perhaps a trip to a video arcade and a few quarters to spend. Table 9-1 shows how this study might be organized. The fictional results of this fictional study are shown in Figure 9-13. If I got this pattern of results, I would conclude that nagging worked a little, but rewards worked better, and both together worked no any better than rewards alone. The logical thing to do, then, would be to make the reward system permanent, at least until my son is a little older.

With more than two variables, the picture becomes so complex that a single sequence will not do it. However, several sequences will work. The central ideas are to change only one thing at a time, to include every possible change of only one thing, and to reverse each change at least once. If you are in a situation that calls for this design, you should get the help of someone familiar with this type of research.

Table 9-1 Design of a Fictional Reversal Design with Two Variables

Label	Description
A	Baseline
B	Nagging alone
A	Baseline
B	Nagging alone
BC	Nagging and rewards
B	Nagging alone
BC	Nagging and rewards
C	Rewards alone
BC	Nagging and rewards
C	Rewards alone
A	Baseline
C	Rewards alone
A	Baseline

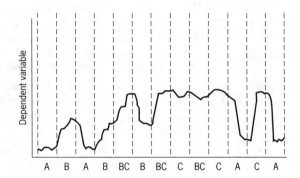

Figure 9-13 Results of a fictional reversal design with two independent variables. The dependent variable is the number of nights per week on which the subject put away his toys. The labels below the graph indicate the periods of the study: A is the baseline condition (no treatment), B is one treatment (nagging alone), C is the other treatment (giving rewards), and BC is a combination of both treatments. This pattern of results would indicate that nagging alone works, but rewards work better, and both together are no better than rewards alone.

Multiple-Baseline Designs

Perhaps you have already spotted the big problem with reversal designs. What if one of the techniques I used to get my son to pick up his toys was so successful that after using it for a while he got into the habit of picking them up and continued to do so after I stopped the treatment? This would surely be a good thing, but in a reversal design it would look like a failure, because in the second baseline period the dependent variable would not return to baseline levels. We use the term **carryover effect** when the effects of a treatment continue into the second baseline period. In many cases, as in this example, the carryover effect is exactly what the treatment is supposed to produce, and reversal designs cannot deal with this result.

To handle carryover effects, you use a simple extension of the before–after single-subject design. This is the **multiple-baseline design**, in which you collect baseline data on several different subjects, or different variables in one subject, and introduce the treatment at a different time in each subject or each variable, looking for a corresponding change in the dependent variable (see Figure 9-14). This avoids some of the problems of the basic before–after design with many subjects because the timing of the treatment is different for each subject, so in most cases it is not likely to correspond with a historical event or the subject's maturation. This reduces the concern about these variables.

For example, consider the study on reading performance in fifth graders by Ayllon and Roberts (1974), mentioned earlier. If the researchers thought that the behavior modification program might produce long-lasting improvement, they could have done a multiple-baseline design, studying, say, six different fifth grade classes, all of which used the same lessons and the same tests. As before, the baseline performance of all the classes would be measured first. Then at some point one class would begin to get points for good performance. A little while later, another class would also begin to get the points, then a while later another class, and so on. Each class would receive the treatment at a different time. If

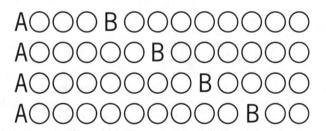

Figure 9-14 Diagram of a multiple-baseline design study. The treatments are applied to the different subjects or variables at different times.

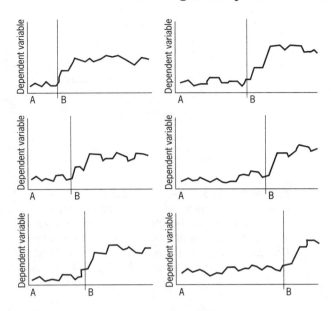

Figure 9-15 Results of a fictional multiple-baseline study. In each subject, the dependent variable changes just when the treatment is introduced, which indicates that the treatment affects the dependent variable.

there were a change in the dependent variable for each class at or just after the change in the independent variable, it could well be that the independent variable had affected the dependent variable. So, if the results from this fictional study were like those in Figure 9-15, the researcher would likely conclude that the point system improved the students' reading performance.

A multiple-baseline design may have one participant, but at least two different dependent variables to measure, which are related to each other but different, so that the treatment can reasonably be expected to affect one of the dependent variables but not the other. For instance, in the research on reading performance, Ayllon and Roberts (1974) could have measured performance on math tests as well as on reading tests. The special rewards for high reading scores would logically affect reading performance without changing math performance much. After measuring both math and reading scores for a time, the special reading incentive program would be introduced, and performance on both tests would still be measured. A successful program would result in a noticeable increase in reading scores, with little change in math scores. Some time later, the incentive program could be expanded to include math performance as well as reading performance, and a successful program should result in an increase in math scores at that point. Results like those shown in

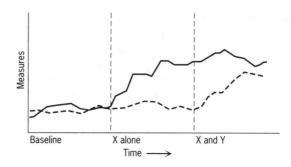

Figure 9-16 Results of a fictional single-subject, multiple-baseline study. Two different dependent variables are measured repeatedly in one subject. At point X, the treatment is applied to only one dependent variable; at point Y the treatment is also applied to the second dependent variable. Each dependent variable changes at the point when treatment is applied to it, which indicates that the treatment affects the dependent variable.

Figure 9-16 would indicate that this special incentive program helped students improve their test scores.

Of course, this is not certain, because not all extraneous variables have been eliminated. This is the inherent limitation of a quasi-experiment. In our example, the children were not assigned randomly to their classes, and the teachers probably knew about the experimental program and what was expected, so there are potential problems. However, in dealing with the complexities of the real world, the control required for a true experiment may not be possible. The partial answers provided by a quasi-experiment are better than no answers at all. As in any research, converging operations are important (see Chapter 4), and if enough quasi-experiments are conducted in different ways with different research designs, and they all reach the same general conclusions, those conclusions become reasonably trustworthy. Just remember, nothing in science is ever completely proven, not even by the strictest, best controlled true experiment.

SUMMARY

A. Quasi-experiments can control some extraneous variables, but not all of them.

B. The simplest quasi-experimental design is the basic before–after design.

  1. In this design, the dependent variable is measured both before and after the independent variable is changed. A change in the dependent variable may be due to the change in the independent variable.

2. In addition to the extraneous variables discussed in Chapter 8, others apply to quasi-experiments.

   a. History effects are caused by events that happen outside the study.

   b. Maturation effects are caused by the fact that the participants are growing older.

   c. Testing effects are caused by the fact that the subjects have been measured before, and will react to the same test differently.

   d. Instrumentation effects are changes in how the measurement applies to the dependent variable.

   e. Mortality effects are caused by participants dropping out between measurements.

   f. Regression toward the mean is a statistical effect in which a variable that is extreme on the first measurement tends to be closer to the mean on the second measurement.

3. The research designs discussed here are variations on the before–after design.

C. Simple variations make no dramatic changes in the design.

   1. Static group comparisons involve finding two groups whose members are as similar as possible except for the independent variable, and measuring the dependent variable in both of them. Subject variables are not controlled.

   2. Before–after nonequivalent groups designs also use similar groups, but the dependent variable is measured before and after the change in the independent variable.

   3. In the simulated before–after design, everyone in a group is exposed to the treatment, but half the people are measured before and the other half afterward.

D. Expanded variations produce more information over more time or from more groups of people than simple ones.

   1. Interrupted time-series designs feature a long series of measurements interrupted at some point by a change in the independent variable, which ought to cause a distinct change in the dependent variable.

   2. Multiple time-series designs feature a long series of measurements on two groups, only one of which gets the treatment and should show a change in the dependent variable.

   3. Regression–discontinuity designs involve measuring all participants on some variable that predicts the future value of the dependent variable. Those who score above (or below) some cutoff value are given the treatment, and then the dependent variable is measured. If the treatment made a difference, there should be a discontinuity in the relationship between the predictor and the dependent variables at the cutoff line.

E. Single-subject designs concentrate on the measurement of a single person (or group), treating it as one unit.

　　1. The reversal design involves measuring under usual conditions, then during treatment, then again under usual conditions. When the conditions return to baseline, the dependent variable should also return to its baseline levels. Usually more than one reversal is used.

　　　　a. Without reversal, this approach is simply a before–after design with only one subject and is very unreliable.

　　　　b. With more than one independent variable it is still possible to plan a reversal design that allows you to compare the effects of all the independent variables alone and in combination with each other.

　　2. Carryover effects prevent the dependent variable from returning to baseline levels when the design is reversed. To handle this, multiple-baseline designs are used. The subjects or variables are all measured under baseline conditions, and then the treatment is introduced separately for each subject or variable, at different times. If the dependent variable changes at just the time that the treatment is introduced for that subject or variable, it is probably being affected by the independent variable.

CHECKPOINT

Check your understanding of the material in this chapter:

- What are the differences between true experiments and quasi-experiments? In what ways are true experiments better than quasi-experiments? In what ways are quasi-experiments better than true experiments?

- What quasi-experimental design is the most basic? Why?

- What are the six basic extraneous variables that can influence quasi-experiments, as listed in this chapter? Define them and give a situation in which each is likely to appear.

- What groups are used in nonequivalent groups designs?

- What is a time series? An interrupted time series? A multiple time series?

- What is a regression? A regression discontinuity? What can a regression discontinuity tell you?

- What is meant by "subject" in single-subject designs?

- What is a reversal design? Why is reversal so important in single-subject designs? How do carryover effects affect reversal designs?

- What is a multiple-baseline design? Under what circumstances is it required? Why?

EXERCISES

9.1 Give some examples of quasi-experimental designs that might be useful in your area of interest. Which extraneous variables are controlled? Which are not?

9.2 Think of an interesting research question for which quasi-experimental research would be necessary. Which quasi-experimental design would you use? Why? What extraneous variables would pose potential problems for this research? Why?

9.3 Find some examples of published research in your area of interest that are quasi-experimental. Why was experimental research not used? Which extraneous variables were controlled? Which were not? Did the uncontrolled extraneous variables in the research present a serious problem? Why or why not? Could the research be done differently to control for those uncontrolled extraneous variables? How? Would this be an improvement? Why or why not?

Part 4

Dealing with Results

Conducting research is not enough. One must know what to do with the results after they have been obtained, and how these results interact with social reality.

In Chapter 10 we look briefly at the concepts behind inferential statistics. This chapter can give the student who has not taken any statistics enough background to talk intelligently with statistical experts and to understand what is being claimed by statistical results in research reports.

Chapter 11 analyzes the composition of a scientific research report and gives the student a step-by-step plan for writing and revising a report.

Chapter 12 explores some global questions about the role of research in society and how the human nature of researchers affects their research. In this chapter we see that science is at its heart a very human activity.

With this section we come to the close of our investigation of the research process. The appendices that follow provide information that might be of use to some readers, including discussions of computers in research, graphs and charts, and computing some selected statistical tests.

Chapter 10

Statistical Decisions

Questions to Consider as You Read

- What sorts of decision can statistics help researchers make about their research?

- Can statistical tests prove that a theory is true? Can they prove that it is false?

- What kinds of error can happen when making statistical decisions?

- Why is it impossible to avoid all errors in making statistical decisions?

- How are the errors in statistical decisions controlled?

- How do scientists go about making statistical decisions in research?

- What different kinds of statistical test are there? What do you need to know about your research to decide which statistical tests to use?

- In writing a research report, how are the results of a statistical test reported?

Y ou have designed an experiment that controls for all the relevant extraneous variables, that meets all ethical criteria, that examines an interesting question in an interesting way. You have performed the experiment, being careful not to contaminate it with a biased selection or assignment of participants or with sloppy experimental procedures. You have collected all your data and calculated the means of the dependent variable for each of your groups. Now what?

What you will probably have to do next is some sort of statistical analysis. This chapter is all about what those analyses are and how they work, but it only skims the surface. For a true understanding of statistical analysis, a student needs courses in statistics, usually two semesters' worth at the undergraduate level. Graduate students typically take more. One chapter obviously cannot provide that understanding.

What this chapter can do is give the student who has no knowledge of statistical analysis an overview sufficient to permit an understanding of what the questions are and what the answers sound like. With just the information in this chapter, a student should be able to follow what an expert is doing when conducting this sort of analysis, even if just how is a mystery. The chapter can also serve as a quick refresher for the student who has taken statistics and needs to be reminded of some of the core concepts.

For example, suppose you were comparing two different techniques for providing special education to learning-disabled children. One group of children used the system that had been applied in the school district for the past five years, while the other group used a set of specialized materials designed with a new theory of intellectual development in mind. Children were randomly assigned to the two groups, and the special education teachers using the materials did not know that one system was traditional and the other experimental. The students' classroom teachers, who also knew nothing about the two different systems, were asked to rate all the students on their performance through the year. From these ratings, each student was given a score on a scale of 10 that measured his or her improvement. Suppose the students in the traditional group got a score of 5.5, while those in the experimental group got a score of 6.8. What does this mean? Does the difference in the average scores imply that the new materials helped the students more than the traditional ones, or is this difference too small to be meaningful? Suppose the new system is much more expensive or requires time-consuming teacher training. Is it worth the trouble and expense of switching systems?

If you are in charge of special education in this school district, which system would you adopt for use next year? If you are a special education teacher, which system would you choose? What information would you need, that I have not yet given, to make these decisions? Before you read on, take a moment to put aside this book and think about these questions.

Inferential Statistics

This chapter is about a type of statistics that researchers use to help make decisions in cases such as these. Back in Chapter 4 a statistic was defined as any number, calculated based on a group of numbers, that summarizes something about those numbers. We have already discussed statistics such as the mean and the standard deviation, which describe the central tendency and the variability of the group of numbers that they summarize. Statistics such as these are called descriptive statistics, because they simply tell about a property of a group of numbers, a sample. **Inferential statistics** are statistics that allow scientists to draw conclusions about some property of the population of numbers from which the sample came from (see Chapter 5 for a discussion of the difference between a population and a sample). Like all statistics, inferential statistics are numbers that are calculated from a set of other numbers, but instead of describing the sample, inferential statistics allow us to make decisions about the population.

There are many different kinds of inferential statistics, designed for use in research situations of many different kinds. Each statistic makes a different set of mathematical assumptions about the kinds of number being analyzed and can be reasonably applied only to situations in which those assumptions are met. It is impossible in a single chapter to even hint at all the different types of statistics available to you or to convey everything you need to know to really understand statistical reasoning. Before actually using the results of any statistical test, you will have to take statistics courses or consult people who are experts in this area. (By the way, if you need to find an expert to help you, one good place to go to is the nearest college with a graduate department in your area of interest. Statistics instructors can recommend graduate students who have taken statistics courses recently and done well, and they are often willing to share their expertise for a modest consultant fee.) As I explained at the outset, this chapter can give only the most general understanding of what statistical tests are about, so that you can ask your expert the right questions and understand the answers.

I hope by now you have thought about the questions I raised above. How would you go about deciding whether the difference between scores of 5.5 and 6.8 is real? What information would you need? One fairly obvious piece of data you would need is the number of children involved in the research. That is, you would want to know the size of the set of numbers on which these means are based. If there are only two children in each group, then a difference of 1.3 is not very impressive. On the other hand, if hundreds of children are involved, the difference is much more important. Another thing you would need is the amount of variability in the scores in each group. Look, for instance, at the two sets of scores in Table 10-1. In both cases the means of the two groups are the same, but the variability differs. In case A there is a lot of variability in each group, which makes the difference between the means look pretty trivial. In case B there is much less variability in each group, and the difference in the means becomes much more important.

This kind of informal reasoning is exactly what inferential statistics does, only more formally. For example, the kind of statistic most commonly used in the sort of case described here uses only five different numbers: the difference between the means, the sizes of each of the groups, and the variability within each group. From these numbers a statistic can be calculated that tells the researcher how much faith can be put in the difference, allowing the researcher to make an inference about whether the treatment of the two groups made a real difference in their performance.

Table 10-1 Two Cases of Experimental Results with Identical Means but Different Variabilities

	A: Large Variability			B: Small Variability	
	Group 1	Group 2		Group 1	Group 2
	3	8		5	8
	5	5		5	6
	4	6		6	6
	3	9		5	7
	5	7		5	6
	9	3		6	7
	7	9		5	7
	3	4		5	6
	7	9		7	8
	9	8		6	7
Means:	5.5	6.8		5.5	6.8

Statistical Reliability

The use of inferential statistics is mathematical and rigorous, and so many people are tempted to think that whatever the statistics say must therefore be true. This is particularly likely because most statistical computations these days are done on computers, so the result as printed out seems to be unchallengeable. However, as we saw in Chapter 2, the scientific method can provide no absolute truths, no matter how many computers or statistics are used. All that statistics can provide for us are probabilities. It is up to us to base our decisions on those probabilities, even knowing that we may be wrong.

All inferential statistics boil down to mathematical answers to one basic question: How likely is it that the results of this particular study are due to random chance, not to any systematic research effects? That is, what is the probability that the result is real, versus the probability that it is just a fluke? Inferential statistics provide the probability of getting results like these if the only factor operating is random chance. In our example, it would be the probability of getting a set of scores from the children like the one that we got if in reality no systematic difference at all existed between the two groups.

Scientists use the term **statistical significance** or **statistical reliability** to refer to the probability that a result is not just the product of random chance. When the probability of a random result is small enough, they say that the result is significant, or reliable. The term "statistical significance" was introduced first, when inferential statistics were first being developed, and it is widely used, but there is something of a movement to replace it with the term "statistical reliability." The word "significant" importance, the likelihood of having a meaningful effect. However, "statistical significance" merely means that the result is probably not a fluke; it implies nothing at all about its importance. This is the meaning of "reliability" we saw in Chapter 4, and it is a common-sense meaning of the word: something is reliable if you can count on it happening again under the same circumstances. In this book, as in most others, these terms are used interchangeably, but in general it is better to use "statistical reliability."

Put in its simplest terms, the process of statistical decision making is to compute an inferential statistic from the data, giving a probability that the result obtained was simply due to random chance. If this probability is small enough, then the scientist will decide that there is a real effect causing the result. If this probability is too large, the scientist will decide that the result was just a fluke.

How small is "small enough?" There is no fixed answer to that question. In each area of research, scientists have decided more or less arbitrarily on a level of probability that they are willing to tolerate. The cutoff is called the **significance level**, because it expresses how reliable a result must be before we will decide it is not likely that it was due to chance. In most of the behavioral sciences, the significance level is set at 5 percent. That is, if the probability of a coincidence is less than .05, it is generally considered to be a reliable result. If the probability of a coincidence is less than .01 (1 percent), it is usually considered to be highly reliable. However, these levels are arbitrary and are not the same in every field of research. In medical research, for instance, it is very important not to give people drugs unless you are really sure they do some good; thus significance levels may be set much tighter, with no result being accepted unless the chance of coincidence is less than .01 or even .005. However, in deciding whether a new teaching method is effective, you may be willing to accept a larger probability that it looks better by chance and may adopt a significance level of .1 or even higher. Reading the literature in the area of your research and talking to other researchers will give you an idea of what the acceptable significance levels are in that area. The one hard rule about significance levels is that you must decide what level you are willing to accept *before* you conduct your experiment. Otherwise, you may be tempted to set your significance level at whatever will allow you to accept your results as real. Only by setting this standard beforehand can you be sure that your decision is appropriate for your type of research, rather than biased in the direction of the level that will make your results come out the way you want them to.

Suppose that a result is statistically reliable. What exactly does this mean? Of course, it has the technical meaning described above, that there is less than a 5 percent chance that the result was due to random chance. But what does it mean for the researcher? It means that you can be 95 percent sure that there is some systematic, nonchance difference between the two groups you are comparing. It does not, however, mean that you can be sure that the result is due to the effect you were looking for. *Anything* that systematically affects the groups differently will show up in the inferential statistics, and it may or may not be the matter of interest to you. For instance, suppose there was some bias in the assignment of participants to groups, so that the children receiving one type of special education were systematically different initially from those receiving the other type. This could easily produce a reliable difference in their scores at the end, because it is not a random factor, but it has nothing to do with the relative effectiveness of the different materials. Or suppose that one teacher, using one of the materials, was more gifted or dedicated than another, using the other type of materials. Again, this discrepancy in ability is not a random factor, so it could produce a reliable result. All that a researcher can safely conclude from a statistically reliable difference is that it is *likely* that *some* systematic factor produced the difference. It is not always obvious what that factor is.

Understanding Errors

Even when there are no problems with control of extraneous variables, and therefore no unknown systematic factors to bias the results, it is still impossible to be absolutely certain about what the results mean. There might, by sheer chance, have been a difference between the two groups when we started the experiment, so that the result is not due to the independent variable at all. Remember, in our experiments we can ensure that the two groups are equivalent by carefully randomizing them, but this does not ensure that they are equal. Statistical analyses deal in probabilities, not certainties, so there is always a chance of making an error.

While we cannot eliminate all errors, we can at least understand them. Consider a simple experiment, designed to test for a specific effect of an independent variable on a dependent variable. After conducting your experiment and computing your statistics, you must make a decision: either the result is reliable, or it is not. In actual fact, in the reality of life, which cannot be observed directly, either there is a real effect of that independent variable or there is not. This gives the four possible outcomes shown in the grid in Table 10-2. Two of these outcomes represent correct decision: you decide the result is reliable, and in reality there is an effect, or you decide the result is not reliable, and in reality there is no effect. The other two outcomes represent errors. Of course, it would be nice if we could avoid making these errors entirely, but, given the probabilistic nature of science and statistics, this is impossible. Random chance might produce two groups that differ in some important way, and this could produce a difference in the result when there is in fact no effect, or it could make the groups come out equal when there is in fact a real effect. Because these errors are real and important, they have been given names. A **Type I error** has occurred when you decide that a result is reliable but in fact there is no real effect. A **Type II error** has occurred when you decide that a result is not reliable but in fact there is an effect. There are also names for the probability of making each error

Table 10-2 Four Possible Outcomes of Any Statistical Decision

	Actual Real-World Situation	
Your Decision	*Real Effect*	*No Real Effect*
Result reliable	Correct decision	Type I error (Probability = alpha)
Result not reliable	Type II error (probability = beta)	Correct decision

in a particular experiment. The Greek letter alpha (α) refers to the probability of a Type I error, and the Greek letter beta (β) refers to the probability of a Type II error. These names are not very descriptive or very memorable, but we are unfortunately stuck with them.

Consider more closely alpha, the Type I error probability. It is the probability of deciding that a result is reliable when, in fact, it is just due to random chance. Sound familiar? This is the probability that is measured in statistical tests. When setting a significance level, a scientist is really determining how large a probability of a Type I error will be tolerated, and calculating an inferential statistic tells how likely it is that it will happen. For this reason, the significance level is often called the **alpha level**. Scientists in general are more concerned about limiting the probability of Type I errors than Type II errors, because it is considered to be a more serious flaw to believe in an effect that is not real than to reject an effect that is real. Remember from Chapter 2 that scientists are concerned about falsification, and they try as hard as they can to prove ideas false before they begin to believe them. Therefore, scientists tend to be very conservative about deciding that results are reliable. By making more "not reliable" decisions, we will automatically reduce the number of Type I errors, but we will also increase the number of Type II errors.

There are ways to reduce the probabilities of both errors at the same time, but not after the experiment is over. Using larger groups (getting more numbers in the sample) will reduce probabilities of both types. So will improving your measurement techniques, because this will reduce the variability in your scores due to irrelevant factors and concentrate on variability due to actual changes in the dependent variable. Increasing the size of the effect, perhaps by strengthening the independent variable in some way, is another way to reduce the likelihood of both errors, and so is choosing a more powerful statistical test. However, simply changing your decision criterion, by changing your significance level, will cause an increase in one error for every decrease in the other.

There are some circumstances in which a Type II error is considered to be more serious than a Type I error. For instance, consider drug testing when the drug is a possible treatment for a disease that is always fatal, such as AIDS. In this case, we would much rather give the patients a drug that is useless than eliminate a drug that might help. Even with problems of side effects and costs, the terminally ill cannot be much worse off with a useless drug than they are with nothing at all. In fact, this is the root of the current controversy over AIDS drug testing. There is tension between two groups of scientists, those concerned about falsifiability and reducing the probability of a Type I error, and those concerned about giving AIDS patients anything at all that might possibly help. As a general rule, Type I errors are more important when comparing two treatments, one of which is "standard" or "accepted," and it is important not to switch to a new treatment unless it is really better. Type II errors are more important when there is no current treatment and almost anything would be better than nothing.

It is important in this discussion of errors to mention once again that random chance is assumed to be the only factor operating, aside from the effect being measured. Any flaw in the experiment that introduces other systematic factors will immediately invalidate any conclusions about the probability of making some kind of error.

Steps in Statistical Inference

When conducting a statistical test of some research result, a researcher must go through several steps. Sometimes the order of the steps varies, and researchers rarely move explicitly from one to another. However, these steps describe the reasoning behind statistical inference, and any researcher using statistical inference ought to know what they mean and how they apply to the research at hand.

To make things a little easier to follow, I have taken as my example a study conducted by Randall Gordon (1987) to demonstrate the social desirability bias. This is the factor that affects survey data when people alter their responses to conform to what they perceive as socially desirable, as we discussed in Chapter 5. Thus people are more likely to admit to drinking decaffeinated coffee than to smoking marijuana, even if they in fact do both.

To demonstrate this effect, Gordon chose a survey of dental hygiene behaviors, things that people do to keep the teeth and mouth healthy. The survey asked people, among other things, how often they brushed their teeth. Two groups of people received different forms of the survey, and it was randomly determined which form each person would receive. The two forms had identical questions, but different instructions. The standard form simply asked people to answer the questions. The modified form stressed how important it was to get accurate information on these questions and asked the respondents to be as honest as possible in answering them. In both cases, the survey was completely anonymous, as no respondents identified themselves on the form. When all the surveys were collected, the average number of reported tooth brushings per day was computed for each group. On average, people who received the standard instructions reported brushing their teeth 2.63 times per day, while those who received the modified instructions reported brushing their teeth only 2.19 times per day. Is this difference real? Statistical inference can help answer that question.

Step 1: When you begin doing your research, you will have an idea of the effect you anticipate finding. The **research** (or **experimental**) **hypothesis** is the effect that will occur if there is a positive result. In this case, Gordon's research hypothesis was that the difference in the instructions would cause people who received the modified instruction, stressing accuracy and honesty, to show less social desirability bias, and therefore to report brushing their teeth fewer times per day.

Step 2: You reverse the experimental hypothesis and predict what will happen if it is *false*. This is the **null hypothesis**, the hypothesis about what will happen if there is no real effect. In this example, the null hypothesis is that there is no difference in the number of times per day the people in the two groups report brushing their teeth. (Remember the importance of trying as hard as possible to prove an idea is false? If not, see again the discussion of falsificationism in Chapter 2.)

Step 3: Set your alpha level, the maximum probability of a Type I error that you will accept. This usually corresponds to the general consensus in your particular area of research, but it may differ in your case for some reason or other. For instance, if you are testing a very controversial theory, you may choose to be stricter than usual and might not consider a result to be reliable unless the chance of a coincidence is less than 1 percent (<.01). In Gordon's case, there was no particular reason to alter the usual practice, so he set his significance level at .05, as is standard in the field.

Step 4: Select and calculate the appropriate test statistic, to determine how likely it is that the results you obtained are the result of random chance. Later in the chapter we discuss how to choose the right statistic for your situation. At the end of this step, you will have calculated the probability of a coincidence causing your results. Gordon used a statistic called *t*. The value he computed for this statistic was 1.92, and this worked out to a probability of a Type I error of less than .03. In other words, there is only a 3 percent chance that some random coincidence, like accidentally getting more dentists' children in one group than the other, caused the result.

Step 5: Compare the actual probability of a Type I error obtained in step 4 with the significance level set in step 3. If the actual probability is *less* than the confidence level, the result is considered to be reliable, and the researcher usually concludes that the research hypothesis is upheld by this study. If the actual probability is *higher* than the significance level, the result is not considered to be reliable, and the researcher usually concludes that the research hypothesis is not upheld. In our example, the actual probability (.03) is less than the alpha level (.05), so the result is reliable, and Gordon concluded that the instructions used in the survey affected how much toothbrushing people reported.

Kinds of Statistical Test

A statistical test is a way of calculating mathematically what is likely to occur by chance in a particular situation. This means that there must be many different types of statistical test to correspond with the many different types of research for which scientists wish to use statistics. In fact, for some less common types of research, no workable statistical test has yet been devised, although new tests are being developed all the time by statisticians.

This section discusses some of the factors that determine the selection of a statistical test. These are the things you must know about your research and your statistical needs before you can select the test that is appropriate in your situation.

Levels of Measurement

Chapter 4 covered the different levels of measurement scientists use. Each different type of measurement allows certain mathematical operations, but not others. For instance, it makes sense to calculate the average of an equal interval measurement such as family income, but not a nominal measurement such as college major. Therefore some statistical tests that involve calculating averages can be applied to equal interval measurements but not to nominal measurements. It is important, therefore, to know what level of measurement your study is using before selecting a statistical test.

The statistics allowable for each level of measurement are cumulative. That is, any test that is permissible for a nominal measurement is also permissible for an ordinal, equal interval, or ratio measurement. There are other tests that are not applicable to nominal measurements but are applicable to ordinal, equal interval, and ratio measurements, and still others are applicable only to equal interval and ratio measurements. (I am not aware of any tests that can be applied to ratio measurements only and not to equal interval measurements, so the distinction between those two is not as important in inferential statistics as the other distinctions.) However, using a test that is appropriate for a level of measurement lower than the one you have will involve throwing away some information in the measurement, thus making the statistical test weaker. Researchers must balance their desire to be mathematically accurate (by avoiding a test from too high a level of measurement) against their desire to be statistically powerful (by avoiding a test from too low a level of measurement).

Sometimes scientists disagree on just what level of measurement is represented by a particular measurement system. One already mentioned is the measurement of intelligence through IQ scores. Many who design and use IQ tests believe that the careful standardization of the tests on populations of thousands of people allows researchers to assume that the intervals between IQ scores are equal everywhere on the scale. Others disagree, saying that the difference between an IQ of, say 90 and 110 (slightly below average to slightly above) is not as great as the difference between 40 and 60 (moderately retarded to mildly retarded). This controversy has two parts. First, there are those who argue that there are no equal interval measurements possible in behavioral sciences, as compared with physical measurements such as temperature or length. These people are in a minority, and most behavioral scientists believe that one can safely consider test scores (percent correct), age in years, family income, IQ scores, number of children, and many other things to be equal interval measures because there is no particular reason to consider one "step" to be any larger or smaller than any other "step."

The other part of the controversy has to do with the difference between a measurement and the construct behind a measurement (see Chapter 4). Even if a measurement, say, percent correct on a test, has equal intervals in itself, the underlying construct of interest to a scientist— say, knowledge of the subject matter—may not have. In that case, the researcher may choose to treat the measurement as ordinal for the sake of more easily applying the results to the underlying construct, which is probably ordinal, and not just to the equal interval measurement itself. (By the way, is test score an equal interval measurement or a ratio measurement? I would say that depends on how the test is constructed and how you define the measurement. For instance, in a multiple-choice test with four choices in each question, someone who knows absolutely nothing about the material, and in fact someone who cannot read the language, would tend to get a score of approximately 25 percent. This might be closer to a "true" zero than an actual zero score on the test would be.)

When deciding what kind of measurement you have, you must balance being conservative against being powerful. If you think your results are strong but might be controversial, it is probably better to assume a slightly lower level of measurement, ordinal rather than equal interval, for instance. Then you will be open to criticism from those who disagree with your decision, and a strong result will come through as reliable even on the weaker statistical tests. However, if most people are likely to agree that a measurement is equal interval, and the effect you are looking for is small, it might be better to assume the higher level of measurement, to increase the chance of finding the effect reliable with a stronger test.

Research Design

The question of research design has to do with the way your study is organized. How many groups did you use? Are they independent or related? Questions like these affect which statistical tests you can use.

First is the question of how many different groups you used, or how many different levels of your independent variable. Some studies have only one group, and the purpose is to compare this group with some sort of standard. The study on dental hygiene mentioned above (Gordon, 1987) included this as one of its purposes, in that the lowest mean number of toothbrushings per day reported in their sample (2.19) was considerably larger than the number reported in a large national health survey (1.60). Gordon attributed this difference to the fact that his survey was done with college students, who might well practice different dental hygiene from a random sample of all Americans. He did not perform the statistical test necessary to show that this difference was not due to random chance, but he could have done so.

In many studies, two groups, or two different levels of the independent variable, are being compared. An example of this was the comparison described above (Gordon, 1987) between the number of toothbrushings per day reported by people whose surveys had different instructions. Then there are many studies with more than two groups of scores, in which the independent variable can take more than two different levels. Each of these cases is handled differently by the statistical analyses. That is, there is one type of statistical test to use when you have two groups, and a different type to use when you have three or more groups.

It also makes a difference whether the scores in the different groups in your study are independent or related. If the participants were randomly divided into the groups, and each participant contributed only one score to only one group, then the groups are independent, because each score in one group has no particular relation to any specific score in another group. However, if all the participants take part in all the groups, contributing a score under each different level of the independent variable, then the groups are related. Each score in one group has a relationship with a particular score in another group, because those two scores were produced by the same individual. (See Chapter 8 for more discussion of designs involving related versus independent groups.) Any factor that creates a special relationship between the scores in the different groups makes the difference between independent and related groups, and the two are handled differently in statistical analyses.

A study that involved related groups was conducted by Friedman (1987), who investigated the effect of taking repeat exams in an attempt to improve one's scores in a college course. Students in Friedman's statistics course were required to take three exams during the course, as well as a final exam. If they wished, the students could repeat each of the three lecture exams as many as three different times, hoping to improve their scores. Friedman then compared the scores on the lecture exams with the scores on the final for students who got a B on the first lecture exam. Students who took no repeat exams at all and those who took only one repeat exam received essentially the same score on the final that they had on their three lecture exams (85.31 on the lecture exams, 86.06 on the final exam). Students who took two or three repeat exams, however, raised their final exam grade by four percentage points, nearly a half a letter grade (85.26 on the lecture exams, 89.32 on the final exam), and many of these students pulled their final course grade up from a B to an A. This is an example of a related groups study because the comparisons are between the lecture exam scores and the final exam scores of the *same* students, so each final exam score is closely related to a particular lecture exam score that came from the same student.

Finally, there are research designs that do not use different groups at all and do not attempt to compare one group with another or with a standard, but instead look for relationships between variables. These are correlational studies, those that measure the same two (or more) variables over and over again in different instances to see whether the two variables seem to be related. For instance, Fernald (1987) examined the effect of textbook writing style on students' preferences. He compared students' ratings of passages from a textbook on introductory psychology that differed in the amount of narrative structure used. (Narrative structure refers to a storylike, continuing flow of information with a beginning and an end. In this experiment, the passages with a heavily narrative structure described the experiences and feelings of an individual person, rather than simply discussing psychological theories and experiments.) Fernald found a correlation between the amount of narrative structure and the students' liking for each passage ($r = .637$). As discussed in Chapter 6, a correlation coefficient such as this one is a descriptive statistic. Inferential statistics are necessary to compute how likely it is that this correlation could have occurred by chance.

Parametric versus Nonparametric Statistics

There is yet another way of organizing inferential statistics: one can use **parametric statistics**, which make fairly strong mathematical assumptions about the data to which they are applied, or **nonparametric statistics**, which make much weaker, simpler assumptions. This means that nonparametric statistics can apply to a much larger collection of situations than parametric statistics, because the former can apply to situations in which the assumptions of the parametric statistics are not met. However, nonparametric statistics are generally weaker statistical tests, in that if you apply both parametric and nonparametric statistical tests to a situation in which the parametric assumptions are met, the parametric statistics might uncover reliable effects that are not indicated by the nonparametric assumptions.

What, exactly, are these assumptions that parametric statistics require and that nonparametric statistics do not? They are:

1. The population from which the sample of observations is drawn must be normally distributed. (See Chapter 5 for a discussion of populations and samples.) To say that something is "normally distributed" means that the values tend to fall into a bell-shaped curve, with most of the observations clustered around a central value and fewer and fewer observations as you approach the extremes. This assumption is a fairly modest one, since most naturally occurring variables seem to be distributed normally. Also, violating this assumption to a certain degree is not immediately fatal to a parametric test, particularly if a fairly large sample size is used. For very small samples, though (less than about 10) this assumption becomes more critical.

2. When samples are drawn from two different populations (which is true any time there are two or more groups in an experiment), not only must both the populations be normally distributed according to assumption 1, but they must both have the same variance. That is, they must show equal amounts of "scatter" or "spread" from the central value. This assumption is somewhat more serious than the first one, because it is easy to imagine that changing conditions could change the amount of variability in a measurement. However, it is probably close enough to being true most of the time, especially when large samples are used. Also, when the sizes of the two samples from the different populations are the same, it is not as important that the variances be the same.

3. The variables being compared must be measured on an equal interval level or a ratio level, so that arithmetic operations such as addition and multiplication of the values can make sense. This is quite a strong assumption. As I have argued earlier, most of the variables we use in the behavioral sciences are not equal interval measurements of the hidden constructs we are trying to measure. Percentage correct on a test may not exactly reflect knowledge of course material; age in years may not exactly reflect emotional maturity; family income may not exactly reflect feelings of wealth or poverty. I personally think that instances of truly equal interval measurements in the behavioral sciences are rare, although behavioral scientists frequently use tests that assume otherwise. It is this assumption that makes the use of parametric tests most questionable in my mind. I must point out, however, that many scientists disagree with my pessimistic view of how unequal the intervals are in behavioral measurements and feel perfectly confident in choosing parametric tests most of the time.

So how do you decide which type of test to use? First of all, if you have any real reason to believe that there are important violations of the assumptions of parametric tests, you must use nonparametric tests. If you are quite sure that all the parametric assumptions hold true in all meaningful ways, it is better to use parametric tests, because all else being equal they are more powerful. If you are in that shadowy in-between land—not quite sure whether your situation fits— then you will have to make a tougher decision. How large is your sample? If it is quite large (say, more than 30) you can probably use parametric tests safely. How strong is your effect? A very strong effect is said to pass the "interocular impact test," which means that it hits you between the eyes. When a glance at your data convinces you that there is a big difference between your groups, use nonparametric tests. They are not likely to miss an effect that strong, and no one can question their validity. Nonparametric tests also can be useful if you know that many of the people you want to convince with your study believe that parametric tests are not appropriate. For more information on nonparametric statistical tests, consult Siegel and Castellan (1988).

Test Selection Summary Chart

Table 10-3 is adapted from one that appears in the book by Siegel and Castellan (1988) mentioned above. It gives some of the more common statistical tests to use in different circumstances. Italicized tests are parametric. Asterisks indicate tests that are discussed in Appendix C of this book; the rest can be found in books on statistical methods.

To use the chart, first decide what level of measurement your study is using to select the appropriate column on the chart. Then decide which type of design best describes your study to select the appropriate row. The tests listed in the appropriate "Form of Data" section can be used in your situation. Remember that any test that is appropriate at one level of measurement (nominal, for example) is also acceptable at a higher level of measurement (ordinal, for instance), although it might not be as powerful. Thus, you can legally use any test in the section that you chose or in any section to the left of it.

For example, in the example of the social desirability bias found in a survey of dental hygiene, Gordon (1987) decided that his study used equal interval data and a design with two independent samples. Of the tests in that section, he chose the Student's *t*-test for independent samples, which is probably one of the most common statistical tests used by behavioral scientists. If he had decided his measurements were ordinal level, he could have used a nonparametric test, such as the Mann–Whitney U test.

Reporting Results of Statistical Tests

When reading a report that gives statistical results, or when writing one, it is important to know how these results are reported. Most behavioral

Table 10-3 Test Selection Chart[a]

Form of Data	Level of Measurement		
	Nominal	Ordinal	Equal Interval
One sample (compare with standard)	Binomial* Chi-square goodness-of-fit test*	Kolmogorov–Smirnov	*t-test for single mean* Z text
Two independent samples	Chi-square test of association* Fisher exact test	Mann-Whitney U test Wald-Wolfowitz runs test Median test	*t-test for independent samples* Randomization test
Two related samples	Binomial test Chi-square test of association*	Wilcoxon signed-ranks test Sign test	*t-test for matched samples* Walsh test Randomization test
More than two independent samples	Chi-square test of association*	Kruskal-Wallis Median test	*Analysis of variance*
More than two related samples	Cochran Q test	Friedman test	*Analysis of variance*
Correlation coefficients (descriptive statistics)	Contingency coefficient Cramer's statistic	Spearman rho* Kendall tau Kendall coefficient of concordance	*Pearson product–moment correlation*

[a] Tests marked with an asterisk are described in this book; Tests shown in italics are parametric.

scientists use a set format, which makes it easier for people to read and understand the reports, provided they know the format.

Ideally, the results of the experiment are given in English first, stating clearly in words what the study showed. (See the next chapter on report writing.) However, some writers tend to give the statistics first and only later tell you in words what they mean. Either way, at some point the writer will say that the difference was (or was not) reliable, perhaps mentioning the statistical test by name, and then will give a string of symbols, often in parentheses. These symbols tell the knowledgeable reader what test was performed, what value was calculated for the test statistic, any other information needed to evaluate that result, and the probability that the result could have happened by chance. For instance, in the study on the dental hygiene survey (Gordon, 1987), the relevant statistical result says:

$$t(46) = 1.92, p < .03$$

The first part of the string, $t(46)$, identifies the test and gives whatever information is needed to evaluate its result. In the study by Gordon, the t identifies the Student's t-test (described in Appendix C) and gives a number called the **degrees of freedom**. Many statistical tests have degrees of freedom, which are related to the number of independent observations in the study and are needed to look up the result in a table and evaluate what it means. (Part of the procedure for calculating a particular test statistic will be the procedure for calculating the corresponding degrees of freedom.) Earlier in this chapter, we noted that results taken from larger samples are more reliable than those taken from smaller samples. The degrees of freedom is one way in which certain statistical tests take this into account.

The second part of the string, $= 1.92$, gives the value that was calculated for the test statistic. In our example, Gordon performed the steps necessary to calculate a value for t, probably with a computer, and the answer he got was 1.92.

The third part of the string, $p < .03$, tells about the value of p, the probability of getting a result like this by chance. In this case the probability is less than 3 percent, so Gordon concluded that the result was not likely to be a fluke, but was reliable. Had the probability been excessively high, Gordon would have reported something like "$p > .05$," and would have concluded that the result was not reliable.

Knowing a little about what inferential statistics are for, how they work, and what they tell us, can improve your ability to evaluate the research reported by others. Of course, you would need more expertise than this book can give before you can analyze your own research results. The best way to get this expertise is to take a course (or two) in statistics. Barring that, you can consult with someone who has the expertise you need, and this chapter gives you enough information to talk intelligently with your expert, providing the necessary information, and asking the right questions. If you should have to conduct some very simple statistical analyses without the benefit of such expertise—for instance, in doing research for this course—you can consult Appendix C for a few basic procedures you might use. You will need to use inferential statistics any time you want to make a scientific decision that is more meaningful than "I don't know, it looks pretty good to me. What do you think?"

━━━━━━━━━━━━━━ SUMMARY ━━━━━━━━━━━━━━

A. Inferential statistics are statistics that are used to help researchers make decisions about the results they obtain in their research, through mathematical computations of how likely it is
   that the results are due to random chance.
   1. Statistical reliability (or statistical significance) is a measure
      of the probability of a certain result occurring by chance. If a
      result is reliable, the probability of its being due to chance is
      small. The cutoff above which a result is *not* considered to be
      reliable varies from discipline to discipline but is often set at
      .05.
   2. Science never gives guarantees, so statistical decisions can be
      wrong. There are two basic types of error. Type I errors occur
      when a researcher decides that a result is reliable when in
      fact there is no systematic effect. The probability of making
      this error is called alpha, or *p*. Type II errors occur when a
      researcher decides that a result is not reliable when in fact
      there is a systematic effect. The probability of this error is
      called beta. In general, Type I errors are considered to be more
      serious than Type II errors, and it is the probability of these
      errors that is computed with statistical tests. All else being
      equal, increasing the probability of one type of error decreases
      the probability of the other type.
   3. When making a statistical inference, the researcher (a) deter-
      mines the experimental hypothesis (what will be observed if
      there is an effect), (b) reverses the experimental hypothesis to
      get the null hypothesis (what will be observed if there is no
      effect), (c) selects a significance level (the maximum value for
      alpha that will allow a decision of reliability), (d) selects and
      calculates a test statistic, giving *p*, the probability of a Type I
      error, and (e) compares the significance level with the actual
      probability, deciding that the result is reliable if p is less than
      alpha ($p < \alpha$).
B. There are many different kinds of statistical test. To select the one
   that is best for your situation, you must know several things
   about your research.
   1. At what level is the dependent variable measured? For in-
      stance, statistics that require adding or multiplying values
      can be performed only on variables measured at the equal
      interval level or higher.
   2. What sort of research design did you use? How many groups
      were there in your experiment, and were they related or
      independent? Are you testing a difference in means, frequen-
      cies or frequency distributions, or a correlation? Different

tests are needed to deal with these different situations.

3. Should you use parametric or nonparametric statistics? Parametric statistical tests make stricter mathematical assumptions about the data than nonparametric tests, which means that the former are sometimes not appropriate. However, parametric tests are more powerful. The researcher must decide which type of test is best in a particular research situation.

4. Having decided on the research design being used and the level of measurement, a test selection chart can help researchers find the appropriate tests to choose among.

C. In a research report, the results of statistical tests are reported in a fairly standard way. Usually, a string of symbols gives first the test that was used and any information needed to evaluate the test, such as the degrees of freedom. Then the value that was calculated for the test statistic is stated, and finally the corresponding value of p, the probability of a Type I error.

CHECKPOINT

Check your understanding of the material in this chapter:

- What are inferential statistics? How are they different from descriptive statistics? How are they the same?

- What probability is measured by inferential statistics?

- What is meant by "statistically reliable"? How does a researcher decide whether the results of a study are statistically reliable?

- What are the two types of error that can be made in statistical tests? Which is generally considered to be the more serious? When is the other type considered to be more serious?

- All else being equal, what effect will an increase in one type of error have on the other type of error? What factors can reduce both types of error?

- List the steps involved in statistical reasoning.

- What is an experimental hypothesis? What is a null hypothesis?

- What is a significance level? What is the other name for significance level, and why is it used? What is the most common choice for a significance level in the behavioral sciences? Why?

- Why is it important to know the level of measurement of the dependent variable when selecting a statistical test to use?

- List the assumptions that parametric tests make that nonparametric tests do not make.

────────────────── **EXERCISES** ──────────────────

10.1 Do you agree or disagree with the opinion that true equal interval measurements are extremely rare in the behavioral sciences? Why? Find out whether your instructor agrees or disagrees with the author's opinion, and why.

10.2 Imagine a research report that contained the following: "The two groups were reliably different ($t(23) = 2.31$, $p<.05$)." What exactly does this sentence mean?

10.3 Think of an example of a type of research you might conduct in your own area of interest. What sort of research design is it? In analyzing the results of this design, would you select parametric or nonparametric statistics? Why? Find the appropriate section on the test selection chart (Table 10-3). Which of the tests listed there would you choose? Why?

Chapter 11

The Research Report

Questions to Consider as You Read

- How is writing a research report different from other types of writing? How is it the same?

- What particular paper format is described in this chapter? How is it the same and different from the format that you will be required to use in your reports?

- What are the major sections of a research report? What comes before and what comes after the report itself?

- What is meant by the word "style" when applied to writing? Does your writing have "style"? Should it have?

- What is the most important goal to keep in mind when writing a research report? How can you achieve that goal?

- What makes it so difficult to judge your own writing? What techniques can help make it easier?

- What procedure do you usually use in writing papers? Do you think it works well? Do you think the procedure suggested in this chapter might have any advantages?

- Do you usually rewrite your reports before turning them in? Do you think you should?

- Do you have a good idea of how to go about rewriting a report? What, according to this chapter, is wrong with the way most student writers go about rewriting?

Almost any research that is worth doing would be worth knowing about to someone else. This is why research reports are written—to tell others about the research you did and what you found, so that they can benefit from your work. In this chapter we look at a classical form of the research report and learn how to write one.

While there are many standard forms for the research report, I will discuss only one of them, the format prescribed by the American Psychological Association (1983). I use it because it is fairly typical of forms used in the behavioral sciences and because it is the form I know best. If you are writing in a field other than psychology, you may have to modify this format somewhat to fit the expectations of your area.

It is one thing to know what a research report looks like, and another thing to know how to go about writing one. That is why this chapter is divided into two sections. The first section describes the structure of the report from beginning to end. The second section describes the process of creating a report. It is generally not best to begin at the beginning and write to the end; this section will explain why. Both sections refer to an example paper (given in Figure 11-5) that permits you to follow the development of a report from beginning to end.

Structure

Most published research reports must follow strict guidelines about structure. Journals require their authors to adhere to the guidelines because the people who read journal articles are very busy people; they do not have the time to read half the articles they would like to read, and they find it much easier and faster to read an article if they know before they begin how the piece is organized. Because anyone writing for publication must learn to follow the rules of format, most instructors require that their students also follow a set of strict guidelines for their term papers.

One requirement that applies to the entire paper is that *everything* must be double spaced. This enchances readability and allows editor's marks (or your instructor's comments) to fit between the lines.

Opening Material

Some components of a report appear at the beginning, before the report itself actually starts. They prepare the reader for the material that is to follow.

Title Page
The **title page** is a single page that contains the title of the report, about a third of the way down from the top, centered left to right. If the title needs more than one line, all the lines are centered. Underneath the title is the name of the author or authors, centered, and underneath that is the author's affiliation. (The affiliation is the organization that sponsored the research or the author while conducting the research. In a report for a class, this information is usually replaced with the name of the course, the name of the teacher, and the date.) In the upper right-hand corner is the **running head**, which is a short version of the title and appears on the top right of every page. The title page is page 1, numbered under the running head.

Abstract
The **abstract** is a brief summary of the report. Its purpose is to allow a busy scientist to decide quickly whether the entire article is worth reading. The abstract should tell why the research is important, giving as well the methods used in the research, a general description of the participants (college sophomores, white mice, nursing home residents, etc.), the main results that were found, and the conclusions drawn from the results. An abstract should generally be about 100 to 150 words, although this varies from area to area. The abstract page is numbered with a 2 in the upper right corner, again under the running head.

What You Did, and Why

The report itself begins with a description of just what research you performed, and why you performed it. By the time the reader finishes this part of the paper, it should be clear why you considered the research worth doing and exactly how you did it.

Introduction
Because the introduction is always the very first part of the report itself, it is not necessary to label it "Introduction." The page after the abstract page has the number 3 under the running head, the title of the paper centered at the top, and then the introduction.

The **introduction** explains why the research was worth doing and why you chose to do it in the way reported in the paper. It should begin with a description of the problem the research addresses and should tell why that problem is important, at least to you. It should also discuss any other related research and why yours is similar but different. Give the reasons for the decisions you made in conducting your research. The introduction leads the reader into your specific study, and often ends with a statement of your research hypothesis (see Chapter 10).

Finding "related research" is not always easy. Sometimes the idea for a research project comes from work done by others, which gives an automatic door into the research literature. At other times the idea comes from your own head. Either way, you will have to consult the library to find out what research has been done that is related to your own research or to the questions you are addressing.

If you have a related research article, begin there. It will have its own references, which will point you to research the author thought was related. Look those articles up and they will point you to others, and so on. This technique is very useful, but it goes only backward. Each article can point only toward articles that had been published before, not those that would come later.

To find more recent articles, there are two basic techniques. The first is to look up all the articles whose authors are referred to in the key articles you found. College libraries usually have a reference work called the *Social Sciences Citation Index*, which for any year gives a list of all the articles in a great many social science journals. All the papers that cited your target article in their reference lists will be found in this resource. A few of these articles might be related to your own research. It might take some time, however, to weed them out from all those that are not.

The other technique is a **bibliographic search**, which looks for all the articles that relate to a certain topic. Most disciplines publish indices, which list all the articles in a given period of time by subject. For instance, the *Social Sciences Index* covers the broad range of most social and behavioral sciences; *Criminal Justice Abstracts* covers criminal activity, police work, rehabilitation, and so on; *Education Index* covers teaching, learning, and evaluation; *Psychological Abstracts* covers psychological and behavioral research; and there are many others. You would have to look up all the key words that pertain to your subject, and then look up all the articles that are listed under those key words. Computers are increasingly used to make this search quicker and more thorough, as discussed in Appendix A.

Usually the indices give the abstracts of the articles to which they refer, so that you can decide from the description in the abstract whether the article is likely to be useful to you. This is yet another reason for the importance of including in your abstract all the information a researcher would need to determine what your study is about and what you discovered. Researchers doing bibliographic searches will be judging the value of your report from its abstract alone.

Actually, the techniques that can be used to find information in the scientific literature are much more subtle and complex than the basic ones I can cover in this section. To get more information, there are two very useful sources. One consists of books written just to help the student dig out the information needed for a report. For instance, Pierian Press publishes a series of Library Research Guides, including guides to education (Kennedy, 1979) and psychology (Douglas & Baum, 1984).

The other source is people. Your instructor, and other professors in your area of interest, will be able to give you hints on where and how to look. There is also the most fabulous, underused resource of all, reference librarians. These workers are specifically trained in how to get information out of the library, and they know just what they have and where to find it. Every reference librarian I have ever consulted has been friendly, helpful, and incredibly competent. The reference desk at your library can also provide you with lists of the indices and journals available, and probably also with pamphlets or other information on how to use the library.

It is important to justify any statement of fact you make in the introduction (and everywhere else in the paper, for that matter) with some sort of citation. Suppose you mention, for instance, that criminals of one race or ethnic background serve longer jail sentences than people from a different racial group convicted of similar crimes. You would have to have some justification for claiming that the offender's race is related to the length of sentence served, giving the reader all the information necessary to locate the exact publication you used to confirm your claim. This is done in two stages. First, in the text itself, you put the **citation**, giving the author and the date of the publication. Second, in the reference list at the end of the report (described later), you put the complete **reference**, with the information the reader would need to find your source.

The sample paper in Figure 11-5, below, gives examples of a few of the most common types of citations and references. Also, this is the format used for references in this book. However, for accuracy you should consult a guide that explains how to cite references of all different sorts. For the APA format described here, the guide to use is the *Publication Manual* put out by the American Psychological Association (1983).

Method
The **method** section describes in some detail exactly how the research was conducted. It is not necessary to begin the section on a new sheet of paper, but put the heading "Method" in the center of the page. This section should give the reader enough information to be able to conduct essentially the same experiment, or to evaluate how well it was done. If there is information that a researcher might need to repeat the research (for instance, a copy of the questionnaire you used), but most readers will not want, you can put it in an appendix at the end of your paper as described later.

The method section is divided into several subsections, some required and some optional. You should include whatever subsections you think will make the overall method section clearest to the reader, making them up if you need to. If, for instance, you used a fairly complex scoring scheme to convert respondents' answers on a questionnaire into measurements, you might want to include a subsection on scoring. Each subsection is identified by a label typed at the left-hand margin and underlined.

The **subjects** subsection, which is required, describes who participated in your experiment. If your participants are people, give their ages and sexes, and information about how they were selected. For instance, you may describe them as "college students between the ages of 18 and 24, equally divided between the sexes, who were participating to fulfill a course requirement." Be careful not to describe the participants as "randomly selected" unless you actually used a random sampling technique such as those described in Chapter 5. If you stood around in the student lounge and asked anyone who looked approachable, this is *not* random selection. You would instead say something like "The students were approached while passing through the student lounge." If your participants were animals, describe the species, strain, sex, age, and weight, and how the animals were housed and treated. As a general rule, describe anything about your participants you think a thoughtful reader or a researcher who wishes to repeat your experiment would like to know.

Also required is the **procedure** subsection, which gives the details of exactly how you conducted your study. Include information about the instructions given to the participants, the materials used, the choices the participants had to make, and how the participants responded. This section should contain enough information to allow the reader to recreate your experiment without having to ask you any additional questions.

Sometimes research reports include a subsection on **materials** or **apparatus**, describing particular equipment that was used in the study. It is not necessary to include this subsection if everything you used was commonplace and easily described in one of the other sections, but if your equipment was more complex, it might help the reader to put it in a separate subsection. Do not describe absolutely everything; there is no need to list pencils, paper clips, staplers, and so on. If you used manufactured or published materials, give the manufacturer's name and model number or the publisher's name and the title of the item (for an intelligence test, for instance). If you built or otherwise created your own materials, describe them well enough for the reader to be able to recreate them essentially the same; illustrations may be helpful. Again, do not go overboard on the detail. It is unnecessary to describe the exact appearance of the form you used to record the data in a phone survey as long as you describe the information that you recorded on that form.

The **design** subsection, also optional, describes the research design used in the study. This subsection is often required by instructors for research students, because it forces the student to be clear about just what research design is being used. This section is probably pretty short, simply specifying that the design used—for instance, three independent groups with participants assigned randomly—and giving the procedures used to assign participants to groups. Be sure to describe the techniques used to control for contamination, such as counterbalancing or control groups (see Chapter 7). Also describe both the independent and dependent variables, giving the method of controlling the independent variable and the operational definition of the dependent variable (see Chapter 4).

What You Found and What It Means

Now is the time to explain what you learned. This material is traditionally divided into two separate sections, but sometimes, particularly with short, simple studies, these two sections are combined into one section, called Results and Discussion.

Results

The **results** section gives the facts about what occurred in your study. It describes the results in words ("Group A scored higher than group B"), in numbers ("The mean for group A was 37.12, while the mean for group B was 25.39"), and in statistics ["This difference was reliable (t (34) = 2.36, $p <. 05$)"]. (See Chapter 10 for a discussion of how to report statistical results.) In a simple study, the Results section might be very short, simply giving the three statements as shown above. In more complex research, the scores of the various groups are often given in tables or graphs or both, making it easier for the reader to see the relationships among the various scores. You should never suggest that two scores are different, or that one score is different from what you might expect, without reporting a statistical test to support this claim.

Discussion

The **discussion** section explains the meaning of the results just described by relating them back to the purpose of the experiment as described in the Introduction. Do not assume that the reader will automatically grasp their importance. The reader is not as tuned in to your research as you are, and is probably reading your report quickly. This is the place to acknowledge any problems that might exist about generalizing from your data and to suggest other research that might be done. End with a broad statement summing it all up, much the same sentence you might use at a party if a new acquaintance asked what you had learned from the experiment.

Closing Material

There are two kinds of material that follow the research report itself. One of these is mandatory, the other optional.

References

Most research reports will include a **reference list**, including all the published sources referred to in the report. This is the second half of the justification procedure mentioned in connection with the Introduction. In the text of the report, you refer to someone else's work (or your own previous work) with the author's name and the date. In the Reference section, these items are listed alphabetically by author, giving the full publication information, so that the interested reader can go back to the original source. A reference list differs from a bibliography in that a bibliography lists many items that might be of interest to the reader, regardless of whether they are mentioned in the report itself, while a reference list gives *only* items that were actually cited in the text. Every item mentioned must be listed, and every item listed must be mentioned. Items that are mentioned more than once in the report appear only once in the reference list.

Most of the people for whom you will be writing reports will have fairly strict rules on just how references should be given. For instance, in the APA format used in this book (American Psychological Association, 1983), there must be parentheses around the date, followed by a period, and so on. Carelessness with references might mean that an interested reader will be unable to look up a related article because some of the necessary information is missing.

Appendices

In general, an appendix is an attachment to something, not really necessary but perhaps helpful. In a research report, an **appendix** contains information that some readers might find useful but most readers would not need; this material would make the report needlessly long and cluttered if it were included in the main text. For instance, if you have designed your own questionnaire for a piece of research, you may choose to append a copy of the questionnaire itself. This way, readers who wish to repeat your study can use the same questionnaire you used, but those who are interested only in your results do not have to read the whole thing. It is important to remember that reading an appendix should not be necessary to comprehend the report. You should include a brief description of the questionnaire, with perhaps a few sample questions, in the report itself. Then mention, perhaps in parentheses, that a copy of the full questionnaire appears in the Appendix.

If you have only one appendix, it is simply called the Appendix. If you have more than one, they get letters: Appendix A, Appendix B, and so on. Every appendix you have should be mentioned at least once in the text. (When there is more than one appendix, you can use the plural form appendixes or appendices, whichever you prefer.)

Writing Techniques

There is no such thing as the one right way to go about writing a report. You will be judged on your finished product, not on how you got there. If you have a method that works well for you, stick with it. However, if you find the idea of writing a report like this worrisome, perhaps some of the suggestions in this section can make it a little easier.

Style

Many people think of "style" in terms of big words and fancy phrases, drawing on poetic metaphors. This is one sort of style, to be sure, but it is not the style used in research reports. **Style** refers to all the decisions any writer must make about what words to choose, how to build sentences, and how to assemble sentences to make a point. Because this must be done any time anyone writes anything, every piece of writing has some sort of style. The purpose of this section is to help you make these decisions so that your report has a style that is appropriate for a research report.

The major goal of any research report is to be clear. This is so important that I will say it again; THE MAJOR GOAL OF ANY RESEARCH REPORT IS CLARITY. It is not always obvious how to accomplish this, however, because you are not the reader of your report. You already know a great deal about what you did, why you did it, and what happened. This means that parts of your report may be perfectly clear to you whereas someone else might not be able to figure out what is happening. You will have to work hard to minimize this problem, and this section gives you some ideas.

Sentence Construction

Students sometimes have the idea that long sentences are better than short ones. This is not true. You should, however, vary the length of your sentences, putting long ones, medium ones, and short ones together in a pleasing mixture. In fact, when clarity is the major goal (and it is, remember), short sentences are often better than long ones. If a sentence is very long, as this one is, the reader may have a hard time, particularly if you try to make too many points all at once or the points are not well related, without sufficient sign points to guide understanding along the way, trying to understand just what you are saying. If you cannot break up long sentences, put in plenty of connecting words to show the reader how all the parts are related. If a sentence begins with "Some researchers believe. . ." and later goes on "while other researchers believe. . .," the reader will know how the parts of the sentence go together.

An important way to shorten sentences is to get rid of unnecessary words. It is amazing how many common words and phrases have become "built in" for many of us and come out regardless of whether they are needed, particularly when the writer is trying to be formal or impressive. For instance, the following sentence appeared in a report submitted in my course: "By obtaining the data and analyzing it [sic] we were able to see that there was a difference between the two groups." The only information in this sentence is that the groups are different; the first 13 words are completely unnecessary. Is there any way to find results other than by obtaining data and looking at them? (As an aside, there is a grammatical error in this sentence. The word "data" is a plural noun, just like "books." Therefore when you analyze data, you are not analyzing *it*, you are analyzing *them*.)

There is another myth among some students that you should never make any parts of any sentence similar to any other parts of any other sentences, or else you will be judged repetitive and boring. There is a grain of truth in this myth, because some structures should not be repeated too often. It looks awkward, for instance, to begin three or four sentences in a row with "However." However, under one condition it is not only all right to repeat a structure, it is practically mandatory.

Many times in scientific writing you want to compare and contrast two different things in one sentence. You want to show how the reactions of group A differ from those of group B, or you want to illustrate the similarities of two different theories. Whenever you write a sentence with two separate but equal parts, with the goal of having the reader compare the two parts, you should use parallel construction. In **parallel construction**, the parts of the two ideas that are the same are expressed in exactly the same words and the same structures, so that the halves of the sentence differ only with respect to the things that are really different between the two ideas. For instance, suppose you read this sentence in the Results section of a report: "The subjects in group A were moved by the documentary, as indicated by the number of tissues they used during the watching, but the ones who did not meet the little girl ahead of time used fewer of the tissues, thus showing less emotionality." You can probably figure out the point the writer is trying to make, but it takes energy, imagination, and perhaps more than one reading. On the other hand, the same idea could be expressed in this way; "Participants exposed to the little girl ahead of time used many tissues during the documentary, indicating a strong emotional response, while participants not exposed to the little girl used fewer tissues, indicating a weaker emotional response." This is, you must agree, a lot clearer. Factors that are constant between the two ideas (use of tissues, exposure to the little girl, emotional response) are expressed in exactly the same words in the same order in both halves of the sentence, so that only factors that are really different (*whether* they were exposed, *number* of tissues used, and the *strength* of the emotional response) are changed. This makes it easy for the reader to tell what is the same and what is different, which makes the text clearer.

There is a controversial area of style that might be important to students. Many people, not just students, believe that a good scientific report must be impersonal and formal. To a certain extent this is true. You do not want a scientific report to read like a letter to a friend at camp. However, in some circles the requirements for impersonality and formality are weakening. It is becoming acceptable for writers of research reports to use first-person pronouns, referring to themselves as "I" or "us" occasionally. In describing part of an experiment, writers used to wonder whether to say something distant and formal, such as "The researchers performed an analysis. . .," or to use a passive sentence construction, such as "An analysis was performed. . . ." There is nothing inherently wrong with either of these choices, but when used over and over and over again, they produce a report that is almost sure to put the reader to sleep. Other choices, such as saying "We analyzed. . ." or even "I analyzed. . ." used to be simply forbidden. Today, however, you can use phrases like these where appropriate, making your reports much less dull. Be careful in applying this advice, however, because many instructors and journal editors strongly disagree with my notion that such change is an improvement and may judge your work to be too casual if you apply it. (At least one reviewer of this book complained that the use of first-person pronouns made it too informal for a college textbook.) When in doubt, ask how formal you should be.

Terminology

When choosing words, as when making any other style decision, remember that your major goal is to be clear. Always choose the words that will make your meaning crystal clear to the reader.

One area in which many writers lose clarity is the use of jargon. Technical jargon exists for a perfectly good reason. When communicating with other people in the same field of work, jargon can allow the speaker or writer to convey a lot of information very quickly. However, you must realize that the audience for your paper probably goes beyond the people in your precise area of interest. Other people might be very interested in your work, if only they could figure out what you were saying.

For instance, when teaching about research methods I had students from a variety of areas of behavioral science. Sometimes they forgot they were writing for someone outside their field. I had a nursing student repeatedly use the term "t_x" in a paper without telling me it was short for "treatment." I had a criminal justice student write an entire paper about "recidivism" without once defining the term as the probability of convicted criminals to be convicted later for another crime. An economics student mentioned that the participants in a study were trying to maximize their "penetration," and all I could think of were sexual meanings until I finally asked the student, and learned that the term was short for "market penetration" or "market share."

There are two ways of dealing with jargon. If a term really does allow you to convey a lot of important information quickly and clearly, you probably will want to use it. Remember, however, to define it clearly the very first time you use it, and to redefine it later in the paper if there is a chance your reader might have forgotten. This rule probably applies to a word like "recidivism." It saves a lot of space to say "The recidivism rate went down" instead of "Fewer criminals were convicted of other crimes after they had finished serving their terms for the first crime." As long as the term is well defined, it is probably appropriate to use it. However, abbreviations like "t_x" for "treatment" are probably never appropriate in a general research report. Saving seven letters each time a short form is used is not worth making your reader learn a new term. In general, abbreviations of any sort are suspect, unless they are terms the reader is likely already to be familiar with. Thus it is fine to write about NASA and the FBI, but even these abbreviations should be spelled out the first time. Spell out technical terms in your area each and every time they are used unless there is a very good reason for doing otherwise. I know it is more difficult to type American Psychological Association than to type APA, but, believe it or not, it is easier to read and comprehend the long form.

Another way to increase clarity is to give meaningful names to the groups or treatments in your study. Instead of group A, call it the Traditional group, or the High Anxiety group, or the Divorced group, or whatever makes sense in your project. This will save the reader from having to look back each time and figure out whether group A was exposed to the traditional method or the experimental method. And once you have chosen meaningful names, do not spoil the device by using abbreviations. Spell it out each time: High Anxiety versus Low Anxiety means a lot more than HA versus LA.

As a final note on terminology, you should know that it is no longer acceptable to use sexist language in a scientific report. The common usage of masculine pronouns (he, his, him) when the sex of the person is not known is not allowed, even if you say in a footnote that you intend the term to refer to women as well as men. Either use the awkward-looking "he or she" construction or, with a little more effort, avoid the issue by avoiding all sexist pronouns. Use the plural ("When the readers finished, they. . ."), but remember that "each," "everyone," and "anyone" are singular and cannot be used with plural pronouns (it is ungrammatical to say "Each reader signed their book."). Use nouns instead of pronouns ("The researcher gave the reader a pencil," not "The researcher gave him a pencil."). Even if your teacher tells you not to worry about this issue, you are going to have to worry about it sooner or later, and you might as well practice doing it right now.

Judging Your Writing

As the researcher, you have so much intimate knowledge of the study you are describing that it is difficult to keep in mind your readers' ignorance. Students are unfortunately familiar with a similar problem, namely teachers who know their material so well that they are unable to explain it in terms beginning students can understand. Just as a teacher has an obligation to make the material understandable to students, so you as a writer have an obligation to make your material understandable to readers.

There are three major techniques for getting a little closer to your readers' perspective. The simplest is to read the paper out loud, listening to yourself and pretending that you are reading it to a friend over the telephone. You will often discover sentences that do not make sense and paragraphs that have lost their meaning. For this trick to work, you must actually read the paper out loud and listen to it; reading it silently to yourself will not work. For this reason, it is not recommended that you try this technique when other people are around.

Another trick that is very useful is the "two-week technique." After you have made the paper as good as you can, put it in a drawer and try not even to think about it for at least two weeks. Whatever was in your head when you wrote the piece is still in your head immediately after, and provides a context your reader will not have. Two weeks later some of that context may have faded, putting you somewhat closer to the reader's state of mind. You will often find that things that were perfectly clear when you wrote them are rather muddy two weeks later.

Finally, the most useful way to find out how a reader reacts to your writing is to get someone to read it and react to it. This reader must not be someone who is as familiar with your work as you are; it will be less helpful to draft your coresearcher for this job than to get your roommate's best friend to do it. Your reader should be fairly intelligent, not too familiar with your work or the field itself, and willing to spend the time and effort to read the paper and talk to you about it. In return, you must *promise* to listen carefully and respectfully to what the reader says. Do not try to defend your paper. If a reader finds a certain paragraph to be unclear, then *by definition* that paragraph is unclear. You may disagree with the reader on how to fix the problem, but you must agree that there is one.

The best way to judge your writing before submitting it to the judgments of others is to apply all these methods, preferably more than once. In writing this book, for instance, I have read many questionable passages out loud (fortunately I work at home, so this bothers no one). After I had finished a chapter, it was read by several anonymous reviewers who sent me comments and suggestions. Then, having finished the entire first draft, I used the reviewers' comments to rewrite the entire thing after nearly a year had passed. Even after three drafts, the editors at Wiley found a great many passages that were confusing, wordy, or downright wrong. And I am sure that there are problems remaining despite their eagle-eyed attention. The moral of this is that a report can benefit from as many readers as you can get. Of course, it all took time. Students frequently find themselves caught by deadlines, and these methods will not work very well if the first draft of a paper due at 4:00 goes into the typewriter at noon (as in Figure 11-1). You might as well resign yourself to the fact that good quality writing takes more time than is needed just to type the words. If you want good judgments from others, you must allow the time for competent judging yourself beforehand.

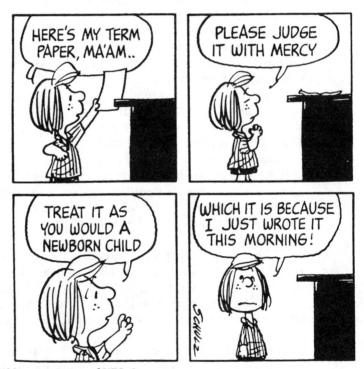

Reprinted by permission of UFS, Inc.

Figure 11-1 Peppermint Patty is right. A newly written report in a teacher's hands has about as much chance as a newborn child in a jungle.

The Writing Process

There are probably as many good ways to write a report as there are writers. However, if you think your method could use improvement, you could do worse than to try the method that works for me and for many other writers.

There are four major steps to this process. It may seem like a lot when you read through it all; it probably sounds much simpler just to roll the paper into the typewriter and begin with the title page. However, by breaking the process into smaller bites, the job actually gets easier to do.

As an overall note before you begin, a good scientific report has what has been described as an hourglass shape, broad at the top and bottom and narrow in the middle (see Figure 11-2). Your report begins by addressing something meaningful in the world at large; this is the broad part at the top. It gradually focuses down on the actual study you did and what you found; this is the narrow part in the middle. Then it relates those findings back to the real-world issue you began with; this is the broad part at the end. You will find this hourglass metaphor cropping up again in the discussion that follows.

Notes

Start by writing down everything you want to say in your report. Do not worry about the terms you use; do not try to make complete sentences or to put things in order. It is unimportant how the ideas are expressed

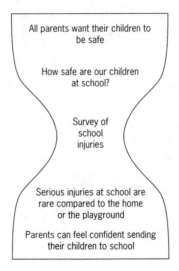

Figure 11-2 A good scientific report has an hourglass shape, broad at the top and bottom and narrow in the middle.

as long as you understand what the notes mean. Some of the notes for our sample paper appear in Figure 11-3.

You might begin by writing down in the fewest possible words just what your study showed. If it had more than one result, write each one down, numbered in order of importance. Make sure that result number one is the one thing you would like your reader to get out of your study. If an acquaintance at a party asked you what you learned from your research, this should be the best answer you can think of to give. Please note that this question is *not* about what you thought you would learn from your research, but what you actually learned. If you were looking for one effect but found something different that was more interesting, forget about your original idea and focus on the interesting finding.

Next, ask yourself what this result means to the real world. Could this result make a difference to any human being besides yourself? Write down all the ways in which your result could satisfy people's curiosity about some aspect of human nature or relate to a problem in the real world, and indicate which you think are most important.

Next, list all the research you know of that relates in any way to your study or the topic your study is about. You may not include all this work

Notes for Paper

Main Question: Are children born to the same parents more likely to have birthdays close together in the year than you'd expect by chance?
Main result: Yes—Brothers and sisters tend to have birthdays closer together than you would expect by chance. Not of major world significance, maybe, but interesting.
Why do I find it interesting? My 2 kids, birthdays 8 days apart
Related research:Couldn't find any!!!
    Closest I come: Ball & Arnaz, on family size; Marx & Marx, on birth order; Commission on Babies, on seasonal fertility.
Participants: Chosen at random from phone book. So population is people w/ listed phone #s in Orange County, NY. Give random sampling technique
Called on phone, asked 3 questions:
  1. Can I ask you some quick questions?
  2. How many children of same parents in your household? (If <2, end interview.)
  3. Give birthdays of oldest and 2nd oldest child.
Continued until I had 20 usable answers.
Analysis: Compute # days between birthdays. Score as "short" if <= 91 days (1/4 year), score as "long" if > 91 days
Research hypothesis: Will have more "short" delays than "long" ones.
Null hypothesis: Will have equal "short" and "long" delays.
Statistical test: Binomial, small sample (see App. B)
Result: Out of 20 families, 16 had children < 91 days apart
    Table C-4 says this is reliable (p<.05)

Figure 11-3 What the first notes for a fictional research paper might look like.

in your paper, but it is easier to take things off the list later than to insert items you omit at this stage. It might be helpful to draw lines connecting each piece of existing research with the other topics in your notes that it relates to.

List all the aspects of conducting the experiment that an interested reader would want to know. Who participated? How were they chosen? What did you do to them, and how did they react? What materials did you use? You will exercise judgment later about how much of this information will actually go into the paper. For now, when in doubt write it down.

Go back through your list to make sure that it includes everything you want to say in your paper. If you think of anything else, add it now.

Organization

The next step is to organize all your information so that it flows logically from one topic to the next. This will produce the organized plan that you follow when you actually write the report.

Take four sheets of paper and label each with the name of one of the major sections of a research report: Introduction, Method, Results, Discussion. Go through your notes, and copy each item onto the page where it makes the most sense. For instance, the statement about how your participants were chosen probably goes into the Method section, so you would copy it onto the Method page. Some items will belong in more than one section. In particular, the major statement about the meaning of your research for the real world should go into both the Introduction and the Discussion. This statement is the broadest part of your hourglass-shaped report, the top and the bottom.

When everything from your notes is copied onto the pages, you must organize the material. (You still are not worried about phrasing or terminology. Just get the ideas down in the order you want them to appear.) You can use the back of the sheets or separate sheets with the same major section headings. On the Introduction sheet, put the major statement about the real-world application of the research first. Then put the related topics in order of importance, each one followed by its reference to previous work. There should be a logical progression from the broad statement through gradually more specific statements until you get to something very close to your own research. You might have to rearrange the topics several times before you have an order that makes sense. At this point you may discover a gap in your reasoning—perhaps there is a leap from one topic to another, and you have no information to fill in that logical gap. In that case, go back to the previous research to find work that relates to the topic in the gap, so that your logical progression can continue.

When your Introduction sheet indicates a smooth path from the broad topic in the real world to the specific research in your report, move on the Method sheet. There you will organize the information into subsections, as described earlier in this chapter. Some of the information will be under Participants (or Subjects), some under Procedure, and so on. You may have to shuffle the information around a good deal until the sheet is organized to include all the relevant information in a sensible group of subsections. Remember that you can add or subtract subsections (except for the two mandatory ones, Subjects and Procedure) to make this section as a whole clear to the reader. You may decide that some of the information belongs in the report but not in the text itself, because most readers will not want that much detail. If that is the case, move it off to a new sheet called Appendix.

Once you have clarified the way the study was performed, move on to the Results sheet. The very first item on the sheet should be the statement about the most important thing to be learned from the research. Double-check to make sure that you have made it clear how this relates to the first statement on the Introduction sheet about what the research means in the real world. After giving the result, describe how you know it, giving the actual numbers or patterns of behavior that lead to that conclusion, and the related statistical test. For instance, if your major result was "Men showed more emotion than women," the justification might be that "Men cried 3.2 mL of tears while women cried only 1.9 mL," and the test might be "$t(41) = 2.32$, $p < .05$." Repeat this procedure for each of the other things you learned from your study, if there is more than one. The results should be given in some sort of logical order, perhaps from most important to least important.

Now that you have covered what your study showed, the Discussion sheet will allow you to relate it back to the real-world issue you discussed in the beginning. In many respects, the Discussion section is a mirror of the Introduction section, beginning with the points closest to the research, with which the Introduction ended, and finishing with the broadest statements of meaning that opened the Introduction. There are two major differences between the Introduction and the Discussion. First, the Discussion is often shorter, because you can move more quickly through the logical progression from experiment to real world the second time. Second, the Introduction will present the real-world issues as problems to be solved, while the Discussion will present them as problems addressed by the result of the study. The Discussion section may include material that was not in the Introduction, such as a mention of where research might go from here. However, even this sort of thing is often usefully addressed in some fashion in the Introduction. (Note that there is absolutely no rule saying that a scientific report must end with a sentence about how "further research is needed to address the many unanswered questions in this area." Of *course* further research is needed. Further research will *always* be needed. No single piece of research has ever answered all the questions there are about any topic whatsoever, so why restate the obvious?) Some of the organized notes for our sample paper appear in Figure 11-4.

ORGANIZED NOTES

INTRODUCTION:
Why do I find it interesting? My 2 kids, birthdays 8 days apart
Main Question: Are children born to the same parents more likely to
    have birthdays close together in the year than you'd expect by chance?
Not of major world significance, maybe, but interesting.
Related research: Couldn't find any!!!
    Closest I come: Ball & Arnaz, on family size; Marx & Marx, on birth
    order; Commission on Babies, on seaasonal fertility.

METHOD
Participants: Chosen at random from phone book. So population is people
    w/ listed phone #s in Orange County, NY. Give random sampling
    technique
Procedure:
    1. Can I ask you some quick questions?
    2. How many children of same parents in your household? (If <2, end
       interview.)
    3. Give birthdays of oldest and 2nd oldest child.
Continued until I had 20 usuable answers.
Analysis: Compute # days between birthdays. Score as "short" if <= 91
    days (1/4 year), score as "long" if > 91 days
Research hypothesis: Will have more "short" delays than "long"
Null hypothesis: Will have equal "short" and "long" delays.

RESULTS
Main result: Brothers and sisters tend to have birthdays closer
    together in the year than you would expect by chance.
Result: Out of 20 families, 16 had children < 91 days apart
Statistical test: Binomial, small sample (see App. B)
    Table C-4 says this is reliable (p<.05)

DISCUSSION
Why might this be true? Intentional planning, or just "seasonal"
    fertility effects in families.

Figure 11-4 What the notes for the fictional paper might look like after they are organized.

Go back now and look again at the four or five sheets you have put together. Read through them in order. Do the points seem to flow from one to another in logical fashion? Does your outline say everything you need it to say? Is all the information the reader will want to know included, without a lot of material that will not interest the reader? If you have a patient friend available, read through the sheets in order to the friend. Feel free to reword or elaborate on every item on the sheets, but make notes of anything that you had to add or explain in detail in order for your friend to understand. Ask your friend to tell you if anything seems disconnected, illogical, meaningless, or confused, so you can fix it now by adding more items or by rearranging the items you have.

Draft
At last you are ready to begin writing. Now is the time to remember all the points of style discussed above. It will be easier now, though, than it would have been if you had tried to handle the writing and the organization all at the same time. A sample of a completed paper is given in Figure 11-5.

Birthdays in Bunches
1

Birthdays in Bunches

Chris Brown
Social Sciences 218-003
Fall, 1991

Birthdays in Bunches
2

Abstract

A representative sample of families with listed telephone numbers in Orange County, NY was polled to determine the birthdays of their two oldest children. The time between these two birthdays was computed to determine whether the birthdays were reliably closer together in the year than would be expected if the birthdays were distributed randomly. Two possible reasons why they might be are the deliberate scheduling of pregnancies to cluster the children's birthdays, and unplanned seasonal fluctuations in couples' fertility.

Figure 11-5 A sample research paper describing a fictional piece of research. Beware: there are ways in which this paper needs improvement.

Birthdays in Bunches

My children's birthdays are just eight days apart. When I mention this to others, they always tell me of a family they know with children whose birthdays are also very close together. Is this a common phenomenon, or simply a series of coincidences that get told and retold?

The scientific literature is silent on this issue. There are many studies on factors governing family size (see Ball & Arnaz, 1987, for a review) and of the effect birth order can have on children (review in Marx & Marx, 1979). One study (US Commission on Babies, 1982) reports seasonal fluctuations in the number of children born around the nation, with more born in winter and early spring, but this study did not examine the relationship between the birthdays of children in one family. The goal of the present study was to determine whether such a relationship does exist.

Method

Participants

A representative sample was selected of 20 families in Orange County, NY who have telephone numbers listed in the telephone directory and who have more than one child of the same parents (see Appendix for random selection technique).

Figure 11-5, continued

Begin with the Introduction. The first sentence you write is important, and you may need to spend a good deal of time on it. This sentence will focus on the broad issue your study addresses, as given in the first item on your Introduction sheet. It should be a sentence about people or about a problem or a phenomenon in the real world, not a sentence about researchers or experiments. That is, you want to avoid beginning with

Birthdays in Bunches

4

Procedure

These families were called and asked to provide the birthdays of their two oldest children. The number of days between these two birthdays was computed, using a calculator programmed to automatically convert a date into the number of its day in the year (so that January 1 is day 1, February 1 is day 32, December 31 is Day 365, and so on), and then finding the difference between these two numbers. February 29 was treated the same as February 28 in this analysis.

Because the smaller number was always subtracted from the larger one, it is impossible to get a difference larger than half a year (182.5 days). If the differences were evenly distributed, the expected mean difference would be a quarter-year, or 91.25 days. The computed differences were divided into two categories: Category A contained short delays (≤91 days), while Category B contained long delays (>91 days). The number of differences in each of these categories was computed.

Results

Of the 20 families polled, 16 (80%) fell into Category A. This percentage is reliably different from chance (50%) by a binomial test (p=q=.50, N=20 r=4, p<.05).

Discussion

It seems that families, at least those in Orange County, NY, are likely to have children whose birthdays are closer together

Figure 11-5, continued

something about "Smith and Wesson (1972) claimed that their interstomal dissection procedure reverses the autokinetic effect, but Remington (1976) disagreed." This might be of interest to the few other experts in this area, but hardly to anyone else. It would be better to begin by saying something like "Most people, most of the time, are law-abiding citizens. What factors make some people, some of the time, break laws and injure other people or

Birthdays in Bunches

5

than we would expect by chance. Why might this be? There are two kinds of reasons one could imagine.

First, there are deliberate plans on the part of the parents. Perhaps they want their children to be able to share birthday parties. Perhaps they would like their children to have their birthdays near holidays, when grandparents visit, or in the summer, when they can have their parties outside. Any of these factors might cause the results we have seen.

Second, there are accidental factors that could cause couples to be more fertile at one time of year than another. Illnesses such as Seasonal Affective Disorders (SAD), in which the individual is severely depressed at one time of year, could easily affect that person's fertility in a particular season. In the far north there might be little else a couple can do together in the winter but conceive a child; in warmer climates, it might be too hot in the summer to get together. One can imagine a couple who, every few years, celebrates their anniversary with a new honeymoon, and nine months later has a child. These factors don't represent deliberate decisions the couple has made, but would nevertheless cause the sort of effect seen in this survey.

Either way, I am now prepared for when I mention my children's birthdays to a stranger, who says, "You know, that really happens a lot." Now I will be able to say, "Yes, I know."

Figure 11-5, continued

property?" This is a lead almost anyone would find interesting.

Then you begin working your way through the ideas on your Introduction sheet, leading the reader from this broad idea to the specific research you have done to address some small part of that important problem. Mostly, you will be converting the rough ideas listed on the sheet into clear, grammatical, well-constructed sentences.

Birthdays in Bunches

6

References

Ball, L. & Arnaz, D. (1987). How many is enough? Family sizes in the US. Family Journal, 22, 143-162.

Marx, G. & Marx, H. (1979). The effects of birth order on intellect and personality. NY: Book Publishing, Inc.

Birthdays in Bunches

7

Appendix

Random Selection Technique

    The following 3-step process was used to select the participants for this study.

    Step 1: A table of random numbers was consulted to select 300 sets of three random numbers each: one between 29 and 363, representing the white pages in the Orange County, NY telephone directory; one between 1 and 4, representing the columns on each page; and one between 1 and 110, representing the number of lines in each column. Each set of numbers specified a telephone number by giving its page, column, and line in the telephone book.

    Step 2: A number was discarded if it was clearly a business, or if it was the same number as one previously selected. After discards, there were 263 usable telephone numbers.

    Step 3: The numbers were called in groups of 20, with the groups scattered throughout the day. Numbers that didn't answer in the morning were called back in the evening, and so on, to catch people at home. Numbers where the person who answered refused to answer the questions, or where the family did not have more than one child, were removed from the list. This process was continued until 20 usable responses were collected.

Figure 11-5, continued

The same procedure applies to the Method section. Using the organized notes on your Method sheet, convert the ideas into sentences, keeping the logical arrangement of information into subsections. One useful trick for writing the Procedure subsection is to think of the study from the point of view of a participant. There is a tendency for researchers to describe what *they* went through, beginning with the hardest methodological problems they had to solve, but this is not usually the best way for the reader to understand the study as a whole. Describe, instead, what a participant in one group experienced, in order. Then, once the reader has a pretty clear idea what your study is like, you can explain the differences for people in different groups.

When writing the Results section, you follow essentially the same procedure, converting all the ideas on your Results sheet into well-constructed sentences. However, there is one additional rule that is very important in writing an understandable Results section. You will have to describe each of the results in three ways: a statement in English of what the result is, a description of the facts that led to that conclusion, and (most of the time) the result of a statistical test backing up that conclusion. The three descriptions should occur in just that order, with the English statement first, the numbers second, and the statistics third. For example, you will want to say something like "Autistic children demonstrated greater powers of concentration in the building task than normal children [this is the English statement of the result], scoring 7.8 out of a possible 10 on the task when the normal children scored 6.2 [this is the statement of the facts supporting the result] $(U(10,10) = 22, p < .05)$ [this is the statistical test that confirms the result]."

Finally, the Discussion section will be made up of sentences constructed from ideas on your Discussion sheet. The major difference in writing the Discussion and the Introduction sections is that the Discussion will present your study as a way of addressing the problems that were raised in the Introduction. It will lead to a broad statement of general interest, answering the broad question that began your Introduction.

After you have written the report proper, you must also write the accompanying opening and closing material. Even though the abstract comes before the result itself, you should write it afterward. Otherwise you may find that important information is omitted from the report proper because it had already been written in the abstract. The reader should *not* have to read the abstract to get the full value of the report. Conversely, people who write the abstract first sometimes do not want to "give away" interesting or critical information. I have read abstracts that left out, for instance, the major result. Writing the abstract after the report makes it easier to remember that it is a summary of the report, not an introduction to it.

Next, write the Reference section. Go through your report carefully, marking every published source of information that is mentioned.

Arrange these citations in alphabetical order by author, with multiple entries from the same author organized by publication date. Then write the complete reference for each source, using the format required in your particular field. Make sure that *every* published source cited in your text appears in the Reference list and that *every* item on the list is referred to somewhere in the text. If you have any information you had set aside for an appendix (or appendices), write it now.

I have not yet mentioned the thing your reader will see first: the title of your report. There is a trend toward of two-part titles in published research reports. One of the parts (either the first or second part) describes the major topic of the study, while the other part indicates something about its purpose or its conclusions. For instance, in my collection of literature I find titles such as "Briefing the Court: Dialectic as Methodological Perspective" (Bannan, 1984); "Right Brain, Left Brain: Fact and Fiction" (Levy, 1985), and *Conversations at Random: Survey Research as Interviewers See It* (Converse & Schuman, 1974). Be sure your title indicates why the report is interesting. For instance, remember the study by Gordon (1987) mentioned in the Chapter 10? He used a survey of dental hygiene habits as a way of demonstrating the social desirability bias. Gordon intended to use the survey of toothbrushing only as a handy way to make the point he wanted to make. He could as easily have used a survey of charitable giving or voting or any other socially desirable behavior. Therefore the title of his report does not even mention dental hygiene, but instead cites the actual subject as the focus of his report: "Social Desirability Bias: A Demonstration and Technique for Its Reduction."

This completes the report. But it does not complete your work, because this is not the best report you could write.

Rewrite

Students know that instructors want them to rewrite their papers, but most students do not know very much about how they are expected to rewrite what they have already written. Nancy Sommers (1980), who has done extensive research on the revision strategies of college students and of experienced writers, has found very interesting differences from which new writers can easily profit. Students rewriting reports typically looked at the individual words and perhaps the phrases they used, trying to find better words and phrases to substitute for the ones they had drafted. Their goal seemed to be to change the fewest possible words. Experienced writers, on the other hand, were much less concerned about the individual words and phrases when rewriting. They were more interested in the overall structure of the work, how it was organized and how the argument progressed from beginning to end. They were more likely to rewrite by moving entire paragraphs around, deleting and replacing whole ideas, adding information that was not in the first draft at all. For instance, in rewriting this book I removed a lot of material from the beginning that my reviewers found unnecessary or redundant, and in the process collapsed two chapters into one. I added several new sections to some chapters and eliminated sections from others. I completely rewrote some discussions the reviewers found confusing. The order of chapters was switched around, and one chapter was eliminated entirely. Except for some disagreements on terminology, the reviewers almost never commented on the individual words or sentences. The entire review process focused on organization and clarity.

When rewriting your report, you will need all the techniques mentioned earlier in connection with judging your work. Read your paper out loud. Put it aside for a time. Have a friend read it and comment on it. Ask yourself questions about how well the report works as a whole, complete entity. You should be as willing to shuffle information back and forth between sections of your paper as you are to change words. Of course, you should also fix any problems in wording and sentence construction that you find, and you should also check to see that the formal details of the structure of the report are correct.

Why do beginning writers focus on words and phrases while experienced writers focus on ideas and arguments? Sommers (1980) blames the way composition is taught in schools, beginning with the earliest grades. Teachers often return papers marked up with corrections of the words and phrases, with little overall comment on the structure of the paper. This teaches students that it is the words and phrases that need fixing. Another reason is that students often find the process of putting words on paper once so painful that they cannot face the thought of doing it over again in a different way. Fiddling around with individual words is much easier. Experienced writers, on the other hand, are less frightened of the idea of having to create a new paragraph from scratch to fill in a hole in the logical development. And besides, if there is a problem with the way a paper is organized, and there often is, then simply substituting words will not fix it. There is nothing else to do but rip it out and write it again.

Several things can make this kind of deep, meaningful revision easier for students. One is to facilitate the writing process itself, thereby making real rewriting less intimidating. The step-by-step method I have described can do this, because each step is easier than just beginning with a blank sheet of paper and producing a report. Plain old practice will help, too. As you write more and more, you will find writing easier and easier to do.

Another thing that can help is technology. Appendix A offers a discussion of computer word processors and how helpful they can be for the writer. Mainly, word processors make revisions much easier to do, such that writers are much more willing to do them. What is painful to write in longhand is even more painful to rewrite, but electronic text can be changed almost as easily as ideas.

No one can tell you that writing a research report is easy, but breaking the process into small bites can make it somewhat easier and may produce a better paper in the end. Using the procedures described here can help you produce a report that will make you proud. Your report will be clear, easy to read, and interesting, and it will earn you the recognition you deserve from your colleagues and your teachers.

SUMMARY

A. Many research reports must follow a strict structural format. This format is widely used in the behavioral sciences.

  1. Two components precede the report itself.

   a. The title page gives the title of the report, the author's name, and information about the author.

   b. The abstract is a short (usually 100–150 words) summary of the main information in the report.

  2. The report itself begins with a description of the problem being addressed and the method of addressing it.

   a. The Introduction defines the problem, relates the study to other related studies, and gives reasons for conducting the study in the way to be described.

   b. The Method section describes just how the research was done. It includes subsections on subjects (or participants), procedure, and whatever else is needed to make the research clear to the reader.

  3. The report closes with a description of what can be learned from the study and what it means.

   a. The Results section states what happened in the study and the conclusions that can be drawn.

   b. The Discussion section states the meaning of the results in relation to the issues raised in the Introduction.

  4. After the end of the report itself, other material usually appears.

   a. Most reports include a Reference section, which lists the full references for all the published material referred to in the report.

   b. Some reports include appendices, with detailed material that might interested some readers.

B. How can you go about producing a good report in this format?

  1. There are some overall considerations of style.

   a. Short sentences are often better than long ones, and long ones need plenty of markers to help the reader follow your train of thought.

   b. Avoid using jargon unless it is really helpful, and then be sure to define it clearly. Give research groups meaningful labels. Avoid the use of masculine pronouns when a person's sex is unknown.

    c. It is difficult for you to judge your report as your reader will see it. It helps to read it out loud, put it away for a time, and get someone to read and comment on it.

2. There are many ways to go about writing a research report, but one good way is this one.

    a. Begin by making random notes of all the information you want your report to include. Be sure to include information about the interesting issues your research addresses.

    b. Sort these notes according to the section of the report to which they pertain; then find the best order within each section. Make sure the sequence is logical and that all necessary information is included.

    c. Write a draft of the report by converting these ideas into complete sentences. Again, make sure the ideas flow logically. Do not be afraid to rearrange your material to reorganize the ideas if necessary.

    d. Wait a time if possible, then rewrite the report, preferably with feedback from a reader. Focus mainly on the overall flow of the report. Only after you are sure it is constructed as well as you can make it should you worry about details.

CHECKPOINT

Check your understanding of the material in this chapter:

- What is the major goal when writing any research report?

- Write a brief description of the report format given in this chapter, including opening and closing material and the major sections of the report itself.

- What are some of the unhelpful myths that students sometimes hold about writing? Did you, yourself, hold to any of them?

- What is meant by "parallel construction" when writing sentences?

- What is jargon? What are the good and the bad points of jargon?

- What kinds of label should be given to experimental groups or other parts of a research study? Why?

- Why it is often difficult to judge your own writing? What techniques can help?

- In the writing procedure presented here, what are the steps involved in writing a report?

- List the main things to keep in mind when writing each of the four major sections of a research report.

- What do student writers focus on when they rewrite? What about experienced writers? What should you try to focus on when rewriting your report?

EXERCISES

11.1 Do you plan to apply some or all of the author's suggestions when writing your next research report? Which suggestions seem most useful to you? Why?

11.2 Dig up a research report you wrote for another class, preferably a year or two ago. Can you still understand it? Is it confusing in places, too long, or otherwise badly written? Does this chapter give you ideas for how it could have been done better? If you were to write that report over again, what would you change?

11.3 Ask whether you can turn in a draft of a research report before the deadline (at least two weeks before) and get the instructor's comments. Then try to rewrite the report, as described here, and turn in a better version on the due date.

11.4 Find some published research in your area of interest that seems particularly well written, and another example that seems uninteresting or confusing. Try to identify just what makes one report better. Is it related to anything in this chapter?

11.5 Examine the sample paper given in Figure 11-5. In what ways does it follow the guidelines in this chapter? In what ways does it not? How might you improve this paper?

Chapter 12

Science as a Human Activity

Questions to Consider as You Read

- What does it mean to say that science is a human activity?

- What sorts of effect can research have on the people who participate in it? On the public as a whole? On the people who make public policy?

- How is behavioral research used in education? By the criminal justice system? By the military? By private industry? How should it be used in these areas?

- How can the stereotype of scientists as completely logical and rational be reconciled with the fact that scientists are human beings?

- What are some of the ways in which our human nature can help us to be better scientists? What are some of the ways in which our human nature can give us problems as scientists?

- What does it mean to say that the way we look at facts is affected by our ideas of what the facts should mean?

- How do scientists react when an observed fact contradicts a widely held theory? How should they react?

- When two conflicting theories are supported by some data and contradicted by other data, how does a scientist choose which theory to support? What does the scientist do next?

- How does the haphazard, human nature of science ever lead us to the truth?

Many people seem to think that science is made up entirely of logic, the kind of clear thinking you do best when alone in a laboratory without other people distracting or confusing you, but this is not true. Logical, clear thinking is, of course, important to good science, but so is the interaction between scientists as individual human beings, and between behavioral scientists and the people they study. Scientists are human, too. They sleep and wake up, eat pizzas and chocolate ice cream, play with their kids, yell at their kids, get involved in love affairs or personal feuds with other scientists, and generally act like human beings. We say that science is a social activity, which means that what a scientist does has profound effects on other people and that other people have a profound effect on what the scientist does. The term "social" implies the interaction between people, how they change and challenge each other. Behavioral science claims as its area of study just about any part of human life, because we realize that our interaction with others is important in work, play, learning, death, crime, buying, selling, and most everything else you can imagine. It is important to realize that what behavioral scientists do is just as much a part of human life as going to the grocery store. Scientists are not rational machines that work only with logic. They are human beings interacting with other human beings. It is those human interactions that this chapter examines.

I will discuss two types of interaction. First, there are the effects that behavioral science research can have on the particular people being studied and on other members of our society. Second, there are the interactions between the scientists themselves and other people, including other scientists, which can affect the research that is done. This type of interaction is not unique to behavioral scientists, and examples will come from other sciences as well. So there are two levels of social activity: the research as it affects society, and the human nature of the scientist as it affects the research.

The Social Effects of Research

Behavioral research affects society, sooner or later, in some way or other. At least, behavioral scientists hope that their research will sooner or later have some effect on society. Otherwise there would be little point in doing the research in the first place. Even the most theoretical, pure, ivory-tower research is supposed to give us a better understanding of what people are like, and such understanding will probably change the way we all think about ourselves and others. Sometimes, however, the effects of research on society are closer and more obvious than this.

Effects on Participants

While some behavioral scientists work with animals, most behavioral science research involves people. It is almost impossible to do anything at all with a person without affecting that person in some way. People react to their environment in extremely complex ways, and a behavioral science experiment is definitely a part of the environment of a research participant. It would be unreasonable to think that such an experiment could have no effect on a participant. However, knowing just what effects it does have is more difficult.

Behavioral scientists frequently point to the positive effects of being in a behavioral science study as justification for conducting the research (Adair, Dushenko, & Lindsay, 1985). Most often, the positive effect mentioned is increased self-knowledge. For instance, a participant who takes a personality test as part of a research project usually is told the results of the test at the end of the research, learning something new in the process. In any case, after the experiment is over, the researcher is supposed to give the participants as much information as possible about what is being studied and what the study shows about human nature. Thus the participants in behavioral research may learn something about people in general and about themselves in particular.

On the other hand, there may be negative effects of participation. These possible effects, discussed at some length in Chapter 3 on ethics, can be summarized as actual harm, invasion of privacy, deception, and coercion. Participants might experience anger or fear as a part of the research situation, they might feel betrayed when they discover that the researcher observed private behaviors or lied, or they might feel a loss of control as a result of being pressured to do something undesirable. These feelings could well extend beyond the research experience itself into a general distrust of behavioral scientists and behavioral science. Such effects are clearly not what behavioral scientists want to create; rather, they are to be avoided if at all possible.

Some of the effects of research on participants are less clearly good or bad, but just reflect ways in which the research situation changes how a person behaves. This is one of the things that makes behavioral science much more difficult than physical science. Humans (and animals, to a lesser extent) display **reactivity**, which means that they respond to being observed in complex, often unpredictable ways. Inanimate objects larger than atoms, as studied by most other branches of science, are not reactive. A hydrogen molecule does not care whether a chemist is observing its interaction with an oxygen atom to produce water. Except in some of the more esoteric branches of quantum physics, most scientists do not have to worry about how their observations affect the things being observed. Behavioral scientists, however, have to worry about that all the time. In some ways this human reactivity is fairly obvious. In most cases, you would expect people to react differently when a large, whirring camera is pointed at them and when they are alone. However, sometimes the ways in which people react to research are completely unexpected.

As an example, consider some work on ethical regulations and its effects on research. Gardner (1978) did a series of experiments on the effects of noise on performance. It had been reported earlier (Glass & Singer, 1972) that when exposed to loud noises, people performed tasks more poorly than before. This result had been replicated several times by many investigators, including Gardner, until Gardner implemented the new federal guidelines on informed consent in research with human subjects. He discovered, to his surprise, that the negative effects of the noise disappeared when participants were fully informed about the experiment and clearly told that they could quit at any time. Apparently, knowing that they could leave if the noise bothered them made the noise less bothersome to participants. This was an unexpected human reaction to the research situation.

This is the essential dilemma of behavioral research. If the human participants know everything there is to know about the research, it will often change their responses, because humans are reactive. If something is hidden from them, then the research might be unethical, because humans have ethical rights. It is this dilemma that makes research with human beings so difficult to do both well and fairly, compared to research with hydrogen atoms or nuclear particles or gypsy moths. If humans were not so much more interesting or important, probably no one would bother doing the research at all.

Effects on the Public

People hear about behavioral research in many different ways from many different sources. Unfortunately, most of what they hear is so simplified or so distorted that it is difficult to understand what it means or to judge whether the research is any good. However, reports about behavioral research still have effect on the people who hear them. Of course, some of these effects are good, and some bad.

When people hear about rampant, unjustified deception in behavioral research, even though such behavior is extremely rare, this undoubtedly has a bad effect on the public and on the field of behavioral science. This is one of the arguments for restricting the use of deception as a technique in behavioral research. Other negative effects occur when a specific group of people become so thoroughly studied by so many different researchers that they make a life style out of being research subjects. This situation becomes a joke in the cartoon in Figure 12-1, but the problem can be serious.

There is a story about a sociologist who was interviewing an old American Indian woman about the life of her people many years ago. He would ask her a question about, say, the rituals surrounding the birth of a child, and the old woman would disappear into her room for a while, and then reappear and tell him about the rituals. After this happened several times, the researcher asked why the woman needed to leave the room before answering. Was she consulting the memory of an even older Indian? No, it turned out she was consulting a book written by a different sociologist about American Indian culture. She enjoyed talking to the interviewer, so she kept him around by feeding him the information from the book.

"Anthropologists! Anthropologists!"

The Far Side cartoons by Gary Larson are reprinted by permission of Chronicle Features, San Francisco, CA.

Figure 12-1 The fact of being studied in social research can often affect the research participants.

Of course, behavioral research can also have good effects on the public. As a behavioral scientist myself I believe that the good effects far outweigh the bad ones. Finding out about how people and cultures and organizations function can help us make them function more successfully. Just think of the changes in the area of child care. Lots of contradictory and troublesome theories have been replaced by beliefs based on empirical research. For instance, studies have followed up on children whose parents used different styles of controlling family life, to see how the children turned out. [This type of research (for instance, Coopersmith, 1967) shows that children whose parents are firmly controlling, imposing rules but enforcing them with some flexibility and discussion, are more independent and have higher self-esteem than children whose parents are either very permissive or very strict. However, most of this research is correlational and has all the problems discussed in Chapter 6.] As research like this becomes better known to the public, perhaps through child-care books or pediatricians, it could have a very positive effect on the next generation.

There has even been research on the effects of research on those who learn about it. Beaman, Barnes, Klentz, and McQuirk (1978) gave a group of college students information about research on the conditions that make it more or less likely for someone in trouble to get help. This sort of research (for example, Darley & Batson, 1973) shows that people are less likely to help someone if there are other people around who are not helping, or if they know there are others around but cannot see what they are doing. In the one case, you tend to think that if there were a real need to help, someone else would be doing it. In the other case, you tend to assume that someone else probably is helping, so you do not bother to do so yourself. Either way, the victim is less likely to be helped than if only one person is aware of the problem.

About two weeks later, the students who had learned about this research, as well as others unfamiliar with it, were presented with a situation in which it seemed that someone needed help. In each case, the student was with another person, a confederate, who acted as though nothing was wrong. The informed students were nearly twice as likely as the uninformed students to offer help to the apparent victim. This is another example of how spreading the news about psychological research can have a positive effect on society in general, by making it more likely that someone in trouble will get help.

Effects on Policy Makers

Often, the effects of behavioral research on society are more deliberate and specific than raising the general level of awareness. Behavioral research is frequently used by policy makers in arriving at decisions that affect important social institutions.

Education

Educators have long been users of behavioral research. Many educational policies have been decided based on research of one sort or another, although some policies have been based on simple personal beliefs. Those who can benefit from behavioral research in education fall generally into three groups: administrators who set overall policies, teachers who control what happens in the classroom, and students themselves.

Education administrators, who must often decide on issues of great public importance, can be helped in their decisions by good behavioral research. For instance, Cook (1985) reports on a series of studies, both experimental and quasi-experimental, on the effects of school desegregation on interracial prejudice. His results indicate that simply placing children of different ethnic groups in the same schools does little to improve relations between the groups. However, certain techniques that can be used in the schools and particularly in the classrooms of integrated schools might significantly improve the way children think about and interact with children of other racial groups. These techniques frequently call for creating situations in which students of different races must work together, helping one another out, in order for any of them to succeed. By applying this research, administrators might make an important contribution to race relations in this country.

Teachers are usually very interested in becoming more effective in the classroom, but sometimes they do not know how to accomplish this. For example, many teachers complain that their students are learning only to repeat back, parrotlike, the information they are given, without learning to think for themselves and evaluate information before making decisions. Such teachers would be quite interested in behavioral research on how to teach critical thinking. For instance, there are descriptive reports of courses that have been designed to teach these skills (for example, Anisfeld, 1987), as well as quasi-experimental evaluations of some teaching techniques (for example, Herrnstein, Nickerson, de Sanchez, & Swets, 1986). Teachers who use the techniques described in research like this might be able to improve their teaching in this important area. For other examples, there are large bodies of research on different ways of teaching the skills involved in writing, some of which are reviewed by Scardamalia and Bereiter (1986), and on controlling behavioral problems in the classroom, some of which are discussed by Lehman (1982).

Students are the group who make the least use of educational research, although they could benefit from this research. Behavioral scientists have learned a great deal about studying that could help the people who do it. To take only one example, consider the phenomenon known in the psychological literature as the spacing effect. The **spacing effect**, sometimes called the **distributed practice effect**, reflects the finding that any specific amount of time spent studying will be much more effective if it is broken up into several small, separate sessions than if it occurs in a few long marathons. Psychologists have known about this effect for more than a century (Ebbinghaus, 1885/1913), and a great deal of research has been done on this phenomenon recently. The spacing effect seems to hold for almost any type of information studied and tested in almost any way, from postal office employees learning to type (Baddeley & Longman, 1966) to classroom students learning meaningful material (Bahrick & Phelps, 1987; Glover & Corkill, 1987; Bower, 1990d). For students, this means that in most of those all-night cramming sessions before tests, they are just wasting time. Instead, they would be better off reviewing their notes and reading small sections in the textbook during the short time gaps that seldom are used for studying, such as the ten minutes before the next class or the fifteen minutes between dinner and a favorite television show. Dempster (1988) reviews some of the recent research on this phenomenon and also documents the fact that this research has had distressingly little effect on how students study, even though it could make their studying time much more effective.

This shows that, in education as in many other areas, behavioral research is being used to benefit many people, but it could and should be used much more than it is. All behavioral scientists have an obligation not only to do the best research they can do, but also to see that the research is used in the best possible ways to help as many people as it can.

The Criminal Justice System

The criminal justice system is a large collection of institutions that deal with preventing, detecting, and responding to crime. It includes police departments, courts, prisons and jails, rehabilitation programs, agencies that assist victims, and probation offices. Behavioral research is used in all these areas to help make their programs more effective.

In studying the causes of crime, behavioral scientists produce research that can and should strongly affect the criminal justice system. For instance, Hill and Atkinson (1988) studied the relationship between delinquency and the controls parents put on their adolescents. These investigators found that parental curfews had no relation to a child's delinquency and parental rules about the child's appearance had only slight effects, but parental support, letting the child know that the parents cared and wanted to help, was more strongly associated with reduced juvenile delinquency. While no one study can possibly answer all the questions we might have on issues of criminal behavior, each one can help us to understand it a little bit better.

For a more complex example, consider the current controversy over pornography. The tension between the First Amendment right to free speech and a sense of moral decency is very old and is not likely to be resolved soon. Recently, however, behavioral research has entered the fray. Some psychologists (for a review, see Donnerstein, Linz, & Penrod, 1987) have shown in laboratory studies that men who watch violent, sexually explicit movies are more negative toward women than men who do not watch violent pornography; they are also more likely to believe that rape victims are responsible for being raped but the rapists are not responsible, and more likely to "punish" female victims with electric shock. It is research like this (along with a host of political and social forces) that led to the recommendations of the Attorney General's Commission on Pornography (1986) that obscenity laws be expanded to limit some of the pornography available in our society. Other researchers, however (Donnerstein, Berkowitz, & Linz, 1986), have indicated that it is the violence, particularly the violence against women, that produces these negative effects, even in material that contains no sexual references at all. This reflects the fact that social issues like pornography are more complex than some people might wish and suggests that even good behavioral research cannot always provide definite answers.

Behavioral research can also contribute to changes in how the judicial system works after a suspect has been brought to trial. For decades, psychologists studying how human memory works have seen evidence that eyewitness testimony in court cases is very likely to be wrong, even when the eyewitnesses are very confident and sure of their judgments (see Loftus, 1979). However, in the courtroom it was considered to be the jury's job to decide on the credibility of an eyewitness account. For a long time psychologists could not testify in court about the weaknesses of eyewitness accounts. As recently as 1988, the *Wall Street Journal* ran a front-page article stating that psychologists were finally being allowed to tell the jurors about this important research (Bishop, 1988). Behavioral science research is also affecting the use of polygraph testing to determine a suspect's guilt (Katkin, 1985; Saxe, Dougherty, & Cross, 1985), pointing out serious problems with the theoretical validity and the practical accuracy of these tests.

In a more controversial vein, psychologists are already being used by legal firms to identify qualities in prospective jurors that are desirable or undesirable for their clients (Patterson, 1986). For instance, research in one case might have indicated the ideal juror to be a white male, 35–40 years old, high school educated, working in a service trade, divorced, no children. Having this information, the attorneys can try to select jurors who fit the mold, thus giving their client the best possible chance of a favorable judgment. While this is clearly counsel's job, the practice of using psychologists to assist in performing it has generated a lot of argument, because it seems to some to be shading over into the area of jury tampering.

Another area in which behavioral scientists have much to tell the courts is the apparent unreliability of testimony retrieved under hypnosis (see Laurence & Perry, 1983). It has been found that hypnotized subjects eagerly follow the lead of the hypnotist into believing that they observed things they did not, and this confidence can remain even after awakening from hypnosis.

Once a criminal has been convicted, there is more behavioral research to do. For instance, research on the effects of living conditions in prison shows that crowding can cause increases in the inmates' ill health (Ruback & Innes, 1988), and research on the relative violence against male and female prison guards yielded the surprising finding that, in California prisons with male prisoners, female officers were assaulted less frequently than male officers (Shawver & Dickover, 1986). All together, behavioral research has had a large impact on the criminal justice system and will no doubt continue to do so.

The Military

Various branches of the military have been interested in behavioral research for some time. For instance, during World War I the Army sponsored the development of intelligence tests to screen recruits (see DuBois, 1970), and during World War II the Air Force sponsored studies of perceptual processes that affect pilots (Gibson, 1947). However, in recent years the use of behavioral research by the military has dropped off. Some scientists believe that this decline in the use of behavioral research by the military has had negative effects, even disastrous effects. For instance, psychologists have testified before the House of Representatives that the use of research on how people make decisions under stress might have prevented incidents like the shooting down of the Iranian passenger airliner by the U.S. Naval vessel *Vincennes* in July 1988 (Bales, 1988). Behavioral scientists claim that the military has shifted its focus to the increasingly sophisticated technology it relies on, sometimes ignoring the human nature of the people who must use the technology. Important research needs to be done on the interactions of humans with these complex new machines, and also on the interactions among human beings who must work and sometimes fight together.

Private Industry

Businesses are often consumers of behavioral research. To mention only a few examples, almost every producer of consumer goods conducts market research to determine who their potential customers are, what products they want, and how to convince them to buy that company's products. Retail stores use research showing that shoppers stay longer and buy more if there is quiet music playing in the store (Greene, 1987). Advertisers use studies showing that simply seeing an object over and over again tends to make us like that object (Zajonc, 1968). Architects use research on the social effects of various designs of living quarters (Baum & Valins, 1977).

In addition to these fairly obvious applications of behavioral research, there are others that are less obvious. For instance, utility companies have an interest in persuading consumers to conserve energy in various ways, to relieve some of the energy demand on the utilities and avoid the need to build more plants or buy power from outside sources. They are not having great success in promoting energy conservation (White, Archer, Aronson, Condelli, Curbow, McLeod, Pettigrew, & Yates, 1984). Behavioral research shows some promise in teaching utilities better ways to spread the word about energy conservation (Constanzo, Archer, Aronson, & Pettigrew 1986); these approaches, if used, would benefit the utilities, the consumers, and the environment. Other behavioral research has helped an automobile company address a concern about expensive equipment that was sitting idle at off times, such as nights and weekends. The auto maker wanted to institute unusual work schedules to use the equipment more completely but faced opposition from workers, who were opposed to the inconvenience of strange timetables and wanted adequate compensation for such nonstandard shifts. The researchers helped design a program that satisfied the needs of both groups, using unusual survey techniques and information distribution methods (Lévy-Leboyer, 1988).

The Behavioral Science of Science

I have pointed out over and over that scientists are human beings, and as such they are capable of excellent science and also of typical human failings. Unfortunately, few scientists know very much about how they function as human beings or as scientists. Behavioral science has much to say about the human behavior of scientists and how it affects the science they conduct.

The Power of Patterns

One of the things we know best about people is that they tend to see things the way they want to see them, rather than the way they actually are. This is a sign of one of our great strengths, but it can sometimes be a real hindrance to the conduct of good science. People are spectacularly good at recognizing patterns. One of my 5-year-old son's favorite games is the "hidden pictures" trick of finding, say, ten musical instruments hidden in a drawing of a racetrack. He is very good at it, which shows how strong this ability is even in little people. We do not lose this skill as adults. We can (usually) pick out the can opener in the drawer full of kitchen junk, or the car keys in the pile on the table by the door, or the recurring theme in a Bach fugue. We can pick out abstract patterns, as when doctors around the country discovered a mysterious respiratory ailment, frequently fatal, in a few isolated men whose family and coworkers had no illness at all. It only took weeks to figure out that all these patients had visited an American Legion convention in Philadelphia, and thus the diagnosis of Legionnaires' disease was born.

The way scientists think about the world, the patterns they look for, will have very strong effects on the kinds of patterns or theories they find. This means that as our ways of thinking change, our theories and the questions we ask will change, too. Thus the patterns we have in our minds can open up new ways of thinking and can make available to us new theories and new research. For instance, it is common these days to use computer metaphors in thinking about people. That is, we think of human behavior as controlled by people's brains and their life experiences, just as a computer's behavior is controlled by its electronic circuitry and its programming. In earlier centuries it was more common to think of people in terms of clockworks, with gears and camshafts and springs, which led to a more mechanical, limited, strictly controlled idea of human behavior. Before the invention of clocks, our conception, not only of human beings, but even of time itself and the very nature of the universe was different. Computer scientist Joseph Weizenbaum describes the ideas of time that existed before the fourteenth century:

> . . . From Classical antiquity until relatively recently, the regularity of the universe was searched for and perceived in great thematic harmonies. The idea that nature behaves systematically in the sense we understand it—i.e., that every part and aspect of nature may be isolated as a subsystem governed by laws describable as functions of time—this idea could not have been even understood by people who perceived time, not as a collection of abstract units (i.e., hours, minutes, and seconds), but as a sequence of constantly recurring events. Times of day were known by events, such as the sun standing above a specific pile of rocks, or, as Homer tells us, by tasks begun or ended, such as the yoking of the oxen (morning) and the unyoking of the oxen (evening). Durations were indicated by reference to common tasks, e.g., the time needed to travel a well-known distance or to boil fixed quantities of water. Seasonal times were known by recurring seasonal events, e.g., the departure of birds.[1]

For people operating under this perspective, certain questions and answers were simply meaningless. How long does it take to boil a quart of water? It takes as long as it takes. How did the world come to be the way it is? It always was and always will be as it is now—Weizenbaum calls this a "complex beating" of repeating, cyclical events. Our modern concept of time as something that can be measured, cut up into smaller and smaller pieces, as something that exists in fixed and absolute perfection independent of whatever happens to be happening, was not

---

[1]From *Computer Power and Human Reason: From Judgement to Calculations*, Joseph Weizenbaum, copyright ©1976 by W. H. Freeman and Company, San Francisco, CA, p. 21. Reprinted by permission.

possible without the idea of the clock. The clock gave us a new perspective to time, a new approach that opened up new ways of relating to the cosmos.

As with most things about us people, this skill has a good side and a bad side. We all need to know how to emphasize this strength when it is positive, and to minimize its effects when it is negative. Our abilities as pattern detectors both help and hinder us as scientists.

Patterns as Positive Forces

Our ability to recognize patterns allows good scientists to look at a collection of confusing information and come up with a single theory that explains everything. Human beings would not be as good at science as they are without being able to do this. There is very little that is less useful to our understanding of nature than a large pile of unsorted, unanalyzed data. Good scientists are the ones who can look through this pile and decide which pieces of data fit with which other pieces, and what they mean.

Take an example from my own area of interest, the psychology of human thought and reasoning. When psychology began, it mostly involved asking people to describe what went on in their heads while they were doing some mental task, such as multiplying two numbers (Wundt, 1904/1907). They would say, for instance, that they saw the numbers in their mind's eye, as though they were written on a blackboard. Some psychologists became convinced that thought was impossible without some sort of mental image, usually a visual one, to represent the thought. Others claimed that imageless thought was possible, and as "proof" of this claim they had reports from people who had thought about something without an image in their heads at all. The first group claimed that these subjects were simply bad observers who failed to notice the subtle images that had to be there. Because nobody can observe the images inside someone else's head, the debate simply boiled down to "I did not!" versus "You did too!" (Notice that this is a problem with the operationalization of the variable, as discussed in Chapter 4. What variable is being measured? What is the operational definition? What is wrong with the operational definition?)

In the early 1900s, a movement called behaviorism became very strong, mostly because it dealt with this problem (e.g., Watson, 1930). In behaviorism, a psychologist may deal only with the visible, measurable behavior of the participant. Thus, a behaviorist avoids the problem of operationalizing the hidden mental constructs by denying the existence of these constructs completely. That is, you can study the words an observer uses to describe what is going on mentally when doing a particular task, but these words are treated simply as sounds, without reference to any ongoing process inside the participant's head. For example, behaviorists might say that a dog had not been given any food for three days, because this was an observable fact, but they would never say that the dog was hungry, because "hunger" is an invisible, internal state of the dog that could not be directly observed. Behaviorists believed that it was sheer, unscientific mentalism to try to talk about unobservable mental processes, because anything that cannot be observed is not scientific. All behavior of humans and animals, they believed, could be explained by studying what the organism does in specific situations. The problem with this approach is that it deliberately ignores a lot of what psychologists found most interesting about people, including thinking.

By the middle of this century, psychologists who were interested in how people think and reason were in a quandary. Behaviorists claimed that it was foolish and unscientific to study something that could not be observed. Besides, the only tool they had for studying mental processes was introspection, which had proven to be hopelessly subjective. What these scientists needed was a new pattern, a new way of looking at human beings. Fortunately, they got it.

Shortly after World War II, the first programmable digital computer was completed (Huskey, 1976). It did not take psychologists long to become interested in this new phenomenon, a machine that could do something that was called thinking when humans did it. Because of our skill at finding patterns and relationships that are below the surface, we could draw parallels between ourselves and these new devices of metal and glass. From wondering what went on inside a person who was multiplying two numbers, it was a short step to wondering what went on inside a computer that was doing the same thing. But while it seemed mystical and unscientific to wonder what the person was doing, it was hardly mystical or unscientific to wonder what the computer was doing.

The computer was the first proof that thinking, or even anything that remotely resembled thinking, could occur without some mysterious, spiritual process that could never, in principle, be studied scientifically. The reasoning went like this. Suppose I gave you a computer, and when you typed certain things into its keyboard, the machine typed certain other things back to you on its screen. You could, scientifically and rationally, do experiments to determine what it would type in response to your inputs, and thus figure out at least some of the program it was using. In the same way, I could do experiments with people, putting them in certain situations (the inputs) and seeing how they respond (the outputs), and therefore I could figure out at least some of the mental processes going on in their heads (the program). If it is scientific to do this with the computer, it can be just as scientific, though more difficult, to do it with a person.

This insight gave birth to a new branch of psychology, called cognitive psychology, which is concerned with thinking, studying, planning, problem solving, reasoning, remembering, and most other intellectual processes. It also affected almost every other area of psychology, and most of the other behavioral sciences as well. For the first time, psychologists realized that they could collect observable data and use this information to draw conclusions about unobservable phenomena. Most of the research discussed in this book came about because of this new insight. A new pattern, a new way of looking at things, opened up enormous, and previously unavailable, possibilities for understanding human beings. And this new insight would have been impossible without our ability to find relationships between things that appear to have little to do with one another.

Patterns as Negative Forces

However, there is a negative side to this skill. We are so good at finding patterns that are buried, we can even find them when they are not there. It is easy to see faces in the flames, or animals in the clouds, even though whatever patterns we may perceive are completely random. And once we have seen a pattern, it becomes difficult to ignore it or to believe it is not real. The pattern controls how we look at things, and what we see, especially when we look at anything as complex as a person (see Figure 12-2). Our ideas, our theories, have an effect on our data that most scientists fail to realize. It is important to recognize this effect so it can be taken into account. Stephen Jay Gould, the biologist specializing in evolutionary theories quoted in Chapter 2, understands this issue well.

> Most scientists maintain—or at least argue for public consumption—
> that their profession marches toward truth by accumulating more and
> more data, under the guidance of an infallible procedure called "the
> scientific method.". . . [However,] new facts, collected in old ways under
> the guidance of old theories, rarely lead to any substantial revision of
> thought. Facts do not "speak for themselves"; they are read in the light
> of theory. Creative thought, in science as much as in the arts, is the
> motor of changing opinion. Science is a quintessentially human activ-
> ity, not a mechanized, robotlike accumulation of objective information,
> leading by laws of logic to inescapable interpretation.[2]

Examples of the power of our beliefs in patterns over what we perceive are many. To take a famous example from the physical sciences, consider the idea that the heavens reflect the unchanging perfection of God and therefore nothing we see when we look at the sky should vary or be imperfect. This idea led to a lot of diligent, patient, important astronomy, as various people studied the stars and planets to find signs of the nature of God. However, it also led to some curious astronomical mistakes. For instance, the light from a relatively nearby supernova became visible in 1054. For days, this exploding star shone brighter than any other star in the sky, and it left behind an expanding cloud of gas

---

[2]From *Ever Since Darwin, Reflections in Natural History*, by Stephen Jay Gould. By permission of W. W. Norton & Company, Inc. Copyright ©1977, pp 161–162; by Stephen Jay Gould. Copyright ©1973, 1974, 1975, 1976, 1977 by The American Museum of Natural History.

Figure 12-2 All of us have preconceptions and assumptions about the world and other people that affect how we see what is really there, but scientists must try especially hard to overcome them. This fellow obviously has a preconception about what Vietnam veterans are like, and it blinds him to reality.

we call the Crab nebula. Chinese astronomers faithfully recorded this event, and it is even thought to be recorded by on the wall of a cave used by ancient people in the American Southwest, but in Europe it was completely ignored. The most likely reason for this is that European astronomers *knew* that new stars did not suddenly burst into flame and then fade out again. The supernova had violated the pattern. It could not have happened. So they never mentioned it.

Behavioral scientists can display the same sort of selective vision. Right at this very moment, in the field of psychology there is a continuing controversy over sex bias in psychological research. In 1986, three women (McHugh, Koeske, and Frieze) published an article on how to eliminate some of the male-dominated bias in psychological research. One of their recommendations was to reduce the emphasis on sex differences when these are found, because extensive reporting of sex differences reinforces the impression that the sexes are very different when in fact they are very similar. Many times, the discovery of a sex difference indicates nothing more than a sex bias on the part of the researcher or the research materials. At other times it is simply a chance occurrence and might disappear if the experiment were repeated. (It is interesting to note that the authors specifically recommend that sex differences not be published if they are not "grounded in a theoretical model"; a clear example of the effect of theory on what we perceive.) Another author (Eagly, 1987) indicated in another article her belief that we should all examine all our data for evidence for sex differences and publish every example that we find, in the interests of expanding the field into a legitimate psychology of women as well as of men.

Later articles have expanded on both these views, with some authors holding that the extensive testing and reporting of sex differences helps to maintain sex biases (Baumeister, 1988) while others argue that only the consistent, diligent search for differences will eliminate the long-term bias that has existed in a field in which twice as many journal articles in one sample used male subjects as female subjects (Rothblum, 1988). Every one of these authors starts from the belief that a researcher's bias toward male-dominant thinking, or toward gender–role stereotypes (beliefs such as "men are logical, but women are emotional"), can have a big influence on the research that is performed, how that research is interpreted, and how it affects the people who read it. Their only disagreement is on how to solve this problem.

For another example, an account of some research on the sleeping patterns of small children (Sweeter slumber. . ., 1990) prompted a challenge on the grounds of researcher bias. The original report discussed some studies showing that, if parents allow their toddlers to sleep in their bed with them more than occasionally, the children show more disturbed sleep patterns over the years and demand to sleep with the parents more and more. The challenge (Schmookler, 1990) restated the result like this: "The more thoroughly parents force their children to sleep alone, the less the children will resist." Schmookler pointed out that in most other societies of the world, infants are expected to sleep with their mothers for at least the first few years. This fulfills the child's inborn need for physical closeness. When we Americans push our babies away, forcing them to sleep all alone, they resist, and we call this resistance "behavior problems." Schmookler labels this "cultural prejudice masquerading as science." We should be teaching parents to fulfill infants' needs, he says, instead of encouraging greater efficiency in thwarting them.

When Theories Collide

Another part of the traditional view of the scientific method is that scientists hold a theory only as long as it is supported by the data. As soon as there is a conflicting piece of evidence, the theory is falsified, and any decent scientist would immediately throw out the old theory and build a new one. This idea fits the concept of a scientist as a supremely logical, rational, passionless person, and therefore is very seldom true, at least with regard to the scientist's major theories. There are two different reasons for a perfectly good scientist to be reluctant to reject a theory that is contradicted by an observation. One of these reasons is very logical and rational, while the other reason is more idiosyncratic.

The logical reason for holding onto a falsified theory is that observations are not perfectly reliable. It might be that the fact is wrong, rather than the theory. To take a familiar example, consider the belief that the earth was the center of the universe, and that the moon, stars, sun, and planets all went around the earth. Today we laugh at this belief and at the people who believed it. In particular, we laugh at the people who continued to believe it after Copernicus came along and told them the true story, namely, that the sun is the center of the solar system, and the earth, moon, and planets go around the sun. Once Copernicus had explained this, only stubborn stupidity could have made people continue to believe the old idea. In actual fact, however, it seemed at the time that the facts contradicted Copernicus's theory. The earth-centered view of the solar system could not be falsified until two things occurred. First, gravitational theory had to advance to the point where people could imagine the earth spinning around without everything on the surface flying off into space. Second, the technology of the telescope had to advance to the point where the planet Venus could be seen to have phases, just like the moon. Without these two advances, the hard facts available lined up behind the traditional view of the cosmos, with the earth firmly at the center.

For a more modern example, consider what happened to the theory of gravity when it was discovered that the planet Neptune was not following the predicted path around the sun. This would seem to be a clear fact falsifying Newton's gravitational theory, but it was not. Scientists got busy trying to figure out what was wrong with the observation of Neptune, or what other factor there might be to explain the observation and still hang onto Newton's theory. As it turned out, they found another factor, and it was thus that the planet Pluto was discovered. On the other hand, when Mercury was observed to slip and slide around the sun in a way that Newton's theory could not predict, scientists trying to fit that fact into the theory of gravity were less successful, and this contradiction led eventually to Einstein's new gravitational theory, special relativity. The moral of these two examples is that even careful, objective, undeniable observations of facts do not always support or falsify current theories. Sometimes a small twist or a new factor will make theory and fact fit perfectly; sometimes the theory will have to go.

Given this confusing state of affairs, what can a scientist do when there is a conflict in the field among rival theories? This is where logic breaks down and the idiosyncratic, emotional, human nature of the scientists involved takes over. What happens is that some individual scientists choose to back one theory, while some choose to back the other, and still others choose to try to create a new theory that incorporates the best of both. Scientists in each group try to collect observations that support their position while figuring out how to explain away the observations collected by the other groups. All scientists recognize the irrational, emotional aspects of this process, although some see it as a lamentable failing while others see it as the spark that keeps science human. A few scientists (most notably Kuhn, 1970) have tried to document how this process works, thus showing that scientific methods can even be applied to scientific methods.

Eventually, one group will become more successful than the others, the issue will be decided, and science can move on to the next controversy. However, "eventually" may not arrive for a long time. To take another example from physics, it was discovered long ago that light is wavelike, in that it spreads out after passing through a slit just as water does. However, it was also discovered that light is made up of particles, in that it can be divided into smaller and smaller packages only up to a certain point, beyond which you simply cannot break it up any smaller. For hundreds of years, the debate over the nature of light continued. It took Einstein, once again, to resolve the issue by demonstrating that light behaves both like a wave and like a particle at the same time. (Actually, Einstein showed that all matter can be explained in this way.) He proposed a theory that could explain both sets of observations at once. In fact, it was this theory that won Einstein his Nobel Prize.

When scientists choose sides in a theoretical controversy, it is often for personal, subjective reasons. A particular individual simply likes one idea more than the other. The physicist and cosmologist James Trefil explains:

> In reality, "soft" considerations such as beauty, elegance, and simplicity play a much bigger role in the way scientists think than people suspect. If an idea isn't sweet—if there is not a brightening of the soul when it is explained—the proponents of the idea may have to accumulate overwhelming evidence before it will be accepted by the scientific mainstream.[3]

Sometimes this sense of the beauty of a theory will not only cause a scientist to choose a particular theory to believe in, it will actually cause the scientist to create a new theory just because it is beautiful. Astronomer Carl Sagan describes how the physicist James Clerk Maxwell, working in the mid-nineteenth century, developed the first set of equations describing the new knowledge about electricity and magnetism:

> The equations exhibited a curious lack of symmetry, and this bothered Maxwell. There was something unaesthetic about the equations as then known, and to improve the symmetry Maxwell proposed that one of the equations should have an additional term, which he called the displacement current. His argument was fundamentally intuitive; there was certainly no experimental evidence for such a current. Maxwell's proposal had astonishing consequences. The corrected Maxwell equations implied the existence of electromagnetic radiation, encompassing gamma rays, X-rays, ultraviolet light, visible light, infrared and radio. They stimulated Einstein to discover Special Relativity. Faraday and Maxwell's laboratory and theoretical work together have led, one century later, to a technical revolution on the planet Earth.[4]

---

[3]From *The Dark Side of the Universe*, by James Trefil. Copyright ©1988 James Trefil. Reprinted by permission of Charles Scribner's Sons, an imprint of Macmillan Publishing Company, p. 106.

[4]Copyright 1979 Carl Sagan, *Broca's Brain*, pp. 32–33. All rights reserved. Reprinted by permission of the author.

And all of this, as Sagan says, grew from "the aesthetic dissatisaction of Maxwell, staring at some mathematical squiggles on a piece of paper" (1979, p. 33).

Choosing to believe one theory over another simply because it is more pleasing has a long and honorable scientific history. Having chosen a particular theory for whatever reason, a scientist is then free to use any method short of outright fraud or personal attacks on opposing scientists to persuade others to accept the theory, too (see Figure 12-3). (Note that there is considered nothing wrong in attacking another scientist's opposing *theory*, only in attacking the other scientist as a *person*. Thus it is all right to say, "That is a stupid idea," but not, "That is a stupid person.") If the arguments the scientist uses are in fact persuasive,

There goes Williams again . . . trying to win support for his Little Bang theory.

The Far Side cartoons are reprinted by permission of Chronicle Features, San Francisco, CA.

Figure 12-3 Williams has his own reasons for developing a Little Bang theory, and then tries to persuade other scientists to support it. This is exactly how scientific revolutions work.

whether based on observable facts or on subjective aesthetics, more and more scientists will come to accept that viewpoint. If the arguments are not persuasive, the scientist's views will not be accepted and will eventually die out.

This is a historical, almost evolutionary view of science. Theories do not survive or die based solely on the objective facts that confirm or deny them. These facts are only part of the human equation. Theories survive if they mesh well with what human scientists want from their theories. One of the things they want is theories that fit with the facts. But they also want theories with elegance, and theories that are aligned with the scientists' perspectives on what the universe is like. It is through a kind of scientific consensus that we arrive at understandings of the universe that are both accurate and inspiring. Whether these understandings are close to some absolute truth about the nature of reality is something that can be decided only by an omnipotent being who knows about the nature of reality. We humans must make do with our observations and our intuitions. Somehow they seem to be bringing us closer and closer to an understanding of the world and our place in it that satisfies our human, scientific needs. I find this an everlasting wonder.

SUMMARY

A. Science is not a mechanical activity. It is completely human, and it has profound effects on the society in which it operates. This is particularly true of behavioral research.

    1. Humans react to the experience of being observed in ways that inanimate objects do not. Some effects are negative, as discussed in the chapter on ethics. Others are positive, as when participants gain new insights into their own behavior or that of other people.

    2. Our understanding of society and of people is affected by the research that we hear about. These ideas may change our ways of interacting with others.

    3. People who make policy decisions often use behavioral research in making their decisions. Some examples:

        a. In education, administrators often use it in determining educational policy; teachers sometimes use it in improving their classroom techniques; and students seldom use it in coping with the demands of learning, although this research has the potential of making them much more successful.

        b. The criminal justice system uses it to understand, prevent, and detect criminal behavior, and to judge suspects and handle convicted criminals.

    c. Military organizations use it to understand leadership and reactions to stress, although there is reason to believe that this use has decreased recently, possibly leading to problems.

    d. Private industry uses it for market analyses and research on how people act in business organizations.

B. Scientists behave in ways that are not entirely logical and rational but nevertheless work quite well in the long run.

1. People are good at picking patterns out of a large quantity of unorganized information.

    a. This helps scientists find the underlying regularities that lead to new theories and a better understanding of the universe. A good scientist can look at the same information viewed by everyone else and see a pattern in it that no one else has seen.

    b. However, we are so good at finding patterns that we may report them when they are not really there. Our biases cause us to interpret data incorrectly. We need to make every attempt to identify our own inner biases and bring them out into the open.

2. When an observation contradicts a theory, the theory is falsified and should be discarded. However, sometimes it is the observation that is wrong, not the theory. So there are often conflicting theories on any topic, neither of which is absolutely disproven. Individual scientists choose which theory they will support based on aesthetic preference or simple whim, and try to persuade other scientists to accept their ideas. Eventually, the majority of scientists will have accepted one or the other of the theories, or a third theory is developed that fits both sets of facts. Thus science grows like an organic structure, somewhat haphazardly, rather than like the proof of a theorem in logic.

CHECKPOINT

Check your understanding of the material in this chapter:

- What are some of the positive effects behavioral research can have on the people who participate in it? What are some of the negative effects?

- What does it mean to say that humans are reactive? How does this make behavioral research more difficult?

- What does it mean to say that humans are good pattern detectors?

- In what ways does our ability as pattern detectors make us better scientists? In what ways does it interfere?

- How do you react to the idea that science advances, not through mechanical logic, but through human judgment and intuition?

EXERCISES

12.1 Can you think of an example of an effect that behavioral research has had on your life?

12.2 Can you think of ways in which behavioral research is *not* being used in your own area of interest, but probably should be?

12.3 In what ways can you, as a behavioral scientist, help to prevent the effects of bias on the research that you perform or use in your job?

12.4 Think of some controversy in your area of interest in which there are two conflicting theories right now. Which theory do you personally support? Why? Do you think your reason for choosing one theory over the other is a "good" reason? Why or why not? How might you go about persuading others in your area of interest to support the theory that you chose?

Part 5

Appendices

Appendix A

Computers in Research

Like most everyone else, researchers are finding themselves using computers more and more in getting their jobs done. Researchers use computers in each of the four phases of the research process: exploring the published literature, conducting the research and collecting the data, organizing and analyzing the data, and communicating the results in a research report. First, though, we should look briefly at the parts that make up a computer.

A Look at Computers

Every computer has four different kinds of parts: a **processor** (also called a **central processing unit**, or **CPU**), which is the part that actually does the computing; a **memory**, which stores data the processor uses and the related instructions; **inputs**, through which information enters the computer from the outside world; and **outputs**, through which the computer communicates information to the world. Computers differ in which specific inputs and outputs they have, how much memory they have, and how powerful their processors are, but the basic parts stay the same.

In general, most computers fall into two broad categories: mainframes and personal computers, often called PCs for short. A **mainframe** is a very large, centralized computer that handles the processing needs of a large number of people at a given facility (university, hospital, etc.). A mainframe's processor is usually powerful and fast. Historically, such computers used decks of punched cards ("IBM cards") for input and lines printed on long rolls of accordion-folded paper for output. While most computers still use printers for output, the punched cards have largely been replaced by systems in which people interact with the computer through a terminal. A **terminal** has a keyboard for input and a TV-like screen for output, and it functions as a communication device for the mainframe. Such a system is often called a timeshare system, because the computer shares its time, split second by split second, among all the people using it at any given moment. By using a terminal on a timeshare system, the user can check that the data were put in correctly and the program is running properly before asking that the results be printed.

A **personal computer**, the familiar Apples and IBMs, is a self-contained computer that can sit on a desk. It is designed to be used by only one person at a time, which is why it is called "personal." Even though these computers can be, and frequently are, linked together in a network, each one is capable of independent function and all the computers in the network are (more or less) equal. The distinction between personal computers and mainframes can get blurry, because a personal computer can, with the right software, pretend it is just a terminal and allow you to communicate with a mainframe. So a particular piece of equipment that is a personal computer might be used at any given moment as part of a timeshare system on a mainframe computer.

A rule of thumb is that a large centralized mainframe computer can handle more complex analyses or larger data sets than a personal computer can, because the former has faster and more powerful processors and more memory. Like all rules of thumb, this one has many exceptions, as technology packs more and more power into smaller and smaller packages. If the particular system you are using cannot handle the job you have in mind, there may well be another system around that can.

Most computers have other input and output devices besides those that communicate with the user. For instance, most personal computers have floppy disks, which can serve as both input and output devices. A computer can write information on the floppy disk at one time (output) and read it back in at another time (input). Because the memory used by most computers goes blank when the electricity is turned off, it may be necessary to write anything you want the computer to know next time onto a floppy disk. Some computers have hard disks, which hold more information than floppy disks and usually can not be removed from the computer. Things you use often you may store on the hard disk, so they will be readily accessible next time you want them.

Hard disks are so convenient, many people whose computers have them wonder whether they would ever use floppy disks again. They will use floppy disks frequently, if they are smart, to make **backups**, copies they will use if anything happens to the main file. Data on hard disks can be damaged. Ask yourself how would you feel if you turned the computer on next time and a particular report, or piece of data, or analysis, was gone? If the idea scares you, then you must make copies onto floppy disks. In particular, remember that instructors (and editors) are not likely to be sympathetic if a promised report is late because "my computer crashed." They are likely to say, "And what about your backups?"

Once you have copies, treat them intelligently. Make more than one copy. Keep the copies up to date. Store the copies in safe places—floppy disks can be damaged by heat, moisture, or exposure to magnetic fields, which surround any electrical appliance. (They say that you should never store disks on the bottom shelf, because when the vacuum cleaner or floor polisher goes by, the data disappear with the dirt.) And be sure not to store all the copies right next to the computer. If something is critical, you do not want the same disaster that takes out the computer to destroy your backups as well. I have copies of this book in my office, my husband's office, and the trunk of my car. The latter is not a great place to keep disks, but if something happened to all the other copies, I might have a chance to recover my files.

Perhaps the most important thing to remember is this: though computers are very fast and very thorough, they are not very smart. If you give a computer the wrong instructions, it will happily compute meaningless quantities, such as an average ID number, or the sum of your participants' ages and their street addresses. The computer deals very well with numbers, but it is up to you to understand what the numbers mean.

Uses of Computers in Research

Having perhaps a little better understanding of what a computer is, let us look at some of the things computers can do to help us with the research process.

Consulting the Literature

Before beginning a research project, and probably while writing the report as well, most researchers will consult the scientific literature to discover what other researchers have found and said about the subject. This topic was discussed briefly in Chapter 11 on writing the research report. Until quite recently the process involved sitting down with a wall full of large books and flipping from page to page, trying to track down the necessary information. These days, computers can help make the process much faster and less painful.

To perform a bibliographic search by computer, you will need access to a data base that includes the abstracts of all the books and articles that were published in a certain field through some period of time, usually years, all indexed by subject. The indexing for every published item is accomplished by someone, either the authors or a paid indexer, who lists the keywords appearing in that article. For instance, an article on teaching remedial reading to retarded teenagers might be indexed under reading, retardation, and teenagers, as well as keywords related to the reading techniques used.

When conducting the computerized search, you will ask the computer how many articles it has indexed under a particular keyword, say, reading. In this case, it would probably reply that there are thousands. You would then restrict the search more and more by specifying additional keywords (teenagers, retarded, or whatever applies in your situation), and also by restricting the time (after 1972, for instance) and the language (usually English only). When the list has been pared down to a more reasonable length, you can have the computer print out the references and their abstracts. This will allow you to examine the abstracts to decide which of these references to read.

Conducting the Research

While research is actually being conducted, there are two jobs computers sometimes have. First, the computer may control what happens in the experiment—for instance, by controlling the presentation of stimuli to the participant. Second, the computer may collect the responses the participant makes, storing them for later analysis. In a variation on this theme, there exist programs that can help conduct content analyses (see Chapter 5) by counting examples of certain words or phrases in a document in its memory.

Computers that control the action of laboratory equipment are often called **laboratory computers**. Such equipment is especially important when the precise timing of events is critical, when a great number of events must appear in precisely the right order and in precisely the right way, or when rapid decisions must be made about calculations based on previous responses. For instance, in biofeedback research, computers can be used to give the participant information nearly instantaneously about various physical variables such as pulse rate and skin temperature. In my thesis research on the perception of moving forms, the forms were generated by a computer according to certain parameters and were presented on a computer monitor. When stimuli are presented by computer, there is less concern about experimenter bias, because the computer (presumably) is not secretly hoping that the participants will respond in a certain way to a certain stimulus.

Unfortunately, there is very little standardization in the area of computer control of laboratory equipment. Dozens of systems exist that allow the computer to control hundreds of different types of equipment, and no two systems are exactly alike. Even if I attempted to review the available products, it would be like trying to hit a target that has moved on between the time I write this and the time you read it. The best way to find out what is available to you is to ask other researchers working with laboratory equipment similar to yours how they are using computers for control purposes.

Regardless of whether the computer controls the situation, its hardware can be used to record the participants' responses. For instance, in my thesis research on moving forms, the participants responded to the forms by pressing various buttons on a special button panel connected to one of the computer's input ports. This allowed the computer to make very detailed records of what button was pressed and exactly when. Computer timekeeping is accurate to milliseconds or even microseconds.

As in the case of laboratory equipment, there is little standardization of computerized data collection. Such standardization would be very difficult, because research requires the flexibility to invent new responses and new types of data for new research questions, which in turn requires new computer input systems to deal with these responses. The most useful aid in developing such systems is a knowledgeable computer technician who can find out what you need and build it for you.

If the purpose is not to conduct original, groundbreaking research, but is instead to conduct laboratory demonstrations of standard experiments, there are numerous programs available to run on personal computers. These can be used either as demonstrations to enhance a lecture course or hands-on exercises for a laboratory course. Such programs are available for most computers, and they vary widely in quality and price. Contact textbook publishers and software stores for catalogs, and look for reviews in teachers' journals.

Analyzing the Data

Once the data are in the computer, they can be treated in a number of different ways. The first step, however, is to make backup copies, as many as possible. If your data are lost or damaged you will have to conduct your whole experiment again from scratch. In addition to the floppy disk copies I discussed before, I also recommend making a print copy of the raw data for each participant and pasting this material into a laboratory notebook. If everything else crashed, you could start over from the raw data without conducting the experiment again.

One of the things computers are best at is handling large quantities of numbers, which makes them perfect for data analysis. They can turn your data into graphs or charts, perform statistical analyses as described in Chapter 10 and Appendix C, print the data sorted by participant, by stimulus, by condition, or by experimenter, and do most any other research manipulation you could ever need. The problem is, the computer makes it so easy that anyone can perform a statistical analysis, even people who do not know what they are doing. This is very dangerous. Anyone using a computer for any analysis should know enough about the procedure to understand what the computer is doing and should have at least a rough idea of the sort of answer to expect. This way, there is a chance of detecting and correcting any problems that may arise.

To perform any statistical analysis, a computer must have a program telling it how to proceed. While some researchers write their own statistical programs, most use **statistical packages**, collections of programs written by others. There are a large number of such packages. Probably the most widely used is **SPSS**, the **Statistical Package for the Social Sciences**, which contains many powerful programs that can perform almost any analysis that a behavioral scientist might expect to use. In fact, anyone who is performing an analysis on a mainframe computer will probably end up using SPSS. Although SPSS usually runs on a mainframe computer, as personal computers become more powerful, more and more of them are able to run large packages such as this one. However, learning to use SPSS can sometimes be tricky. If you have occasion to summon all this power, try to find someone who knows how to use the system to help you. Most college computer centers have available operators who can give you some pointers once you have figured out the basics but are having trouble getting your particular analysis to run properly.

If you are performing an analysis on a personal computer, the choices are wider and therefore more complicated. It is possible to buy small statistical packages that cost little more than the floppy disks they come on and will perform little better than a programmable calculator. It is also possible to buy SPSS to run on a personal computer, though it may have some limitations compared with the mainframe version—for instance, there may be limits on the number of data values it can handle, or it may not be able to perform some analyses at all. In between are countless small packages, all differing in the type of analyses they perform and the type of data they can handle, and more are being offered every month. These packages are advertised in scientific journals for behavioral scientists. Before buying a package, it is best to talk to a user, and, if possible, try it out for a while. This will tell you whether the software is compatible with your needs.

When using a statistical package, you will have to be very careful about how the data are entered. Remember that computers are not intelligent. If you have established, for instance, that the first piece of information for each participant is a telephone number, and you leave this area blank for a participant who has no telephone, a person would figure it out. A computer, however, will not: either it will give you an error message and refuse to perform the analysis at all, which is very frustrating, or it will take the next item, say, the participant's test score, and treat it as a telephone number, which is even more frustrating. You must specify every detail of how every possible sort of information is to be given to the computer. This is sometimes called **coding** the data, because you follow a detailed procedure to convert your information into a particular form. If, for instance, the participants' sex is recorded, you will likely have to convert the usual M for male and F for female into numbers, say 0 for male and 1 for female. All your data will be coded in this way, and it is crucial that the coding procedures be followed exactly.

A typical procedure for using a statistical package involves two steps. First is the data entry. All the data are coded into the proper form for input, and the result is stored somewhere. It can be stored in a deck of punched cards, or more likely in a computer file. A **file** is just a collection of related data that is given a name that permits both the computer and the user to access the unit later. Files can be copied and transferred from one place to another. On a mainframe computer a file may be stored on a disk, a cylinder, a tape, or some other device, and it is not necessary to know exactly where, as long as you know the file name. On a personal computer a file may be in memory, on the hard disk, or on a floppy disk. Because computer memory requires electricity to function, a file that has not been saved will disappear when the power goes off. If it is on the hard disk only, it might be damaged. Make multiple copies on floppy disks and store them in various places.

Once you are satisfied that all the data have been properly coded, you can go on to the next step, which is the actual analysis. You will run whatever program or package you are using, and tell it to get its data from your file or your deck of cards. The program will give you its analysis either in another file or on the printer or both.

When you have a computer printout in your hand, it is very easy to believe that because the computer says so, it must be true. Computers do not make mistakes (assuming the hardware is functioning correctly), but they frequently do give wrong results because of small errors in their instructions or their data. As much as possible, check whether the results make sense, and if not, double-check the data and the program. If you report that group A scored reliably higher than group B, but the mean of group A is 12.7 and that of group B is 12.9, your instructor will not be sympathetic, even if you produce a printout that indicates a reliable result. There must be an error somewhere, either in the means or the test, and you should have caught it.

Reporting the Results

Research that is not reported to others is sterile. Writing a research report is as much a part of the research project as collecting the data. And computers have an important niche in this aspect of research also.

There are two ways computers are used in writing a research report. The first, and by far the more common, is the **word processor**, a program or collection of programs that allows the user to type, correct, revise, format, and print a variety of documents, research reports included. Word processors take a little more effort to learn to use than typewriters, because there are so many different things they can do, and the user must learn the necessary commands. For instance, with a word processor the user can delete individual letters, sentences, or whole passages; move sections of text from one place to another; find every occurrence of a specific word, phrase, or telephone number; change every occurrence of a phrase to another phrase, and so on. Some word processors allow the user to check on the correct spelling of a word, to find appropriate substitutes for an overused word, to count all the words in the document, and so on. The user can typically decide how to arrange the lines on the page and what margins to use; it is also possible to instruct the word processor to number the pages of a report.

If you already have a typewriter, why invest the energy in learning to use a word processor? The main reason is that it makes the revision process, discussed in Chapter 11, much less painful. If you have typed a draft or written it in longhand, revisions involve lots of crossing out, squeezing in, and circles and arrows showing how things are to be rearranged. Then the revised draft must be retyped. This process is clumsy, confusing, and time-consuming, and it makes anyone reluctant to do major rewriting. With a word processor, you can shuffle things around very easily, and you will be freer to experiment with new ideas to find out what works best. When first learning to use a word processor, people often feel that they *would* get the report done faster if they just used a typewriter. Stick with it, though. Remember that it took time and energy to learn to drive, but once you learned, it was a lot faster than walking.

The other application of computers to the research report is much rarer than word processors but gaining in popularity. There exist some programs specifically designed to guide the scientist through the process of developing a research report. For instance, the American Psychological Association has developed program with which a user can produce a report that meets the format specified by the APA. The program will check, for instance, that all the proper sections appear in the proper order, that all the references cited in the text appear in the reference list, and that all the items in the reference list are given in the right order and the right format. I expect this sort of program to become more common in the future.

Conclusions

A one-sentence summary of this appendix might be that computers can be very helpful in virtually every stage of the research process, but you will have to talk to local experts to find out just what is available and how to use it. This book cannot be more helpful for two reasons. First, the number and variety of machines and programs available is so large I would have had to spend prohibitive amounts of time just finding out what is there. Second, even if I had done that exhaustive research, it would have been outdated by the time you read this book.

Good sources of information on computers can usually be located through stores specializing in computers and software. In addition, there are organizations that publish newsletters and reviews of available software for different sorts of users: teachers, researchers, writers, and so on. Try to find these publications. They can help you locate just what you need to automate your own research project.

Appendix B

Displaying Data

Research often (though not always) generates a lot of data. These data may consist of the number of observations that fell into each of several categories or the numerical scores assigned to each observation. In either case, it is usually useful to present the data you obtained in visual form, making it easier for you and your audience to understand. This appendix will show some of the more common ways of presenting data.

Frequency Data

You have frequency data when your measurements are on the nominal level (see Chapter 4). That is, you classify each of your observations into one of several different categories and take the frequency or the number of cases in each category. Chapter 4 offered an example from the study by Waters, Kemp, and Pucci (1988) on how often college students used different sorts of terms to describe their best and worst college teachers (see Table 4-1 on page 84). Each descriptive term was classified as to whether it described a characteristic of the teacher personally, of what went on in the classroom, or of how the teacher related to the students.

There are basically three ways to present this type of data. The first is a frequency table, as given in Table 4-1. Each category is identified, and the number of cases in each one (the **frequency**) is given. Often the frequency is converted into a percentage by dividing it by the total number of observations and multiplying the answer by 100. This is done because when the number of observations is not the same from distribution to distribution, it is easier to compare percentages than actual frequencies.

Another way to present frequency data is to convert the list of descriptors and their frequencies into a more visual representation. A **bar chart** applies to nominal data. First, draw a horizontal line and mark positions on it that correspond to your various groups. Draw a vertical line on the left, mark on the top of it the number of observations in your largest group, and divide it into smaller units so it can be used as a frequency scale. Then draw a line or a bar upward from each category position that goes up to the proper level, as marked on the vertical line, corresponding to its frequency. Figure B-1 shows the same data displayed in Table 4-1, but in a different form. When there are two or more different frequency distributions to be compared, as in Figure B-1, the bars for the different distributions are given in different colors or with different patterns. In one variation the points are connected to each other, instead of showing lines drawn up from the bottom, making a line graph. Sometimes the ends of the line are connected down to the bottom of the graph, as in Figure B-2; this configuration is called a **frequency polygon**, because it encloses a shape made up of many straight lines.

Another way to show frequency data for nominal measurements is to use the corresponding percentages to draw a **pie chart**. In this form, you draw a circle and mark the center point. If you know the diameter of the circle, you can multiply it by pi (a mathematical constant symbolized by π and equal to approximately 3.14159) to find out the circumference, or the distance around the circle. A pie chart can show only one frequency distribution at a time, so it is less useful than a bar chart for comparing different distributions. Let us suppose that I make a pie chart for the data in Table 4-1, showing the best teachers only (since a pie chart cannot display both distributions at once). The result might look like Figure B-3. If I have a circle 10 cm across, this gives a circumference of 10π: 10 x 3.14159 = 31.42 cm. I would pick any point on the circumference of the circle and mark it, then draw a line from there to the center. Then I would multiply the first percentage in my table by 31.42 and divide by 100, to get the number of centimeters around the edge of the

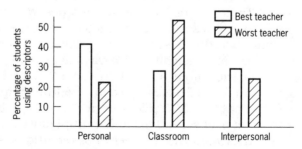

Figure B-1 A bar chart drawn from the frequency table given in Table 4-1. (From Waters, Kemp, & Pucci, 1988.)

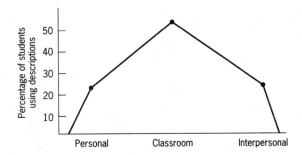

Figure B-2 The "worst teacher" data from Table 4-1 and Figure B-1, redrawn as a frequency polygon. (From Waters, Kemp, & Pucci, 1988.)

circle between the first mark and the next one. Since my first percentage (42%) gives 13.2 cm to the next mark; I draw a line from the 13.2 mark to the center and label it with then name of the first category, in this case "personal characteristics". (Measuring around the circumference of a circle with a straight ruler is not easy. One way to do it is to use string. Hold the string straight against the ruler, pinch off the proper distance (in this case, 13.2 cm) with your fingers, and lay the string along the curve of the circle to find the next point.) If I continue until I have used up all the categories, I should end exactly where I started.

If the measurement is at the ordinal, equal interval, or ratio level, the frequencies are not the number of observations in a certain well-defined group, but the number of measurements that fell between two values. For instance, on a scale of 10, you might want to show the frequencies for ratings from 1 to 3, 4 to 5, 6 to 7, and 8 to 10. A **histogram** is a visual representation of the frequency distribution of a numerical variable such as this. Begin by drawing a horizontal line to represent the variable, and mark on it the points that are the boundaries between the groups whose frequencies you will be showing. In our example, you will put marks at 3.5, 5.5, and 7.5. Then draw a vertical line representing frequency, and

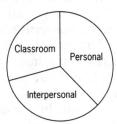

Figure B-3 The "best teacher" data used for Table 4-1 and Figure B-1, redrawn as a pie chart. (From Waters, Kemp, & Pucci, 1988.)

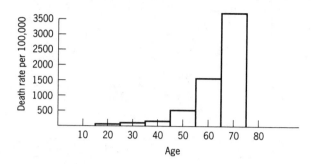

Figure B-4 A histogram of death rates of white male prison inmates. (From Ruback & Innes, 1988.)

plot a vertical bar representing each group that extends vertically to the point corresponding to its frequency. The difference between a histogram and a bar chart is that a histogram represents the frequency of some numeric variable, while the bar chart represents the frequency of some nominal variable. The bars on a bar chart do not touch each other, while the bars on a histogram do touch, because the frequency represented by a histogram bar covers the entire region between the marks. Figure B-4 shows a histogram of frequency data compiled by Ruback and Innes (1988) on the death rate of male prisoners of various ages.

In general, frequency tables are used when it is not as important to compare directly the frequencies of the different groups. Use histograms or bar charts when you want to show at a glance which groups are larger or smaller than other groups. Use a pie chart when you want to emphasize how some large group of things is sliced up into sections.

Multivariate Data

Multivariate data consist of data arrived at by simultaneously measuring two or more variables. If you collected a group of people and simultaneously measured their intelligence and their shoe size, your result would be multivariate data. Alternatively, we use multivariate data when each observation consists of one or more independent variables (assigned, not measured) and a dependent variable (measured). With frequency data, each observation consists of a category and nothing more; here there are two values given to each observation.

Multivariate data displays always have two things in common. First, they have a horizontal line or axis across the bottom, called the **abscissa**, which corresponds to the values of one variable. The abscissa is usually used for the independent variable, or the predictor variable in correlational research. The second component is a vertical line or axis at the left-hand side, called the **ordinate**, which corresponds to the values of the other variable. The ordinate is usually used for the dependent variable, or the predicted variable in correlational research. Both axes have their lowest values at the lower left corner, and the values increase upward and to the right. Each observation is shown in the graph by a dot or other mark at the point directly above its value on the abscissa and directly to the right of its value on the ordinate.

A scatterplot (see Chapter 6) is a multivariate data display for correlational data, in which each point consists of simultaneous measurements of two separate variables. (Actually, scatterplots are **bivariate**, which means they have exactly two variables per observation.) For example, Figure 6-5 (on page 134) shows a scatterplot for some data collected in my class. Each dot on the plot corresponds to one student, with two scores, one on the abscissa and one on the ordinate. In scatterplots there is no particular order to the points, and they are never connected by lines.

A **graph** is another kind of multivariate data display that is typically used for experimental or quasi-experimental data, where there is an independent and a dependent variable. The abscissa corresponds to the independent variable and is labeled with the levels of the variable or with the names of the various groups in the experiment. The ordinate is labeled to correspond to the measured values of the dependent variable. The scores on the dependent variable are averaged for each group, and then they are plotted as a single point on the graph. This point is over the label for that group on the abscissa, and to the right of the average score on the ordinate. For example, the graph shown in Figure B-5 gives the results of Gordon's (1987) study of reported toothbrushing, as discussed in Chapter 10. It is a very simple graph, with only two points. One point indicates the number of times per day people given no special instructions reported brushing their teeth (2.63 toothbrushings per day.) When the instructions were modified to emphasize the importance of answering the question honestly and accurately, however, respon-

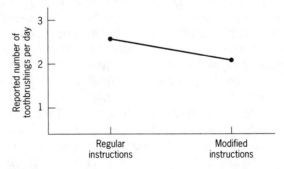

Figure B-5 A very simple multivariate graph, showing the results of the study by Gordon (1987).

dents no longer claimed to have done such a good job (only 2.19 toothbrushings per day), as indicated by the second point.

When there are only two points to show, a graph is probably not much more useful than just giving the numbers, as I did above. Most graphs give data on observations that have more than two variables. Typically these graphs show the results of factorial experiments (see Chapter 7), where each observation is associated with a certain level of each of two independent variables, plus a dependent variable measurement. For example, Figure 7-3 (on page 161) shows the results of the study by Chaiken and Pliner (1987) of how people's perceptions of men and women are affected by how much they eat. Each observation is categorized on two independent variables: meal size (small vs. large), and the sex of the person being evaluated (male vs. female). The observation also has a measurement of the dependent variable, in this case how concerned that person seemed to be about his or her appearance. When there are two independent variables like this, only one can go on the abscissa (in this case, meal size). The other one is expressed by plotting the points separately for each level of the variable (in this case, separate points for males and for females at each meal size), each point plotted across from the average score for appearance concern for all the people in that group. To make it clearer, all the points for one level of the second independent variable are connected by lines, to help keep them separate from the points for the other level. In this case, the points for the men are connected and the points for the women are connected. Then the lines are labeled, so the reader can tell which points correspond to which level of the independent variable. With this sort of graph, it is easy to visualize the interaction effect the authors reported. The line for the men is almost flat, which means that men got virtually the same score for appearance concern no matter what size meal they ate. The line for the women, however, is steeply sloped. The women seemed to be much more concerned about their appearance (got higher scores on the dependent variable) when they ate small meals and much less concerned (got lower scores) when they ate large meals.

Sometimes a graph of multivariate data can generate confusion even with the lines drawn, especially if some of the lines fall very close together. In such cases it is often useful to use different symbols for the different groups instead of dots. For instance, the graph in Figure 9-5 (on page 201) shows data from two different years, for national surveys and for Atlanta surveys, for blacks and for whites. That is, there are three different independent variables: year (1970 and 1976), region (national and Atlanta), and group (blacks and whites). Again, only one falls on the abscissa, in this case the year. The other two have to be plotted separately, giving four separate lines on the graph. This would be quite confusing if all the points were marked with dots. Instead, this graph uses circles for the national figures and triangles for the Atlanta figures, and open shapes for the whites, and solid shapes for the blacks. The legend on the side of the graph describes all this for the reader.

Appendix C

Statistical Computations

While a complete presentation on statistics is way beyond this book, most of the students using it will find themselves conducting some sort of research as a course requirement, and this research will often call for the use of statistical computation. Therefore, this appendix discusses some of the most common statistical values and tests: what they are for, how to perform them, and how to interpret their results.

A Note on Computations

Most researchers today use computer programs to perform their statistical analyses, as discussed in Appendix A. If you have access to such a thing, by all means find out how to use it to analyze your data. However, in case such electronic assistance is unavailable to you, you will be happy to know that all the **statistical tests** described here can be performed with a simple calculator given a little time and diligence. [Note that some of the tests require a calculator with a square-root ($\sqrt{\ }$) key.]

Even the simplest statistical analysis requires many separate calculations, so it is crucial that steps be taken to ensure accuracy. The best way to do this is for two people to use the same starting data and, without communicating with each other, compute the final statistic. If the results agree, you can be reasonably sure that there were no small slips of the calculator keys, although both analysts might have made the same mistake in interpreting the procedure. If the results disagree, you will have to go over the analysis step by step until the point of disagreement is found, and then you will have to figure out the correct path. Work carefully. It will be helpful to use clean pieces of paper, writing down all your intermediate results and labeling them clearly so that any errors can be located and corrected.

If you are working alone, perform the complete calculation once, working neatly and keeping all intermediate results as described above. Then take a blank piece of paper and do it all again from the beginning, preferably after taking a break to minimize the chances of repeating one of your mistakes. Always remember that teachers usually take a very dim view of careless errors in computation, especially if they should have been easy to catch, as when a student of mine reported that scores "ranged from 15 to 28 points, with an average of 32.3 points."

Correlation Coefficients

A correlation, as described in Chapter 6, is a number, between -1.0 and +1.0, that describes the strength and direction of the relation between two variables. If the coefficient is zero, then there is no relation. If it is positive, it means that the two variables go in the same direction, so that if one gets larger, the other also tends to get larger. If it is negative, it means that the variables go in the opposite direction, so that if one gets larger, the other tends to get smaller.

There are many different correlation coefficients, calculated in different ways from variables of different types. We will look at the two most common, the Pearson product–moment correlation, called r, and the Spearman rank–order correlation, called **rho** (ρ; also symbolized by r_s).

Pearson Product–Moment Correlation (r)

The Pearson r is probably the most common correlation coefficient and is generally that one that is meant if a researcher does not specify which correlation was used. It is the most powerful coefficient, in that it will find relations that other correlations miss, as long as they are straight-line relations between parametric variables (see Chapter 10). If the variables being measured are not parametric, or if the relation between them cannot be represented by a straight line, then either the variables must be redefined to make them fit these criteria or another correlation should be used.

To calculate a Pearson r, you must first arrange all the measurements into pairs, with one measurement of one variable paired with its corresponding measurement of another variable, and find the total for each variable. The first variable is named X and the second is named Y. The sum of each set of observations is shown by using the Greek letter **sigma**, so that the sum of the X scores is ΣX and the sum of the Y scores is ΣY. For instance, the first two columns of Table C-1 contain the measurements of two variables, students' grades on the first and second research papers in a research methods course. These data, shown in a

Table C-1 Calculating the Pearson *r* Correlation Coefficient.

First Score:	Second Score:	First Score Squared:	Second Score Squared:	First x Second Score:
X	Y	X²	Y²	XY
54	68	2916	4624	3672
57	65	3249	4225	3705
62	62	3844	3844	3844
65	63	4225	3969	4095
68	73	4624	5329	4964
70	79	4900	6241	5530
72	70	5184	7900	5040
73	84	5329	7056	6132
75	82	5625	6724	6150
78	80	6084	6400	6240
80	82	6400	6724	6560
82	95	6724	9025	7790
84	88	7056	7744	7392
87	94	7569	8836	8178
88	95	7744	9025	8360
89	89	7921	7921	7921
90	87	8100	7569	7830
91	93	8281	8649	8463
92	89	8464	7921	8188
95	98	9025	9604	9310
Σ: 1552	1636	123,264	139,330	129,364

$N = 20$

$$r = \frac{N(\Sigma XY) - (\Sigma X)(\Sigma Y)}{\sqrt{\left[N(\Sigma X^2) - (\Sigma X)^2\right]\left[N(\Sigma Y^2) - (\Sigma Y)^2\right]}}$$

$$r = \frac{20(129,364)) - (1552)(1636)}{\sqrt{\left[20(123,264) - (1552)^2\right]\left[20(139,330) - (1636)^2\right]}}$$

$$= \frac{2,587,280 - 2,539,072}{\sqrt{\left[20(123,264) - 2,408,704\right]\left[20(139,330) - 2,676,496\right]}}$$

$$= \frac{48,208}{\sqrt{(56,576)(110,104)}} = \frac{48,208}{78,925} = .61$$

scatterplot in Figure 7-5, are arranged in Table C-1 so that each pair contains the grades of the same student. At the bottom of each column appears the total of all the grades in that column.

Next, take the **square** of each of the *X* scores in the first column (that is, multiply the number by itself), put these squared scores in a new column, X^2, and calculate the sum of all the scores in the column, ΣX^2. Then do the same thing with the *Y* values in the second column to create a new column, Y^2, and its sum, ΣY^2. Finally, make a fifth column containing the product you get by multiplying together the two scores in each pair from columns 1 and 2. The last column is called *XY*, and its sum is ΣXY. The only other thing you need for the calculation is the total number of pairs of scores, called *N*.

Once you have all this information, you plug it into the equation shown in Table C-1 and repeated here:

$$r = \frac{N(\Sigma XY) - (\Sigma X)(\Sigma Y)}{\sqrt{\left[N(\Sigma X^2) - (\Sigma X)^2\right]\left[N(\Sigma Y^2) - (\Sigma Y)^2\right]}}$$

That is, you insert data from your table into the equation for r. In this case, you multiply the number of pairs (*N*) by the sum of the product column (ΣXY) and subtract from it the product of the two sums of scores (ΣX times ΣY) to get the numerator. Then you take the sum of the *X* scores, square it, subtract it from the sum of the *X* squared scores, and multiply by the number of pairs. Do the same for the *Y* scores, and multiply these two numbers together. Take the square root, and this gives the denominator. Divide the numerator by the denominator, and this is the value of *r*, as worked out in Table C-1.

After calculating something this complex, you will have to check your work, or better yet, get someone else to check it for you. In particular, you know you have made a mistake if the number is outside the -1.0 to +1.0 range. If you have drawn a scatterplot of your data (see Chapter 6), you can decide whether the coefficient should be positive or negative, and perhaps roughly how strong it should be. If your result does not match, you probably have made an error in arithmetic. This is why it is better to use a computer if you can.

Spearman Rank–Order Correlation (rho)

The Spearman *rho*, a correlation based solely on ranks, applies to variables measured on an ordinal scale (see Chapter 4), which makes it a nonparametric statistic (see Chapter 10). It can find any relationship between variables with equal power, provided only that the relationship is monotonic, which means that as one variable gets larger, the other always tends to get larger (or always smaller), without reversing itself and going the other way. That is, if you followed a graph of the relationship from left to right, the curve would either always go up or always go down, but it would never go one way for a while and then reverse itself (see Figure C-1).

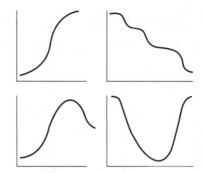

Figure C-1 The top two curves are montonic, because they do not reverse themselves but either consistently increase or consistently decrease as you go from left to right. (They can have flat plateaus, but no hills or valleys.) The bottom two curves are not monotonic, because they start to go in one direction and then switch.

To calculate the Spearman rho, you begin by collecting your pairs of scores, just as with the Pearson *r*. Table C-2 shows the number of hours a group of students spent studying, paired with each student's grade in the course, which are shown in a scatterplot in Figure 7-6. Number the pairs from 1 to *N*. Then take all the scores on one variable and rearrange them in rank order, making sure to keep track of which pairs of numbers go together. One way is to write the number of the pair next to the score in parentheses. You will put the lowest score first, the second-lowest score next, and so on. When all the scores are in order, write next to them the rank for each score. (If two or more scores are the same, take the ranks they would be assigned if they were different—1, 2, 3, and 4 in the case of the zero scores in Table C-2—and calculate their average, by adding those ranks and dividing by the number of paired scores (1 + 2 + 3 + 4 = 10/4 = 2.5). Then assign this averaged rank to each score in the tie.) You now have three things on each line: the pair number, the score, and its rank. Do the same for the scores on the other variable.

Now you must calculate a difference score, called *D*, for each pair. To do this, find the rank for that pair's score on the first variable and subtract from it the rank for its score on the second variable. Once you have computed all the D scores, square each one (by multiplying it by itself) to get a group of squared differences, D^2. Add all these squares, to get the sum of squared differences, ΣD^2. Finally, use this number and the number of pairs (*N*) in the following formula:

$$\rho = 1 - \frac{6\Sigma D^2}{N^3 - N}$$

(where N^3 means "*N* cubed," or *N* multiplied by itself 3 times).

Table C-2 Calculating the Spearman rho Correlation Coefficient

Pair Number	Hours	Rank	Grade	Rank	D	D²
1	0	2.5	76	12.5	-10	100
2	0	2.5	82	14	-11.5	132.25
3	0	2.5	85	16	-13.5	182.25
4	0	2.5	96	18	-15.5	240.25
5	10	6.5	52	2	4.5	20.25
6	10	6.5	68	8	- 1.5	2.25
7	10	6.5	75	11	- 4.5	20.25
8	10	6.5	88	17	-11.5	132.25
9	15	10	67	7	3	9
10	15	10	72	9.5	0.5	0.25
11	15	10	83	15	- 5	25
12	20	13	43	1	12	144
13	20	13	62	4	9	91
14	20	13	76	12.5	0.5	0.25
15	30	15.5	65	6	- 0.5	0.25
16	30	15.5	72	9.5	6	36
17	40	17.5	57	3	14.5	210.25
18	40	17.5	63	5	12.5	156.25
N = 18						ΣD² = 1502

Sorting Grade Variable

Grade	Pair Number	Rank	Calculating rho
43	12	1	
52	5	2	$\rho = 1 - \dfrac{6\Sigma D^2}{N^3 - N}$
57	17	3	
62	13	4	
63	18	5	$\rho = \dfrac{6 - 1502}{(18)(18)(18) - 18} = -1496 / 5814 = -.26$
65	15	6	
67	9	7	
68	6	8	
72	10	9.5	
72	16	9.5	
75	7	11	
76	1	12.5	
76	14	12.5	
82	2	14	
83	11	15	
85	3	16	
88	8	17	
96	4	18	

As you can see, the actual calculations are much simpler for the Spearman correlation than for the Pearson. The Spearman has the other advantage of applying to a broader range of data, because it is a nonparametric test. The main disadvantage of the Spearman correlation compared to the Pearson is that, if the assumptions of a parametric test are met (see Chapter 10), and if the relationship between the variables is a straight line, the Pearson correlation could find a relationship that is considerably weaker than any that the Spearman correlation could find.

Four Common Statistical Tests

This section briefly describes four tests that are commonly used by students in analyzing their research projects. The type of data to which they apply, the specific values needed for the computation, and the type of result produced are described for each of the tests. This should enable you to decide whether one of these tests is suitable for your project.

Testing a Frequency (Binomial Test)

The binomial test is used to determine whether the results of one group differ from some standard value. Thus it is a one-sample statistic, in that there is only one level of the independent variable and all measurements fall into only one group. In particular, the binomial test is used when there are only two possible results for each observation, and the measurement consists of determining which of the two results occurred in each case. (A measurement like this is at the nominal level, and therefore this is a nonparametric statistic.) The **binomial test**, then, is used when all observations fall into one of two categories, and you wind up with the number of cases out of the total that fell into each category. This is a frequency, or it can be divided by the total number of cases and multiplied by 100 to give a percentage.

To calculate how likely a particular proportion is, you will need to know n (the total number of things that were classified into the two groups), p (the probability that any particular observation would go into the first group just by chance), and r (the actual number of observations that fell into the smaller of the two groups). Then you can compute q (the probability that an observation would go into the second group just by chance), which will be $1 - p$. Once you have these values, n, p, q, and r, you are ready to begin calculating the probability that the particular frequency x would occur by chance.

There are two methods for doing a binomial test, depending on how big your sample is (n) and what your probabilities are (p and q). If both p and *q* are equal to 1/2 , and *n* is less than 25, then you have a small-sample case. If your probabilities are different from 1/2 or *n* is 25 or larger, then you have a large-sample case.

In a small-sample case, you will use Table D-4 in Appendix D. Simply find your value of *n* down the side of the table, and the number of cases in your smaller group (*r*) across the top. The value in the cell is the probability of getting that frequency by chance. For instance, if your value of *n* was 10 and you had 2 cases in your smaller group, you would find that your probability was .1094. If this is less than your cutoff probability, you can conclude that your result is reliable.

For example, Barthol and Ku (1955) performed a study of the effects of stress on performance. They taught 18 college students two different ways to tie the same knot. Half the students (randomly selected) were taught method A first, and the other half were taught method B first. Then all the students were subjected to the stress of taking a four-hour exam, at midnight. After the exam all the students were asked to tie the knot. The dependent variable was the method each student would select to use: the one learned first, or the second one. The research hypothesis (see Chapter 10) was that the participants would use the method they had learned first; the null hypothesis was that there would be no difference in the probability of selecting one method or the other. Of the 18 students, 16 chose to use the method they had learned first. The researchers believed that the stress caused the students to regress to the simplest method they knew, which was the one they had learned first. But to make this claim, they had to show that this frequency (16 out of 18, or 89%) was reliably different from what you would expect by chance (9 out of 18, or 50%). Because their probabilities *p* and *q* were both $^1/_2$ and their *n* was less than 25, this is a small-sample case. Table D-4 in Appendix D shows us that, for *n* = 18 and an *r* of 2, the probability is .0013, so Barthol and Ku concluded that their result was reliable.

A table to give probabilities for the large-sample case would be larger than this book. Instead, an approximation is used that is close enough. It is called the normal approximation, because it uses the standard normal table, given in this book as Table D-5 of Appendix D. To use the table, convert your binomial frequency *r* to a standard normal score **z** by using the formula:

$$z = \frac{|r-(np)|-.5}{\sqrt{(np(1-p))}}$$

The vertical bars indicate "absolute value," which means that if the subtraction gives you a negative value, you should throw away the minus sign. DO NOT throw away minus signs in any other place. Also note that you can use this formula for any values of *n*, *p*, and *r*. Just be careful that *p* and *r* both refer to the same category of observations.

Having computed z, look for this value in the first column of Table D-5. (If the z value you computed is negative, ignore the minus sign.) Your z value will probably fall between two of the numbers given, in which case the probability of getting that result by chance is somewhere between the corresponding two probabilities in the second column of the table. If the larger probability is less than your cutoff frequency, your result is reliably different from chance.

There is no specific symbol for the result of a binomial test, so to report their results, Barthol and Ku would not be able to use a string of symbols like those described in Chapter 10. Instead, they would say that their result was reliable by the binomial test, and then, in parentheses, give the particulars ($n = 18$, $r = 2$, $p < .0013$).

Testing a Frequency Distribution (Chi-Square)

The **chi-square test** (also written with the Greek letter χ^2) can be used to compare one frequency distribution with another frequency distribution. As mentioned in Chapter 4, a frequency distribution is a description of a variable measured on a nominal level, which lists the number of observations that fall into each of the possible categories. A grade distribution, giving the number of A's, B's, C's, and so on in a particular class, is one example of a frequency distribution. Because this is another nominal measurement, the chi-square test is also a nonparametric test.

The chi-square test can be used in a one-sample case, to compare a measured distribution with some standard distribution, or in a multiple-sample case, to compare two or more different measured distributions with each other. The chi-square test will not tell you that one distribution is larger or smaller or anything like that, but it will tell you whether the distributions are different.

The **chi-square goodness-of-fit test** applies to the one-sample case, because what you are doing is testing how well your measured distribution fits the standard distribution. Usually, the standard to which researchers are comparing is a flat or even distribution, in which all categories are equally likely. Sometimes, however, there is a different standard. It does not matter where the standard distribution comes from, as long as it can be used to produce expected frequencies in each category. Then the basic chi-square arithmetic can convert the observed and expected frequencies into the probability that the observed frequencies came from the standard distribution.

In the multiple-sample case, the chi-square test is comparing different observed frequency distributions. That is, you measure how a variable is distributed in one set of conditions and also how it is distributed in another set of conditions, and compare the distributions. This is called a **chi-square test of association**, because it allows you to determine whether two variables are associated: the variable that you are counting to give the frequencies, and the variable that determines the different conditions of measurement. In a test of association, the expected frequencies are not provided by a standard distribution. Instead, you must calculate them according to a formula. Then you apply the usual chi-square method to the observed and expected frequencies to determine how likely it is that the distribution is the same under the different condition.

To compute chi-square, make a row for each of the distributions you are comparing. (There will be only one row for the goodness-of-fit test.) Label the rows according to the distribution they come from, and label the columns according to the category of observations they represent. In each cell write the observed frequency, the actual number of cases found in that category in that distribution. Label the observed frequencies *o*.

Next, calculate the row and column totals. (This step applies only to the test of association.) Add all the observations in each distribution and write the total at the end of the row. These are the row totals, labeled *r*. Then add all the observations in each category and write the totals under the columns. These are the column totals, labeled *c*. Add up all the row totals and then all the column totals. The sum of the row totals and the sum of the column totals should be the same. This number is the grand total, labeled *T*. Write it in the lower right-hand corner.

The next step is to calculate the expected frequencies. In the goodness-of-fit test, the expected frequencies will be given by the standard distribution to which your observed distribution is being compared. In the test of association you will calculate the expected frequencies from your row and column totals. In each cell, multiply that cell's row total by that cell's column total, and divide the result by the grand total. Write the expected value in the cell, and label it *e*.

Finally, in each cell you will calculate a departure from the expected value. First, subtract the expected value from the observed value, and square the result. Divide the result by the expected value. Call this number *x* and write it in the cell, too.

You now have three values in each cell: *o*, the observed frequency in the cell; *e*, the expected value, which is given by the standard distribution in the goodness-of-fit case or by the formula $(c \times r) / T$ in the test of association; and x, the departure from the expected value, given by the formula $(o - e)^2 / e$. To calculate chi-square, simply add all the *x* values in all the cells. That is:

$$x = \Sigma \frac{(\mathrm{obs} - \mathrm{exp})^2}{\mathrm{exp}}$$

Having calculated chi-square, you must next calculate the **degrees of freedom** (df) of your study. This is a number that reflects the number of independent observations in your study, which for mathematical reasons is not the same as the number of measurements you made. The theory behind the degrees of freedom is beyond this book, but calculating them is easy. For the test of association, this is equal to one less than the number of rows in your table times one less than the number of columns: $(R - 1)(C - 1)$. For the goodness-of-fit test, it is simply one less than the number of columns, or $C - 1$. Now you can look up your result in Table D-2 of Appendix D. Find the number of degrees of freedom (df) down the left side, and look across the row until you find two numbers on either side of the calculated value. The probability that the differences in your distributions are due to chance falls between the two probabilities given at the tops of those two columns. If the larger of the two probabilities is equal to or less than your cutoff probability, you can conclude that the distributions are reliably different from each other or from the standard.

For an example of the goodness-of-fit test, consider the work of Carroll (1986), who reported on a method for encouraging cooperation among college students in laboratory and discussion courses. The approach was called the jigsaw technique because each student was obliged to make a small, unique contribution to the project, like a piece of a jigsaw puzzle. Caroll applied the technique in a one-credit laboratory course in which students were learning to use the concepts of research design in a general topic area by planning and conducting an original research project. In four years of experience, he was dissatisfied with the course because students were unhappy with it, and in fact in one semester one-third of them failed to complete the course at all. After the jigsaw technique had been applied, however, students were much happier with the course and tended to complete it on time. Caroll reported that the method was very successful.

Carroll's (1986) article was largely descriptive, but he gave enough information to permit the use of a chi-square test to see whether the percentage of students completing the course on time actually changed when the jigsaw technique was introduced (see Table C-3). The research hypothesis (see Chapter 10) is that the frequency distribution is different before the change and after; the null hypothesis is that no change occurred. The percentage of students finishing on time, finishing late, or never finishing at all over the first four years provided the expected frequencies in the chi-square analysis. When compared with the observed frequencies under the jigsaw technique, the chi-square analysis shows clear evidence of a change. That is, the difference is highly reliable $\chi^2(2)$(i.e., chi-square with 2 degress of freedom) = 16.2, and from Table D-2 we find $p < .001$).

For an example of the test of association, consider a study by Schatz and Best (1987) on why students change answers on multiple-choice tests and whether these changes helped or hurt them. The investigators gave students in their course a multiple-choice test and asked them to

Table C-3 Calculating Chi-Square from Data by Carroll (1986)

On Time	Late	Drop/F
o: 40	o: 1	o: 5
e: 29.4	e: 13.3	e: 3.2
x: 3.82	x: 11.37	x: 1.01

df = 3 - 1 = 2
$\chi = \Sigma x$
χ^2 = 3.82 + 11.37 + 1.01 = 16.2
The distributions are reliably different: $\chi^2(2)$ = 16.2, $p < .001$.

Table C-4 Calculating Chi-Square from Data by Schatz and Best (1987)

Reason	Answer Changing Outcome			
	Wrong-to-Wrong	Right-to-Wrong	Wrong-to-Right	Row Totals
Wrong space	o: 5	o: 1	o: 14	20
	e: 4.9	e: 4.0	e: 11.1	
	x: .002	x: 2.25	x: .758	
Misread question	o: 3	o: 6	o: 30	39
	e: 9.6	e: 7.7	e: 21.6	
	x: 4.54	x: .375	x: 3.27	
Better guess	o: 22	o: 20	o: 23	65
	e: 16.0	e: 12.9	e: 36.1	
	x: 2.25	x: 3.91	x: 4.75	
Clue in later question	o: 6	o: 2	o: 14	22
	e: 5.5	e: 4.4	e: 12.2	
	x: .045	x: 1.31	x: .266	Grand Total:
Column totals: 36		29	81	146

e = row total x column total / grand total
df = (# rows - 1) x (# columns - 1) = (4 - 1) x (3 - 1) = 3 x 2 = 6
$\chi^2 = \Sigma x$ = .002 + 2.25 + .758 + 4.54 + .375 + 3.27 + 2.25 + 3.91 + 4.75 + .045 + 1.31 + .266
The variables are reliably related: $\chi^2(6)$ = 23.73, p < .001.

identify each answer they changed on the test and to indicate their reason for making the change. The reasons had to be selected from a list of four possible choices: accidentally marked the wrong answer, misread or misinterpreted the question the first time, were unsure of the first answer and decided the second answer was a better guess, and read something in a later item that gave a hint about the item that was changed. For each of these four reasons, the researchers calculated the number of times the change went from one wrong answer to another wrong answer, from wrong to right, or from right to wrong. That is, there were four frequency distributions, one for each of the four reasons, and three categories, corresponding to the three possible types of changes. The researchers performed a test of association to find out whether the reason for changing an answer was related to the type of change that it made, that is, whether the four frequency distributions were different (see Table C-4). The research hypothesis was that the distributions were different; the null hypothesis was that they were the same. The result was that the variables were reliably related. When the students changed an answer to a "better guess," they were just as likely to make their score worse as better, but when they changed for any other reason, the change tended to improve their score. These results were reported with the string: $\chi^2(6) = 23.73$, $p < .001$.

Testing a Difference in Means (t-Test)

A very common experimental situation is to compare the mean value of the dependent variable in two different groups, each with a different level of the independent variable. This is what Gordon (1987) did in his study on the social desirability bias in reported dental hygiene, discussed in Chapter 10. When comparing the means or averages of two different groups, the most common statistical test is the *t*-test. [This test is formally known as **Student's t**, because W. S. Gosset, the inventor, wrote about it in a series of papers that he signed, not with his own name, but just with "Student" (1908).] Because this test requires the computation of means (or its mathematical equivalent), which involves adding and dividing the scores, the measurements must be at least at the equal interval level of measurement, and this is a parametric test. The *t*-test should not be used when the assumptions of parametric tests are not met (see Chapter 10).

The *t*-test can be used with either independent groups, as in Gordon's study, or with related groups. However, the procedure is slightly different in the two situations. With independent groups (see Table C-5), you first calculate several basic numbers from your data: N_1 is the number of observations in group 1; ΣX_1 is the sum of all the values in group 1; M_1 is the mean of the values in group 1; ΣX_1^2 is the sum of the squared values in group 1; and N_2, ΣX_2, M_2, and ΣX_2^2 are the correspond-

Table C-5 Calculating the Value of *t* from Two Independent Samples (Fictional Data)

X_1	X_1^2	X_2	X_2^2
16	256	19	361
23	529	15	225
18	324	17	289
22	484	14	196
21	441	21	441
24	576	16	256
19	361	15	225
16	256	17	289
20	400	19	361
19	361	16	256
Σ: 198	3988	169	2899

$M_1 = 19.8$
$M_2 = 16.9$
$N_1 = N_2 = 10$
3988 - 10(19.8)+2899-10(16.9)

$$s^2 = \frac{\Sigma X_1^2 - N_1 M_1^2 + \Sigma X_2^2 - N_2 M_2^2}{N_1 + N_2 - 2}$$

$$s^2 = \frac{3988 - 10(19.8)^2 + 2899 = 10(16.9)^2}{10 + 10 - 2}$$

$$= \frac{3988 - 3920 + 2899 - 2856}{18} = \frac{111}{18} = 6.17$$

$$t = \frac{19.8 - 16.9}{\sqrt{(6.17/10) + (6.17/10)}} = \frac{2.9}{\sqrt{1.23}} = \frac{2.9}{1.11} = 2.64$$

df = 10 + 10 - 2 = 18
This difference is reliable [$t(18) = 2.64$, $p < .05$]; see Appendix D, Table D-3.

ing values for group 2. From these numbers, you calculate s^2, an estimate of the variance, using the formula:

$$s^2 = \frac{\Sigma X_1^2 - N_1 M_1^2 + \Sigma X_2^2 - N_2 M_2^2}{N_1 + N_2 - 2}$$

Then you plug this number into another equation to calculate the value of *t*:

$$t = \frac{M_1 - M_2}{\sqrt{s^2 / N_1 + s^2 / N_2}}$$

There is one other thing you will need, which is the degrees of freedom (df) of your test. This is just the total number of observations in both groups, minus 2 (df = $N_1 + N_2 - 2$).

To decide whether your groups are reliably different, use Table D-3 of Appendix D. First find your value of df down the side of the table. Then look across the row until you find the two numbers on either side of your value for t. The probability that your means are really the same will be somewhere between the two probabilities at the top of those two columns. If the larger of the two probabilities is less than or equal to your cutoff probability, the two groups are reliably different. Gordon's study found a reliable difference between the means of the two independent groups, and this result could be reported with the string: $t(46) = 1.92$, $p < .05$.

The technique with related groups is somewhat different (see Table C-6). First you produce a set of scores that is the *difference* between the related scores in the two different groups; that is, you subtract each score in group 2 from the related score in group 1. You wind up with only one score for each related pair, a difference score. The value of t is calculated from the difference scores (D) and the squares of the difference scores (D^2) using the formula:

$$t = \frac{\Sigma D}{\sqrt{\left[N\left(\Sigma D^2\right)-\left(\Sigma D\right)^2/(N-1)\right]}}$$

Table C-6 Calculating the Value of t From Two Related Groups, Using the Same Data as in Table B-1

	Data			Calculations
X_1	X_2	D	D^2	
16	19	-3	9	
23	15	8	64	$t = \dfrac{\Sigma D}{N\left(\Sigma D^2\right)-\left(\Sigma D\right)^2/(N-1)}$
18	17	1	1	
22	14	8	64	
21	21	0	0	$t = \dfrac{29}{\sqrt{\left[10(229)-841\right]/9}} = \dfrac{29}{\sqrt{1449/9}} = \dfrac{29}{\sqrt{161}}$
24	16	8	64	
19	15	4	16	
16	17	-1	1	$= \dfrac{29}{12.7} = 2.28$
20	19	1	1	
19	16	3	9	
Σ:		29	229	

$(\Sigma D)^2 = 841$

$N = 10$

df = 9

This difference is reliable: $t(9) = 2.28$, $p < .05$.

In this formula, ΣD represents the sum of all the difference scores, (ΣD^2) is obtained by squaring each score and adding these totals, $(\Sigma D)^2$ is obtained by adding all the scores first and then squaring, and N represents the total number of difference scores. The degrees of freedom for this test is $N - 1$. You look your value up in Table D-3 of Appendix D just as you did for the independent sample t test discussed above.

In Friedman's (1987) study on the effect of taking repeat exams in a statistics course, discussed in Chapter 10, the two groups are not independent, because the final exam scores are compared with lecture exam scores produced by the same students. (What are the research and the null hypotheses in this example?) The difference in scores between the lecture exams and the final exams, for B students who took two or three repeat exams, was more than 4 percentage points, and this difference was reliably different from zero. This result was reported with the string: $t(18) = 3.66$, $p < .001$. There was no reliable difference for B students who took one repeat exam or none, which implies that the repeat exams helped improve the grades of the students who took them.

Testing a Correlation (t-Test)

Finally, there are ways to test the reliability of a correlation coefficient. You will recall from Chapter 6 that a correlation coefficient is a number that varies from -1.00 to +1.00 and measures the strength of the relationship between two variables. If the coefficient is very near zero, there is no relationship. The further the number is from zero, the stronger the relationship. If the number is positive, there is a positive relationship between the variables, so that large values of one variable are associated with large values of the other variable. If the number is negative, the relationship is negative, so that large values of one variable are associated with small values of the other variable.

You may also remember that there are different correlation coefficients, although the Pearson product–moment correlation, r, is the most common. The Pearson r is a parametric statistic and is not appropriate for situations in which the variables are not measured at the equal interval or the ratio level. It is also poor at finding curved relationships between variables, because it looks for straight lines. A nonparametric correlation coefficient, useful for ordinal level data and for curved relationships, is the Spearman rank–order correlation, r_s, also called rho. Formulas for calculating both these statistics appeared earlier in this appendix. Other correlation coefficients exist for use in different circumstances, many of which are described in Siegel and Castellan (1988).

After you have calculated a correlation coefficient, it is often useful to find out whether the correlation is reliably different from chance. Fernald (1987) was in this situation after finding the correlation between how much narrative structure there was in textbook chapters and how much students liked them, as discussed in Chapter 10. The correlation he used was the Spearman rho, (can you follow the reasoning that caused him to choose this coefficient?) and the value he calculated was $r_s = .637$, but what does this mean? Is this number high enough to permit us to feel confident that narrative structure is really related to preference? To test this, Fernald conducted a test of the reliability of his value of rho. (Can you identify the research and the null hypotheses in this example?)

To test the reliability of a correlation, you use the coefficient to compute another statistic, the **test statistic**. In the case of both the Pearson *r* and the Spearman rho, the test statistic used is the now-familiar Student's *t*. The conversion is pretty simple, and requires that you know only the value of the correlation coefficient (*r* or r_s) and the number of observations on which it is based (*N*, the sample size). The formula is the same for both these coefficients. The formula for calculating t (where "coeff" refers to the Pearson r or the Spearman rho) is:

$$t = \frac{\text{coeff}}{\sqrt{1 - \text{coeff}}} \sqrt{N - 2}$$

The degrees of freedom for this test is *N* - 2, and the result can be looked up in Table D-3 of Appendix D as for any other *t*-test.

When we apply this formula to Fernald's Spearman rho, we get $t(7) = 2.19$, $p < .05$, which means that the correlation is reliably different from zero. (Actually, for small samples such as the nine different chapters Fernald used, tables exist that will give the probability *p* directly without converting from rho to *t*. This is what Fernald did, so he did not report a value for *t*, because he never actually calculated one. Either way, however, the value of *p* comes out to be less than .05.)

Appendix D

Statistical Tables

Table D-1 Random Numbers

```
096157 097019 764932 398534 698290 967967 850803 718794 042150
660453 619913 778071 059056 749891 075305 533179 605649 343297
145423 140938 743208 386953 068056 314272 888161 247925 596654
752687 835072 828199 653760 399272 034837 383297 173984 082833
384424 497268 789796 038194 523306 986017 978300 048003 918478
308909 321249 521927 395942 448598 334834 516052 708370 344996
578588 981405 149430 214435 900048 327817 587882 052328 516205
243238 354440 170394 869258 467190 898040 839096 428589 207740
838507 943754 470245 156315 076032 609243 586290 528566 938898
722603 348874 117620 424550 108322 536094 822677 838040 946219
563669 907546 089142 144512 262008 277831 104300 763871 641317
692450 379382 253163 692356 337728 237436 175894 430636 291366
878573 995010 505459 667488 335911 234481 429309 513994 802507
349871 825367 494507 238274 154279 122582 936200 330610 754053
869414 591690 103136 337980 172081 317678 733051 361597 196590
544012 937296 039641 069306 098720 563464 883203 953285 102243
737022 802981 744458 706557 529729 781610 886816 861786 220046
414918 360857 002688 888059 102567 156661 021818 796832 132313
```

Table D-1, continued

450851 339410 716322 574884 998734 389112 697320 562805 844845

136026 140762 717240 341058 049604 192883 267153 475034 263924

369138 479803 909948 573954 067565 561881 881399 017685 945864

471597 713655 672705 810518 905842 477301 563823 561336 632634

535169 084504 315372 162630 805819 984600 938150 395944 515378

260844 603451 510214 316177 889889 166733 652036 905602 511739

792675 504659 896099 946793 313237 039009 505136 645879 732604

762989 297837 377796 802392 019864 139044 973305 474188 109017

578896 650884 661823 101995 430221 331760 455341 306206 676244

146745 025619 738555 301508 354110 377005 887366 568361 007080

288846 743947 347996 959999 067474 764773 134512 257388 507476

573825 063323 881111 761335 685261 728952 917955 487451 011764

889596 673502 577468 181945 948330 469471 167111 676744 367321

242420 316561 829148 175753 829208 114426 757250 545067 824868

597498 036415 127911 317301 170983 108273 227269 230534 869126

417169 766989 971208 400088 633996 884819 593635 591771 726642

929096 459895 788805 892290 662395 466931 397507 928429 971936

536122 061248 839199 032549 181616 225832 546783 473661 915284

269355 804060 977387 177611 712419 123688 425093 588612 625374

117857 389934 092306 311255 262542 859255 848171 328460 357737

689877 470402 365376 362975 549581 834414 019292 998899 590803

288331 876235 335608 809011 702731 642094 440712 833387 894338

743803 314606 053845 172401 448405 461271 159906 057449 427292

602474 888612 957144 810779 346192 329050 348878 691893 767461

334449 700734 858821 492757 803230 065057 861966 232161 937016

339732 581643 992579 026163 659815 581466 511004 289039 163529

064052 375710 291148 140714 084730 368171 670140 628979 790514

134653 696369 849974 556903 193927 105206 011217 384853 961620

969565 693232 162495 139446 668854 394998 456711 503952 485858

142054 870554 285894 532937 972854 147196 158376 633805 070800

490557 227895 250165 769200 329962 916013 428217 151318 229190

Table D-2 Probability Distribution of Chi-Square*

Degrees of Freedom	Probability That χ^2 Equals or Exceeds the Value by Chance					
	.20	.10	.05	.01	.005	.001
1	1.642	2.706	3.841	6.635	7.88	10.83
2	3.219	4.605	5.991	9.210	10.60	13.82
3	4.642	6.251	7.815	11.345	12.84	16.27
4	5.989	7.779	9.488	13.277	14.86	18.47
5	7.289	9.236	11.070	15.086	16.75	20.51
6	8.558	10.645	12.592	16.812	18.55	22.46
7	9.803	12.017	14.067	18.475	20.28	24.32
8	11.030	13.362	15.507	20.090	21.95	26.12
9	12.242	14.684	16.919	21.666	23.59	27.88
10	13.442	15.987	18.307	23.209	25.19	29.59
11	14.631	17.275	19.675	24.725	26.76	31.26
12	15.812	18.549	21.026	26.217	28.30	32.91
13	16.985	19.812	22.362	27.688	29.82	34.53
14	18.151	21.064	23.685	29.141	31.32	36.12
15	19.311	22.307	24.996	30.578	32.80	37.70
16	20.465	23.542	26.296	32.000	34.27	39.25
17	21.615	24.769	27.587	33.409	35.72	40.79
18	22.760	25.989	28.869	34.805	37.16	42.31
19	23.900	27.204	30.144	36.191	38.58	43.82
20	25.038	28.412	31.410	37.566	40.00	45.31
22	27.301	30.813	33.924	40.289	42.80	48.27
24	29.553	33.196	36.415	42.980	45.56	51.18
26	31.795	35.563	38.885	45.642	48.29	54.05
28	34.027	37.916	41.337	48.278	50.99	56.89
30	36.250	40.256	43.773	50.892	53.67	59.70
35	41.778	46.059	49.802	57.342	60.27	66.62
40	47.269	51.805	55.758	63.691	66.77	73.40
45	52.729	57.505	61.656	69.957	73.17	80.08
50	58.164	63.167	67.505	76.154	79.49	86.66

*To use Table D-2, look your value up in the row corresponding to the number of degrees of freedom of your test. If it is to the right of your **cutoff value**, then your result is reliable. This is a **one-tailed test**.

Table D-3 Probability Distribution of Student's t*

Degrees of Freedom	Probability That t Exceeds Value by Chance					
	.20	.10	.05	.01	.005	.001
1	1.376	3.078	6.314	31.821	63.657	318.31
2	1.061	1.886	2.920	6.965	9.925	22.33
3	0.978	1.638	2.353	4.541	5.841	10.21
4	0.941	1.533	2.132	3.747	4.604	7.173
5	0.920	1.476	2.015	3.365	4.032	5.893
6	0.906	1.440	1.943	3.143	3.707	5.208
7	0.896	1.415	1.895	2.998	3.499	4.785
8	0.889	1.397	1.860	2.896	3.355	4.501
9	0.883	1.383	1.833	2.821	3.250	4.297
10	0.879	1.372	1.812	2.764	3.169	4.144
11	0.876	1.363	1.796	2.718	3.106	4.025
12	0.873	1.356	1.782	2.681	3.055	3.930
13	0.870	1.350	1.771	2.650	3.012	3.852
14	0.868	1.345	1.761	2.624	2.977	3.787
15	0.866	1.341	1.753	2.602	2.947	3.733
16	0.865	1.337	1.746	2.583	2.921	3.686
17	0.863	1.333	1.740	2.567	2.898	3.646
18	0.862	1.330	1.734	2.552	2.878	3.610
19	0.861	1.328	1.729	2.539	2.861	3.579
20	0.860	1.325	1.725	2.528	2.845	3.552
22	0.858	1.321	1.717	2.508	2.819	3.505
24	0.857	1.318	1.711	2.492	2.797	3.467
26	0.856	1.315	1.706	2.479	2.779	3.435
28	0.855	1.313	1.701	2.467	2.763	3.408
30	0.854	1.310	1.697	2.457	2.750	3.385
35	0.852	1.306	1.690	2.438	2.724	3.340
40	0.851	1.303	1.684	2.423	2.704	3.307
45	0.850	1.301	1.679	2.412	2.690	3.281
50	0.849	1.299	1.676	2.403	2.678	3.261

*To use Table D-3, look your value up in the row corresponding to the number of degrees of freedom in your test. If it is to the right of your cutoff value, then your result is reliable. This is a one-tailed test.

Table D-4 Values of the Binomial Distribution*

						r (the smaller observed frequency)							
n	0	1	2	3	4	5	6	7	8	9	10	11	12
5	.0625	.3750	1.000	—	—	—	—	—	—	—	—	—	—
6	.0313	.2188	.6875	—	—	—	—	—	—	—	—	—	—
7	.0156	.1250	.4531	1.000	—	—	—	—	—	—	—	—	—
8	.0078	.0703	.2891	.7266	—	—	—	—	—	—	—	—	—
9	.0039	.0391	.1797	.5078	1.000	—	—	—	—	—	—	—	—
10	.0020	.0215	.1094	.3438	.7539	—	—	—	—	—	—	—	—
11	.0010	.0117	.0654	.2266	.5488	1.000	—	—	—	—	—	—	—
12	.0005	.0063	.0386	.1460	.3877	.7744	—	—	—	—	—	—	—
13	.0002	.0034	.0225	.0923	.2668	.5811	1.000	—	—	—	—	—	—
14	.0001	.0018	.0129	.0574	.1796	.4240	.7905	—	—	—	—	—	—
15	.0001	.0010	.0074	.0352	.1185	.3018	.6072	1.000	—	—	—	—	—
16	.0000	.0005	.0042	.0213	.0768	.2101	.4545	.8036	—	—	—	—	—
17	.0000	.0003	.0023	.0127	.0490	.1435	.3323	.6291	1.000	—	—	—	—
18	.0000	.0001	.0013	.0075	.0309	.0963	.2379	.4807	.8145	—	—	—	—
19	.0000	.0001	.0007	.0044	.0192	.0636	.1671	.3593	.6476	1.000	—	—	—
20	.0000	.0000	.0004	.0026	.0118	.0414	.1153	.2632	.5034	.8238	—	—	—
21	.0000	.0000	.0002	.0015	.0072	.0266	.0784	.1892	.3833	.6636	1.000	—	—
22	.0000	.0000	.0001	.0009	.0043	.0169	.0525	.1338	.2863	.5235	.8318	—	—
23	.0000	.0000	.0001	.0005	.0026	.0106	.0347	.0931	.2100	.4049	.6776	1.000	—
24	.0000	.0000	.0000	.0003	.0015	.0066	.0227	.0639	.1516	.3075	.5413	.8388	—
25	.0000	.0000	.0000	.0002	.0009	.0041	.0146	.0433	.1078	.2295	.4244	.6900	1.000

*Table D-4 is to be used only when $p = q = 1/2$, and $5 \leq n \leq 25$. Each cell contains the probability of an r that small or smaller by chance. Find the cell in the row corresponding to your number of observations and in the column corresponding to your smaller observed frequency. If the value in the table is less than or equal ($\leq$) to your chosen cutoff value, your result is reliable. This is a one-tailed table.

Table D-5 Values of the Standard Normal Distribution*

Probability that z ≥ value by chance	Value of z
0.200	0.842
0.100	1.282
0.050	1.645
0.010	2.326
0.005	2.576
0.001	3.090

*To use Table D-5, find your z value on the bottom line. If it is to the right of your cutoff value, your result is reliable. This is a one-tailed table.

Table D-6 Needed Sample Sizes*

	Desired Accurancy		
Pop.	*.05*	*.03*	*.01*
50	46	48	49
55	50	53	55
60	53	57	59
65	59	63	65
70	59	67	69
75	64	72	75
80	68	76	79
85	71	82	85
90	75	84	89
95	79	89	95
100	79	93	99
110	90	100	108
120	93	110	118
130	99	116	128
140	106	125	138
150	110	133	148
160	117	140	157
170	119	150	167
180	126	155	177
190	130	165	187
200	135	168	197
210	139	180	206
220	140	184	216
230	150	191	226
240	150	199	236
250	155	204	246

Table D-6, continued

Pop.	Desired Accurancy		
	.05	.03	.01
260	159	214	253
270	159	216	263
280	170	225	273
290	170	233	283
300	170	234	293
320	179	250	310
340	184	265	330
360	190	272	350
380	199	284	367
400	199	299	387
420	210	302	402
440	210	316	422
460	210	327	442
480	219	333	457
500	219	350	477
550	230	367	522
600	239	385	567
650	250	414	610
700	250	433	653
750	259	450	699
800	259	467	744
850	270	484	787
900	270	499	828
950	279	516	867
1000	279	516	906
1100	290	550	995
1200	299	567	1071
1300	299	599	1150
1400	310	616	1228
1500	310	633	1299
1600	310	650	1379
1700	319	667	1450
1800	319	684	1522
1900	319	699	1599
2000	330	699	1657
2200	330	733	1799
2400	339	750	1932
2600	339	767	2050
2800	339	784	2183
3000	339	799	2299
3500	350	833	2581
4000	359	850	2850
4500	359	867	3089

Table D-6, continued

| | *Desired Accurancy* | | |
Pop.	.05	.03	.01
5000	359	884	3299
6000	359	916	3699
7000	370	933	4050
8000	370	950	4399
9000	370	967	4650
10000	370	967	4899
15000	379	999	5899
20000	379	1016	6499
30000	379	1033	7299
40000	379	1050	7750
50000	379	1050	8099
75000	390	1067	8550
100000	399	1084	8799
200000	399	1084	9199
300000	399	1084	9350
400000	399	1084	9399
500000	399	1084	9499

*The first column of Table D-6 is the size of the population being sampled. The other columns represent the desired accuracy. For instance, the entries in the column labeled ".05" will give the size of a randomly chosen sample needed to be sure, at the 95% confidence level, that the the sample proportion will be within $\pm$.05 of the population proportion.

References

Abney, F. G., & Hutcheson, J. D., Jr. (1981). Race, representation, and trust: Changes in attitudes after the election of a black mayor. *Public Opinion Quarterly, 45,* 91–101.

Adair, J. G., Dushenko, T. W., & Lindsay, R. C. (1985). Ethical regulations and their impact on research practice. *American Psychologist, 40,* 59–72.

American Psychological Association. (1983). *Publication manual of the American Psychological Association* (3rd ed.). Washington, DC: Author.

American Psychological Association, Committee for the Protection of Human Participants in Research. (1982). *Ethical principles in the conduct of research with human participants* (2nd ed.). Washington, DC: Author.

Anisfeld, M. (1987). A course to develop competence in critical reading of empirical research in psychology. *Teaching of Psychology, 14,* 224–227.

Aronson, E. (1969). Some antecedents of interpersonal attraction. In W. J. Arnold & D. Levine (Eds.), *Nebraska Symposium on Motivation, 1969.* Lincoln: University of Nebraska Press.

Attorney General's Commission on Pornography: Final Report. (1986, July). Washington, DC: U.S. Department of Justice.

Ayllon, T., & Roberts, M. D. (1974). Eliminating discipline problems by strengthening academic performance. *Journal of Applied Behavior Analysis, 7,* 71–76.

Babbie, E. (1986). *The practice of social research* (4th ed.). Belmont, CA: Wadsworth.

Baddeley, A. D. (1972). Selective attention and performance in dangerous environments. *British Journal of Psychology, 63,* 537–546.

Baddeley, A. D., & Longman, D. J. A. (1966). The influence of length and frequency of training sessions on rate of learning to type. Unpublished manuscript, Medical Research Council Applied Psychology Unit, Cambridge. Described in Baddeley, A. D. (1976). *The psychology of memory.* New York: Basic Books, pp. 26–29.

Bahrick, H. P., & Phelps, E. (1987). Retention of Spanish vocabulary over 8 years. *Journal of Experimental Psychology: Learning, Memory, and Cognition, 13,* 344–349.

Bailey, W. C. (1975). Murder and capital punishment. In W. J. Chambliss (Ed.), *Criminal law in action.* New York: Wiley.

Bales, J. (1988, December). *Vincennes:* Findings could have helped avert tragedy, scientists tell Hill panel. *APA Monitor,* pp. 10–11.

Bannan, R. S. (1984). Briefing the court: Dialectic as methodological perspective. *Journal of Contemporary Law, 10,* 121–139.

Barash, D. P. (1974). Human ethology: Displacement activities in a dental office. *Psychological Reports, 34,* 947–949.

Barthol, R. P., & Ku, N. D. (1955). Specific regression under a nonrelated stress situation. *American Psychologist, 10,* 482 (Abstract).

Baum, A., & Valins, S. (1977). *Architecture and social behavior: Psychological studies in social density.* Hillsdale, NJ: Lawrence Erlbaum Associates.

Baumeister, R. F. (1988). Should we stop studying sex differences altogether? *American Psychologist, 43,* 1092–1095.

Baumrind, D. (1985). Research using intentional deception. *American Psychologist, 40,* 165–174.

Beaman, A. L., Barnes, P. J., Klentz, B., & McQuirk, B. (1978). Increasing helping rates through information dissemination: Teaching pays. *Personality and Social Psychology Bulletin, 4,* 406–411.

Berkowitz, L., & Green, R. G. (1967). Stimulus qualities of the target of aggression. *Journal of Personality and Social Psychology, 5,* 364–368.

Bishop, J. E. (1988, March 2). Memory on trial: Witnesses of crimes are being challenged as frequently fallible. *Wall Street Journal,* pp. 1, 18.

Bourke, P. D. (1984). Estimation of proportions using symmetric randomized response designs. *Psychological Bulletin, 96,* 166–172.

Bower, B. (1990a). Defensiveness reaps psychiatric benefits. *Science News, 137,* 309.

Bower, B. (1990b). Anxiety weighs down pregnancies and births. *Science News, 138,* 102.

Bower, B. (1990c). Subliminal deceptions. *Science News, 138,* 124.

Bower, B. (1990d). College classes spur lifelong math memory. *Science News, 138,* 375.

Bower, B. (1991). True believers: The thinking person may favor gullibility over skepticism. *Science News, 139,* 14–15.

Bradburn, N. M., Rips, L. J., & Shevell, S. K. (1987). Answering autobiographical questions: The impact of memory and inference on surveys. *Science, 236,* 157–161

Brady, J. V. (1958). Ulcers in "executive" monkeys. *Scientific American, 199,* 95–100.

Broad, W., & Wade, N. (1982). *Betrayers of the truth.* New York: Simon & Schuster.

Bureau of Justice Statistics (1983). *Report to the Nation on Crime and Justice.* U.S. Department of Justice. Washington, DC: Government Printing Office.

Carey, J. T. (1969). Changing courtship patterns in the popular song. *American Journal of Sociology, 74,* 720–731.

Carroll, D. W. (1986). Use of the jigsaw technique in laboratory and discussion classes. *Teaching of Psychology, 13,* 208–210.

Ceci, S. J., & Peters, D. (1984). Letters of reference: A naturalistic study of the effects of confidentiality. *American Psychologist, 39,* 29–31.

Chaiken, S., & Pliner, P. (1987). Women, but not men, are what they eat: The effect of meal size and gender on perceived femininity and masculinity. *Personality and Social Psychology Bulletin, 13,* 166–176.

Chambers, W. V. (1986). Inferring causality from corresponding variances. *Perceptual and Motor Skills, 63,* 475–478.

Cheatwood, D. (1988). Is there a season for homicide? *Criminology, 26,* 287–306.

Converse, J. M., & Schuman, H. (1974). *Conversations at random: Survey research as interviewers see it.* New York: Wiley.

Cook, S. (1985). Experimenting on social issues: The case of school desegregation. *American Psychologist, 40,* 452–460.

Coopersmith, S. (1967). *The antecedents of self-esteem.* San Francisco: Freeman.

Costanzo, M., Archer, D., Aronson, E., & Pettigrew, T. (1986). Energy conservation behavior: The difficult path from information to action. *American Psychologist, 41,* 521-528.

Cox, V. C., Paulus, P. B., & McCain, G. (1984). Prison crowding research: The relevance for prison housing standards and a general approach regarding crowding phenomena. *American Psychologist, 39,* 1148-1160

Cressey, D. R. (1953). *Other people's money: a study in the social psychology of embezzlement.* Glencoe, IL: Free Press.

Critelli, J. W. & Neumann, K. F. (1984). The placebo: Conceptual analysis of a construct in transition. *American Psychologist, 39,* 32–39.

Darley, J. M., & Batson, C. D. (1973). "From Jerusalem to Jericho": A study of situational and dispositional variables in helping behavior. *Journal of Personality and Social Psychology, 27,* 100--108.

Davenport, B. C., & Nutall, R. L. (1979). Cost-effective Medicaid mental health policies: Design and testing. In L.-E. Datta & R. Perloff, (Eds.), *Improving evaluations.* Beverly Hills, CA: Sage.

Dempster, F. N. (1988). The spacing effect: A case study in the failure to apply the results of psychological research. *American Psychologist, 43,* 627–634.

Descartes, René (1955). *Philosophical works.* (Elizabeth S. Haldane & G. R. T. Ross, tran.). New York: Dover Press. (Original work published 1641.)

Devesa, S. S., Blot, W. J., & Fraumeni, J. F., Jr. (1989). Declining cancer rates among young men and women in the United States: A cohort analysis. *Journal of the National Cancer Institute, 81,* 1568–1571.

Donnerstein, E., Berkowitz, L., & Linz, D. (1986). *Role of aggressive and sexual images in violent pornography.* Unpublished manuscript, University of Wisconsin—Madison.

Donnerstein, E., Linz, D., & Penrod, S. (1987). *The question of pornography: Research findings and policy implications.* New York: Free Press.

Douglas, N. E., & Baum, N. (1984). *Library research guide to psychology.* Ann Arbor, MI: Pierian Press.

Driscoll, J. W., & Bateson, P. (1988). Animals in behavioural research. *Animal Behaviour, 36,* 1569–1574.

DuBois, P. H. (1970). *A history of psychological testing.* Boston: Allyn & Bacon.

Duncan, B. L. (1976). Differential social perception and attribution of intergroup violence: Testing the lower limits of stereotyping of blacks. *Journal of Personality and Social Psychology, 34,* 590–598.

Eagly, A. H. (1987). Reporting sex differences. *American Psychologist, 42,* 756–757.

Ebbinghaus, H. (1913). *Memory.* (H. A. Ruger & E. C. E. Bussenius, Tran.). New York: Teachers College. (Original work published 1885.)

Education index. (1929-present). New York: W. H. Wilson.

Farbstein, J. (1986). *Correctional facility planning and design.* New York: Van Nostrand Reinhold

Fernald, L. D. (1987). Of windmills and rope dancing: The instructional value of narrative structures. *Teaching of Psychology, 14,* 214–216.

Fisher, K. (1988, September). Confidential survey holds plea for help. *APA Monitor,* p. 5.

Friedman, H. (1987). Repeat examinations in introductory statistics courses. *Teaching of Psychology, 14,* 20–23.

Gardner, G. T. (1978). Effects of federal human subjects regulations on data obtained in environmental stressor research. *Journal of Personality and Social Psychology, 36,* 628–634.

Gibson, J. J. (1947). *Motion picture testing and research.* AAF Aviation Psychology Research Report Number 7. Washington, DC: Government Printing Office.

Glass, D. C., & Singer, J. E. (1972). *Urban stress: Experiments on noise and social stressors.* New York: Academic Press.

Glover, J. A., & Corkill, A. J. (1987). Influence of paraphrased repetitions on the spacing effect. *Journal of Educational Psychology, 79,* 198–199.

Goodman, W. (1982, August 9). Of mice, monkeys, and men. *Newsweek,* p. 61.

Gordon, R. A. (1987). Social desirability bias: A demonstration and technique for its reduction. *Teaching of Psychology, 14,* 40–42.

Gould, S. J. (1977). *Ever since Darwin: Reflections in natural history.* New York: Norton.

Gould, S. J. (1983). *Hen's teeth and horse's toes: Further reflections in natural history.* New York: Norton.

Greene, A. (1987). The tyranny of melody. *Etc., 43,* 285–290.

Grotevant, H. D., & Carlson, C. I. (1987). Family interaction coding systems: A descriptive review. *Family Process, 26,* 49–74.

Guida, F. V. (1987). Naturalistic Observation of Academic Anxiety Scale. *Journal of Classroom Interaction, 22*(2), 13–18.

Hearnshaw, L. S. (1979). *Cyril Burt, psychologist.* London: Hodder & Stoughton.

Herrnstein, R. J., Nickerson, R. S., de Sanchez, M., & Swets, J. A. (1986). Teaching thinking skills. *American Psychologist, 41,* 1279–1289.

Hewish, A., Bell, S. J., Pilkington, J. P. H., Scott, P. F., & Collins, R. A. (1967). Obeservations of a rapidly pulsating radio source. *Nature, 217,* 709–713.

Hill, G. D., & Atkinson, M. P. (1988). Gender, familial control, & delinquency. *Criminology, 26,* 127–149.

Huskey, H. D. (1976). The development of automatic computing. In D. Van Tassel (Ed.), *The compleat computer.* Chicago: Science Research Associates.

Johnson, W. T., Petersen, R. E., & Wells, L. E. (1982). Arrest probabilities for marijuana users as indicators of selective law enforcement. In J. C. Weissman & R. L. DuPont (Eds.), *Criminal justice and drugs: The unresolved connection.* Port Washington, NY: Kennikat Press.

Katkin, E. S. (1985). Polygraph testing, psychological research, and public policy: An introductory note. *American Psychologist, 40,* 346–347.

Kennedy, J. R., Jr. (1979). *Library research guide to education: Search strategy and sources.* Ann Arbor, MI: Pierian Press.

Kiesler, S., Siegel, J., & McGuire, T. W. (1984). Social psychological aspects of computer-mediated communication. *American Psychologist, 39,* 1123–1134.

Kimmel, A. J. (1980). *Ethics and values in applied social research.* Newbury Park, CA: Sage.

Kuhn, T. (1970). *The structure of scientific revolutions.* Chicago: University of Chicago Press.

LaFrance, M. (1979). Non-verbal synchrony and rapport: Analysis by the cross-lag panel technique. *Social Psychology Quarterly, 42,* 66–70.

Landers, S. (1988, September). Adolescent study presents dilemma. *APA Monitor,* p. 5.

Langer, E. J., & Rodin, J. (1976). The effects of choice and enhanced personal responsibility for the aged: A field experiment in an institutional setting. *Journal of Personality and Social Psychology, 34,* 191–198.

Laurence, J.-R., & Perry, C. (1983). Hypnotically created memory among highly hypnotizable subjects. *Science, 222,* 523–524.

Lehman, J. D. (1982). *Three approaches to classroom management: Views from a psychological perspective.* New York: University Press of America.

Lerner, M. J. (1980). *The belief in a just world: A fundamental delusion.* New York: Plenum Press.

Levy, J. (1985, May). Right brain, left brain: Fact and fiction. *Psychology Today,* pp. 38–44.

Lévy-Leboyer, C. (1988). Success and failure in applying psychology. *American Psychologist, 43,* 779–785.

Linn, R. L. (1982). Ability testing: Individual differences, prediction, and differential prediction. In A. K. Wigdor & W. R. Gardner (Eds.), *Ability testing: Uses, consequences, and controversies* (Part II). Washington, DC: National Academy Press.

Loftus, E. (1979). *Eyewitness testimony.* Cambridge, MA: Harvard University Press.

Longo, D. J., Clum, G. A., & Yaeger, N. J. (1988). Psychosocial treatment for recurrent genital herpes. *Journal of Consulting and Clinical Psychology, 56,* 61–66.

McAlister, A., Perry, C., Killen, J., Slinkard, L. A., & Maccoby, N. (1980). Pilot study of smoking, alcohol and drug abuse prevention. *American Journal of Public Health, 70,* 719–721.

McClelland, D. C. (1961). *The achieving society.* Princeton, NJ: Van Nostrand.

McHugh, M. C., Koeske, R. D., & Frieze, I. H. (1986). Issues to consider in conducting nonsexist psychological research: A guide for researchers. *American Psychologist, 41,* 879–890.

McNemar, Q. (1942). *The revision of the Stanford–Binet Scale: An analysis of the standardization data.* Boston: Houghton Miflin.

Middlemist, R. D., Knowles, E. S., & Matter, C. F. (1976). Personal space invasions in the lavatory: Suggestive evidence for arousal. *Journal of Personality and Social Psychology, 33,* 541–546.

Mikhail, A. A. (1969). Genetic predisposition to stomach ulceration in emotionally reactive strains of rats. *Psychonomic Science, 15,* 245–247.

Milgram, S. (1963). Behavioral study of obedience. *Journal of Abnormal Psychology, 67,* 371–378.

Nelson, W. R. (1986). New generation jails. *Corrections Today, 45,* 108–112.

Orne, M. T. (1962). On the social psychology of the psychological experiment: With particular reference to demand characteristics and their implications. *American Psychologist, 17,* 776–783.

Parke, R. D. (1981). *Fathers.* Cambridge, MA: Harvard University Press.

Patterson, A. H. (1986). Scientific jury selection: The need for a case-specific approach. *Social Action and the Law, 11,* 105–109.

Peele, S. (1983, April). Through a glass darkly. *Psychology Today, 17*(4), 38–42.

Pendery, M. L., Maltzman, I. M., & West, L. J. (1982). Controlled drinking by alcoholics? New findings and a reevaluation of a major affirmative study. *Science, 217,* 169–175.

Pinder, C. C. (1976). Additivity vs. non-additivity of intrinsic and extrinsic incentives: Implications for work motivation, performance, and attitudes. *Journal of Applied Psychology, 61,* 693–780.

Plato (1956). *The Great Dialogues of Plato.* (W. H. D. Rouse, Tran.). Eric H. Wormington & Philip G. Rouse (Eds.). New York: New American Library. (Original work never published, written 427–347 BC.)

Plumb, E. (1986). Validation of voter recall: Time of electoral decision making. *Political Behavior, 8,* 302–312.

Popper, K. (1965). *Conjectures and refutations.* New York: Harper Torchbooks.

Premo, S. (1990, August 18). Lane found. . . [Letter to the editor]. *Science News,* p. 99.

Psychological abstracts. (1927–present). Washington, DC: American Psychological Association.

Roethlisberger, F. J., & Dickson, W. J. (1939). *Management and the worker.* Cambridge, MA: Harvard University Press.

Rosenthal, R., & Fode, K. L. (1961). The problem of experimenter outcome-bias. In D. P. Ray (Ed.), *Series research in social psychology.* Symposia studies series, no. 8, Washington, DC: National Institute of Social and Behavioral Science.

Rothblum, E. D. (1988). More on reporting sex differences. *American Psychologist, 43,* 1095.

Ruback, R. B., & Innes, C. A. (1988). The relevance and irrelevance of psychological research: The example of prison crowding. *American Psychologist, 43,* 683–693.

Sagan, C. (1979). *Broca's brain: Reflections on the romance of science.* New York: Random House.

Saxe, L., Dougherty, D., & Cross, T. (1985). The validity of polygraph testing: Scientific analysis and public controversy. *American Psychologist, 40,* 355–366.

Scardamalia, M., & Bereiter, C. (1986). Writing. In R. F. Dillon & R. J. Sternberg (Eds.), *Cognition and instruction.* New York: Academic Press.

Schaie, K. W., & Geiwitz, J. (1982). *Adult development and aging.* Boston: Little, Brown.

Schaie, K.W., & Hertzog, C. (1986). Toward a comprehensive model of adult intellectual development: Contributions of the Seattle Longitudinal Study. In R. J. Sternberg (Ed.), *Advances in the psychology of human intelligence.* Hillsdale, NJ: Lawrence Erlbaum.

Schatz, M. A., & Best, J. B. (1987). Students' reasons for changing answers on objective tests. *Teaching of Psychology, 14,* 241–242.

Schmidt, H. O., & Fonda, C. P. (1956). The reliability of psychiatric diagnosis: A new look. *Journal of Abnormal and Social Psychology, 52,* 262–267.

Schmookler, A. B. (1990). American antagonism? [Letter to the editor]. *Science News, 138,* 211.

Shawver, L., & Dickover, R. (1986). Exploding a myth. *Corrections Today, 48,* 30–34.

Sherif, M. (1966). *In common predicament: Social psychology of intergroup conflict and cooperation.* Boston: Houghton Mifflin.

Siegel, S., & Castellan, J. (1988). *Nonparametric statistics for the behavioral sciences* (2nd ed.). New York: McGraw-Hill.

Simon, C. (1988, April). A care package. *Psychology Today,* pp. 42–49.

Sobell, M. B., & Sobell, L. C. (1973). Alcoholics treated by individualized behavior therapy: One year treatment outcome. *Behavior Research and Therapy, 11,* 599–618.

Social sciences citation index. (1969–present). Philadelphia: Institute for Scientific Information.

Social sciences index. (1974-present). New York: W. H. Wilson.

Sommer, R., Estabrook, M., & Horobin, K. (1988). Faculty awareness of textbook prices. *Teaching of Psychology, 15,* 17–21.

Sommers, N. (1980). Revision strategies of student writers and experienced adult writers. *College Composition and Communication, 31,* 378–388.

Sroufe, L. A., Fox, N. E., & Pancake, V. R. (1983). Attachment and dependency in developmental perspective. *Child Development, 54,* 1615–1627.

"Student." (1908). The probable error of a mean. *Biometrika, 6,* 1.

Sweeter slumber for tots who sleep solo. (1990). *Science News, 138,* 87.

Tajfel, H. (Ed.) (1982). *Social identity and intergroup relations.* New York: Cambridge University Press.

Tobacco researchers say smoking harms. (1991). *Science News, 140,* 59.

Trefil, J. (1988) *The dark side of the universe: A scientist explores the mysteries of the cosmos.* New York: Scribner's.

Wason, P. C., & Johnson-Laird, P. N. (1972). *Psychology of reasoning: Structure and content.* Cambridge, MA: Harvard University Press.

Waters, M., Kemp, E., & Pucci, A. (1988). High and low faculty evaluations: Descriptions by students. *Teaching of Psychology, 15,* 203–204.

Watson, J. B. (1930). *Behaviorism* (Revised ed.). Chicago: University of Chicago Press.

Wawra, M. (1989). Vigilance patterns in humans. *Behaviour, 107,* 61–71.

Webb, E. J., Campbell, D. T., Schwartz, R. D., & Sechrest, L. (1966). *Unobtrusive measures: Nonreactive research in the social sciences.* Chicago: Rand McNally.

Weiss, J. M. (1972). Psychological factors in stress and disease. *Scientific American, 226,* 104–113.

Weiss, R. (1990). Sweet tooth, rotten kid: A theory gone sour. *Science News, 138,* 84–85.

Weizenbaum, J. (1976). *Computer power and human reason: From judgement to calculation.* San Francisco: Freeman.

Wells, L. E., & Rankin, J. H. (1988). Direct parental controls and delinquency. *Criminology, 26,* 263–285.

White, L. T., Archer, D., Aronson, E., Condelli, L., Curbow, B., McLeod, B., Pettigrew, T. F., & Yates, S., (1984). Energy conservation research of California's utilities: A meta-evaluation. *Evaluation Review, 8,* 167–186.

Wilson, E. O. (1975). *Sociobiology: The new synthesis.* Cambridge, MA: Harvard University Press.

Winter, D. G. (1987). Leader appeal, leader performance, and the motive profiles of leaders and followers: A study of American presidents and elections. *Journal of Personality and Social Psychology, 52,* 196–202.

Wohlstein, R. T., & McPhail, C. (1979). Judging the presence and extent of collective behavior from film records. *Social Psychology Quarterly, 42,* 76–81.

Wundt, W. (1907). *Outlines of Psychology.* (C. H. Judd, Tran.). New York: Stechert. (Original work published 1904.)

Zajonc, R. B. (1968). The attitudinal effects of mere exposure. *Journal of Personality and Social Psychology Monograph Supplement, 9*(2).

Zeller, A. F. (1950). An experimental analogue of repression. II: The effect of individual failure and success on memory measured by relearning. *Journal of Experimental Psychology, 40,* 411–422.

Glossary

Abscissa In a graph, the horizontal line at the bottom that represents the predictor or the independent variable.

Abstract In a research report, the summary of the research and its major findings that appears before the report itself.

Alpha In inferential statistics, the Greek letter (α) used to symbolize the probability of committing a Type I error.

Alpha level See **significance level**.

Alternate form reliability A version of split-half reliability in which the two halves of a long list of items are separated into two distinct forms of a test, given at different times, and the scores on the two forms are compared.

Anonymity A behavior is anonymous if the person who performed it believes that no one can identify him or her as having performed that behavior and therefore no one can tell anyone else about it. A researcher who observes anonymous behavior, determines who performed it, and tells others, has committed a violation of ethical principles.

Apparatus In a research report, an optional subsection of the Method section that describes any special equipment used.

Appendix In a research report, material that is unnecessary for an understanding of the study but might be useful for some readers, which is collected into a special section at the end of the report.

Applied research A type of research whose purpose is to answer a question of immediate, practical application, thereby solving some important problem. Frequently considered to be the opposite of theoretical research.

Archival research A type of unobtrusive research using data collected by other researchers for other purposes, for instance, data collected by the U.S. Census Bureau.

Backup In a computer, a copy of information in some durable form (often a floppy disk) from which it can be recovered if the main files are lost.

Bar chart A way of visually portraying frequency distributions, similar to a histogram but applied to a nominal variable. The variable is represented on the abscissa and is divided into ranges. The number of observations that fell into each range are indicated by the height of the bar over that range.

Baseline A measurement of the behavior of the participants before any treatment is applied, to determine the standard of comparison when looking for a change. Common in single-subject reversal research.

Basic research See **theoretical research**.

Before–after design The most basic type of quasi-experimental design, which consists of measuring the dependent variable before and after some change in the independent variable, looking for a change that might be due to the change in the independent variable.

Before–after nonequivalent groups design A quasi-experimental design in which two pre-existing groups that differ in the independent variable are measured before and after one of them receives the treatment, to look for a change in the dependent variable in the treatment group.

Behavioral measurement A measurement in which the actual behavior of interest is observed directly, rather than inferred from indirect observations. For instance, directly observing acts of violence in kindergarteners would be a behavioral measure; asking teachers to rate the children's violence would not.

Beta In inferential statistics, the Greek letter (β) used to symbolize the probability of committing a Type II error.

Bibliographic search A search for all published research that is related to the subject of a research report, so that the current research can be related to the body of scientific knowledge.

Bimodal A set of measurements is bimodal if it has more than one mode, or most common value.

Binomial test A statistical test that is used to determine whether the observed frequency of a category in a nominal measurement is different from what would be expected by chance.

Bivariate data A set of observations, each of which represents two different variables; either two measured variables, as in a correlation, or an independent and a dependent variable, as in an experiment.

Blind design Any research design in which the participants do not know to which group they have been assigned and therefore do not know how they are expected to react. A solution to the problem of reactivity effects.

Carryover effect A long-term effect of treatment that continues even after the treatment is removed. Can cause difficulties in interpreting the results of reversal designs.

Causation A relationship between variables such that a change in one variable has a direct, deterministic effect on the other variable, with all else equal.

Cause Something that directly produces an effect in something else, such that a change in it (i.e., the cause) will produce the effect even when all else is equal.

Central processing unit (CPU) See **processor.**

Central tendency One property of a set of measurements, describing the "typical," "middle," or "most common" measurement. Three important measures of central tendency are the mean, the median, and the mode.

Chi-square test A statistical test used to determine the probability that a frequency distribution is what would be expected by chance, or that two or more frequency distributions are different. Symbolized by χ^2

Chi-square goodness-of-fit See **goodness-of-fit test**.

Chi-square test of association See **test of association**.

Citation In a research report, a place in the text of the report that mentions other research, giving the author(s) and the date.

Cluster sampling techniques Probability sampling techniques that work best with very large populations that have no single list but are divided into clusters that do have lists. The technique is to select at random a few clusters, and then select a random sample of examples from each cluster.

Coding The process of transforming data into a form that can be analyzed by a computer.

Coercion Any action on the part of a researcher that tends to persuade unwilling people to participate in research. Coercion is a violation of ethical principles.

Cohort effects Similarities among people of roughly the same age (a cohort), caused by experiences they have in common that make them different from other people of different ages. The Great Depression had a cohort effect on people born between 1880 and 1925.

Conceptual variable A variable that is not observable, but can be imagined; another term for **construct**.

Concurrent validity One type of criterion validity, in which the outside standard of comparison is available at the present time. Usually it involves giving the measurement to two groups, one of which is known to have more of the property of interest than the other, and looking for a corresponding difference in the measurements.

Confederate Someone who works with the researcher by pretending to be a participant or a bystander. The use of a confederate is inherently deceptive because the real participants in the research do not know that he or she is playing a part.

Confidentiality A behavior is confidential if the person who performed it expects that the person who observes it will not tell anyone else who performed it. If a researcher observes confidential behavior and then tells who performed it, a violation of ethical principles has occurred.

Confirmed In the falsificationist approach, a failed attempt to falsify a statement is said to be a confirmation of the statement. Note that the statement is not said to be "true."

Confound See **confounding variables**.

Confounding variables Any extraneous variables, not one of the independent variables, that are systematically different in the different groups of an experiment. A confounding variable automatically produces a rival hypothesis, invalidating the conclusions drawn from the experiment.

Construct A hypothetical property of an object or event, one that is not directly observable but can be constructed out of observations and theories and can be measured through those observations and theories.

Construct validity The type of validity that is demonstrated when the measurement of one construct shows the expected relationships with measurements of other, related constructs.

Content analysis A type of unobtrusive research that analyzes the meanings of recorded messages, including books, diaries, letters, songs, and television commercials.

Content validity The type of validity that is demonstrated when experts on a particular construct agree that the measurement addresses all the theoretically important aspects of the construct it is supposed to measure.

Continuous sampling A type of systematic observation, in which the behaviors are observed and recorded continuously as they occur.

Control One of the goals of science, along with description, prediction, and explanation. Control involves being able to influence which events happen or the way in which they happen, in order to make them happen in a desired way.

Control group In an experiment, a group that is included for comparison purposes in which the value of the independent variable either is zero or is what might have been expected under normal circumstances.

Control group effect Any of a number of possible reactivity effects that are due to a participant's response to being in the control group rather than the treatment group. May include demoralization or overachievement.

Convenience sample A type of nonprobability sampling technique in which the examples are chosen for the sample on the basis of how easy or comfortable they are to study.

Converging operations Several different operational definitions of a single underlying construct, all of which ought to agree on a measurement of the construct. This principle is very important, because a set of converging operations can reduce or eliminate many of the problems that can exist with any single operational definition.

Correlation A relationship between two variables that allows you to predict something about one variable if you know something about the other.

Correlation coefficient A number between -1.0 and +1.0 that describes the relation between two variables. A coefficient of 0 indicates an absence of relationship. A correlation of -1.0 means there is a perfect negative relationship; a correlation of +1.0 means there is a perfect positive relationship. Other coefficients imply relationships of differing strengths.

Correlational research Descriptive research in which variables of interest are not controlled or manipulated, but are measured as they naturally occur, to help researchers in looking for relationships between the variables.

Cost–benefit analysis The measurement of all the positive effects (benefits) and all the negative effects (costs) of some event, in an attempt to determine whether the results are worth the cost outlay. Cost–benefit analyses may be part of evaluation research, when determining whether a program should be continued, or part of an ethical evaluation of a piece of research, when determining whether ethical problems outweigh the potential benefits to science.

Counterbalancing A technique for controlling for order effects by making sure that each condition appears equally often in each ordinal position in the experiment, and follows and precedes each other condition equally often.

Covert research Research in which the people being observed do not know that the research is taking place, but instead think that the observer is actually a participant in the setting. This can create ethical questions.

Criterion validity The type of validity that demonstrates that compared with an outside standard, a measurement is measuring what it is supposed to measure. There are two types of criterion validity: concurrent validity and predictive validity.

Cross-sectional techniques Research intended to examine how things change with time, by sampling a group of objects of different ages all at the same time. Generally easier to conduct than longitudinal research, but open to more problems with cohort effects.

Cutoff value See **significance level**.

Debriefing The procedure whereby a participant who was deceived for a research project is afterward filled in on the true situation. Debriefing can reduce but does not entirely eliminate the ethical problems of deception.

Deception Any act that deliberately causes a person to believe something that is false or to be unaware of something that would be important to the individual if it were known. Excessive or careless use of deception is a violation of ethical principles.

Deduction One major type of rationalistic thinking, which produces knowledge by reasoning from general principles to specific conclusions. If the general principles are correct, and the reasoning is careful, then deduction leads to correct conclusions. However, deduction cannot be used to prove the truth of the general principles, and if they are not true the conclusion may easily be false.

Definitional statement A type of nonfalsifiable statement that must be true because it is based on the definitions of the words. Example: Fire produces heat.

Degrees of freedom (df) A number related to the number of observations or the number of groups, used in various statistical tests to determine the reliability of a result.

Demoralization A type of control group effect, which occurs when participants assigned to the control group in an experiment become resentful of being denied the benefits of treatment and give up, thereby performing worse than they would have otherwise.

Dependent variables In an experiment, the variables that the experimenter does not directly control, which are measured to determine whether the independent variable made a difference. A change in the dependent variable is the presumed effect in the cause–effect relationship being tested.

Description One of the goals of science, along with prediction, explanation, and control. Description involves systematically observing and recording what happens under certain specific circumstances.

Descriptive research A type of research whose purpose is to tell about a particular situation or event without necessarily explaining how it came to be that way. Phenomena can be described without being understood.

Descriptive statistics Statistics that describe some property of the group of numbers on which they are calculated. Common descriptive statistics are the mean, median, mode, variance, standard deviation, and range.

Design In a research report, an optional subsection of the Method section that describes the logical structure of the study. Rare in published papers, it is often required for student papers.

Determinism A philosophy in which one event produces a direct, inevitable effect without any additional intervention.

Deviation Mathematically, the difference between a single score and the mean of all the scores in the sample. It is used in computing the variance and the standard deviation, two measures of the variability of a set of scores.

Discussion In a research report, the last section of the report itself, which interprets the results and examines how they relate to the broader issues addressed by the research.

Distributed practice effect See **spacing effect**.

Double-blind Any experiment in which neither the participants nor anyone who has any contact with the participants nor anyone who is associated with the recording or interpretation of responses knows the groups to which participants have been assigned, such that no one has expectations as to how individual participants should behave. Useful for controlling for experimenter expectancy effects.

Empiricism One source of knowledge about the world, in which knowledge is derived from observations of actual events in the real world. Empiricism is the opposite of rationalism, in which only thought produces knowledge. Science is primarily an empirical endeavor.

Equal interval measurements One level of measurement, with labels assigned to properties such that not only does one label imply more of the construct than another does, but the difference between adjacent labels is equal everywhere. Temperature, on, say, the Celsius scale is measured in equal intervals because the difference between 100 and 101°C is the same as the difference between 10 and 11°C.

Equivalent Two groups in an experiment are equivalent if there exist no systematic differences between them except for those planned and controlled by the experimenter. This is usually accomplished through random assignment.

Ethics Systems of moral beliefs about what is right and what is wrong. In research, systems of moral beliefs about what a researcher can and cannot do to research participants, human and animal.

Ethics oversight committees Groups whose purpose is to evaluate the ethical acceptability of research that is proposed by the members of an organization, or to investigate claims of unethical research practices after the research is conducted.

Evaluation research A type of applied research whose purpose is to assess the effectiveness of a program or treatment, perhaps leading to a decision about how to improve it or whether to continue it.

Experimental group In an experiment, the group exposed to a new or unusual value of the independent variable, to see whether it causes a change in the dependent variable.

Experimental hypothesis See **research hypothesis**.

Experimenter bias See **experimenter expectancy effect**.

Experimenter expectancy effect A type of experimenter variable in which the experimenter's expectations have unintended but important effects on the behavior of the participants.

Experimenter variables Extraneous variables that describe properties of the people conducting the experiment.

Explanation One of the goals of science, along with description, prediction, and control. Explanation involves being able to give a coherent set of reasons telling why the events that were observed happened in one way and not another way.

Exploratory research A type of research whose purpose is to investigate and describe a phenomenon about which very little is known. It is generally used not to test specific theories but to gather as much information as possible for the development of a more thorough understanding.

External validity A property of a piece of research that can safely be generalized to the real world, or to other situations outside the actual study itself. Field research typically has more external validity than laboratory research, because it is conducted in more natural settings. Usually compared with internal validity.

Extraneous variables In an experiment, any of a multitude of variables that are not greatly interesting to the researcher. The proper control of extraneous variables determines the strength of the conclusions drawn from an experiment.

Face validity The type of validity demonstrating that a measurement appears to nonexperts to be related to the property of interest. Not usually considered to be of great scientific importance.

Factorial research Experimental research in which two or more independent variables are manipulated such that each level of each independent variable is combined with each level of every other independent variable. Factorial research makes it possible to examine possible interactions between the independent variables.

Factors A term for the independent variables in factorial research.

Falsifiable A statement is said to be falsifiable if there is some imaginable, logically possible set of observations which, if true, would prove the statement false. If a statement is not falsifiable, it cannot be a scientific theory, because science is founded on the constant attempt to prove its theories false.

Falsificationism An empirical system of knowledge in which no statement can be thought of as true; rather, all statements are constantly subjected to attempts to prove them false. Science is primarily conducted using the falsificationist approach.

Field research Any type of research that involves studying events as they occur naturally in the world, without staging or manipulating them, as opposed to laboratory research, in which the events are manipulated by the researcher.

File A collection of related data stored by a computer system and given a name so that it can be accessed later by name. For instance, the responses of the participants in a study may be in one file, and the research report describing the study may be in another file.

Fixed-response questions Survey questions that offer the respondent several possible answers from which to make a selection. This format allows the respondent much less freedom of response than open-ended questions.

Formative evaluation research A type of evaluation research designed primarily to diagnose areas in which a program or treatment is weak and to make recommendations for its improvement. Usually contrasted with summative evaluation research.

Frequencies Sets of numbers telling how many examples were observed to fall into each of several categories. Frequencies are the only meaningful numbers that can be derived from nominal level measurements, though they can be applied to other levels as well.

Frequency distribution The set of all the frequencies of the various categories in a set of nominal observations. May be described in a frequency table, a histogram, or a pie chart.

Frequency polygon A way of visually protraying frequency data in which the categories of measurement are arranged on the abscissa and the number of observations in each category is represented by the height of a point drawn above the category. Lines are then drawn to connect the points, and to connect the endpoints down to the abscissa.

Frequency table The simplest way to describe a frequency distribution, just by listing all the categories and their frequencies. The frequencies are often given as percentages.

Generalization The process of drawing conclusions about a population from observations that were made on a sample chosen from that population. The more representative the sample, the more valid the generalization.

Goodness-of-fit test A chi-square test used to compare a single frequency distribution to the distribution that would be expected by chance.

Graph A visual portrayal of the data produced by an experiment in which an independent variable is plotted on the abscissa and the dependent variable on the ordinate; the mean of each group is shown as a dot corresponding to its value on the two variables.

Haphazard sampling techniques Non-probability sampling techniques in which examples are chosen from the population with no systematic sampling plan, just by virtue of which ones happen to come along.

Hawthorne effect A type of placebo effect observed when any change in the environment produces a short-term increase in the dependent variable, just as a reaction to the change. Named after the General Electric plant at which it was first systematically observed.

Hidden observations A type of unobtrusive research in which the person observed is unaware that the observations are occurring. This research technique is, of course, subject to ethical difficulties.

Histogram A way of visually portraying one or more frequency distributions using an abscissa to represent the various groups and the ordinate to represent the frequencies or the percentages, with the number of observations in a group indicated by the height of the bar over that group.

History effects Potential confounding variables in many quasi-experiments, which are present whenever an event that occurs outside the research has an effect on the participants that might be responsible for changes observed in the dependent variable.

Impact evaluation research A type of evaluation research that assesses the influence a program or treatment has had, regardless of its stated objectives. Usually contrasted with process evaluation research.

Inclusive statement A type of nonfalsifiable statement that includes all possibilities, so that no alternatives that could possibly prove it false have been omitted. Example: Chris is either a male or a female.

Independent groups Experimental design in which there is no particular association between any score in one group and any one score in any other group. Usually contrasted with related groups designs

Independent variables In an experiment, the variables whose value are determined by the experimenter, independently of other factors. The presumed causes of the cause–effect relationship being tested in the experiment.

Inferential statistics Statistical analyses that compute the probability that a result could have occurred just by chance, allowing the researcher to decide whether to accept a result as real.

Informed consent Agreement given beforehand by participants in a study, knowing just what will be happening in the research. Informed consent can reduce or eliminate many of the ethical problems a study might otherwise have.

Inputs The devices through which information enters a computer from the outside world. Keyboards and joysticks are examples of input devices.

Instrumentation effects Potential confounding variables in quasi-experiments, which occur when the effectiveness or meaning of a measurement technique changes between one measurement and the next, producing a change in the dependent variable.

Interaction effect In factorial research, an effect that can be described only by taking two or more independent variables into account, because the effect of one variable depends on the level of the other variable, and vice versa.

Internal validity The result of the elimination of the maximum possible number of rival hypotheses, so that it is clear within the situation of the research just what caused what to happen. Usually compared with external validity.

Interrater reliability One way of measuring the reliability of a measurement, by comparing the judgments of two or more different observers. A high interrater reliability implies that the judgments are relatively objective.

Interrupted time-series design A quasi-experimental design in which a long series of measurements is taken before and after the change in the independent variable, so that a change due to the independent variable can be more easily spotted.

Interview A type of research in which one person asks another person questions and records the answers. Interviews may have more or less structure.

Introduction The first part of a research report, which explains why the research was conducted and how it relates to other published research.

Invasion of privacy Occurs whenever a researcher observes behaviors the participants would expect not to be observed. This is a violation of ethical principles.

Laboratory computers Computers that are primarily used for controlling research equipment, collecting data, and analyzing results.

Level (of an independent variable) The value of the independent variable that is assigned to a particular group by the experimenter.

Level of measurement A description of the type of relationship specified by a measurement between the property being measured and the system of labels used as measurements. There are four levels of measurement: nominal, ordinal, equal interval, and ratio. (Sometimes called scale of measurement.)

Locus of control A construct important in social psychology, which has to do with the sorts of factors a person believes cause the important events in life. People who feel that they have a lot of control over their lives have an internal locus of control; those who feel that outside forces (luck, personality conflicts, God, etc.) are most important have an external locus of control.

Longitudinal techniques Research that studies how things change with time by observing a group of objects again and again over a long period. Generally considered to be more accurate than cross-sectional research despite some problems occasioned when participants drop out of the study.

Main effect In factorial research, a direct effect of one independent variable on the dependent variable(s), with all other independent variables equal.

Mainframe A computer used to serve the needs of many different people. Generally the users of a mainframe do not need to be physically near the computer; they communicate with it through terminals.

Matched groups design A type of related groups design in which there are different participants in each group, but each participant is matched with a participant in another group who is similar on some variable that is related to the dependent variable.

Materials In a research report, an optional subsection of the Method section that describes any special items used, such as questionnaires or tests.

Maturation effects In many quasi-experiments, the participants might change between measurements just because they are getting older, with this change in turn perhaps producing a change in the dependent variable. It is necessary to compensate for these potential confounding variables.

Mean An important measure of central tendency, often called the average, which can be applied to measurements at the equal interval or ratio level. It is calculated by adding up all the scores and dividing by the number of scores in the sample.

Mean square The average value of a squared quantity. It is calculated by squaring each item, adding up the squared values, and dividing by the number of items.

Measurement A relationship between a system of labels and a property of an object or event, which allows you to assign specific labels to the objects or events based on their properties.

Median A measure of central tendency that can be applied to measurements at the ordinal, equal interval, or ratio level. It is the middle value, which has an equal number of scores above it and below it.

Memory In a computer, the system in which information and instructions are stored while they are being used. Usually the memory is temporary, and information stored there will disappear when the power is turned off.

Method In a research report, the section that describes how the research was conducted. Composed of two or more subsections.

Mode A measure of central tendency that can be applied to any level of measurement. It is the most common score observed. A set of numbers that has a tie for the most common measurement is said to be bimodal.

Monotonic A relationship between two variables is montonic if, when one variable increases, the other variable either always increases or always decreases without ever reversing itself and going the other way.

Mortality effects Potential confounding variables in many quasi-experiments, which occur whenever participants drop out of the study between one measurement and the next, raising the question of whether there is a systematic difference between the participants who remained and those who left.

Multiple-baseline design A type of single-subject design in which different subjects receive the treatment at different times, which should cause the dependent variable to change for each subject just when the treatment is applied. Used to deal with carryover effects.

Multiple time-series design A quasi-experimental design in which interrupted time series are obtained from two or more groups that differ in the treatment program to which they are exposed.

Multistage cluster sampling techniques Methods for producing probability samples of populations in which the members are organized into clusters, which are themselves organized into clusters, and so on. First a sample of clusters from the top level are chosen, and then a sample from each level down within each of those first clusters, and so on, until you reach the lowest level of actual examples of the population. For instance, a sample of elementary school children could be selected by choosing first four states, then three counties in each state, then two school districts in each county, then one school in each district, then 10 children in each school, to give a representative sample of 240 children.

Multivariate data A set of observations, each of which is described by two or more variables: measured variables in correlational research, or one or more dependent and independent variables in experimental research.

Multivariate design Experimental research in which there are two or more dependent variables. The researcher looks for effects of the independent variable(s) separately on each of the dependent variables.

Negative correlation The relationship that exists between two variables when the value of one variable goes up as the value of the other goes down, and vice versa. On a scatterplot, a negative correlation tends from upper left to lower right.

Nominal measurement One level of measurement, in which the labels are simply categories, with no inherent order. For instance, labels of political affiliation (Democrat, Libertarian, Republican, Other) are nominal measurements.

Nonparametric statistics Inferential statistics that make very weak assumptions about the data to which they are applied and therefore can be applied safely in many situations. Not as powerful as parametric statistics.

Nonprobability sampling techniques Sampling techniques in which every member of the population does not have an equal chance of being in the sample. In general, nonprobability samples are not representative of the population.

Null hypothesis The statement of the result that will occur in an experiment if there is no effect. Usually a result of no difference or no effect, a null hypothesis that proves to be true indicates that the relationship being tested is false.

Objective An observation is objective if different observers will agree on just what the observation was. For instance, different observers with accurate clocks will agree how long it took a student to finish a test. Opposite of subjective.

One-tailed test In statistics, a test that considers only one direction of difference between two scores, not both. For instance, when testing whether the scores of group A were reliably higher than those of group B, it would be a one-tailed test. When testing whether the scores of group A were reliably different from group B, without caring whether they were higher or lower, it would not be a one-tailed test.

Open-ended questions Survey questions in which the respondent may make any answer desired, in writing or orally. No choices are offered, as in fixed-response questions.

Operational definition A specification of exactly how a hidden construct will be measured, describing the operations, or steps, that will be conducted to obtain the measurement. An important concept in the theory of measurement.

Order effects Possible extraneous variables in within-subjects designs, which can occur if one condition always follows another condition in all the subjects. Counterbalancing or randomization of order is required to control for order effects.

Ordinal measurements One level of measurement, in which the labels have an inherent order, such that one label implies more of the construct than another does, but the difference between adjacent labels is not known. For instance, assigning letter grades to term papers is ordinal, because an A paper has more quality than a B paper, but there is no reason to think that the difference between A and B is the same as the difference between D and F.

Ordinate In a graph, the vertical line along the side that represents the value of the dependent variable or the predicted variable.

Outputs The devices through which information passes from the computer to the outside world. Monitors and printers are examples of output devices.

Overachievement (overcompensation) A type of control group effect in which participants resent being denied the benefits of the treatment and react by trying extra hard to overcome this handicap, thereby performing better than they would have otherwise.

Overt research Any research in which the participants know what is being observed by whom for what purpose, so that the research is not a secret.

Parallel construction In writing, the use of two sentences or two halves of a sentence that are identical in every way except for the specific parts the writer wants to contrast, making it easier for the reader to know what is the same and what is different.

Parametric statistics Inferential statistics that make certain assumptions about the data to which they are applied, including a normal distribution, equal variances, and equal interval or ratio levels of measurement. When these assumptions are met, parametric statistics make for very powerful tests, but when they do not fit, nonparametric statistics should be used instead.

Pearson product–moment correlation (r) One correlation coefficient, the most powerful for finding straight-line correlations between variables measured on the equal interval or ratio level.

Percentage A number that tells how many times a category was observed out of 100 cases. It is calculated by dividing the frequency of the category by the total of all the observations, and multiplying by 100. Percentages make it easier to compare frequencies in different distributions when the number of observations in each distribution is not equal.

Personal computer A computer designed to be used by only one person.

Pie chart A way of drawing a frequency distribution, using a circle divided into wedges proportional to the various frequencies.

Placebo A condition that provides the general benefits of most treatments, particularly the participant's expectations of improvement, without providing the specific benefit of the treatment that is being tested.

Placebo effect A type of reactivity effect in which the participant's expectation that a treatment will cause improvement is enough, by itself, to cause the improvement, even though the treatment really has no effect.

Population The entire group of objects, people, or events that a piece of research is attempting to find out about. Usually a small part of the population, called a sample, is actually observed.

Positive correlation The relationship that exists between two variables when the value of one variable goes up and the value of the other does also, and vice versa. On a scatterplot, a positive correlation tends from lower left to upper right.

Power In statistics, the ability of a statistical test to uncover a weak effect. If a treatment improves test scores, but only by a small amount, a weaker test might find no reliable difference, while a more powerful test might produce a reliable result.

Prediction One of the goals of science, along with description, explanation, and control. Prediction involves making statements about what events will occur in the future and then comparing the future events with the predictions to test their accuracy.

Predictive validity One type of criterion validity, in which the outside standard will not be available until some future time. Usually the measurement is administered and used to predict the future behaviors of the objects measured. Later the actual behavior is compared with the prediction to determine whether the measurement was related to the correct property.

Predictor variable In correlations, regressions, or regression–discontinuity research, a variable that has some actual or presumed relation to another variable and is used to predict the future value of that variable.

Pretest-posttest design See **before–after design**.

Pretest sensitization The phenomenon whereby the experience of being tested or measured before treatment changes the way a participant experiences the treatment, thereby changing the dependent variable. May be a confounding factor in any before–after type design.

Probability sampling techniques Sampling techniques in which every member of the population has an equal chance of being in the sample. In general, these techniques produce representative samples.

Procedure In a research report, a subsection of the Method section that describes just how the study was conducted.

Process evaluation research A type of evaluation research that analyzes in detail how the program or treatment functions, with particular attention to areas of the process that need improvement. Usually contrasted with impact evaluation research.

Processor The part of the computer that performs computations and manipulates information according to its instructions.

Qualitative research A type of research that emphasizes the personal meaning of events to the people who experience them, typically using measurement on the nominal level if at all. Usually contrasted with quantitative research.

Quantitative research A type of research that emphasizes the numerical measurement of variables at the ordinal level or higher. Usually contrasted with qualitative research.

Quasi-experimental research Research in which some, but not all, rival hypotheses are eliminated, allowing the researcher to draw some conclusions about causality but always leaving other possibilities open. Generally conducted when true experiments are not possible.

Quota sampling techniques Nonprobability sampling techniques in which examples are chosen deliberately to match the known distribution of the population on certain variables. This technique can produce representative samples only if the quotas are chosen carefully and the important variables are accounted for; otherwise the samples will not be representative.

r The standard abbreviation for the Pearson product–moment correlation coefficient.

r_s The standard abbreviation for the Spearman rank-order correlation coefficient. The Greek letter rho (ρ) is also used.

Random assignment The use of a procedure that produces numbers with no predictable relationship to determine which participants in an experiment will be assigned to which groups, or levels of the independent variable(s). An important technique for ensuring the equivalence of the groups.

Random sampling techniques Another term for probability sampling techniques, because these techniques use random factors to give every member of the population an equal chance of being selected.

Range One measure of the variability of a set of scores, computed by subtracting the lowest score from the highest and then adding in one of the unit of measurement used. It can be applied to measurements at the ordinal, equal interval, or ratio level, but because the range grows with the sample size, it is most useful in comparing different samples of the same size.

Ratio measurements One level of measurement, which has all the properties of an equal interval measurement and in addition has a true zero point, such that a measurement of zero means that there is absolutely none of the property. The measurement of temperature on the Kelvin scale is in the ratio category because 0 °K is absolute zero, below which it is not possible to go. This is the only level of measurement in which it is meaningful to calculate ratios, and say, for instance, that 100 °K is twice as hot as 50 °K.

Rationalism One source of knowledge about the world, in which knowledge is figured out by the intellect alone, reasoning from assumptions to conclusions without involving actual observations. It is the opposite of empiricism, in which knowledge derives from observations.

Reactivity A property of humans and animals but not of inanimate objects, in that the subjects' behavior may change in complex, unpredictable ways as a result of being observed.

Reactivity effects Any extraneous variables affect a participant's response to being in a particular group or condition of the experiment.

Reduction of variability The main reason for using related groups designs: variability due to simple subject factors (intelligence, age, or whatever) will disappear from the analysis, since scores will be compared within people who are similar or the same on those variables.

Reference The item in a list at the end of a research report that describes a certain authority cited with full publication or other access data, allowing the reader to consult the source if desired.

Reference list The complete list of references to all publications cited in a research report.

Regression equation A mathematical formula used for predicting the value of one variable from another. Related to, but slightly different from, a correlation.

Regression toward the mean A potential confounding variable in many quasi-experiments, which can occur whenever scores are selected because they are extreme on the first measurement. Just by chance, the next measurement would tend to have scores closer to the mean, producing a change in the dependent variable.

Regression–discontinuity design A quasi-experimental design in which participants are measured on some variable that predicts the dependent variable; those that score above or below a predertermined cutoff are given a treatment program. Later, the dependent variable is plotted against the predictor variable; if the treatment made a difference, there should be a discontinuity or break in the regression line at the cutoff value.

Related groups An experimental design in which there is a particular relationship between one score in one group and a certain score in another group, perhaps because both scores come from the same participant.

Reliability (of a measurement) A property of a measurement, determined by how consistent or repeatable it is. A measurement that yields completely different scores each time is not very reliable.

Reliability, statistical See **statistical reliability**.

Representative A sample is representative of a population if conclusions based on that sample are accurate for the population. In general, probability samples are more representative than nonprobability samples.

Research A systematic way of answering questions about the world, generally using scientific methods such as the ones described in this book.

Research hypothesis The statement of the result that will occur in an experiment if the causal relationship being tested is true.

Respondents The people who answer questions or give opinions in a survey or an interview.

Response style A respondent's tendency to select a particular reply to almost any question, regardless of the actual answer. May include tendencies to answer "no," "yes," or with an answer that is socially more acceptable or more shocking.

Results In a research report, the section that describes the observations collected in the study, as well as any statistical analyses performed and how they relate to the research hypotheses.

Reversal design A design in which the dependent variable is measured before treatment, during treatment, and after treatment has ceased. Usually more than one reversal is used. Common in single-subject research.

rho The Greek letter (ρ) used to represent the Spearman rank–order correlation coefficient.

Rival hypothesis Any explanation for the effect observed in an experiment other than the planned variation in the independent variable. Rival hypotheses, which are produced whenever there is a confounding variable, can invalidate an experiment's conclusions.

Running head In a research report, the brief version of the title that appears in the top right-hand corner of every page.

Sample The group of examples, selected from the entire population of interest, that are actually observed in a study.

Sampling techniques Procedures for selecting which members of a population will be in the group actually observed in a piece of research. The type of technique used will determine the sample's representativeness with respect to the population.

Scale of measurement See **level of measurement**.

Scatterplot A visual representation of the relationship between two variables. One variable increases horizontally from left to right, the other increases vertically from bottom to top. Each observation is indicated by a point defined by its value on the two variables. Useful in understanding correlations.

Self-selected sample A type of haphazard sample in which the particpants volunteered or otherwise controlled themselves whether they would particpate in the research. Because those who chose to participate may differ from those who did not, this type of sample does not permit generalization to the population at large.

Sigma The Greek letter (Σ) used to represent the sum of a group of numbers.

Significance level The level of reliability a result must reach before it is accepted as not due to simple chance. Put another way, the probability (α) of a Type I error that will be tolerated when declaring a result reliable.

Simple random sampling techniques Probability sampling techniques in which examples are chosen at random from a list of all members of the population. If the population is large, this technique is unwieldy, but it yields representative samples.

Simulated before–after design A quasi-experimental design in which a group of participants scheduled to receive a treatment is randomly divided into two groups, one of which is measured before the treatment and the other one after.

Single-subject design A quasi-experimental design in which one subject (which may be a single participant or a group that is treated as one unit) is observed while changes are made in the independent variable, looking for related changes in the dependent variable.

Situational variable A type of extraneous variable that describes properties of the situation or environment in which the experiment is conducted.

Sources of variability Factors that can cause the value of a measurement to vary, or change, from one measurement to another. Can include actual changes in the underlying property being measured, changes in irrelevant properties, and random error.

Spacing effect In education, the phenomenon that most types of learning occur better if the work is spread out in several relatively short sessions than if it is done in one long session.

Spearman rank–order correlation A correlation coefficient that is useful for finding monotonic relationships in variables measured at the ordinal, equal interval, or ratio level. Abbreviated r_s or *rho* (ρ).

Split-half reliability One way of measuring the reliability of a measurement, by comparing the score obtained from half the items on a test with the score on the other half.

SPSS See **Statistical Package for the Social Sciences.**

Squared A number is squared by multiplying it by itself: 2 squared is 4; 3 squared is 9.

Standard deviation (s.d.) A measure of variability, computed as the square root of the variance. It can be applied to measurements at the equal interval or ratio level.

Static group comparisons A quasi-experimental research design in which two preexisting groups that differ in the independent variable are compared for differences in the dependent variable.

Statistic A quantity calculated by applying a mathematical procedure to a group of other numbers. Two important types of statistics are descriptive and inferential statistics.

Statistical package A group of computer programs that will organize, analyze, and display the results computed from a set of data.

Statistical Package for the Social Sciences (SPSS) A powerful collection of computer programs for performing a variety of statistical analyses on many different types of data. Probably the most commonly used statistical package in the social or behavioral sciences.

Statistical reliability The probability that a particular result of a study would not have occurred just by chance, but reflects a real effect.

Statistical significance See **statistical reliability**.

Statistical test A particular mathematical procedure used to calculate a quantity that measures the statistical reliability of a result.

Stratified sampling techniques Probability sampling techniques in which quotas are chosen to match the known distribution of certain variables in the population, just as in quota sampling. In the next step, however, representative samples are chosen of each quota, or stratum, by a random technique.

Structured interview An interview in which the questions are specified quite clearly in advance, usually as some form of survey. There is less freedom to explore issues than in unstructured interviews, but the results are easier to interpret.

Student's t A statistical test (*t*-test) used to compare the means of two groups of scores to determine whether they are reliably different.

Style The many small decisions any writer must make in composing a piece of writing, which give it its overall tone and make it clear or confusing, dull or interesting, and so on.

Subject variables Extraneous variables that describe relatively stable properties of the participants in the research.

Subjective An observation is subjective if different observers will disagree on what was observed because they cannot all make the same observation at the same time. The opposite of objective.

Subjects In a research report, a subsection of the Method section that describes the research participants and tells how they were selected.

Summative evaluation research A type of evaluation research that measures the effectiveness of a program at achieving its stated goals, without regard to why it is or is not achieving them. Usually contrasted with formative evaluation research.

Survey A set of standardized questions that are asked of a sample of people, whose answers are combined to represent the responses of an entire population.

Syllogism A standard type of deductive reasoning, which begins with a general principle (for example, All men are mortal) and a specific assumption (for example, Socrates is a man), and leads to a specific conclusion (for example, Socrates is mortal).

Systematic observations The name for one observational technique, in which specific, well-defined observations are made, usually of naturally occurring behaviors, which can produce objective descriptions of what occurred.

Systematic sampling techniques A variation on simple random sampling in which the first selection is made at random from the first part of the list, and each successive item is selected a certain distance farther down the list. Easier to deal with for large lists, it can create samples that are not representative if there exists a systematic cycle to the order of the list that matches the cycle of the systematic sampling.

t-test See **Student's t**.

Terminal A device through which a user communicates with a mainframe computer. A terminal usually consists of a keyboard, a monitor, and a processor running a program to handle the communications.

Test of association A chi-square test used to compare frequency distributions obtained under different circumstances to determine whether they are different, thereby measuring whether the frequencies are associated with the situations under which they were measured.

Test statistic A statistic calculated on one or more samples of scores to determine whether the results obtained are reliable.

Test-retest reliability A measure of the reliability of a measurement, achieved by conducting exactly the same measurement again and comparing the two results.

Testing effects Potential confounding variables in many quasi-experiments, which occur whenever the act of being observed or measured changes how the participant reacts to the measurement a second time, producing a change in the dependent variable.

Theoretical (basic) research A type of research whose purpose is to test and evaluate theories about the causal relationships between variables by specifically attempting to falsify particular theories. Often considered to be the opposite of applied research, which is used to make important real-world decisions.

Theoretical (conceptual) variables Variables whose existence and nature are derived from theories, not from direct observations. Another word for construct.

Time-interval sampling A type of systematic observation in which the behaviors are observed during certain predetermined intervals.

Time-point sampling A type of systematic observation in which the behaviors are observed at certain predefined instants in time.

Title page The first page of the research report, which contains the full title and the author's name and affiliation.

Trace measures An unobtrusive research technique that uses the marks that a behavior leaves behind. For instance, researchers might examine tire skid marks at an intersection to determine how dangerous it is.

Type I error In inferential statistics, the probability of accepting a result as reliable when there is in fact no real effect. Its probability is alpha (α).

Type II error In inferential statistics, the probability of rejecting a result as unreliable when there is in fact a real effect. Its probability is beta (β).

Unobtrusive research techniques Research that has no potential to change the behavior being observed, usually because those being observed are not aware of it.

Unstructured interviews Interviews in which specific questions are not planned, but only general areas to be explored, allowing for much more freedom than is possible in structured interviews.

Validity A property of a measurement, determined by whether it measures the property it is supposed to measure or whether it is strongly influenced by other sources of variability. Counting a person's freckles is not a valid measurement of the individual's intelligence.

Vapor statement A type of nonfalsifiable statement so vague that it makes no specific predictions that could possibly be false. Example: Some people like asparagus.

Variable Any quantity that can vary when measured in different objects under different circumstances.

Variability The name for the differences in the measurements of a single variable under different conditions. Some measurements will have more variability than others, which means they will differ more when measured under different conditions.

Variance A measure of variability, computed by finding the difference between each score and the mean of all the scores, squaring these differences, adding them, and dividing by the number of scores minus one. It can be applied to measurements at the equal interval or ratio level.

Within-subjects design A type of related groups design in which each subject (participant) is exposed to each of the levels of the independent variable, so that any difference found in the dependent variable will occur between scores on the same participant (that is, the difference will show up within a subject).

Word processor A computer program that allows a writer to enter, change, and print text.

Yoked Two things are yoked if they are connected in such a way that what happens to one of them affects what happens to the other.

Yoked design A research design in which two participants are linked so that what happens to one affects what happens to the other. For instance, one participants's responses may control what happens to both participants.

z A variable distributed according to the standard normal distribution. Statistical tests often produce variables distributed this way for use in determining the reliability of a result.

Index

Abney, F. G., 200–201, 341
Abortion, 28
Abscissa, 135, 312–314, 347
Academic anxiety, 116
Adair, J. G., 277, 341
Adolescents, 48, 124, 163, 165,
    177, 203, 205, 282
AIDS, 13–15, 57, 230
Alcoholism, treatment of, 56-57
Alpha, probability of Type I error,
    229–230, 232, 241, 347
Alpha level, *see* Significance level
American Association for the
    Accreditation of Laboratory
    Animal Care, 57
American Psychological
    Association, 40, 48, 50, 60,
    246, 249, 252, 256, 308, 341
Animals, ethics of research with,
    56–57, 59, 62–63
Anisfeld, M., 281, 341
Anonymity, 45-48, 56, 62, 231, 347
Archer, D., 285, 342, 346
Armed forces, 48, 52-53, 284
Aronson, E., 161–162, 285,
    341, 342, 346

Astrology, 33–34
Astronomy, 55, 181, 289–290
Atkinson, M. P., 282, 344
Attachment, in infants, 29
Attorney General's Commission
    on Pornography, 283, 341
Author's affiliation, 247
Ayllon, T., 209–211, 214–215, 341

Babbie, E., 95, 97, 341
Backups, for computers, 302–
    303, 305, 347
Baddeley, A. D., 53, 282, 341
Bahrick, H. P., 282, 341
Bailey, W. C., 199–200, 341
Bales, J., 284, 341
Bannan, R. S., 270, 341
Barash, D. P., 116, 341
Bar chart, 310, 312, 347
Barnes, P. J., 280, 342
Barthol, R. P., 322–323, 342
Baseline, 209–214, 218, 347
Bateson, P., 57, 343
Batson, C. D., 184, 192, 280, 343
Baum, A., 284, 342

Baum, N., 249, 343
Baumeister, R. F., 291, 342
Baumrind, D., 51, 58, 342
Beaman, A. L., 280, 342
Before–after design, 192–198,
    203–204, 208, 211, 214,
    216-217, 347
Before–after nonequivalent
    groups design, 199–200, 202,
    217, 348
Behavior modification, 209–211, 214
Behavioral measures, 104
Behaviorism, 287–288
Bell, S. J., 55, 344
Bereiter, C., 281, 345
Berkowitz, L., 104, 283, 342, 343
Best, J. B., 325–327, 345
Beta, probability of Type II error,
    229–230, 241, 348
Bibliographic search, 248, 303, 348
Bimodal, 85, 348
Binomial test, 239, 321–323,
    337, 348
Bishop, J. E., 283, 342
Bivariate data, 313, 348
Blind designs, 179–180, 186, 348
Blot, W. J., 191, 343
Blunders, effects on liking, 161–
    163
Bourke, P. N., 107, 342
Bower, B., 30, 127, 130–131,
    178, 282, 342
Bradburn, N. M., 105, 342
Brady, J. V., 156–157, 172, 342
Broad, W., 55, 342
Bureau of Justice Statistics, 123, 342
Burt, C., 55

Campbell, D. T., 113, 346
Capital punishment, 199–200
Card-choice problem, 30–31, 37
Carey, J. T., 112–113, 342
Carlson, C. I., 116, 343
Carroll, D. W., 325–326, 342

Carryover effects, 214, 218
Castellan, J., 238, 330, 345
Causation, 129–132, 135, 137,
    139–140, 147-148, 165, 348
Ceci, S. J., 49–50, 342
Central tendency, 84–86, 90, 348
Chaiken, S., 159–161, 164, 191,
    314, 342
Chambers, W. V., 130, 342
Charlie Brown, 24, 69
Cheatwood, D., 123, 342
Chernobyl nuclear disaster, 194
Chi-square test, 239, 323–326,
    335, 348
Clocks, 286–287
Clum, G. A., 158, 163, 177, 179,
    344
Coding, of data, 306–307
Coercion, 52-54, 56, 62, 277,
    348
Cognitive psychology, 288
Cohort effects, 103, 348
Computers:
    controlling research, 304–305
    and data searches, 11, 248, 303–
        304
    description of, 301–303
    as metaphors for people, 286, 288
    and random numbers, 172
    and report writing, 272, 307–308
    and statistical computations,
        305–307
Computer-mediated communication,
    10
Conceptual variables, *see* Constructs
Concern for appearance, 159–
    161, 164, 191
Condelli, L., 285, 346
Confederates, 42, 46, 49, 54,
    104, 185, 280, 349
Confidentiality, 47–50, 62, 349
Confirmation, 34, 36, 349
Confound, *see* Variables,
    confounding
Constructs, 70–75, 78, 80–83,

89–90, 113, 164, 234, 237, 287, 349

Content analysis, 112–113, 118, 349

Control, as a goal of science, 23, 35, 146, 349

Control group, 151–152, 177–180, 186, 198, 349
  effects, 178–180, 186, 350

Converging operations, 74–75, 112, 113, 164, 216, 349

Converse, H., 270, 342

Cook, S., 281, 342

Coopersmith, S., 280, 342

Corkill, A. J., 282, 343

Correlation, 121–140
  definition, 122
  positive *vs.* negative, 123–124

Correlation coefficient, 132–134, 140
  calculation of, 316–320
  definition, 132
  meaning of, 133–134
  Pearson product-moment, 137–138, 239, 316–317, 330–331, 356
  Spearman rank-order, 137, 239, 318–321, 330–331, 359
  testing reliability of, 330–331

Correlation is not causation, 129–132, 135, 137, 139–140

Cost-benefit analysis:
  in ethical decision-making, 58–59, 63, 350
  in evaluation research, 13–14, 16–17, 350

Costanzo, M., 285, 342

Counterbalancing, 175, 350

Cox, V. C., 11, 342

Crab nebula, 289–290

Creationism, 33

Cressey, D. R., 109, 342

Crime rate and temperature, 122–124

Criminals, interrogation of, 138–139

Criminal justice, 34, 122, 138–139, 248, 255, 282-284, 295

Critelli, J. W., 177, 342

Critical thinking, teaching of, 281

Cross, T., 283, 345

Cross-sectional research, 101–103, 117, 350

Crowding, in prisons, 11, 284

Curbow, B., 285, 346

Darley, J. M., 184, 192, 280, 343

Davenport, B. C., 15, 343

de Sanchez, M., 281, 344

Debriefing, 51, 350

Deception:
  active *vs.* passive, 49
  ethics of in research, 49–52, 56, 58-59, 62, 277–279, 350
  informed consent in, 49–50, 342

Deduction, 26, 28, 350

Degrees of freedom, 240, 324–325, 329-331, 350

Demoralization, 179, 186, 350

Dempster, F. N., 282, 343

Dental hygiene, 231–232, 235, 238, 240, 270, 313–314, 327, 329

Descartes, R., 25–26, 343

Description, as a goal of science, 20, 35, 350

Determinism, 129, 351

Devesa, S. S., 191, 343

Deviation, 86–88, 90, 351

Dewey, T., 95

Dickover, R., 284, 345

Dickson, W. J., 210–211, 345

Discrimination, racial, 21–23, 28, 195, 281

Distributed practice effect, *see* Spacing effect

Doctor Who, 62

Donnerstein, E., 283, 343

Double blind designs, 183–184, 186, 351

Dougherty, D., 283, 345

Douglas, N. E., 249, 343

Driscoll, J. W., 57, 343

DuBois, P. H., 284, 343

Duncan, B. L., 21, 343
Dushenko, T. W., 277, 341

Eagly, A. H., 290, 343
Ebbinghaus, H., 282, 343
Einstein, A., 292–293
Elderly, research concerning, 9,
    101–103, 150–151, 153
Elections, presidential, 95–96, 112
Electricity and magnetism, 293
Empiricism, 27–29, 35, 71, 351
Equal interval measures, see
    Levels of measurement
Equivalence, 170–171, 351
Estabrook, M., 9, 346
Ethics, 39–63, 114, 118, 277–
    278, 295, 351
  concerning animals, 56–57
  definition, 40
  oversight committees, 59–60,
    63, 351
  questionable activities, 40–56
Experimental group, 151, 177,
    179, 186, 351
Experimental hypothesis, see
    Research hypothesis
Experimenter bias, see Experimenter
    expectancy effects
Experimenter expectancy effects,
    154–155, 166, 183–186
Experimenter variables, 154,
    166, 181–183, 186, 351
Explanation, as a goal of science,
    22, 35, 146, 351
Expressiveness, 164
Eyewitness testimony, 283

Factorial design, 159–162, 164,
    166, 212, 314, 352
Falsifiable statements, 31–34, 36, 352
  vs. nonfalsifiable statements, 32–33
Falsificationism, 29–36, 158,
    185, 230, 232, 352

Farbstein, J., 34, 343
Femininity, 164
Fernald, L. D., 236, 330–331, 343
Field research, 190
Files, on computers, 302–303,
    307, 352
Fisher, K., 48, 343
Fixed-response vs. open-ended
    questions, 106–107, 109,
    112–113, 352, 356
Floppy disks, on a computer,
    302, 305–307
Fode, K. L., 154, 183, 345
Fonda, C. P., 80, 345
Fox, N. E., 29, 346
Fraumeni, J. F., Jr., 191, 343
Frequency data:
  descriptions of, 83–84, 90,
    309–312, 347, 353
  measurement of, 76
  reliability of, 239, 242, 321–
    327, 335, 337
Frequency distributions, 83–84, 242,
    310–311, 323, 325, 327, 352
Frequency tables, 83, 90, 309–
    310, 312, 352
Friedman, H., 235–236, 330, 343
Frieze, I. H., 290, 344

Gallup, G., 95–97
Gardner, G. T., 278, 343
Geiwitz, J., 101-103, 345
Generalization, 95–97, 116, 352
"Get Smart," 76
Gibson, J. J., 284, 343
Glass, D. C., 278, 343
Glover, J. A., 282, 343
Goodman, W., 57, 343
Goodness-of-fit test, see Chi-
    square test
Gordon, R. A., 231–232, 235, 238,
    240, 270, 313, 327, 329, 343
Gosset, W. S., 327
Gould, S. J., 33, 289, 343

Government officials, trust of, 200–201, 314
Graphs, 312–314, 355
Green, R. G., 104, 342
Greene, A., 284, 343
Grotevant, H. D., 116, 343
Guida, F. V., 116, 343

Hard disks, on a computer, 302, 307
Harm, physical and mental, 41–43, 56–57, 62
Hawthorne effect, 210–211
Head Start program, 157, 179
Hearnshaw, L. S., 55, 343
Helping behavior, 184–185, 192, 280
Herpes, 158–159, 163, 177–179
Herrnstein, R. J., 281, 344
Hertzog, C., 103, 345
Hewish, A., 55, 344
Hidden observations, 113–114, 118, 353
Hill, G. D., 282, 344
Histogram, 311–312, 353
History effects, 194, 217, 353
Honesty, 70–74, 81–83, 125, 129
Horobin, K., 9, 346
Huskey, H. D., 288, 344
Hutcheson, J. D., Jr., 200–201, 341
Hypnosis, 283–284

Independent groups *vs.* related groups, 173–176, 185, 187, 235–236
  statistical test of, 327–329
Informed consent, 43–44, 46–50, 53, 56–57, 62, 278, 353
Innes, C. A., 284, 312, 345
Inputs, of a computer, 288, 301, 353
Instrument decay, *see* Instrumentation effects

Instrumentality, 164
Instrumentation effects, 195, 198, 217, 353
Intelligence tests, 98, 102, 126, 128, 233–234, 284
Interaction effects, 160–162, 166, 314, 353
Interrupted time-series designs, 203–204, 209, 217, 353
Interviews, 108–111, 117, 353
Invasion of privacy, 45–46, 277, 354

Jargon, 255–256, 273
Johnson, W. T., 111, 344
Johnson-Laird, P. N., 30–31, 346
Jury selection, 283
Just world phenomenon, 22
Juvenile delinquency, 124, 131, 163, 282

Katkin, E. S., 283, 344
Kemp, E., 84, 309–311, 346
Kennedy, J. P., Jr., 249, 344
Keywords, in bibliographic searches, 248, 303–304
Kiesler, S., 10, 344
Killen, J., 203, 205, 344
Kimmel, A. J., 40, 344
Klentz, B., 280, 342
Knowles, E. S., 45–47, 59, 344
Koeske, R. D., 290, 344
Ku, N. D., 322–323, 342
Kuhn, T., 292, 344

LaFrance, M., 115, 344
Landers, S., 48, 344
Langer, E. J., 150–151, 153, 344
Laurence, J.-R., 283, 344
Lehman, J. D., 281, 344
Lerner, M. J., 22, 344
Letters of reference, 49–50

Level of an independent variable, 150–151, 162–163, 354
Levels of measurement, 75–79, 89, 233–234, 238–239, 242, 354
Levy, J., 270, 344
Lévy-Leboyer, C., 285, 344
Lindsay, R. C., 277, 341
Linn, R. L., 128, 344
Linz, D., 283, 343
Locus of control, 82, 354
Loftus, E., 283, 344
Longitudinal research, 101–104, 117, 354
Longman, D. J. A., 282, 341
Longo, D. J., 158, 163, 177, 179, 344
Lung disease, 191

McAlister, A., 203, 205, 344
McCain, G., 11, 342
McClelland, D. C., 112, 344
Maccoby, N., 203, 205, 344
McGuire, T. W., 10, 344
McHugh, M. C., 290, 344
McLeod, B., 285, 346
McNemar, Q., 126, 128, 344
McPhail, C., 114, 116, 346
McQuirk, B., 280, 342
Main effects, 160, 164, 166, 354
Mainframe, type of computer, 301–302, 306–307, 354
Maltzman, I. M., 56, 345
Marijuana, 111
Masculinity, 164
Matched groups designs, 174–176, 185, 354
Matter, C. F., 45–47, 59, 344
Maturation effects, 194, 202, 204, 214, 217, 354
Maxwell, J. C., 293–294
Meal size, 159–161, 164, 314
Mean, 85–86, 354
Mean square, 86, 354
Measurement:
 definition, 68–70

levels of, 75–79, 89, 233–234, 238–239, 242, 354
theory of, 67–91
Median, 85–86, 90, 354
Medicaid, effectiveness of, 15–16, 343
Memory, of a computer, 301
Middlemist, R. D., 45–47, 59, 344
Mikhail, A. A., 157, 344
Milgram, S., 42–43, 50–51, 54, 58, 345
Military personnel, 48, 53
Mode, 85–86, 90, 354
Monkeys, 156–157, 172
Monotonic, 122, 138, 318–319, 355
Mortality effects, 195, 202, 217, 355
Multiple-baseline designs, 213–216, 218, 355
Multiple-choice tests, 325–327
Multiple time-series designs, 204–205, 217, 355
Multivariate data, 312–314, 355
Multivariate designs, 163–166, 355
Museum, exhibit popularity, 113
Music, in stores, 284

Nelson, W. R., 34, 345
Neumann, K. F., 177, 342
Nickerson, R. S., 281, 344
Noise, effects of, 278
Nominal level of measurement, see Levels of measurement
Nonequivalent groups, see Before–after nonequivalent groups design
Nonparametric statistics, 137, 236–238, 242, 318, 321, 323, 330, 355
Null hypothesis, 232, 241, 322, 325, 327, 355
Nutall, R. L., 15, 343

One-tailed tests, 336–338, 355
Open-ended *vs.* fixed-response
    questions, 106–107, 109,
    112–113, 352, 356
Operational definitions, 73–74, 89
Order effects, 175, 185, 356
Ordinal level of measurement,
    see Levels of measurement
Ordinate, 135, 313, 356
Orne, M. T., 54, 345
Outputs, of a computer, 288,
    301–302, 356
Overachievement, 179, 356

Pancake, V. R., 29, 346
Parallel construction, 254, 356
Parametric statistics, 236–239,
    242, 316, 321, 327, 330, 356
Parenting, 124, 131, 280, 282
Parke, R. D., 46, 345
Patterson, A. H., 283, 345
Paulus, P. B., 11, 342
Pearson product-moment
    correlation, 137–138, 239,
    316–319, 330–331, 356
Peele, S., 56, 345
Pendery, M. L., 56, 345
Penrod, S., 283, 343
Percentages, 84, 90, 96, 309–310
Perry, C., 203, 205, 283, 344
Personal computer, 302, 306, 307, 356
Peters, D., 49–50, 342
Petersen, R. E., 111, 344
Pettigrew, T. F., 285, 342, 346
Phelps, E., 282, 341
Pie chart, 310–312, 356
Pilkington, J. P. H., 55, 344
Pinder, C. C., 27, 345
Placebo effects, 176–178, 184,
    186, 356
Plagiarism, 54–55, 62
Plato, 25–26, 345
Pliner, P., 159–161, 164, 191,
    314, 342

Plumb, E., 105, 345
Polygraph testing, 283
Popper, K., 29, 345
Population, 94–97, 101, 105,
    116, 237
Pornography, 282–283
Posture, of teachers and
    students, 115
Prediction, as a goal of science, 21,
    35, 124–129, 132, 134, 140, 357
Pregnancy, anxiety in, 127, 131
Premo, S., 131, 345
President, 95, 112
Pretest–posttest design, *see*
    Before–after design
Pretest sensitization, 201, 357
Prison guards, 284
Prisons, 11, 34–35, 52, 284, 312
Processor, of a computer, 301, 357
Pucci, A., 84, 309–311, 346
Punched cards, for computers,
    301, 307
Pyramid power, 147–148

Quota sampling techniques, 96–97

Random assignment, 172–174,
    179, 185, 202, 357
Random numbers, 97, 172, 333
Random number generators,
    computerized, 172
Range, 88–90
Rankin, J. H., 124, 131, 346
Ratio level of measurement, *see*
    Levels of measurement
Rationalism, 25–27, 28, 35, 358
Reactivity effects, as extraneous
    variables, 176–180, 186,
    277–278, 358
Reading, in children, 209–211,
    214–215
Reduction of variability, 175–176,
    358

Regression equation, 126, 358
Regression toward the mean, 196–197, 217, 358
Regression-discontinuity designs, 205–208, 217, 358
Related groups designs, 174–176, 185–186, 235–236, 327, 329, 358
Reliability:
  of a measure, 79–81, 89
  statistical, 227–228, 241, 360
Repeat exams, 235–236, 330
Representativeness, of a sample, 95–99, 108, 116–117
Research:
  applied, 11–15, 17, 23, 347
  archival, 111–112, 113, 118, 347
  basic, *see* Research, theoretical
  correlational, 21, 121–140, 191, 312–313, 349
  covert, 44, 350
  definition, 8
  descriptive, 8–9, 17, 21, 121–122, 350
  evaluation, 11–15, 17, 351
  experimental, 143, 146–186, 190, 192
  exploratory, 9–10, 17, 114, 351
  factorial, 159–162, 164, 166, 314, 352–353
  formative evaluation, 12, 15, 352
  impact evaluation, 13, 353
  multivariate, 163–165, 355
  overt, 44, 356
  process evaluation, 13, 357
  qualitative *vs.* quantitative, 16–17, 21, 76, 357
  quasi-experimental, 189–216, 281, 313, 357
  single-subject, 208–218, 359
  summative evaluation, 12, 15, 360
  theoretical, 10–11, 15, 17, 22–23, 361
  unobtrusive, 111–114, 117, 361

Research hypothesis, 231–232, 241, 248, 322, 325, 327, 358
Research report, 221, 245–273, 301, 307–308
  parts of, 246–252
  sample paper, 264–268
  writing techniques, 253–272
Respondents, 105–111, 113, 117, 231, 358
Response style, 180–181, 186, 359
Responsibility, and health, 146, 150–153
Restricted range, 127–129
Rest rooms, 45–47, 59
Reversal designs, 208–216, 218, 359
Rewards and punishments, 150, 209–215
Rips, L. J., 105, 342
Rival hypotheses, 148, 156–158, 165–166, 170–171, 185, 190–192, 359
Roberts, M. D., 209–211, 214–215, 341
Rodin, J., 150–151, 153, 344
Roethlisberger, F. J., 210–211, 345
Rosenthal, R., 154, 183, 345
Rothblum, E. D., 291, 345
Ruback, R. B., 284, 312, 345

Sagan, C., 293–294, 345
Sample, 86–89, 94–101, 105–106, 108, 116–117, 225, 237, 321, 359
  definition, 94
Sample size, 88–89, 99–101, 117, 133, 237, 331, 338
Sampling techniques, 94–99, 116, 359
Saxe, L., 283, 345
Scardamalia, M., 281, 345
Scatterplot, 134–139, 140, 206, 313, 317–319, 359

Schaie, K. W., 101–103, 345
Schatz, M. A., 325–327, 345
Schmidt, H. O., 80, 345
Schmookler, A. B., 291, 345
Schwartz, R. D., 113, 346
Scott, P. F., 55, 344
Sechrest, L., 113, 346
"Sesame Street," 20, 31
Sex differences, in research, 290–291
Sexism, in language, 256
Shawver, L., 284, 345
Sherif, M., 23, 345
Shevell, S. K., 105, 342
Siegel, J., 10, 344
Siegel, S., 238, 330, 345
Sigma, symbol for summation,
    85–86, 88, 316–317, 324,
    328–329, 359
Significance level, 227–228, 230,
    232, 241, 359
Significance, statistical, *see*
    Statistical reliability
Simon, C., 9, 345
Simulated before-after designs,
    201–202, 217, 359
Singer, J. E., 278, 343
Single-subject research, 208–
    218, 359
Sleeping patterns, in children,
    291
Slinkard, L. A., 203, 205, 344
Smoking, 131–132, 148, 152,
    178, 190–191, 203–205, 231
Sobell, L. C., 56, 345
Sobell, M. B., 56, 345
Social desirability bias, 231–232,
    238, 270, 327
Sociobiology, 22
Socrates, 25
Sommer, R., 9, 346
Sommers, N., 270–271, 346
Songs, popular, 112–113
Spacing effect, 281–282, 359
Spearman rank-order
    correlation, 137, 239, 316,

    318–321, 330–331, 359
SPSS, *see* Statistical Package
    for the Social Sciences
Sroufe, L. A., 29, 346
Standard deviation, 86–88, 90, 360
Standard normal distribution,
    322, 338
Static group comparisons,
    198–199, 217, 360
Statistical package, for a computer,
    306, 360
Statistical Package for the Social
    Sciences, 306, 360
Statistical regression, *see*
    Regression toward the mean
Statistical reliability, 227–228, 241,
    360
Statistical significance, *see*
    Statistical reliability
Statistics:
    descriptive, 83, 350
    inferential, 223–242, 353
    parametric *vs.* nonparametric,
        236–239, 242, 355–356
    reporting results, 240, 242
Stratified sample, 98, 117
Stress:
    created by research, 41–43,
        45–46, 53, 56, 58
    and herpes, 158–159, 163, 177–178
    in monkeys, 155–156
    and performance, 322
    and pregnancy, 131
"Student," *see* Gossett, W. S.
Student's *t*, *see* *t*-test
Studying and grades, 135–136
Subliminal messages, 178
Sugar, effects on behavior,
    163–165, 177
Supernova, 289–290
Survey techniques, 105–108, 117
Swets, J. A., 281, 344
Syllogism, 26, 360
Systematic observations, 114–116,
    18, 360

t-test, 232, 238–240, 327–331, 336
Tajfel, H., 21, 23, 346
Teachers, evaluations of, 84, 309–311
Terminal, for a computer, 302, 361
Test of association, *see* Chi-square test
Testing effects, 194–195, 200–201, 217, 361
Textbooks:
  comparisons of, 236, 330–331
  prices of, 9
Theoretical variables, *see* Constructs
Three-Mile Island, nuclear accident at, 194
Timesharing, on a computer, 302
Toothbrushing, 231–232, 235, 238, 240, 270, 313–314, 327, 329, 343
Trace measures, 113, 361
Traditionalism, 24–25
Trefil, J., 293, 346
Type I *vs.* Type II errors, 229–232, 241–242, 361

Ulcers, 156–157
Uniform Crime Reports, 111
Urination, 45–47, 59
Utility companies, 284–285

Validity:
  external *vs.* internal, 191–192, 351, 353
  of a measure, 80–83, 89–90, 127, 129, 183, 283, 361
  types of, 81–83, 90, 349–350, 352
Valins, S., 284, 342
Variability, sources of, 71–73, 79, 89, 359
Variables:
  confounding, 155–158, 166, 170–171, 185, 202, 349
  definition, 71
  dependent, 152–153, 163–166, 170–171, 350

experimenter, 154–155, 166, 181–186, 351
extraneous, 153–155, 166, 169–187, 190, 352
independent, 150–152, 159–163, 165–166, 353
situational, 155, 166, 359
subject, 154–155, 166, 171–176, 185–186, 360
theoretical, *see* Constructs
Variance, 86–88, 90, 237, 328, 362
Vigilance, 115
Vincennes, U.S. Naval vessel, 284

Wade, N., 55, 342
Wason, P. C., 30–31, 346
Waters, M., 84, 309–311, 346
Watson, J. B., 287, 346
Wawra, M., 115, 346
Webb, E. J., 113, 346
Weiss, J. M., 156, 346
Weiss, R., 163, 165, 346
Weizenbaum, J., 286, 346
Wells, L. E., 111, 124, 131, 344, 346
West, L. J., 56, 345
White, L. T., 285, 346
Wilson, E. O., 22, 346
Winter, D. G., 112, 346
Within-subjects designs, 174–175, 185, 362
Wohlstein, R. T., 114, 116, 346
Word processors, 307–308, 362
Working and grades, 135–136
Wundt, W., 287, 346

Yaeger, N. J., 158, 163, 177, 179, 344
Yates, S., 285, 346
Yoked designs, *see* Matched groups designs

Zajonc, R. B., 284, 346
Zeller, A. F., 41–42, 346

Printed by
Fong & Sons Printers Pte Ltd